THE DEATH OF
BUY AND HOLD

How *Not* to Outlive Your Money
—Investing for, and in, Retirement

© 2015 by Capital Strategies Press LLC

All rights reserved. Printed in the United States of America

18 17 16 15 14   1 2 3 4 5

Published by Capital Strategies Press LLC

305 Ferris Lane, New Britain, PA 18901

David Moratto, cover and interior design

Library of Congress Control Number: 2014921000

ISBN: 978-0-9862253-0-7

THE DEATH OF BUY AND HOLD

How *Not* to Outlive Your Money —Investing for, and in, Retirement

Chris Minnucci

CAPITAL STRATEGIES PRESS, LLC

CSP
CAPITAL STRATEGIES PRESS

NEW BRITAIN, PENNSYLVANIA

To my mother, Dorothy Minnucci, with love
(and apologies for the tables and graphs)

October. This is one of the peculiarly dangerous months to speculate in stocks in. The others are July, January, September, April, November, May, March, June, December, August and February.
—Mark Twain

CONTENTS

PART III
PUTTING WELL-DIVERSIFIED PORTFOLIOS TO THE TEST

PART IV
HOW TO BUY

PART V
HOW TO HOLD

INTRODUCTION

~ک~

I'm often asked whether the markets behave rationally.
My answer is that it all depends on your time horizon.
Turn on CNBC at 9:31 AM any weekday morning
and you're faced with a lunatic asylum described by the Three Stooges.
—**William Bernstein,** *The Four Pillars of Investing*

I t was several years ago when I first heard the news—at least, it was news to me. The TV was tuned to CNBC, and a distinguished-looking gentleman was on camera. He spoke with an air of supreme confidence and authority. An éminence grise, no doubt about it. He was talking about the Lost Decade, those ten years beginning in 2000 when the stock market went down, then up, then down, and then up again—only to finish pretty much in the same place it started.

And then he delivered the grim news: "Buy and hold is dead."

How, he asked, can you possibly earn any returns simply holding your positions year in and year out, when the stock market has been moving sideways for a decade? Instead, he offered us viewers this advice: we would need to become "stock pickers." We would need to be nimble, to dart quickly in and out of positions, catching a stock with a little upward momentum here and there and then quickly dumping it before it goes back down. This approach is, he said, the only way to make money in a market going nowhere fast.

The stockbrokers watching that day were no doubt gladdened by his news, and by his advice on what we should do about it. After all, investors who just sit there holding the same old investments year after year don't generate commissions. "Buy and hold is dead? Well, good riddance," the brokers might well have been thinking.

And similar thoughts might have been passing through the heads of the CNBC on-camera personalities, their off-camera colleagues, and others who earn their living providing a 24/7 stream of market news and advice. After all, buy-and-hold investors have no need for the media's short-term investment advice. "Buy and hold is dead? Then by all means," the pundits, newsletter writers, and investment advisors might have thought to themselves, "follow Mr. Éminence Grise's advice and become a stock picker. Don't fret, Mr. Jones and Ms. Smith. We'll be more than happy to sell you our latest, greatest market predictions."

★★★

Yes, it was no doubt the kind of news to warm the hearts of stockbrokers, stock-picking gurus, and others eyeing *your* purse or wallet. But that doesn't mean it wasn't true. After all, consider the evidence in support of buy and hold's demise. Our friend on CNBC was speaking just two years after the stock market meltdown of 2008. Just about every asset class in existence plummeted in value during that debacle. U.S. stocks, international stocks, emerging market stocks, high-yield bonds—you name it, it lost money big time. Beginning in October 2007, and continuing until March 2009, the S&P 500 dropped a whopping 55.3 percent—the worst stock market loss since the Great Depression.

And the 2007–9 bear market began only five years, to the day (October 9), after the 2000–2002 bear market ended. Between March 2000 and October 2002, the S&P 500 dropped 47.4 percent. These two bear markets served as bookends to the second worst ten-year stretch for investors since 1926. Between 2000 and 2009, the S&P 500 managed to deliver, on average, annualized returns[1] of *negative* 1 percent. A $10,000 investment in the S&P 500 made on January 1, 2000, would have been worth only $9,090 by December 31, 2009.[2] And that's not even taking into account the mutual fund fees and other costs you would have incurred. That's *ten years* adding up to nothing but losses. The so-called aughts produced naught for a lot of investors.

It's no wonder, then, that so many responded by fleeing stocks in favor of bonds and other fixed-income investments. From 2008 through 2012, investors in the world's ten largest economies pulled $1.1 trillion from stock mutual funds, while adding $1.3 trillion to bond mutual funds.[3] The stampede out of stocks finally began to reverse itself in 2013. Of course, at this point, investors returning to stocks had already missed out on the 129 percent returns generated by the S&P 500 between the market bottom on March 9, 2009, and December 31, 2012. Buy and hold? It sure doesn't look like that's what many investors did in the wake of the financial crisis. But nor did they follow our CNBC friend's advice. "Dump and run" is what happened, as in dump stocks and run to the safety of bonds.

So maybe buy and hold *is* dead, at least in the sense that most average investors are not using it, regardless of its advantages or disadvantages. But still, there was one question someone should have put to that gentleman on CNBC: when you say buy and hold is dead, exactly *what* investments are you talking about buying and holding? Yes, the S&P 500 had negative returns over the past decade. But none of the books I've read on buy and hold recommend putting all of your money into the S&P 500. *Diversification* is the cornerstone of the buy-and-hold approach to investing. A portfolio invested 100 percent in the S&P 500 is *not* diversified. Would you believe a *well-diversified* buy-and-hold portfolio, split 60 percent stocks and 40 percent bonds, purchased on January 1, 2000, and rebalanced back to 60/40 each year since then, would have more than doubled in value by December 31, 2009? It's true. Such a portfolio, based on the principle underpinning modern portfolio theory (MPT) and including *high-volatility hedges, return boosters,* and *low-volatility hedges,* would have yielded annualized returns of 8.1 percent between 2000 and 2009. A $10,000 investment in this portfolio made on January 1, 2000, would have been worth $21,848 by December 31, 2009. And this is *after* taking into account average mutual fund fees and trading costs. This portfolio would have generated modest *positive,* not negative, returns during the 2000–2002 bear market. True, this same portfolio would have lost about 21 percent of its value in 2008. However, the loss would have been made up, in its entirety, by December 31, 2009—just ten months after the great bear market of 2007–9 ended. We study this portfolio—the advanced moderate portfolio—and other similar portfolios in detail in Part III.

As Mark Twain might have said, reports of the death of buy and hold are greatly exaggerated. As for the so-called Lost Decade, it is a myth to those investors who maintained a well-diversified buy-and-hold portfolio throughout the 2000s. A difficult decade? Yes, for sure. But by no means was it a lost decade—despite what the financial gurus on CNBC might say.

But what about all those individual investors fleeing stocks and buying bonds? Isn't it reasonable to move to bonds given the riskiness and poor returns of stocks over the past decade?

Well, maybe. If some investors had too large a share of their assets in stocks going into 2008, it may have made sense for those particular individuals to lighten up a bit on stocks. But that massive move away from stocks and toward bonds was probably motivated more by fear than by reason. This is unfortunate and may prove counterproductive to the bond buyers. Yes, stocks are risky. But bonds come with their own risks. By fleeing one type of risk—the short-term risk posed by stock market volatility—investors caught up in the rush to bonds (and also CDs, bank savings accounts, and other fixed-income investments) may be taking on another, more insidious and potentially more dangerous risk—the long-term risk of returns that cannot keep pace with inflation. This risk is all the greater today given that bond yields and interest rates are at historic lows. Because bond prices move up when bond yields go down, the many investors who piled into bonds paid a hefty price for those low yields. When interest rates and bond yields return to more normal levels—as they probably will—bond prices will drop.

★★★

All this takes us to our central topic. This is a book about risk—specifically, risk to your retirement—and how to manage and minimize it. Successful investing for, and in, retirement basically comes down to mitigating a single, key risk—the risk of outliving your money. Throughout this book, we refer to this risk as the *retirement risk*. If you manage to live out the entirety of your golden years comfortably and enjoyably, without having to make sacrifices in your standard of living, and without becoming a financial burden on your family, you will have successfully navigated the retirement risk.

Unfortunately, retirement seems to be becoming more and more about sacrifice, scrimping, saving—and working. The Center for Retirement Research at Boston College estimates that more than half of all workers risk being unable to maintain their standard of living in retirement.[4] Given current trends, 30 percent of workers currently in the middle class will become low-income retirees.[5] Many people delayed their retirements because their 401(k)s and IRAs took major hits in 2008. Seventy percent of adults recently surveyed by Wells Fargo plan to work during retirement—in many cases because they cannot afford to retire full time.[6] Many already in retirement are returning—or trying to return—to the workforce for the same reason. Not only are older workers who want to retire finding it necessary to continue working, but these same workers are occupying jobs that would otherwise go to younger people who want to work but can't find employment. This is not how it should be.

But neither is it surprising. With the demise of pension plans and their replacement with defined contribution plans—401(k)s and the like—responsibility for successful investing for, and in, retirement has been transferred from professional pension fund managers to individual Americans like you and me. But the knowledge and skill needed to invest successfully and avoid the risk of running out of money have not been transferred along with the responsibility. It is as if we have all been given a new job—Money Manager in Charge—without receiving any job training. No wonder, then, that the prospects for a comfortable retirement are slipping away for so many.

Well, like it or not, you've been given the responsibility of managing your retirement portfolio. Of course, you can always outsource the job to a professional financial planner. That was what I was planning to do myself, back when I was getting ready to retire. In fact, I did hire a financial planner to create my retirement plan and was expecting to use him to manage my nest egg going forward—until he told me the fee for his services! That's when I decided to try the do-it-yourself approach. With some trepidation, I started to read up on the subject of investing. It proved to be not too difficult, so I kept at it. And then a strange thing happened: much to my surprise, I discovered I actually *liked* learning about investing and putting my newfound knowledge to work. What started out as a chore became a hobby and then something of an obsession. After a few more years went by, I found myself sitting down to write a book about what I had learned.

And so here we are. I can't promise you you're going to find drama, suspense, fun, and excitement in the world of investing—or in the pages of this book. Unless you're a math-loving, number-crunching geek like me, that's just not very likely. But what you *will* find here is the accumulated knowledge of a self-taught, pretty good amateur investor who has read a lot of the great books on investing and distilled them into what, I hope, is a clear, comprehensible, and not too unbearable read. So if you've decided to have a go at the DIY approach to investing (or even if you're going to hire a professional but want to be able to check up on what he or she is doing with *your* money), it's time now to roll up your sleeves, put on your green eye shade, and get to work. The goal of this book is to help you learn your new job. More specifically, the book's goal is to help you construct and manage an investment portfolio that will minimize the retirement risk—the risk of running out of money before running out of time. Understanding the retirement risk in all its dimensions is a prerequisite to understanding how to construct a portfolio that will last your entire lifetime. Therefore, we begin with a consideration of the retirement risk, and only after considering this risk in some depth do we proceed to the question of how best to invest your nest egg for, and in, retirement. The retirement risk will not only serve as our starting point—it will also be our touchstone throughout this book.

If you are a young person, please do not get the wrong impression by my use of the term *retirement risk*. This book is intended for all age groups—young workers far from retirement as well as retirees and those nearing retirement. As we shall see, the principles I'll be sharing work to reduce risk just as well for young investors as for older investors. These principles do not discriminate by age. There are some differences in the ways a younger person should approach the all-important task of developing an asset allocation plan, but Chapter 11 provides advice tailored to those still working, separate from the advice for retirees and near-retirees. Also, Chapter 10 includes guidance for estimating the amount of money workers will need to be able to retire comfortably and how much workers need to be saving to grow their nest eggs to the required size.

★★★

In this book, we will consider a broad array of solutions to the problem posed by the retirement risk. We will learn how to combine these solutions into a holistic risk-reduction approach providing *defense in depth* against the risk of bankruptcy. The first half of the book (Parts I–III) will focus on one of these solutions: diversification using the principles of *correlation* and *compromise*.

But before we can even begin to consider these solutions, we must first, in Chapter 1, learn all we can about the problem these solutions seek to address—the retirement risk. When it comes to investing, the term *risk* is often used interchangeably with the term *market volatility*. But too much (negative) volatility is only one aspect of the retirement risk. The other aspect—not earning enough returns to outpace inflation — is just as important to understand and guard against. Viewing risk as equivalent to volatility can blind investors to the less terrifying but equal danger of insufficient returns. This blindness is often manifested in an overreliance on investments like bonds, CDs, and money market funds—investments that will, to be sure, reduce an investor's exposure to market volatility, but only at the expense of an increased risk of not earning enough returns to keep up with inflation. This latter risk is especially dangerous today, when the yields for bonds and other fixed-income investments are at historic lows and the future outlook for these investments is not promising.

There is, fortunately another way besides bonds and other fixed-income investments, to reduce the risk posed by too much volatility while still realizing good returns. The approach to asset allocation I'll be sharing, beginning in Chapter 2, is based on the fundamental insight underlying modern portfolio theory (MPT). Don't worry —you will not need to learn MPT to apply the principle that underlies the theory. The mathematics behind MPT is formidable; but the *principle of correlation*, on which MPT is based, is simple. As we will learn, this principle is *uniquely* well suited to addressing the risk of too much market volatility *without* forcing us to give up returns. You can think of diversification based on the correlation principle as *judo investing* —or, better yet, *black belt investing*. A black belt in judo uses the force of a bigger, stronger opponent to throw that opponent off balance and defeat him. Similarly, when you use the correlation principle to construct a well-diversified portfolio, you take the risk posed by market volatility and turn that risk against itself. We cannot change the volatile nature of the stock market, but in this book, you will learn how to make volatility your friend.

Harry Markowitz won the 1990 Nobel Prize in Economics for developing MPT. I want to stress this point—the principle of correlation you will be learning in Parts I–III underpins a *Nobel Prize–winning investment strategy*. There are never any guarantees when it comes to investing in the stock market, but I *will* guarantee you one thing: none of the pundits on the financial networks who declared the death of buy and hold ever won a Nobel Prize for their investment ideas.

Of course, theories, even Nobel Prize–winning theories, are all well and good, but when it comes to investing, *results* are what matter. I wouldn't be writing a book on the correlation principle unless that principle had proven its worth over and over again, by growing and protecting not only my own portfolio but those of many others. The fact is, MPT and the principle of correlation have been successfully applied for many years both by small-time amateur investors like me and by professional money managers responsible for multi-billion-dollar portfolios. David Swensen, the manager of the Yale endowment, used MPT to help generate annualized returns of greater than 16.5 percent from 1985 to 2008, while the Harvard endowment used MPT to produce annualized returns of greater than 15 percent—not bad for a period when the S&P 500 yielded only 12.6 percent.[7]

If you diligently apply the principle of correlation, will you, like Swensen, be able to beat the stock market by 4 percentage points per year for the next twenty-five years? Absolutely not. You're not David Swensen, and you don't run a multi-billion-dollar portfolio like he does.[8] But you can apply the correlation principle to achieve the kind of modest success I and other small investors have enjoyed. It is not a secret, nor is it difficult to master—and though you can't come close to Swensen, you may well be able to do *better* than me.

There's nothing new about a book on the principle of correlation. Many investment books describe or apply this principle. My personal favorites are Burton Malkiel's *A Random Walk Down Wall Street* and William Bernstein's *The Intelligent Asset Allocator*. These two books are investment classics. You should beg, borrow, or steal them, read them, read them again, and then stick to the lessons they teach you through thick and thin.

This book approaches the subject of correlation from a somewhat different angle than these classics. In addition to using the retirement risk as our starting point and touchstone, I will *show* you how diversification based on the principle of correlation, combined with the complementary *principle of compromise* (i.e., using bonds to reduce portfolio volatility), would have worked to protect and grow portfolios over the past four decades. We will focus less on theory and more on market history. I hope that this will make the book more accessible to normal, nongeeky people (such as my mother, who, when she first heard that I was writing a book on this subject, made a face and asked if it was going to contain a lot of math and statistics). I will explain how the principle of correlation works as a risk-reduction tool and will show how various portfolios based on this principle would have performed during all of the major bear and bull markets of the last forty years. In the process, I will debunk the myths of the Lost Decade and the death of buy and hold.

***

Again, the principles of correlation and compromise are the focus of Parts I–III. Part I explains the two manifestations of the retirement risk—too much (negative) market volatility and not enough returns to outpace inflation. It then goes on to explain the two principles.

Part II describes the various asset classes that can be used to construct and hedge (protect) an all-weather, buy-and-hold portfolio based on the principles of compromise and correlation. We consider the risk and reward profile of each asset class and how well each one meets the three main criteria of a good hedge: (1) *low correlation* with other asset classes, (2) *high expected returns*, and (3) *high volatility*. We also examine how each asset class has actually performed during the major bear markets and market corrections of the past forty years.

In Part III, we use the asset classes examined in Part II to build a variety of portfolios based on the principles of compromise and correlation. We consider simple portfolios for those with modest savings as well as more complex portfolios for people with larger nest eggs. We also look at portfolios for the risk averse versus portfolios for those willing to accept more volatility. Each portfolio is put to a rigorous backtest using historical return data for mutual fund categories from Morningstar's excellent investor website.[9] Reliance on Morningstar's data helps to ensure that the backtests provide the most realistic representation possible of the kinds of returns a typical, real-world investor might have achieved. Unlike data on market indices (such as the Dow Jones or S&P 500), the Morningstar mutual fund data capture the impact of real-world costs, including management fees and trading costs, on returns. Also, because the Morningstar data are averaged across all mutual funds in a given asset class, the backtest results assume neither superior nor inferior fund selection skills on the part of the typical investor. The backtests show us how each portfolio would have performed during bull and bear markets stretching back to 1972.

★★★

In the second half of the book (Parts IV and V), we turn to the practical issues involved in implementing and maintaining an all-weather portfolio, such as how to develop a personalized asset allocation plan, how to select the specific investments that will compose your portfolio, how to check on and maintain your portfolio's health, and how to stick with a buy-and-hold approach through thick and thin. In the process of explaining these and other how-tos, we expand our scope beyond investing to the related fields of retirement planning (including saving for retirement) and taxes. As we explore these fields, we will discover potential solutions to the retirement risk beyond the principles of correlation and compromise. For example, in Part IV, we will learn that establishing a low withdrawal rate (the rate at which money is withdrawn from a retiree's portfolio to meet expenses) is an excellent way to minimize both components of the retirement risk (too much volatility and not enough returns to outpace inflation). In fact, a low initial withdrawal rate is even more effective than the principle of correlation at reducing the retirement risk.

Other solutions to the retirement risk considered in Part IV include index investing, liability-matching bond portfolios, dollar cost averaging, tax loss harvesting, and rebalancing. By reducing the percentage of returns you must give up to mutual fund managers and to Uncle Sam, index investing and tax loss harvesting reduce the risk posed by insufficient returns without simultaneously increasing the risk posed by market volatility. Dollar cost averaging is a reliable, disciplined way to "buy low" while saving for retirement—again, reducing the risk posed by inflation. As we will see in Chapter 12, implementing a liability-matching bond portfolio (LMBP) can virtually eliminate both components of the retirement risk—at least for a while, and possibly for the duration of your retirement. Finally, rebalancing your portfolio on a regular basis will afford you opportunities to buy low and sell high, thereby possibly yielding a rebalancing bonus that will reduce the inflation component of the retirement risk while simultaneously keeping your portfolio's volatility from rising over the long term.

In Part V, we turn to the emotional aspects of investing. You will learn why simply holding your investments is almost always the best strategy, and you will learn how to control your emotions and stick to a buy-and-hold approach through thick and thin. We address not only the strengths of buy and hold but also its weaknesses. The strategy contains a major flaw: although holding your investments is almost always the best way to protect yourself from the retirement risk, exceptions to this rule are possible. Given a big enough drop in the stock market, you may suffer losses so large that bankruptcy becomes a near-certainty. If inflation gets out of control (as happened during the 1970s), your portfolio's returns may prove insufficient to outpace inflation, forcing you to draw down on your principal until it is entirely gone. Because investors have no way of knowing the difference between situations that truly threaten their portfolios' survival and situations that are merely scary but pose no real risk, they often make what is arguably a rational decision to sell their stock holdings rather than risk the slim possibility of a catastrophic loss. This fundamental uncertainty in part accounts for the unpopularity of the buy-and-hold strategy among amateur investors. In the last two chapters of Part V, we address the uncertainty underlying the buy-and-hold approach head-on, by providing tables of historical portfolio survival rates that you can use to gauge the probability that your portfolio will survive future market meltdowns. In addition, you will be given a hierarchy of actions you can take, ranging from reducing your withdrawal rate to selling your stocks, if and when the tables indicate that you are approaching a true danger zone.

The many solutions to the retirement risk we explore—the principles of correlation and compromise, a low initial withdrawal rate, an LMBP, index investing, rebalancing, dollar cost averaging, tax loss harvesting, and others—work well separately. But when they are combined within the framework of a buy-and-hold investment strategy, they form a very powerful "defense in depth" to protect your nest egg. You can never completely eliminate the risk of outliving your money, but this defense-in-depth approach will give you the best prospect of managing and minimizing this risk—and enjoying a comfortable, secure retirement.

PART I

THE RETIREMENT RISK: PROTECTING YOUR RETIREMENT WITH A WELL-DIVERSIFIED PORTFOLIO

CHAPTER 1

OUTLIVING THEIR MONEY: A SHORT STORY ABOUT THE RETIREMENT RISK

To an older man it must have seemed inevitable that we were heading for a crash but to most of us it seemed that we were in a "New Era" which would never end.
—**Benjamin Roth,** *The Great Depression: A Diary*

As recently as the 1970s, as inflation soared around the world, the bond market made a Nevada casino look like a pretty safe place to invest your money.
—**Niall Ferguson,** *The Ascent of Money*

Imagine for a moment that you are James Bond. You have been locked in a vault by an arch villain. Inside the vault is a doomsday device set to explode in one hour. It is up to you to disarm it and save the world. You have no idea how this particular device works and no means of communicating with anyone outside the vault. Besides you and the device, the vault is empty, except for two books. One is a lengthy manual that explains clearly and in detail how the device works but offers no solutions for how to disarm it. The other is a short manual offering quick descriptions of one hundred possible solutions; however, only one of those solutions will work. It will take you nearly the entire hour just to read the long manual, but you could quickly read and try a couple dozen of the possible solutions in the short manual.

The clock on the device is ticking more and more loudly. The background music grows more ominous. The beautiful woman waiting in bed for you is getting impatient. What would you do?

Well, Bond would probably mutter a joke, cut the red wire, and, with his incredible luck, save the world. But if you wanted to attempt a solution that relied less on luck and more on brains, you might start by considering what Einstein once said: "If I had one hour to save the world, I would spend fifty-five minutes defining the problem, and only five minutes finding the solution." Einstein would probably read the long manual first, and then, based on his understanding of how the device operates, he would search for and find the one solution in the short manual that made the most sense.

Of course, most of us don't think like Einstein, nor do we possess James Bond's ability to remain cool under extreme duress. Fortunately, unlike Bond, we are not called on to save the world on a routine basis. But we do face financial challenges that, if solved incorrectly, could blow up our own little worlds. For many of us, by far the biggest of these challenges is the risk of running out of money in retirement. Just how big a deal is this risk? According to AARP, most people fear running out of money in retirement more than they fear death.[10]

In this book, I refer to the risk of bankruptcy in retirement as the retirement risk. Although you may face other financial challenges, such as saving and investing for your kids' college education or to buy a home, in this book, we focus exclusively on the mammoth challenge posed by the retirement risk. I am using the term *retirement risk* because it is in retirement (when you begin to spend your savings) that the risk of outliving your money will manifest. The retirement risk is the risk that you will go broke when you are seventy, or eighty, or ninety years old, and the only jobs still open to you might be Wal-Mart greeter or fast-food burger flipper.

Although we focus exclusively on the retirement risk, do not assume that this book is intended only for retired people. In fact, the cost of funding a comfortable, happy, worry-free retirement is so large that you should begin saving and investing for it decades in advance. This book is for everyone, regardless of age. Whether you are young or old, just embarking on a career, nearing retirement, or already retired, you need to be working on solving the challenge posed by the retirement risk *now* and throughout the rest of your life.

So how do we do this? We could do worse than follow Einstein's lead. After all, he was a genius. Einstein's point is really simple—before you try to solve a problem, first you must understand it. Unfortunately, when confronted with a stressful problem, most humans have a tendency to give short shrift to studying it and instead try to jump quickly to a solution. We don't read the lengthy "problem" manual; we skip right to the short "solutions" manual. Nowhere is this tendency more pronounced than when the problem to be solved is the retirement risk. And it is not just amateur investors who exhibit this unfortunate tendency; financial advisors and other finance professionals are just as guilty.

The financial pros often equate "risk" to "volatility." In this view, investment risk boils down to the possibility of losing money during a period of high negative volatility—that is, a sharp stock market downturn, or bear market. Understanding risk in this way leads to an obvious solution: because, in investing, volatility and returns increase and decrease together, the way to reduce risk is by buying lower-returning investments like bonds. Essentially, you give up the money that comes with higher returns, and in exchange, you get lower risk. Many investors, taking this solution to its logical extreme, sold all of their stock holdings during the 2008 financial crisis and went to bonds, CDs, and other fixed-income investments.

This solution makes perfect sense if risk and volatility are in fact one and the same. But volatility is only one aspect of the really big, monumental risk investors face—the risk of running out of money in retirement.

Now, this is where Einstein's point becomes really important. A solution that is not based on a clear, full understanding of the problem is not only likely to prove inadequate; in some cases it can be downright dangerous. So it is with the retirement risk. For although putting all your money in low-returning investments like bonds will definitely reduce the *volatility* of your portfolio, it may well increase the *risk* that you will run out of money in retirement. Even if you manage to reduce your retirement budget to match the low returns you can expect from bonds, you may encounter unexpected expenses (such as medical bills) that bankrupt you—but that you might have been able to afford had you been earning higher returns on your investments.

It is so obvious that low returns can put you at increased risk of bankruptcy (not to mention an uncomfortable retirement), everyone intuitively grasps the concept. And yet paradoxically, for many investors—amateurs and pros alike—the only way to reduce "risk" is by buying low-returning investments like bonds. Seemingly, you are exchanging dollars for safety. Few see this exchange for what it really is—reducing the risk of a dramatic, fast, and terrifying ride to the poorhouse during a market crash by increasing the risk of a slow, insidious slide to the exact same destination.

Why is it that we know low returns could put us at *increased* risk of bankruptcy, and yet we seek to *reduce* risk by shifting to low-returning investments in the wake of a market crash? The answer lies in the human psyche. The dramatic, terrifying dangers grab our attention and keep us awake at night, not the mundane, everyday ones. After the September 11 terrorist attacks, airline ticket purchases dropped dramatically, as many would-be fliers decided to drive to their destinations instead. This happened despite the fact that the chances of being a passenger on a hijacked plane are much lower than the odds of being in an automobile accident. Clearly those who switched from flying to driving did so without a clear-eyed understanding of the true risks involved in getting from point A to point B. Blinded by their fear of a dramatic, terrifying, and extremely unlikely event, they wound up *increasing* their travel risks. The solution they adopted did not match the problem. Similarly, investors who are blinded by the fear of another financial crisis equate risk with volatility, and don't clearly see the problem posed by the retirement risk. They are in danger of adopting a solution that may at best merely trade one route to bankruptcy for another, while leaving themselves with less money to enjoy in retirement. Those who have shifted most or all of their savings from stocks to bonds and cash have probably increased their risk of running out of money, while at the same time condemning themselves to a poorer retirement.

I am not suggesting that you should completely avoid bonds. On the contrary, as we shall see, a *moderate* allocation to bonds is an absolute necessity for most investors. Rather, what I'm saying is that the confusion of risk with volatility has misled many investors seeking to *reduce* their risk into allocating too much of their savings to bonds, thereby *increasing* their risk.

A solution that is not based on a clear understanding of the problem is no solution at all. Therefore, in this book we approach the problem posed by the retirement risk as the brainy Einstein (not the lucky James Bond) would have done. We take the time, here in Chapter 1, to come to a full and clear understanding of the problem. Then, in the subsequent chapters, we proceed to a solution.

If we can simply understand, and mitigate, the various ways in which our money might run out before we do, we will have solved the retirement riddle. Although the specifics are many and varied, in general, there are two ways we can go broke in retirement. Either we can encounter too much (negative) market volatility or not earn enough returns to keep up with our inflation-adjusted living expenses.

John Stockman and the Great Crash of 1929

To illustrate these two paths to financial ruin, I'd like to begin with a short story. Our story concerns two very different (fictional) characters, both of whom happened to be born in the same small town in rural Iowa on January 1, 1897. Both lived to be ninety-five years of age—a remarkable achievement for two people born before 1900 but no longer such an unusual occurrence. John Stockman was born on the east side of town, the only child of a successful local merchant. John was a mischievous kid, always getting into trouble. He graduated from high school at the bottom of his class of twelve in 1915 and, bored with small-town life, moved to New York City. When the United States entered World War I in 1917, he joined the navy "for the adventure of it," and as a sailor on a destroyer, he was cited for bravery on two separate occasions.

After the war, Stockman found work as a bartender in an upscale Manhattan nightclub. He proved very popular with the club's wealthy patrons as well as the club's owner, who took him under his wing and taught him the business. Stockman proved to be a fast learner. The club became a speakeasy when Prohibition became the law of the land, and not long after, Stockman came up with the idea of adding a gambling parlor. As he put it, "We're paying off the cops anyway, so we ought to make the most of it." Stockman helped raise the capital needed for the expansion from his rich friends, and as a reward, the owner made him a junior partner in the business and put him in charge of the gambling operation. As the 1920s progressed, the club became ever more popular, and Stockman enjoyed the high life his position and growing income brought him.

And what a time it was to be young and on the move up! The United States had emerged from the war an economic powerhouse. In the Roaring Twenties, signs of the nation's newfound prosperity were everywhere—in the extension of the electric grid to the majority of homes; in the vast market accessible electricity created for new conveniences like refrigerators, vacuum cleaners, radios, toasters, washers, and dryers; and above all in the rise of the automobile from a plaything of the wealthy to the ultimate middle-class status symbol. Between 1922 and 1928, gross national product rose nearly 40 percent and real wages 22 percent, while the standard workweek shrank.[11] In New York, Chicago, and other big cities, jazz clubs, flappers, and boot-leggers were plentiful and ready to help young, single men like Stockman spend their newfound dollars and leisure time.

The stock market more than kept pace with the booming economy. Between January 1924 and September 1929, the Dow Jones Industrial Average rose from 94.88 to 386.10 — a 300 percent rise in fewer than six years. Whereas the market had been largely a staid preserve of Wall Street bankers and wealthy investors prior to the 1920s, now, for the first time, the broader public began to get in on the game. In a widely read article published in *Ladies Home Journal* and titled "Everybody Ought to Be Rich," John Jacob Raskob, a member of GM's board of directors, showed that anyone who could invest $15 a month in sound common stocks would be worth $80,000 (more than $1 million in today's dollars) in twenty years.[12] As the decade progressed, many people took Raskob's advice. More than a few became obsessed with the stock market and what they saw as the opportunity for quick riches. Like the forty-niners of the gold rush, they upended their lives in pursuit of the paper gold sold on the stock exchanges, going deep into debt to buy stock on margin. Some even quit their jobs so they could spend their weekdays trading stocks and watching the ticker tape at the new branch offices brokerages were opening throughout the country. It was widely believed that a "new era" of unending prosperity had dawned. The highly respected and well-known economist Irving Fisher lent credence to this belief when he proclaimed that "stock prices have reached what looks like a perma-nently high plateau."

Stockman was one of the many caught up in the market mania. Though in his earlier years, he had loved to gamble, as part owner of his own casino, he learned just how high the odds were stacked in the house's favor. And anyway, now that he worked every night in his own gaming mecca, the excitement of the casino environ-ment gradually wore off for him. Gambling, he knew, "was for losers," and he need-ed a new thrill. In the late 1920s, the stock market provided all the thrills of a real casino — but with the important difference that this casino was turning out many more winners than losers. Stockman became less and less interested in his business, showing up late or sometimes not at all. Instead, he spent most of his time at his broker's office just off Wall Street. In spring 1929, he decided to quit his job and sell his ownership stake in the club to raise more funds for stock purchases. He became what we would today call a day trader, living off of his speculative returns. He was pretty good at it, too. It helped that he knew a lot of rich investors from among the clientele at the club. Occasionally they passed him privileged information (insider trading was legal back in the 1920s). He returned the favor by helping them spread negative rumors about stocks they had targeted in bear raids — which involved pool-ing their funds to sell a stock short and drive down the price. (Conspiring to ma-nipulate stock prices was also legal in the 1920s, believe it or not. Beer, however, wasn't. Different times, different values.) Stockman had always envied the wealth and privilege enjoyed by his rich friends. Now he figured that if he just kept at his stock trading for a few more years, he would be one of them. Riches were within his grasp. He just *knew* it.

★★★

Looking back from the twenty-first century, we know this story cannot have a happy ending. When the stock bubble finally burst, Stockman was a witness to history. On Black Thursday, October 24, 1929, he was in the customers' room at his broker's office as wave after wave of sell orders flooded the stock exchange and the stock ticker fell hours behind. Without access to up-to-the-minute price quotations, investors and speculators had no way of knowing just how much money they had lost. "The uncertainty led more and more people to try to sell. Others, no longer able to respond to margin calls, were sold out. By eleven-thirty, the market had surrendered to blind, relentless fear."[13] In his classic account of the crash, John Kenneth Galbraith described the scene unfolding in New York's financial district:

> Outside the Exchange in Broad Street a weird roar could be heard. Police Commissioner Grover Whalen became aware that something was happening and dispatched a special police detail to Wall Street to insure the peace. More people came and waited, though apparently no one knew for what. A workman appeared atop one of the high buildings to accomplish some repairs, and the multitude assumed he was a would-be suicide and waited impatiently for him to jump. Crowds also formed around the branch offices of brokerage firms throughout the city and, indeed, throughout the country. Word of what was happening, or what was thought to be happening, was passed out by those who were in sight of the board or the Trans-Lux. ... Rumor after rumor swept Wall Street and these outlying wakes. Stocks were now selling for nothing. The Chicago and Buffalo Exchanges had closed. A suicide wave was in progress, and eleven well-known speculators had already killed themselves.[14]

On the afternoon of October 24, the city's leading bankers organized a pool to buy up major stocks in an effort to quell the panic. The pool worked, selling gave way to a rally, and the market closed only slightly down for the day. But the respite proved brief, as the panic returned with renewed vengeance the following week. By the end of June 1930, the Dow stood at 48.11 — a decline of 87.5 percent from the high reached less than a year previously. Stockman managed to scrape up enough money to meet a series of margin calls and held on to his few remaining investments as long as he could in the belief that the market would eventually recover. He was right — it did recover. But the recovery came too late to help him. In 1934, as the Depression ground on, with no job and no prospects, he was forced to liquidate the last of his shares to buy a few weeks' worth of groceries.

At this point, the trail goes cold on Stockman's life. It was rumored that he spent a few years riding the rails as a hobo, but we cannot say if this is true. We must instead leave John Stockman in the midst of the Depression and turn to his fellow Midwesterner, born on that same winter's day in 1897, on the west side of the same small town.

Joe Bondsman and the Stagflation of the 1970s

Joe Bondsman may have been born at the same time and place as John Stockman, but he couldn't have been more different in life experience or temperament. His father was a farmer who was seriously injured in an accident and forced to sell the farm before Joe, the youngest of nine, was born. After the accident, Joe Sr. moved to the west side of town, where he barely earned enough as a bank teller to keep his family in poverty. Young Joe might have been a playmate of John Stockman's growing up if he had had the time to play, but his was a short childhood. He left school at age ten to work various odd jobs. At age fourteen, he landed a job at the local meatpacking plant—a brutal job but one that paid well for someone his age. Almost all of his earnings went toward helping his family get by, but he was able to deposit a few pennies each week in his own account at the bank where his father worked. He never spent anything on himself. When America entered the Great War in 1917, Joe joined the army. "It's my duty as a citizen," he said at the time. Private Bondsman shipped out to France in a convoy guarded by Seaman Stockman's destroyer. It was almost, but not quite, the last time their paths would cross.

During the war, Bondsman was gassed and bombed and suffered from trench-foot—all of which he endured with great equanimity and resolve. His company commander admired his toughness and leadership qualities, and within a few months, he was promoted to sergeant.

After the war, Bondsman returned home and found his old job at the slaughterhouse waiting for him. Soon after he returned, his father died of complications from the old farming injury, and his mother passed away not long afterward. At the age of twenty-one, Bondsman was on his own, but by twenty-two, he had married a local girl, Emily, age nineteen. Two years later, Emily gave birth to a son, Joseph Bondsman III, who was followed in short order by three sisters and a brother.

As Joe's family grew, he slowly worked his way up to more responsible positions at the plant. By 1924 he was a foreman. Meanwhile, he took a series of correspondence courses in bookkeeping, in the hope that he would someday be able to leave the slaughterhouse floor for an office job. And all the while, while meeting the bills and avoiding debt, he managed to add slowly to his savings account at the bank.

But Joe's gains were nearly all lost as the Roaring Twenties gave way to the Great Depression. These were frightening times for the Bondsmans and their fellow Midwesterners. Many lost their farms to foreclosure, and their life savings to bank failures.

Nor was it just the economy that brought hardship to rural Americans; the land itself turned against them. More than once the Iowa sun was blotted out by vast dust clouds carried on the wind from the Dust Bowl states of Nebraska and Kansas.

Joe's employer was forced to lay off more than half the workforce at the meatpacking plant. Bondsman lost his position as a foreman to a more experienced supervisor, but he was just barely able to hold on, through a number of layoffs, to a position as a laborer in the plant's stockyard. Another close call came in 1933, when rumors that the local bank was insolvent threatened a bank run. Fortunately for Joe and Emily, the new president, Franklin Roosevelt, declared a bank holiday just as these rumors were about to reach a critical mass. Roosevelt's first fireside chat, intended to calm depositors and stop the bank runs, was arguably one of the most effective speeches in history. When the banks reopened, long lines once again formed outside their doors—but this time people lined up to deposit, not withdraw, their money. Nonetheless, Bondsman, who thought his money was safe at the bank, never forgot the sinking feeling he got when he first heard the insolvency rumors. It was during those dark days of 1933 that he first began to consider alternatives to his savings account. Stocks were out of the question—if Bondsman was too risk averse to buy stocks in the Roaring Twenties, he certainly wasn't going to do so in the depths of the Depression. Bonds seemed much safer, although "Go Slow Joe," as his friends called him, would take years before finally buying his first bond mutual fund.

In the meantime, the Depression finally came to an end as the nation's factories geared up for World War II. The slaughterhouse returned to hiring mode, and Bondsman, after a short stint in his old foreman's job, became supervisor of the day shift. Throughout the Depression, Bondsman had kept up with his nighttime studies, and he earned an accounting degree and passed the CPA exam. When the plant's bookkeeper finally retired in 1942, Bondsman got the job. He actually had to take a pay cut at first, but he believed he was positioning himself for improved job prospects in the future. He was right. In 1945, he was transferred to the company's headquarters in Chicago. By 1949, he was head of the accounting department, and during the 1950s, he rose through the executive ranks. He and Emily put all five of their children through college, bought a fine house in the Chicago suburbs, hired a live-in housekeeper, and enjoyed travel abroad. And when Bondsman retired in 1962 at age sixty-five, he had built up a sizeable nest egg worth $625,000—invested entirely in bond mutual funds. Joe Bondsman, a survivor of the Great Depression, never overcame his fear of stocks. It was a fear that would eventually doom him and Emily to poverty.

Joe Bondsman's Retirement Plan Meets a Harsh Reality

Bondsman had a detailed financial plan all worked out for his golden years with Emily. He had estimated their budget and planned to withdraw 4 percent of the money in his portfolio—$25,000—to cover living expenses in their first year of retirement ($25,000 in 1962, the year Bondsman retired, is worth more than $100,000 in today's dollars). After that first year, by his calculations, he would be able to increase the amount withdrawn from the portfolio by 3 percent per year to cover inflation. These withdrawals, plus the $5,000 per year he expected from Social Security, should have enabled the Bondsmans to enjoy a comfortable retirement in their suburban home, with little danger of running out of money.

In 1962, Joe's all-bonds portfolio sustained a 5.2 percent loss. (This and all of the following return figures in Joe Bondsman's tale represent actual average historical returns for investment-grade, intermediate-term bond funds, calculated from data on Morningstar's website.) The first few years of retirement are crucial to the survivability of a retiree's portfolio, and there is nothing unluckier than starting off the first year with a loss. Fortunately, the next two years saw improved bond returns of 9.8 and 8.0 percent, and by the end of 1964, Joe's portfolio had recovered to $616,000 —only $9,000 less than his starting value of $625,000. But 1964 was the high water mark. Over the next six years, Bondsman's *best* annual returns were only 5.6 percent, and in two of those years, returns were negative—including a huge double-digit loss of 15.7 percent in 1969. By 1970, when Bondsman turned seventy-three, his portfolio had shrunk to $437,000.

The years 1973–74 brought the Arab oil embargo and spiraling inflation. President Nixon tried, but failed, to stop inflation with wage and price controls. By the late 1970s, "stagflation"—high unemployment coupled with double-digit inflation that seemingly could not be stopped—had settled in. Joe Bondsman, a former CFO, was financially astute enough to have taken inflation into account in his retirement plans. Recall that he planned to withdraw $25,000 from his portfolio to cover living expenses in the first year of his retirement and then to *increase* this amount by 3 percent per year to cover the effects of inflation. In the low-inflation environment of the early 1960s, 3 percent seemed more than adequate. But the inflation rate gradually rose above 3 percent in the late 1960s, and between 1977 and 1982, the inflation rate averaged 9 percent—*three times* the rate Joe had expected.

Beginning in 1973, the Bondsmans began to cut back on their living expenses. In 1975, with inflation showing no sign of abating, they made the painful decision to sell their house and move into a much smaller duplex near the city limit. The moved helped their finances, but not enough. The inflation rate kept increasing, and the Bondsmans simply couldn't make ends meet with the 3 percent adjustment. In 1977, at Emily's insistence, Joe increased the inflation adjustment to 9 percent to match actual inflation. Joe and Emily planned to return to a more sustainable, 3 percent adjustment once the inflation rate returned to more normal levels. But stagflation dragged on into the 1980s. Meanwhile, their bond fund returns had dwindled. Between 1977 and 1981, returns on intermediate-term bond funds averaged a measly 2.8 percent—nowhere near enough to keep up with inflation. By 1981, the Bondsmans' nest egg had declined to $156,000, pressured on both sides by low returns and rapidly increasing withdrawals.

It was around this time that Federal Reserve chairman Paul Volcker, by raising interest rates to double-digit levels, finally brought an end to stagflation and ushered in the great 1980s–90s bull market in stocks and bonds. In 1982, the average investment-grade, intermediate-term bond fund returned a whopping 32.4 percent. For the remainder of the 1980s, the average return of these same funds remained more than 8 percent in every year but one. Unfortunately, all this came too late for Joe and Emily Bondsman. They reduced their inflation adjustment back to 3 percent starting in 1983, but despite the much better returns and the tamed inflation, their remaining nest egg was now too small to recover. In 1984, the year Joe turned eighty-seven and Emily eighty-four, they ran out of money. They sold their duplex unit and move back to their old Iowa hometown to live with their youngest daughter and her husband —himself a retiree on limited income. The Bondsmans had outlived their money. Joe Bondsman, who had been financially independent since age fourteen and hated the thought of being a burden on anyone, let alone his own daughter, would have to survive on her charity and a small stipend from Social Security for the remaining eight years of his life.

Stockman's and Bondsman's Two Paths to Ruin

Let's now analyze what happened to Stockman and Bondsman. In Stockman's case, it's pretty obvious. His road to financial ruin is the one all investors know about, and fear. Over the long run, stocks have proven to be an excellent investment, yielding annualized returns of about 10 percent from the 1920s to the present. But these returns have been anything but steady. During the Depression, the Dow lost a staggering 89 percent of its value. More recently, the S&P 500 dropped 47 percent in the 2000–2002 bear market and 55 percent in the 2007–9 financial crisis. It is difficult enough to watch these kinds of losses ravage your savings when you enjoy steady income from a secure job. But if you are retired and, like Stockman, entirely dependent on the stock market for your income, such losses can lead to bankruptcy.

But it was not just the magnitude of his losses that sent Stockman to the poorhouse. It was also the timing of those losses. Stockman began his retirement in spring 1929, only a few months before the October crash. Retirees who encounter a major bear market soon after retiring are in much greater danger of losing everything than those who retire in the early or middle years of a bull market. The latter retirees will have time to grow their portfolios, and this early growth will help to offset their losses when the inevitable bear market finally arrives. But for those who have the bad luck of retiring shortly before a major market crash, the investment losses, coming on top of the need to keep withdrawing money from a dwindling nest egg to meet living expenses, can spell financial doom.

The risk posed by the timing of market losses is referred to as sequencing risk. Sequencing risk in turn combines with the magnitude and frequency of market crashes to compose the risk posed by market volatility—one of the two components of the retirement risk, and the undoing of John Stockman.

★★★

What happened to Joe Bondsman is less obvious. The financial route that Bondsman followed through his retirement seemed *much* safer than Stockman's. Stockman's road was a short one that sent him over a cliff. Although much longer and less dramatic, Bondsman's road ended at the same destination—bankruptcy. Bondsman was bound and determined to reduce the risk posed by market volatility to an absolute minimum. It was for this reason that he invested his entire life savings in bonds. What Joe Bondsman didn't know—what he couldn't possibly have known—is that the first twenty years of his retirement would parallel a long bear market in bonds. A bond bear market looks, and feels, much different than a bear market in stocks. During this entire period, Joe lost money in only five years. Furthermore, the worst loss was only 15.7 percent, in 1969. Compare this with the 90 percent loss suffered by Stockman during the Depression, and it is clear that bonds are indeed much less "risky" than stocks—if by "risky" we mean *only* less volatile.

But it is an ironclad rule of investing that risk and return go together. Buyers of a high-risk (meaning highly volatile) investment, such as a stock, are compensated for the risk they undertake with high expected returns. Investors in low-risk (i.e., low volatility) bonds must expect low returns. Over the twenty-year period of 1962–81, the average investment-grade, intermediate-term bond fund generated annualized returns of only 3.2 percent. In 1962, Joe withdrew 4 percent of his portfolio for living expenses, and increased his withdrawals each subsequent year. It is clear that you cannot keep taking out 4 percent or more of the value of a portfolio that is growing only 3.2 percent per year and expect it to last.

The Night Thief

But while he couldn't have done it forever, Bondsman *could* have taken a flat $25,000 per year for the twenty years that the bear market lasted, and he would have been able to recover financially once the bear market ended. It was inflation—the need to keep increasing the withdrawal rate to keep up with rising prices—that bankrupted Bondsman. Whereas John Stockman was done in by too much market volatility, Joe Bondsman was financially ruined by returns insufficient to keep up with inflation. The effect of inflation on Bondsman's portfolio is illustrated in Figure 1.1. This figure compares the actual trajectory of Joe's portfolio, with the original 3 percent inflation adjustment and the 9 percent adjustment he used from 1977 through 1982, with the trajectory it would have taken if Joe had lived in some inflation-free fantasyland where he could have kept his annual withdrawals for living expenses at a flat $25,000.

The difference between the two trajectories is stark. By 1984, just twenty-two years into Joe's retirement, the portfolio subject to the inflation adjustments went bust, but in that same year, the fantasy portfolio with no annual inflation adjustment would have been worth $596,000.

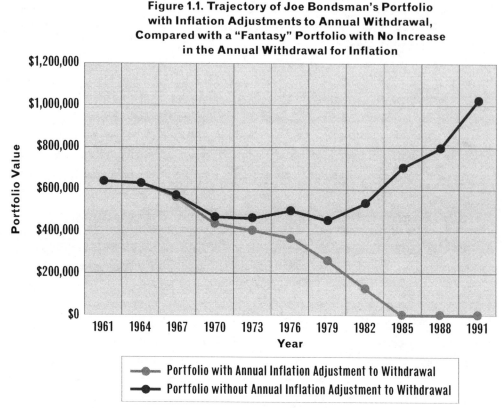

Figure 1.1. Trajectory of Joe Bondsman's Portfolio with Inflation Adjustments to Annual Withdrawal, Compared with a "Fantasy" Portfolio with No Increase in the Annual Withdrawal for Inflation

Source: Developed by the author using data from www.morningstar.com.

And this isn't the worst of it. Even if stagflation hadn't occurred and Bondsman didn't have to increase the inflation adjustment starting in 1977, the portfolio *still* would have gone bust by the time Joe turned ninety-one (and Emily eighty-eight). In that same year, the fantasy, no-inflation portfolio would have grown to $798,000. Increasing the inflation adjustment from 3 percent to 9 percent between 1977 and 1982 didn't cause the Bondsmans' financial ruin—it just hastened it.

Why does a small, 3 percent increase in the annual amount withdrawn from the portfolio have such a huge impact on the portfolio's final value? The answer is simple. The effects of inflation compound over time, in the same way as the interest you earn on a savings account. A few years ago, I took a night class on retirement planning. The instructor had a colorful way of warning us against two key risks to our nest eggs. There are, he would say, two thieves we must guard against. First, there is the bold thief who comes in the broad daylight and demands a cut of everything we earn. This daytime thief is also called "the taxman." Then there is the much sneakier burglar who comes in the night, while we sleep, and raises the prices of everything we need and want. The price increases are very small—almost imperceptible—so we barely notice what has happened. But he comes back the next night and raises prices again. And the next night. And the night after that. And even though each time the night thief—also called "inflation"—strikes, the effect on prices is barely perceptible, over time the effect compounds in the same way that interest earned on a savings account compounds.

Over the very long term, the rate of inflation has averaged 3 percent. Owing to the effects of compounding, a 3 percent inflation rate will cause prices to *double* every twenty-four years. Or, viewed another way, a 3 percent inflation rate will reduce the *real* value of $1 million to $491,934 in twenty-four years and to $241,999 in forty-eight years. This constant, insidious reduction in the real purchasing power of your retirement savings is the biggest long-term problem you and every investor face. It is why you *must* earn a long-run rate of return that significantly exceeds the rate of inflation if you are to grow the purchasing power of your nest egg and beat the retirement risk. Bondsman's 3.2 percent returns barely exceeded the long-run inflation rate. He could not grow his portfolio on such meager returns and was forced to dip more and more deeply into his principal to meet expenses. The old story claiming that Einstein said compound interest is the most powerful force in the universe is probably apocryphal, but certainly compounding is one of the most powerful forces in the *financial* universe. And it can be a force for evil (inflation) as well as good (compound interest).

Joe Bondsman was done in by the second of the two great risks to retirement— investment returns too small to keep up with the compound effect of inflation. What is the lesson here? Although bonds are much more effective than stocks in limiting an investor's exposure to market volatility, they are much less effective at safeguarding an investor from inflation—especially unexpectedly high inflation such as we experienced in the 1970s and early 1980s. Unlike stock dividends, which can grow over time with inflation, the dividends you earn from a bond will remain the same, year in and year out, regardless of whether inflation remains tame or rises. Furthermore, whereas the price of a stock can move higher as the stock's earnings per share increase with inflation, a bond's price can rise only so far before it eventually converges back toward the bond's face value—the principal that must be paid when the bond matures. When there is an unexpected rise in inflation, the value and price of a fixed-income investment like a bond will decline, not increase. And we should add that cash investments like money market funds, CDs, and savings accounts are even worse than bonds at protecting you from inflation.

Unfortunately, memories are short. With the extreme stock market volatility we experienced in 2008 still fresh in their minds, many investors—professional traders as well as amateurs—have long since forgotten the less dramatic but no less catastrophic stagflation of the 1970s and early 1980s. Yet inflation has been a fact of life ever since the rulers of antiquity discovered that they could make their tax revenues go further by debasing (reducing the gold or silver content of) their coinage. And it is a fact that as government debt rises—as it is doing across the globe today—the temptation governments face to inflate their way out of that debt (by paying it off in debased dollars, euros, yen, etc.) also rises. The night thief is still with us today, and he could still surprise us by going on a rampage, as he did back in the 1970s. The investor in bonds should never lose sight of this possibility and the risk it poses for her bond portfolio.

That said, we can perhaps take some comfort from the fact that Joe Bondsman didn't run out of money until he was eighty-seven years old. After all, what are the odds of living eighty-seven years or more?

To a Long Life (and a Merry One)

Well, according to actuarial tables from the Social Security Administration, the odds are pretty high. If a male makes it to retirement age (sixty-five), he has a 33 percent chance of living until at least eighty-seven. For a female, the odds increase to 46 percent.[15] And what are the odds that at least one spouse of a couple, both age sixty-five, will make it to age eighty-seven or more? These odds can be estimated easily from the two preceding numbers. I've done the calculation, and the result is 64 percent.[16] Chances are better than even that at least one spouse will live to age eighty-seven, or longer.

In Table 1.1, I've used the Social Security data to calculate the odds of making it to other advanced ages. The table gives the probabilities that a sixty-five-year old male, a sixty-five-year old female, and at least one member of a sixty-five-year-old couple will live to at least eighty-five, ninety, ninety-five, and one hundred. For example, at least one member of a 65-year-old couple has a 19 percent (nearly one in five) chance of making it to age 95.

Table 1.1. Probabilities of Living to Advanced Ages for Sixty-Five-Year-Old Males, Females, and Couples

Age (years)	Probability for 65-Year-Old Male (%)	Probability for 65-Year-Old Female (%)	Probability for 65-Year-Old Couple (%)
85 or older	42	54	73
90 or older	21	33	47
95 or older	7	13	19
100 or older	1	3	4

Source: Calculated by the author from the Social Security Administration's 2009 Actuarial Life Table, www.ssa.gov/oact/STATS/table4c6.html.

Take a good, long look at the probabilities in Table 1.1. The good news is that life expectancy in the United States has increased significantly over the years. The downside is that, if you don't want to wind up flipping burgers at McDonald's when you're ninety, you'd best make financial preparations for a long retirement.

A Postscript

We lost track of John Stockman in Depression-era New York, but in 1948, he reappeared as the owner of a small restaurant in Los Angeles, with a wife (Brenda) and son (Anthony). In the mid-1950s, he hit upon the idea of expanding his small business by opening a chain of restaurants to serve travelers along the interstate highway system then being built by the Eisenhower administration. His interstate restaurant chain was small but growing rapidly by the late 1950s, and he was able to sell the business for the then-sizable sum of $625,000 in 1962. Thus he entered into retirement at the same time, and with the same-sized nest egg, as Joe Bondsman. And although he didn't plan his retirement out with anything like the same precision as Bondsman, he nonetheless wound up withdrawing 4 percent in the first year to cover his and Brenda's living expenses and then adjusting the withdrawal upward 3 percent per year—just like Bondsman. And like Bondsman, he had to increase the inflation adjustment to 9 percent between 1977 and 1982, before going back to 3 percent after 1982. The only difference is that whereas Bondsman invested all of his savings in bond mutual funds, Stockman invested 100 percent of his nest egg in large cap (large company) stock mutual funds.

Although Stockman's total reliance on stocks had proven disastrous in the 1930s, it worked out okay for him in the 1960s and 1970s. Figure 1.2 shows the trajectory of Stockman's portfolio compared with Bondsman's. There were a few rough patches for Stockman—especially 1973–74, when the average large cap mutual fund lost 38.8 percent of its value. In 1974, Stockman's portfolio hit a low of $355,000. But by 1984, the year Joe Bondsman went broke, Stockman's portfolio had recovered to $505,000. John's nest egg lasted his entire lifetime, and was still worth $476,000 when it was passed on to his son Anthony.

As would be expected, and as Figure 1.2 confirms, Bondsman's all-bond portfolio followed a much smoother path than Stockman's all-stock portfolio. But that smooth path led to a much different destination.

In 1987, Brenda Stockman passed away, and John, still in good mental and physical health at age ninety, decided to visit his Iowa birthplace for the first time in more than seventy years. His son Anthony agreed to take him there. On the drive from the Des Moines airport, he noticed an old, run-down clapboard house on the west side of town. In a rocking chair on the porch sat a very old man. Staring at the man's ancient face, a sense of recognition, or connection, passed over Stockman.

It was a vaguely disquieting feeling. But it quickly passed as the light turned green and they continued their drive to Stockman's childhood home on the east side of town.

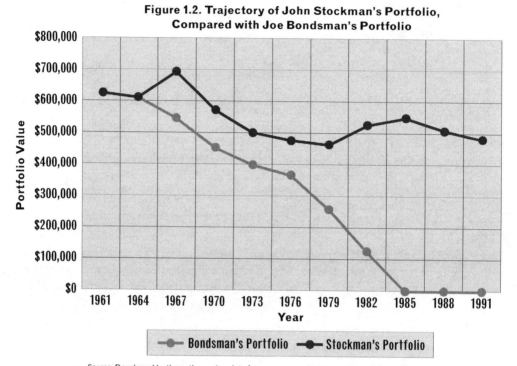

Figure 1.2. Trajectory of John Stockman's Portfolio, Compared with Joe Bondsman's Portfolio

Source: Developed by the author using data from www.morningstar.com.

TWO PATHS TO DIVERSIFICATION

Say to yourself every day, "I cannot predict the future, therefore I diversify."
—**William Bernstein**, *Rational Expectations*

T hanks to John Stockman and Joe Bondsman, we now have a clearer understanding of the problem we are seeking to solve in this book. That problem is the retirement risk—the risk of outliving your money. It is now clear that there are two components to this risk—too much (negative) volatility (Stockman's undoing) and not enough returns to outpace inflation (Bondsman's path to the poorhouse).

Diversifying Using the Principle of Compromise

We also have the beginnings of a solution to the retirement risk problem. Clearly John Stockman and Joe Bondsman brought on their own financial ruin by failing to diversify their portfolios. Had Stockman mixed some bonds in with his stocks, he could have survived the 1929 Crash. For example, Vanguard's venerable Wellington mutual fund, which invests in a mix of stocks and bonds, lost only 59 percent of its value during the 1929 Crash,[17] as compared to the Dow's 89 percent loss. Similarly, had Bondsman added a large helping of stocks (70 percent or more) to his bond investments he would have made it to his ninety-fifth birthday without going bankrupt. A possible solution to the retirement risk is simply to mix stocks with bonds.

But this solution does not quite fit the problem. Mixing stocks with bonds, or bonds with stocks, *reduces* one part of the retirement risk by *increasing* the other part. This is the fundamental dilemma that Stockman and Bondsman faced—and that you and I face.

If, like Bondsman, your personality drives you to keep volatility to a minimum, you must accept low returns—and the risk of bankruptcy stemming from those low

19

returns. Adding stocks to an all-bond portfolio will increase the portfolio's returns, but only at the cost of increased volatility. If, like Stockman, you want to maximize returns, you must accept high volatility—and the risk of bankruptcy that comes with volatility. You can add bonds to an all-stock portfolio to reduce its volatility, but that will compromise your goal of high returns.

A truly satisfactory solution to the problem of the retirement risk would address both of its component parts. It would enable you to reduce volatility while increasing, or at least not reducing, returns. What we really need is an investment that combines high returns with low volatility.

Unfortunately, there's no such investment. But there *is* a way to construct a *portfolio* of investments that minimizes volatility and maximizes returns. So far, we've talked about mixing stocks with bonds. This is one way to diversify your portfolio. It works—and works well—simply by blending a set of low-volatility, low-return investments with high-volatility, high-return investments. The resulting mix has characteristics somewhere between stocks and bonds. You wind up with a portfolio that is not as volatile as stocks but more volatile than bonds, and that generates returns larger than bonds but not as large as stocks. This way of diversifying works on the principle of *compromise*—you give up some returns to reduce volatility. In essence, you are balancing one component of the retirement risk against the other component.

The second way to diversify your portfolio actually gives you a way of reducing volatility without having to give up returns (in some cases, it may even boost your returns, as we shall see). It is a very powerful diversification strategy that works on the principle of *correlation* rather than *compromise*. The principle of correlation is a key foundation of modern portfolio theory (MPT), the Nobel Prize–winning strategy for optimizing the risk-return profile of investment portfolios. While the optimization mathematics composing MPT is complicated and not particularly useful from a practical standpoint, the principle of correlation on which MPT is based is simple and extremely useful. In this book, we borrow the simple principle without delving into the complicated theory.

Diversifying Using the Principle of Correlation

To understand how the principle of correlation works, we must first draw a sharp distinction between a *single investment* and a *portfolio* of investments. And before we can talk about how to build portfolios that maximize returns while minimizing risk, we first need to understand why single investments can never do this. Every single investment that offers the potential of high returns comes with high volatility. Every single investment that offers low volatility comes with low expected returns. It is an ironclad rule of investing—risk and reward go together. It *must* be this way. To understand why, consider what would happen if this rule were ever to be broken. Suppose, for example, that two different bonds, each priced at its face value of $1,000 and maturing in one year, will pay back the $1,000 principal plus a coupon of $50 at the end of the year. One bond has a credit rating of AAA—the highest rating possible, indicating that the risk of default on the bond is minimal. The other bond is rated CCC, indicating that it is a junk bond with an elevated risk of default. Given that both bonds are priced at $1,000 and will pay $1,050 in one year—an expected return of 5 percent—why would anyone purchase the higher-risk CCC bond? They won't, and because all buyers will choose the AAA bond instead, its price will rise relative to that of the CCC bond. As the price of the AAA bond rises and that of the CCC bond drops, the expected return on each bond changes. Suppose, for example, that the price of the AAA bond rises to $1,010, whereas that of the CCC bond drops to $970. In this case, the yield on the AAA bond will be $40—the $1,050 you will receive in one year minus the price of $1,010 you paid for the bond. In percentage terms, the bond's expected return would be 3.96 percent (calculated by dividing the $40 return by the $1,010 purchase price). The expected return on the CCC bond will be $80 ($1,050 − $970) divided by the $970 purchase price, or 8.25 percent. The lower-risk bond will be priced by the market in such a way as to ensure that it will come with a lower expected return than the higher-risk bond. The market *can always* be counted on to price investments perceived as having low risk—in other words, low volatility—in such a way as to ensure lower expected returns for these investments. If you want higher returns, you must take on higher volatility, and to reduce volatility, you must accept lower returns. If anyone ever offers you an investment with high expected returns and low volatility, don't fall for it. The person making you the offer is either a fool or a con artist.

So how do you get around the ironclad rule of risk and return? By recognizing that a single investment is not the same thing as a group of investments—a portfolio. Let me draw an analogy between investing and baking. Like me, you may never have baked a cake in your life, but you've probably tasted one or two. And like me, you're probably at least vaguely aware that a cake is made out of a bunch of different ingredients: things like flour, eggs, butter, baker's chocolate, and sugar. The interesting thing about a cake is that it neither looks nor tastes like any single ingredient that went into it—although each ingredient plays a role in the overall "cakeness" of the cake. For example, a cake does not look anything like a stick of butter, nor does it have the texture of butter, although it may be buttery tasting. A cake is more than the sum of its parts. You can taste all or at least some of the ingredients that went into it, but it has a character all its own.

A portfolio constructed according to the principle of correlation is like a cake. It combines investments with different characteristics—different levels of volatility and expected returns—into a single portfolio that is greater than the sum of its parts. Most interestingly, using the correlation principle, you can combine two investments with high volatility into a portfolio that is *less* volatile than either individual investment. To understand how, let's consider a hypothetical example. XYZ Company makes and sells widgets. We'll pretend widgets are made by combining a substance called "wid" with another substance, "get." Wid is produced by ABC Corporation. The prices of ABC's and XYZ's stocks can be quite volatile, and hence the expected returns provided by each stock are high (remember that high volatility comes with high rewards). But the price movement of one is often related to the movement of the other. In particular, when the price of wid rises, ABC's stock price may tend to go up, while that of XYZ may tend to go down. Why? The wid producer's profit margin depends directly on the price of its product. When the price of wid rises, ABC's profits go up, and its stock price is likely to follow. However, wid is a key ingredient in the production of widgets. When the price of wid rises, XYZ's production costs rise, reducing its profit margin and quite possibly its stock price.

So in this example, we have a single event—a rise in the price of wid—that tends to lower the price of the widget manufacturer's stock, while causing the price of the wid producer's stock to rise. Similarly, a drop in the price of wid may result in a decline in the wid producer's stock price and an increase in the widget company's stock price. The two stocks have a tendency to move in opposite directions.

Suppose now that we combine the two stocks in a single portfolio. When the wid producer's stock drops, the resulting loss tends to be offset by a rise in the widget manufacturer's stock, and vice versa. When one stock *zigs*, the other *zags*, and as a result, the volatility of the portfolio is less than the volatility of either stock. But because both stocks come with high expected returns, the portfolio's expected return is also high. The result is a portfolio with high expected returns and low volatility.

Figure 2.1 illustrates this example. Here we see that the price of each stock, considered in isolation, zigzags up and down a lot in the short run, although both stocks follow an upward trend in the long term. Notice that when the widget maker's stock goes down, the wid company's stock tends to go up, and vice versa. The two stocks are said to be *negatively correlated* to each other.

Now take a look at Figure 2.2. Here we have combined the two stocks in a portfolio consisting of 50 percent widget manufacturer stock and 50 percent wid producer stock (represented by the dotted line in the figure). Notice that the portfolio captures the long-term upward trend of both stocks but smoothes out the short-term fluctuations. In our example, the return of the portfolio as a whole is exactly the same as the return of each stock ($25 on a $20 investment, for a return of 125 percent), but the portfolio achieves this return with much lower volatility than either stock.

Combining assets that zig with assets that zag minimizes volatility for a given level of expected returns. It is the *only* way we can get around the ironclad rule of investing and reap large returns without taking on large risks. Consider for a moment how this idea of combining zigging and zagging stocks might help investors facing the retirement risk. As we have seen, the retirement risk—the risk of outliving our money—manifests itself in two main ways. We can encounter either too much (negative) market volatility or not enough returns to outpace inflation. Using the *principle of compromise* to diversify, we must balance high-return, high-volatility assets with low-return, low-volatility assets. In other words, we must either give up some returns to reduce our portfolio's volatility, or we must take on more volatility to increase our returns. The dilemma this poses is clear—to reduce one risk to our portfolio, we must increase the other risk.

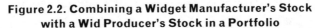

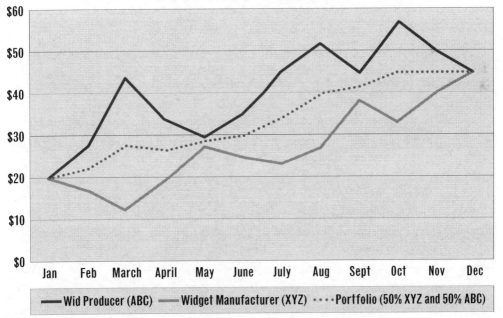

Figure 2.1. Price Trends of a Widget Manufacturer's Stock and a Wid Producer's Stock

Figure 2.2. Combining a Widget Manufacturer's Stock with a Wid Producer's Stock in a Portfolio

But if we use the *principle of correlation* to diversify, combining zigging assets with zagging assets, we can actually reduce our portfolio's volatility without having to give up much, if any, of our returns. Instead of having to balance risks—reducing one risk to our nest egg by increasing the other risk—we can have our cake and eat it too. *This* is what makes diversification based on the correlation principle such a powerful investment strategy. It is the *only* way we can expect to get around the ironclad rule of investing and reap large returns without taking on large risks.

Applying the Principle of Correlation in Practice

We can now begin to consider how to use the principle of correlation to construct a truly well-diversified portfolio. To do so, we first need to make an assumption—that the core *asset class* composing our portfolio will be the stocks of large companies ("large cap" stocks). We are making this assumption because in most real-world portfolios, stocks—particularly large cap stocks—are the dominant asset class. This reflects the fact that large cap stocks account for 70 percent of the total value of the U.S. stock market. You cannot be truly diversified if such a large segment of the market is not represented in your portfolio. The best way to own large cap stocks is not individually but through a low-cost index mutual fund or exchange traded fund (ETF) that covers a broad swath of the market. There are many such investments, including, for example, funds that are designed to track the S&P 500.

So which characteristics should we look for in *other* asset classes—for example, bonds and other categories of stocks—that will help us to protect, or hedge, our portfolio from suffering massive losses when our core large cap stock fund drops in value? The ideal characteristics of a hedge to large caps are as follows:

- *Low correlation* with large caps

- *Expected returns* similar to those of large caps

- *High volatility* (yes, you read that right!)

Of the preceding three characteristics, *low correlation* is the most important. Two asset classes can be said to be *positively correlated, negatively correlated,* or *uncorrelated* with one another. Correlation is measured by statisticians on a scale of −1 to +1. If one asset always yields below average returns when another asset produces above average returns, and vice versa, then the two assets have perfect negative correlation (a *correlation coefficient* of −1). Two assets that always experience either above average returns or below average returns at the same time have perfect positive correlation (a correlation coefficient of +1). An asset that exhibits no tendency to either under-perform or outperform its average when another asset outperforms (or underper-forms) is *uncorrelated* to the other asset (correlation coefficient of 0). Correlation coefficients can take on any value between −1 (perfect negative correlation) and +1 (perfect positive correlation). For example, if two assets have a correlation coefficient of +0.8, then when one of the assets outperforms, the other will usually, but not always, follow suit.

Ideally, the other asset classes to be combined with large caps in our portfolio would have strong negative correlation with large caps—that is, correlation coefficients ranging from −0.5 to −1. But unfortunately, in the real world, there are no such asset classes. In fact, even asset classes that exhibit weak negative correlation with large cap stocks (correlation coefficients ranging from −0.5 to 0) are rare. The sad fact is that in the investment world, asset classes tend to move in sync with each other. When the S&P 500 is up, most other assets go up right along with it—and most assets follow the S&P 500 down as well.

This lack of asset classes with strong or even weak negative correlation to large cap stocks has very important implications. We will return to these implications later. But for now, let's focus on a happier fact: combining asset classes with anything less than perfect positive correlation can reduce a portfolio's volatility. Of course, the weaker the positive correlation, the better. In practice, this means that the best way to "hedge" our investment in large cap stocks is to find asset classes with weak positive correlation (correlation coefficients between 0 and +0.5).

So which asset classes fit the bill? One of the most important is bonds. Stocks and bonds are characterized by low positive (and, in the case of some types of bonds, low negative) correlation. Why? One reason is that when the stock market is going down, people have a tendency to reduce their risks by shifting money out of stocks and into safer investments, including bonds. Thus bond prices often (though not always) rise when stock prices fall. This is a very important point, because it means that bonds reduce portfolio volatility in *two* ways. As we have already seen, bonds work on the principle of compromise, reducing the volatility of a stock portfolio because they are low-volatility investments. But bonds also work on the principle of correlation, reducing portfolio volatility because they often tend to move in the opposite direction of stocks. This makes bonds a particularly powerful volatility-reducing asset class. There are, of course, many different types of bonds—Treasuries, agency bonds, corporate bonds, municipal bonds, high-yield bonds, and foreign bonds, to name a few—and their volatility-reducing power varies across type. In Chapter 5, we will discuss bonds, their characteristics and many varieties, in detail. For now, you should know simply that adding bonds to our large cap portfolio is the single most important step we can take to reducing the portfolio's volatility.

That said, there are also some major drawbacks to using bonds as a hedge for large cap stocks. In fact, if we return for a moment to the three key characteristics of an ideal hedge—low correlation, similar returns, and high volatility—we notice that bonds meet only one of these characteristics (low correlation). Bonds are *low-*volatility, not *high-*volatility, investments. Even more important, at least over the last nine decades, bonds have averaged significantly lower returns than large cap stocks (about 5.5 to 6 percent for bonds vs. about 10 percent for large cap stocks). As we have already seen, adding bonds to a stock portfolio requires that we give up some returns to get reduced volatility—a compromise increasing the risk that the portfolio will not keep up with inflation over the long term. Hence, although they have a low correlation with stocks, bonds work primarily on the basis of the principle of compromise. Remember that the promise of the principle of *correlation* lies in its potential to reduce portfolio volatility without reducing portfolio returns. Bonds clearly do not fulfill this promise (though they remain crucially important components of an investor's portfolio because, as we shall see, the principle of correlation sometimes doesn't work!). To realize the promise of the correlation principle, we need to find some asset classes that combine *low correlation* to large cap stocks with *high expected returns*.

And we need to find asset classes with *high volatility*. This may be surprising, although in at least one way, it shouldn't be. Because we are looking for asset classes with high expected returns, it necessarily follows that we are looking for asset classes with high volatility. Remember, we can't have one without the other.

Black Belt Investing

But this is not a situation where, to get high returns, we have to grudgingly accept a lot of volatility. On the contrary, for the purpose of hedging a portfolio, we should *welcome* volatility as a good thing in and of itself. Keep in mind that highly volatile asset classes tend to fluctuate sharply upward as well as downward. If an asset class combines this characteristic of sharp upward and downward swings with a tendency to move opposite the direction of large cap stocks, it will be more effective at smoothing out the downturns in large caps than a hedge characterized by low volatility. If, for example, large caps decline by 50 percent, a highly volatile investment has a much better chance than a low-volatility investment of increasing by a similar amount, thereby significantly offsetting the large cap losses.

I have a name for portfolio diversification using high-volatility hedges. I refer to it as *black belt investing*. In judo, a black belt can defeat a larger, stronger opponent by throwing the opponent off-balance. In effect, the black belt takes the opponent's advantages of size and strength and uses those advantages against him. Similarly, an investor who applies the principle of correlation using high-volatility hedges is taking the stock market's main danger—high volatility—and using it to her advantage. By including in her portfolio investments with high volatility and low correlation to the broader stock market, she can take the risk posed by the market's high volatility and use it to reduce her own risk.

You must invest in stocks or risk winding up, like Joe Bondsman, with insufficient returns to outpace inflation. But as John Stockman's experience shows, the volatility of stocks can be your greatest enemy. Black belt investing, based on the principle of correlation and using high-volatility hedges, makes a friend of this enemy.

Good Hedges

So again, to hedge our core portfolio holding of large cap stocks using the principle of correlation, we are looking for asset classes that combine three key attributes — low correlation with large cap stocks, expected returns similar to large caps, and high volatility. Very few asset classes manage to deliver all three of these characteristics; a short list of potential good hedges is as follows:

- Gold (including gold mining stocks, also known as precious metals equities, or PME)

- Emerging-market bonds (bonds issued by governments and corporations in emerging-market countries)

In addition to gold and precious metals equities (PME), the observant reader will notice that a type of bond managed to slip onto the preceding list. As we will see in Chapter 4, emerging-market bonds have been characterized by returns closer to those of stocks than other types of bonds over the past two decades. This may well change in the future, but at least for now, we will treat them as potential high-volatility, high-return hedges.

The Principle of Correlation Still Works — but It Is Not a Panacea

Black belt investing, based on the correlation principle, is a very powerful investment strategy. But it is far from perfect. Remember a while back when we were discussing correlation coefficients, and we learned that there are no asset classes with strong negative correlation to large cap stocks, and few with even weak negative correlation? What this means, in plain terms, is that you cannot count on your hedges to move in the direction opposite to large caps all the time. In fact, high-volatility hedges have an unfortunate tendency of failing to act like hedges right when you most want them to work. For example, during the 2007–9 Great Recession, pretty much every type of investment went right down the drain, along with large cap stocks. Gold was an exception to the general downward trend, although PME declined along with the broader stock market.

Although most bonds also declined along with stocks in 2007–9, bond losses were much more limited. As a result, portfolios including a healthy helping of bonds held up much better than stock-heavy portfolios. The low volatility of bonds provides ballast to a portfolio, thereby keeping the portfolio from overturning and sinking during stock market storms. As we shall learn in Chapter 5, this low volatility is an inherent and stable characteristic of bonds. Low correlation, conversely, tends to be a less constant characteristic of the hedges we identified in the preceding section.

When these hedges maintain their low correlations to the broader stock market, as they did during the 2000–2002 bear market, they can significantly offset a portfolio's losses. But when correlations rise, as happened in 2007–9, they prove less effective as hedges.

Combining the Two Principles

It is because the principle of *correlation* doesn't always work that we still need to make use of the principle of *compromise*. Although bonds require us to compromise on returns, they provide more reliable protection against stock market volatility than the higher-volatility, higher-returning hedges like PME. What we will refer to in the remainder of this book as a well-diversified portfolio will therefore include *both* high-volatility hedges that work on the principle of correlation and low-volatility hedges (bonds) that work mainly on the principle of compromise. Each set of hedges has its own role, or job, to perform in protecting a well-diversified portfolio from the retirement risk. The high-volatility hedges *might* offset the well-diversified portfolio's losses during a market crash, *without* increasing the portfolio's exposure to the second component of the retirement risk—not enough returns to outpace inflation. These hedges form the well-diversified portfolio's first line of defense against volatility. This first defensive line is less reliable than the second line of defense provided by bonds, but it is also less expensive in terms of reduced returns. Think of the role of bonds in a well-diversified portfolio as a sort of fail-safe mechanism. If correlations rise during a stock market crash, the low volatility of the bonds will still provide some protection from losses. Each set of hedges—low-volatility and high-volatility—has its benefits and drawbacks, but when combined in a well-diversified portfolio, the two types are complementary.

Critics of the Correlation Principle

Diversification based on the correlation principle has its share of critics. Some say that although it was once a good strategy, it just doesn't work anymore. These critics often point to the 2007–9 bear market as proof of their contention.

But it is dangerous to draw general conclusions from a single event—especially a very unusual event. The 2007–9 mortgage meltdown and subsequent financial crisis was no ordinary, run-of-the-mill bear market. The first phase of the downturn, running from October 2007 to September 2008, seemed ordinary enough. A bubble burst (this time in the housing market), leading to recession and some problems in the markets for credit and certain derivatives. The stock market trended downward, but selling was relatively orderly. However, when Lehman Brothers failed in mid-September, the downturn morphed into something quite extra-ordinary. That a venerable, seemingly rock-solid institution like Lehman Brothers could go bankrupt sent a shock wave down Wall Street. Suddenly, the interest rate banks charge each other for overnight loans skyrocketed. Understand that we are talking here about the rate charged by big banks for very short-term loans to other big banks. Big Wall Street Bank A wanted a lot more interest on its loans to big Wall Street Bank B—because A was no longer quite so sure that B would still be in business *the next morning*. And B had the same doubts about A. Trust—the ultimate foundation of capitalism—was in short supply. We were staring into the potential imminent collapse of the global financial system—something that hadn't happened since the 1930s, and that would've almost certainly caused another depression. Panic seized the markets, as investors from Wall Street to Main Street sold everything that wasn't nailed down. The major indices were swinging up and down (mostly down) wildly, like a pressure gauge on an old, leaky steam engine about to blow up. *Capitulation* is the word sometimes used to describe these market events. In September and October 2008, the markets capitulated.

The fear of another depression that helped drive the sell-off is *not* a normal characteristic of run-of-the-mill bear markets. Isn't it possible, we might ask the critics, that the correlation principle didn't work well in the unusual circumstances prevailing in 2008, rather than that it has stopped working altogether? Correlations between asset classes have long been known to increase during fear-driven sell-offs. Perhaps the increases in correlations were more pronounced and encompassed more asset classes in 2008, because the fear level was abnormally high during that particular sell-off.

Let me draw an analogy. In 2011, the northeastern United States, where I live, experienced a freak weather event—an October snowstorm. Claiming, as some critics do, that the correlation principle failed in 2007–9 and therefore won't work in the future is a bit like saying that because the precipitation we got in October 2011 came in the form of snow, we should expect snow instead of rain in future Octobers. It is simply false logic. (A psychologist might refer to this as an example of recency bias—a tendency to place undue emphasis on some events over others because the former happened more recently.)

That said, there is some real substance behind the criticism that the correlation principle doesn't work as well as it once did. The gist of this argument is that the rise in the popularity of index investing and exchange-traded funds (ETFs)—funds containing all of the stocks that make up an index like the S&P 500—have led to an across-the-board increase in asset class correlations. Instead of individual stocks, many traders increasingly rely on ETFs to buy and sell broad swathes of the stock market. When shares of an individual stock are traded, only the price of that stock is affected. But when shares of an ETF are sold, the price not only of the ETF but of all of the stocks the ETF comprises goes down. The rising popularity of ETFs means that stocks are now bought and sold together in large blocks, causing their prices to move up and down in tandem with one another.

And the news gets worse. The impact of ETF trading is most pronounced during market sell-offs, like the one that occurred in autumn 2008. Reliance on ETFs makes it that much harder to discriminate between "good" and "bad" stocks when the market panics. If what you own is an ETF, not individual stocks, and you are driven by the prevailing mood to dump a large portion of your holdings, you can't pick and choose the individual stocks you'd still like to keep. You have to sell shares of the ETF and, therefore, of *all* the stocks in the ETF. And when investors are selling their ETFs during a panic, all the stocks in those ETFs move in the same downward direction. The tendency of all stocks to nosedive together during a market rout or capitulation is not something new—it has long been known that the correlations between different asset classes increase, often dramatically, during major sell-offs. But ETFs and index mutual funds have undoubtedly exacerbated this unfortunate tendency.[18]

So we must concede that the critics of the correlation principle have a point. The number of asset classes that exhibit low correlation with large cap stocks, particularly during market sell-offs, has declined with the rise of ETFs. But this number has not gone to zero. And I don't believe it can *ever* go to zero, for a simple reason: when investors sell their shares during a panic, the cash they raise *has* to go somewhere. Even in the worst-case scenario, there should be at least one asset class—one safe haven—that sees an inflow of cash when all the other asset classes experience an outflow. That single asset class should go up when all the others go down. And even if we are left with only one asset class capable of bucking the downward trend, we still have one way to implement the principle of correlation.

Mark Felt, better known as Deep Throat, offered a famous bit of advice to reporter Bob Woodward. "Follow the money," he said. Woodward and his partner Carl Bernstein took that advice, and they followed the leads from the Watergate break-in all the way to the Oval Office. Later in this book, we're going to take the same advice. We're going to "follow the money" that was raised during the 2008 market sell-off and find out where that money was invested. (Don't worry, unlike Woodward, you won't have to meet any shady characters in underground parking garages.) We will show that the money trail leads to not one but two asset classes that proved capable of generating positive returns during the worst market storm since the Great Depression. These two asset classes (along with one other closely related asset class) should serve investors well in future downturns.

There is a second point to be made in response to the critics of the correlation principle. They are quite right when they note that correlations between asset classes tend to rise, often dramatically, when the market goes into a tailspin. But this means the opposite is also true. Correlations return to lower levels when the market is not in the grips of a panic sell-off. What are the implications of this point? There are periods of relative calm during even the worst bear markets, and correlations can, during these calms, revert to lower, more normal levels. Consider once again the 2007–9 bear market. Figure 2.3 breaks this bear market down into three distinct periods, which I'll cleverly refer to as the Calm before the Storm, the Storm, and the

Calm after the Storm. The figure shows how the S&P 500 fared during each of these three periods, compared with one of the three asset classes we mentioned earlier as making for a good hedge—PME. Specifically, the figure shows the average total returns (including dividends as well as capital gains or losses[19]) of PME mutual funds in each of the three periods. In both the Calm before the Storm (October 10, 2007, to July 14, 2008) and the Calm after the Storm (October 25, 2008, to March 9, 2009), PME funds were moving up while the S&P 500 was trending down. It was only during the height of the panic leading up to and including the failure of Lehman Brothers (July 15, 2008, to October 24, 2008), that PME funds reversed course and moved in the same direction as the broad market. Because PME funds participated in only the worst part of the financial crisis, and worked to hedge stocks during the Calms surrounding the Storm, over the entire length of the bear market, the losses these funds suffered (22.6 percent) were less than half the S&P 500's losses (55.3 percent). And though we picked PME funds to illustrate this point, the other two hedges we mentioned earlier (gold and emerging-market bonds) also moved opposite the stock market during at least some portions of the 2007–9 bear market.

The return to low correlations that often occurs during the calmer periods of short-term (or *cyclical*) bear markets has very important implications for long-term (or *secular*) bear markets (like the Lost Decade of 2000–2009). A secular bear market is defined as a prolonged period of abnormally low returns. Typically, a secular bear market lasts a decade or longer. Total cumulative returns may not be negative over such a long period, but they are anemic.

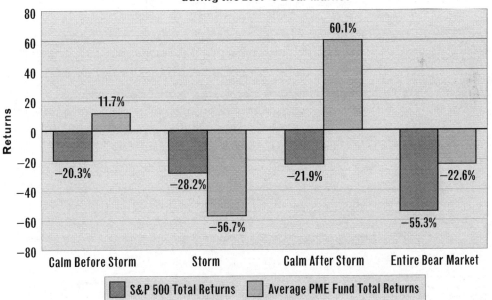

Figure 2.3. Average Returns of PME Funds versus the S&P 500 during the 2007–9 Bear Market

Source: Developed by the author using data from www.morningstar.com.

A secular bear market looks, and feels, very different from a short-term, cyclical bear market. Short bursts of fear and outright panic may punctuate a secular bear market, but the prevalent market mood is more typically frustration (with the pathetically low returns). Although asset class correlations rose dramatically during certain limited periods of the Lost Decade—most notably during the panic sell-off in the latter half of 2008—they remained at more normal levels most of the time. As we've already seen, PME funds moved opposite the stock market during the Calms that surrounded the Great Storm of 2008. And all three hedges—PME, gold, and emerging-market bonds—moved opposite the stock market during the entire period making up the 2000–2002 bear market. As a result, these hedges did not suffer nearly as much damage as the broader stock market during the early and later years of the Lost Decade. Partly because they avoided damaging losses, our hedges did *not* move sideways with the S&P 500 over the past decade. On the contrary, PME, gold, and emerging-market bonds generated outsized returns. How big? We'll see in Chapter 4. (Hey, I have to create *some* suspense here to keep you reading!)

Why does this distinction between cyclical and secular bear markets matter? It is the *length*, not the *depth*, of a bear market that often poses the greatest risk to a retiree's portfolio. And secular bear markets are, by definition, much longer than cyclical bear markets. The fear engendered in investors by sharp, short-term (*cyclical*) bear markets exceeds that of shallow, long-term (*secular*) bear markets. For a retiree who must continually withdraw money from her portfolio to meet living expenses, the need to dip into her principal for a couple of years while at the same time suffering major losses may be daunting. But it pales in comparison to the prospect of living mainly on principal for *a decade or more*. During a secular bear market, the retiree's need to keep withdrawing money to meet living expenses, year after year, from a portfolio that isn't growing or, at best, is growing anemically can severely weaken the portfolio. It is the superior ability of the correlation principle to mitigate the impact of *secular* bear markets that really cuts the retirement risk down to size. And this ability is not severely affected by the tendency of asset class correlations to rise during the relatively brief periods corresponding to the storms at the center of cyclical bear markets.

So while black belt investing using the correlation principle sometimes fails in the short run, over the long run, it remains the best way to maximize returns and minimize risks. In Part III, we will use actual average return data for different mutual fund classes to demonstrate just how well portfolios built using the principle of correlation would have held up over the so-called Lost Decade.

The Long View: In Defense of Ancient History

But don't think that black belt investing can't help you during short-term bear markets, too. The critics of the correlation principle, perhaps suffering from recency bias, tend to focus on the last (2007–9) bear market. We had to focus on that one, too, to address their criticisms. But in the remainder of this book, we will be taking the long view. We will look at the performance of well-diversified portfolios built on the correlation principle over *all* of the major bear markets and market corrections of the past forty years. And once we peer back into history beyond 2007, we will see some of this principle's stunning successes.

For example, the correlation principle worked beautifully during the 2000–2002 bear market. Many well-diversified portfolios built on this principle would have *increased* in value during 2000–2002, despite the fact that the S&P 500 dropped 47.4 percent.

★★★

However, before we delve deep into history, I have some explaining to do. I've been warned, by a very knowledgeable former publishing executive, that most readers of this book won't be interested in anything that happened more than fifteen years ago. Perhaps foolishly, I have ignored his warning. But before I drag you, perhaps kicking and screaming, through a tour of what might seem like ancient history, I at least owe you an explanation as to why I think such a tour is necessary.

My explanation will take the form of a pleasant analogy. Imagine that you have just retired at the age of sixty. Thanks to many years of hard work and successful investing, you have built up a sizeable nest egg. You've purchased a fine beachfront property on Florida's Gulf Coast, where you plan to spend your evenings watching the sunset over the water while sipping margaritas.

First, however, you must build your dream house. Two different home builders have submitted their plans to you; you must pick the one you like best. Both plans look beautiful, similar in some ways but different in others. One of the key differences is that Plan A calls for the house to be raised five feet above ground level, whereas Plan B incorporates a fifteen-foot elevation. Upon inquiring about this difference, the Plan A builder tells you that he has checked the records for your property going back fifteen years, and a five-foot elevation would have protected the house from the highest storm surge recorded over that period. In contrast, the Plan B home builder has reviewed the storm surge data for the past eighty-five years—as far back as the records go. She found three hurricanes that brought storm surges exceeding five feet, including a monster surge of eleven feet forty-two years ago. Which plan, A or B, would you choose?

Like the Gulf Coast dream house, your retirement portfolio must be built to last you a lifetime. Of course, you can never know what future storms the stock market may bring, and whether your portfolio will stand up to those storms. But like a beachfront home builder who must construct her houses to withstand decades of violent weather, you can at least make sure that your portfolio is equal to the challenges of the past. As the Plan B home builder in our example understood, the key to minimizing the risk of a catastrophic loss is to review the historical records as far back as they go. What has happened in the past—even the distant past—can happen again.

Only by reviewing the entire historical record can we be sure that we have captured, and protected against, the worst case scenarios of the past. I use the plural "scenarios" for a reason. To continue our analogy, the main threats different hurricanes pose vary, from coastal storm surges to wind damage to flooding rain. A house built to withstand the worst storm surge on record that is not likewise constructed to weather the highest recorded wind speeds is at risk of being blown away. Similarly, recessions, financial crises, bursting bubbles, and runaway inflation test the strengths of portfolios in different ways. By extending our review of market history as far back as the data will allow, we are able to capture not only the worst case scenario but the widest possible diversity of conditions that may stress a portfolio.

If possible, I would extend our review of asset class performance data at least as far back as the 1920s, to capture the 1929 Crash and subsequent depression. In fact, in Chapter 18, where we tackle the critically important task of estimating survival probabilities for simple two-asset-class portfolios, we extend our analysis all the way back to 1926. Unfortunately, though, for most of the asset classes of interest to us, the available data stop well short of the 1920s and 1930s. In the upcoming chapters, we make do with the data we have and follow them as far back as possible. For many asset classes, that means the 1960s or 1970s; in a few cases, we will be limited to the 1990s. If this be ancient history, then so be it.

★★★

We have likened our ultimate goal—building an investment portfolio that will last you a lifetime—to the construction of a beachfront home. This analogy has proved useful, but like all analogies, it has its limits. There is a crucial difference between building a house and building a portfolio. The materials used to build a house, such as concrete, bricks, and wood, change little with time. Today's concrete is similar in its performance characteristics—its strength in compression, in tension, and so forth—to the concrete used one hundred years ago. In contrast, the characteristics of materials that compose portfolios—that is, asset classes like large cap stocks, bonds, and gold—can and do change, sometimes dramatically, with time. Most importantly, as we have learned, correlations between asset classes have been rising because of the increasing popularity of index investing and ETFs. This development raises a critically important question: how do we know that the asset classes we hope to use as hedges will behave in the future as they have in the past? As we embark in the following chapters on our tour of "ancient" market history, you should keep this question in the back of your mind. We will address it in due course.

But before we can do so, we first need to come to a better understanding of the building blocks we have at our disposal. We have thus far been comparing a portfolio built on the principle of correlation to a beachfront home. I'm now going to switch metaphors and liken such a portfolio to a gourmet meal. To know how to prepare such a meal, the master chef begins by learning all he can about each ingredient.

The chef must understand not only the unique flavor and texture of each ingredient but also how these flavors and textures will mix together into a savory dish that is greater than the sum of its parts.

You are now well on the road to becoming the master chef of your own well-diversified portfolio. You have learned the two manifestations of the retirement risk—too much market volatility and not enough returns to outpace inflation. You have learned the two principles you can use to diversify your portfolio and solve the problem of the retirement risk—the principle of compromise, based on finding a balance between returns and volatility, and the principle of correlation, which may enable you to reduce volatility without sacrificing returns. You have some idea of the specific asset classes you can use to cook up your portfolio. Now we will delve into these asset classes in greater detail, focusing in particular on how each one measures up in terms of the three ideal characteristics of a good hedge: low correlation, high returns, and high volatility. In Chapter 3, we discuss the core holding—the "meat" of your gourmet meal—large cap stocks, both U.S. and foreign. In Chapters 4 and 5, we turn to the hedges that will help you reduce the volatility of your portfolio. Chapter 4 describes the vegetables, the high-volatility hedges—gold, PME, and emerging-market bonds—that will enable you to apply the principle of correlation to your portfolio. In Chapter 5, we consider the potatoes, bland but sustaining—the low-volatility hedges, including bonds of all kinds, which enable you to make use of the principle of compromise.

In Chapter 6, our focus shifts from hedging your portfolio against volatility to protecting it against the equally dangerous risk of not earning enough returns to outpace inflation. This chapter thus describes the special sauces that will spice up your portfolio without making it too hot—asset classes like value stocks and small cap stocks that can boost your portfolio's returns. Finally, in Chapter 7, we return to the question first raised earlier in this section: how do we know that the asset classes we hope to use as hedges and return boosters will behave in the future as they have in the past?

BUILDING YOUR PORTFOLIO: THE ASSET CLASSES

CHAPTER 3

U.S. AND INTERNATIONAL LARGE CAP STOCKS: THE MEAT OF YOUR PORTFOLIO

L arge cap stocks are the stocks of large companies. The term *cap* is shorthand for "market capitalization." Market capitalization is the total value of a company's stock shares. For example, a company with a stock that sells for $20 and that has 10 million shares available has a market capitalization of $200 million. The Morningstar website defines large cap stocks as the 70 percent of all publicly traded stocks with the largest market capitalizations. Hence, by definition, large cap stocks compose 70 percent of the total stock market.

U.S. Large Caps

Most of the companies you've probably heard of—GE, McDonald's, ExxonMobil, Wal-Mart—are large cap stocks. The Dow Jones Industrial Average is the most famous index tracking the ups and downs of large caps. But the Dow includes only thirty of the biggest of the large caps. A much better measure of the performance of large caps is provided by the S&P 500, comprising 500 stocks selected by Standard & Poors. We will be using the S&P 500, not the Dow Jones, in this book.

You cannot be effectively diversified if 70 percent of the stock market is not well represented in your portfolio. In fact, given that large caps compose the bulk of the entire value of the stock market, they are typically the core holdings of many, if not most, portfolios. This is not always the case. Individuals who are particularly risk averse, or who are wealthy enough to be able to get by on low returns, might construct their portfolios around a core consisting of bonds. But even if bonds are going to be your core holding, you should still include a good helping of large caps in your portfolio. A small allocation to stocks will not have a major impact on your portfolio's volatility, and it could spell the difference between staying ahead of inflation or watching your nest egg get slowly eaten away by the night thief's machinations. Just ask Joe Bondsman.

So regardless of whether they will form the meaty core or a tasty side dish, large cap stocks belong in your portfolio. A good, low-cost way to own U.S. large caps is through a mutual fund that tracks the S&P 500 index. There are many such index funds available. But before you buy one, you should have a clear idea of what you are getting yourself into in terms of the risks (volatility) and the potential rewards (returns).

U.S. Large Cap Returns

I occasionally come across articles complaining that the market and the mutual fund industry are rigged against the small investor, who cannot hope to make money in stocks. Nonsense! Between 1966 and 2013, the annualized return of U.S. large cap blend mutual funds averaged 8.8 percent. A $10,000 investment in the average large cap fund on January 1, 1966, would have grown to $584,925 by December 31, 2013[20]—and this is after taking into account mutual fund fees and expenses. Not bad for a market and industry supposedly rigged against the small investor. Simply buying and holding an average large cap mutual fund would have produced these results—no attempt to diversify using the principles of correlation or compromise, no superior fund selection, no attempt to "time" the market, and no work trying to outthink the stock manipulators, inside traders, con artist stockbrokers, and fee-greedy mutual fund management companies (all of whom really do exist) required. Stocks—particularly the stocks of large U.S. companies—have proven themselves to be excellent money generators for investors large and small with the patience and self-discipline necessary to follow a buy-and-hold approach.

U.S. Large Cap Volatility

But as you know, with high returns comes high volatility. There have been sixteen bear markets since 1929. A bear market is defined as a decline of at least 20 percent, but that's just the minimum loss. The *average* bear market has seen a whopping decline of 40 percent and has lasted nineteen months. The stock market has been in bear territory for twenty-four of the last eighty-one years—30 percent of the time. Since 1970, we have seen four major bear markets, which, listed in order starting with the worst, were as follows:

1. October 9, 2007, to March 9, 2009 (housing bubble bursts, financial crisis): S&P 500 down 55.3 percent

2. March 24, 2000, to October 9, 2002 (Internet stock bubble bursts, 9/11): S&P 500 down 47.4 percent[21]

3. January 11, 1973, to October 3, 1974 (Arab oil embargo, high inflation): S&P 500 down 44.8 percent

4. August 25, 1987, to December 4, 1987 (October 87 market crash): S&P 500 down 32.9 percent

A young person can withstand losses of 30, 40, or even 50 percent of her portfolio because she has plenty of time to recover. (That said, she would probably prefer *not* to experience these kinds of losses, and for this reason, she should keep reading!) But for a retiree depending on his investment returns to help meet his living expenses, such huge losses can lead to financial ruin. It is events like those listed that necessitate the use of both low-volatility and high-volatility assets to hedge a core investment in large cap stocks. In the next two chapters, we will turn to these hedges. But first, let's consider adding some international large cap stocks to our core holding of U.S. large caps.

International Large Caps

Globalization means that national boundaries matter less and less to communications, trade, and the free flow of capital and people. Boundaries no longer pose a hindrance to investors either. It is just as easy to buy a mutual fund investing in international stocks as it is to purchase a domestic U.S. stock fund. And there are benefits to be gained by adding international stocks to your portfolio. The United States accounts for less than half of the total market capitalization of all publicly traded stocks across the world. In a global economy, you cannot be truly diversified if you limit your portfolio to stocks of a single country representing less than half of the universe of investable equities.

That said, we shouldn't overestimate the diversification benefits of international stocks. At one time, correlations between the U.S. and foreign stock markets were relatively low, but this is no longer the case. With globalization, correlations have increased dramatically. These high correlations are reflected in the performance of international stocks during the two big bear markets of the last decade. Table 3.1 shows average returns for mutual funds investing in the large cap stocks of Europe, Japan, and emerging markets. In both bear markets, these international funds followed the U.S. stock market down the tubes. In fact, in most cases, they did even worse than the S&P 500. Unlike the asset classes we will be discussing in the next two chapters, international stocks offered investors no shelter from the major market storms of the last decade.

Table 3.1. Average Returns of Large Cap Mutual Funds Investing in European, Japanese, and Emerging Market Stocks during the 2000–2002 and 2007–9 Bear Markets

Region	Mar 2000–Oct 2002	Oct 2007–Mar 2009
Europe	−51%	−62%
Japan	−60%	−58%
Emerging markets	−47%	−61%
U.S. (S&P 500)	−47%	−55%

Source: Developed by the author using data from www.morningstar.com.

However, recall that as long as asset classes are not perfectly correlated with each other, they will provide at least some diversification benefits. In the case of highly correlated asset classes, such as international large caps and U.S. large caps, these benefits tend to show up in the long term rather than the short term. Figure 3.1 shows average annualized returns of international large cap mutual funds over the Lost Decade (2000–2009). During this period, the S&P 500 yielded *negative* returns of 0.9 percent per year. Returns for other developed markets were mixed, with Europe doing better but Japan worse than the United States. However, emerging-market funds shone during the decade, yielding average annualized returns of 8.7 percent. Even a limited allocation to emerging-market funds would have provided a helpful boost to overall portfolio returns.

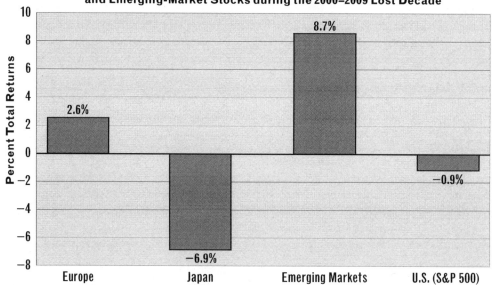

Figure 3.1. Average Annualized Returns of Large Cap Mutual Funds Investing in European, Japanese, and Emerging-Market Stocks during the 2000–2009 Lost Decade

Source: Developed by the author using data from www.morningstar.com.

Emerging Markets Outperform during the Lost Decade

The outperformance of emerging markets during the Lost Decade can be traced back to events during the late 1990s. In July 1997, Thailand adopted a floating exchange rate, with the result that its currency (the baht) suffered a 20 percent devaluation. Investors in emerging markets tend to be a skittish bunch, and when one country runs into problems, investors will often flee other emerging markets. Hence the sell-off of the Thai baht quickly spread to other Asian currencies. Foreign capital, which had been flowing into the emerging markets of Asia, reversed course. With the outflow of capital, Asian economies stalled, and their stock markets tanked. The currency crisis eventually spread to Russia, which defaulted on its debt in 1998. At this point, the U.S. stock market followed emerging-market stocks down. The S&P 500 dropped 19.2 percent in just six weeks in summer 1998. But the average emerging-market stock fund declined a much larger 31.0 percent over the same period.[22]

Whereas the U.S. market quickly recovered, investors remained wary of emerging-market stocks for the remainder of the 1990s. As a result, emerging-market equities entered the Lost Decade slightly underpriced relative to their earnings potential.[23] In contrast, the U.S. stock market was dangerously overpriced owing to the formation of a bubble in Internet stocks during the late 1990s. Although both U.S. and emerging-market stocks dropped when the bubble burst in 2000, the latter were priced for a more robust recovery when the market bottomed in 2002.

This bit of history helps to explain why, despite globalization and high correlations in the short run, stock returns for different regions of the world can nonetheless diverge significantly over the longer term. The ripple effects of an event such as the Thai currency crisis will quickly travel to every corner of the world in today's global economy, forcing all stock markets to move in the same *direction*. But the *magnitude* of the moves may differ from country to country, and the long-term effects of these differences can be very significant. The diversification benefits of adding emerging-market stocks, as well as international developed-market stocks, to your core U.S. stock holdings are real and may help you in the long run if not the short term.

And there are a couple of other points to consider. Although it is true that globalization and its resulting free flow of capital and goods across borders has brought about a dramatic increase in U.S. and foreign stock market correlations, you should *never* assume that a trend will continue indefinitely. The possibility exists that the globalization trend could reverse itself. In fact, history provides many examples of such reversals, stretching back to the fall of the Roman Empire and even earlier. For a more recent example, we need only go back one century. In the late 1800s and early 1900s, new transportation and communication technologies, including railroads, steamships, and the telegraph, combined with the expansion of Europe's colonial empires to bring about a vast increase in international trade and cross-border flows of people and capital. But this first modern era of globalization came to a dramatic and abrupt end with World War I. History does not move in a straight line, globalization is not *necessarily* here to stay, and there is at least a possibility that the recent trend toward high correlations among the world's stock markets could reverse itself.

Keep in mind, too, that the twentieth century—the American Century—saw the U.S. stock market's capitalization grow from about 22 percent to 54 percent of the world's total.[24] In the wake of World War II, most of Europe lay in ruins, and even Britain was essentially bankrupt. Alone among all countries, the United States emerged victorious in all senses of the word, physically and financially unscathed, with our factories and infrastructure intact and the dollar poised to become the world's reserve currency. In short, America held an enormous competitive advantage over the rest of the globe after World War II. It is little wonder that our stock market powered past those of other countries. But those unique postwar advantages are now past and unlikely to be repeated. We can hope that the United States will continue to prosper as it has, but investing should never be based on hope alone. Diversifying your investments across the globe will help protect your savings should the next century prove less kind to Americans than the last.

Currency Diversification

There is one other point to be gleaned from the 1997–98 emerging-market currency crisis, and that is the importance of diversifying your portfolio across currencies as well as countries. When you buy the stock of a foreign company, your dollar investment is converted into an investment in the local currency—for example, yen if you are buying a Japanese stock. Your returns on the stock are then equal to the returns of the stock in yen, *adjusted to take into account fluctuations in the exchange rate between dollars and yen.* If the yen appreciates in value relative to the dollar, your returns will be adjusted upward; if the yen declines in value, your returns will be adjusted downward. By investing in the stocks of a diversified set of foreign countries, you are in effect hedging your portfolio against the possibility of a devaluation of the dollar (and a resulting increase in the costs of imported goods that could lead to high inflation). During the late 1990s, it was currencies like the Thai baht and the Malaysian ringgit that came under pressure; more recently, the euro weakened during the European debt crisis of 2011. Who is to say that it won't be the dollar the next time around? With the U.S. government running massive trillion-dollar deficits and its credit rating already cut one notch, there is ample reason for concern. A significant decline in the dollar could lead to reduced foreign demand for U.S. Treasury bonds.[25] This in turn would put upward pressure on interest rates—which is usually a negative for both the stock and bond markets. And putting these issues aside, it makes no more sense to be invested in a single currency than it would to put all of your money in a single stock or mutual fund—even if that currency is the almighty dollar.

Returns of International versus U.S. Large Caps

Developed-market returns. You can get the currency and other diversification benefits of international stocks without having to significantly compromise on long-run returns. Annualized returns (including dividends) of the MSCI EAFE index (a large cap index covering all developed-market countries excepting the United States and Canada) were 10.1 percent from 1970 through 2013—not far behind the 10.6 percent annualized returns of the S&P 500 over the same period.

Emerging-market returns. Whereas developed-market stocks have nearly kept pace with the U.S. stock market, emerging-market stocks have lagged a bit behind U.S. large caps, owing in part to their poor performance since 2011. From 1990 (the earliest year for which data are available) through 2013, annualized returns for mutual funds investing in diversified emerging markets averaged 7.7 percent, versus 8.3 percent for U.S. large cap funds.[26] However, a 0.6 percent difference in long-run returns is a reasonable price to pay for the outperformance of emerging-market stocks during the Lost Decade, when investors in U.S. stocks were most in need of a boost to their portfolios' returns.

Summary

Table 3.2 summarizes the characteristics exhibited by U.S. and international large caps, along with the role each of these assets can play in a well-diversified portfolio. Remember, although international equities are highly correlated with U.S. large caps, they nonetheless offer real diversification benefits over the long run. They also provide an opportunity to hedge your portfolio against possible future declines in the value of the dollar. For these reasons, you should make a place for international stocks—both developed-market and emerging-market equities—in your portfolio.

Table 3.2. Summary of Large Cap Characteristics and Roles

Asset Class	Correlation with U.S. Large Caps	Volatility	Expected Returns	Role in Portfolio
U.S. large caps	—	High	High	Core holding; produce high returns to beat inflation risk
International developed-market large caps	High	High	High	Long-run diversification benefits; currency diversification
Emerging-market large caps	High	High	High	Long-run diversification benefits; currency diversification

CHAPTER 4

BLACK BELT INVESTING: REDUCING PORTFOLIO VOLATILITY WITH HIGH-VOLATILITY HEDGES

Gold ... never changes ... has no nationality and ... is eternally and universally accepted as the inalterable fiduciary value par excellence.
—**Charles de Gaulle**[27]

If we think of large cap stocks as the meaty core of our portfolio, then the high-volatility hedges can be thought of as the vegetables. Now, I have a confession to make. I never did much like vegetables. When I go to a restaurant and order a nice, juicy steak, it usually arrives with a side of peas and carrots or some other vegetable dish. Chances are I'll devour the steak and leave the vegetables untouched. After all, if I eat those vegetables, I'll have less room for the steak. I might even wind up having to bring part of the steak home in a doggy bag. My dog will be eternally grateful—but I'll feel like I cheated myself out of the best part of the meal. Of course, I shouldn't think like this. As our mothers taught us, vegetables are good for us.

So, too, are high-volatility hedges. Granted, when we add them to our portfolios, they take up room that otherwise could have been devoted to those nice, juicy, high-returning large caps. And it's true that they tend to act as a drag on our returns during bull markets. After all, if they have low correlation with large cap stocks and go *up* when the rest of the market is going down, then it follows that they'll also tend to go *down* when the market is rising. It's hard to watch investments in gold and other hedges drag down returns when the stock market is going gangbusters. Back in the 1990s, when the S&P 500 posted annualized returns of more than 18 percent, mutual funds investing in precious metals equities (PME) *lost* an average 4.4 percent of their value each year. Just thinking about it leaves a bad taste in my mouth—like some vegetables.

But PME, and other high-volatility hedges, can be real life savers during bear markets. These assets are the ingredients that enable us to take the principle of correlation and apply it to real-world portfolios. Like vegetables, high-volatility hedges need not form a large portion of our portfolios to do us good. They can and should be small side dishes to the meaty core of large cap stocks. In this chapter, we will see how a little bit of gold and other high-volatility hedges can sometimes go a long way.

Gold

On the morning of May 18, 1864, New York City awoke to reports that President Lincoln had ordered the conscription of four hundred thousand men into the Union Army. This news came as a shock to the financial community and the broader public, as the Union had grown hopeful that an end to the four-year-old Civil War was finally in sight. Coming as it did less than one year after the New York Draft Riots, the news portended serious trouble. Stock prices dropped, while the price of gold skyrocketed.

The news of the draft order had appeared in two city newspapers, the *New York World* and the *Journal of Commerce*. The two papers cited rather vague reasons for the order, including "the situation in Virginia" and "the general state of the country" —not exactly a compelling case. More puzzling, though, the news of Lincoln's order was not covered in any of the other New York City newspapers. Crowds gathered at the *New York World*'s and *Journal of Commerce*'s offices demanding answers, but the editors of both papers produced the Associated Press (AP) dispatch showing that the news came from a credible source. Yet the AP soon issued a statement that it had not issued the dispatch, and secretary of state William Seward declared the dispatch to be "an absolute forgery."

The puzzle of the dispatch was eventually resolved when its real source was traced back to one Joseph Howard, the city editor of the *Brooklyn Eagle*. Howard, working with one of his reporters (Francis Mallison) as an accomplice, had crafted a realistic forgery of an AP news dispatch. He then sent the forgery out to the New York papers in the early-morning hours, when he knew there would be few personnel available to verify the news. Although only two of New York's many newspapers were fooled, two was enough. Before his ruse, Howard had purchased as much gold as he could on his margin account; he sold the gold at a huge profit before the news was discredited.[28]

Here's the question the Civil War Gold Hoax raises for us: how did Howard know that his phony dispatch would cause the price of gold to soar? It didn't take a financial genius. Bad news and rising gold prices have gone together like peanut butter and jelly for centuries. As we will soon see, they go hand in hand as much today as in the Civil War era. To understand why, we first need to learn a bit about the precious yellow metal.

★★★

Gold, unlike many other metals, has surprisingly few practical uses. It is an excellent conductor of electricity but is too expensive to be used for this purpose, except in very small quantities. It is also used, again in tiny amounts, as a lubricant and insulator in aerospace applications, and it has certain specialized uses in medicine. But most of the time, gold just sits there looking pretty in the form of jewelry, or else it remains hidden from view and under heavy guard, in forts and vaults built for no purpose other than to protect the precious metal inside.

Yet despite the dearth of practical uses, gold has been coveted by humans since time immemorial. Cultures separated by great expanses of time and distance, from ancient Rome to modern India, have shared a love of gold. In the sixteenth century, visions of gold brought the Spanish conquistadors to the New World, where they fought the Aztecs and Incas to the death to get their golden treasures. In the nineteenth century, gold fever drove tens of thousands of men (and a few women) to risk life and limb to reach the new gold discoveries in the wilds of California, the Rockies, and the Klondike. We might not agree on much, but humans everywhere, and at all times, have agreed on one thing: gold is *intrinsically* valuable.

It is precisely this combination of limited practical use and high *intrinsic* value that makes gold an excellent hedge. Unlike silver, crude oil, corn, and other commodities, all of which have many practical uses and are therefore subject to the ups and downs of the business cycle, gold is not as closely tied to industrial or consumer demand. True, purchases of gold jewelry will tend to decline during hard times, but this decline is often more than offset by a sharp increase in investors' demand for gold bullion and gold coins.

So why do investors flock to gold when the news turns bad? Because, unlike all of the other assets we are considering in this book, the value of gold does *not* depend on the promise of some future payoff. We buy bonds because the borrower issuing the bonds has *promised* to pay back the principal, with interest. We buy stocks because the companies issuing those stocks have *promised*, either explicitly or implicitly, to pay us dividends or to increase the share price by growing earnings. We accept cash payment in dollars, or euros, or pounds sterling, because the governments issuing those currencies have made an implicit *promise* to us that they will manage their affairs such that those currencies will have pretty much the same value tomorrow that they have today.

What happens, then, when war, recession, or financial crisis causes disruptions in commerce, widespread bond defaults, and stock market losses, or when spiraling government debt and inflation cause us to question the soundness of our currencies? We lose faith in the promises backing up bonds, stocks, and currencies; we sell these paper assets; and we use the proceeds to buy the one tangible asset whose value does not depend on a promise—the one *tangible* asset with *intrinsic* value. As the forger Joseph Howard no doubt understood, gold is the ultimate safe haven.

"Follow the Money"

No recent events illustrate gold's safe haven role better than its performance during the 2007–9 bear market. This market crash began in October 2007, but it wasn't until September 2008, and the failure of Lehman Brothers, that it graduated from a run-of-the-mill market correction into an all-out panic. Stocks of all types, along with most types of bonds, sold off as professional money managers were swept up in the panic along with amateur investors.

With everyone selling stocks and bonds indiscriminately, virtually every asset class plummeted. But when investors large and small sell their investments, the cash they raise has to go somewhere. If we take Deep Throat's advice and "follow the money," it should lead us to those very few asset classes that investors saw as safe havens during the great 2008 financial storm.

Some of the money from the sell-off went into money market funds, CDs, and savings accounts. Beyond these obvious safe harbors, there were only two asset classes that saw an inflow of money—gold and U.S. Treasury bonds. I'll have more to say about Treasuries in the next chapter. For now, let's focus on what happened to gold. According to data from the World Gold Council, the total demand for gold in the third quarter of 2008 spiked 53 percent. Gold demand fell off a bit in the fourth quarter of 2008, owing to a reduction in jewelry consumption and industrial demand, but it still remained 29 percent higher than second-quarter demand.[29]

With the exception of Treasuries, no other asset class besides gold managed to produce positive returns during the 2007–9 bear market. Of course, every bear market is different, characterized by its own unique conditions. Just because gold worked as an excellent hedge in 2007–9 doesn't mean it will do so during the next bear market. That said, gold tends to work as a hedge in a much wider range of economic environments than other asset classes. For example, bonds generally perform poorly in inflationary environments (as Joe Bondsman learned during the 1970s). Gold, conversely, tends to hold its value when inflation rages. It is, after all, a commodity, and it will tend to rise in price along with other commodities. But paradoxically, gold has also done well during times marked by deflation, or at least the fear of deflation. Back in autumn 2008, there was real fear that we were heading for a deflationary depression similar to what we experienced in the 1930s. Federal Reserve chairman Ben Bernanke and Treasury secretary Hank Paulson stressed that this was a real possibility when they argued for the need to bail out the big Wall Street banks. In fact, deflation did take hold during the height of the panic. The Consumer Price Index declined by 3.5 percent between July 2008 and February 2009. Over this same period, the price of gold *increased* by 3.7 percent.

It was not deflation per se that caused gold to rise but rather fear of the events that often accompany a deflationary spiral, including credit crunches, bank runs, debt defaults, and, ultimately, depression. Nonetheless, unlike all other commodities, gold has exhibited a tendency to rise in price during periods marked by inflation and also by fears of deflation.

Gold is also likely to benefit when investors worry about the possibility of currency crashes. Today, growing government debt has begun to chip away at our confidence in the soundness of the currencies of the developed world. Too much government debt in countries like Greece and Italy has threatened the stability and even the survival of the euro, while the recent downgrade of the United States' credit rating reminds us that the dollar is not immune to the problems caused by debt overload. In the face of our growing currency concerns, gold is still viewed as a potential currency alternative. Worries about the euro and the dollar likely contributed to the dramatic rise in the price of gold between December 31, 2008, and December 31, 2011, when it increased 82 percent.

The Historical Record for Gold

Given gold's versatility as a hedge in a wide variety of different conditions—including inflation, financial crises, military conflicts, currency collapses—we would expect to find that it performed well in most of the big bear markets of the last forty years. And that is in fact the case. Table 4.1 shows us how gold and PME mutual funds (which invest in the stock of gold mining companies[30]) have performed during the worst market downturns of the past forty years.[31] For comparative purposes, the returns of the S&P 500 are also shown. We will come back to the data for the PME mutual funds later; for now, let's focus on physical gold—gold coins, gold bars, and gold ingots—in the middle column of the table.

Table 4.1. Average Returns of Gold and PME Mutual Funds during Past Bear Markets and Market Corrections

Time Period	S&P 500 Total Returns	Gold Price Returns	Average PME Fund Returns
Bear Markets:			
Oct 2007–Mar 2009	−55.3%	+25.5%	−22.6%
Mar 2000–Oct 2002[a]	−47.4%	+12.1%	+46.6%
Jan 1973–Oct 1974	−44.8%[c]	+139.4%	+57.5%
Aug 1987–Dec 1987	−32.9%[c]	+6.2%	−17.1%
Corrections:			
Nov 1980–Aug 1982[b]	−20.0%[c]	−46.0%	−43.0%
Jul 1990–Oct 1990	−19.2%	+6.8%	−8.8%
Jul 1998–Aug 1998	−19.2%	−6.9%	−29.0%
Apr 2011–Oct 2011	−18.6%	+7.8%	−18.3%

[a]Combines the 2000–2001 and 2002 bear markets.
[b]Officially a bear market.
[c]Estimated for partial months based on monthly return data.
Sources: Developed by the author using data from www.morningstar.com. Gold returns based on London Gold Market Fixing prices.

In all four of the past bear markets, the price of gold increased while the S&P 500 plummeted. In the two most recent bear markets (2000–2002 and 2007–9), gold posted double-digit gains, while in the 1973–74 bear market, the price of gold skyrocketed more than 100 percent.[32] Gold also rose during the 2011 and 1990 market corrections (whereas a bear market is defined as a loss of over 20 percent, a market correction is a loss of 10 to 20 percent). And although the gold price fell during the 1998 correction, it did not decline nearly as much as stock prices. Of the eight big bear markets and market corrections of the past forty years, gold completely failed as a hedge in only one instance—the 1980–82 market correction, when the S&P 500 declined by 20 percent but gold dropped by 46 percent.

Table 4.1 shows gold's performance during cyclical, or short-run, bear markets. Of at least equal concern are secular, or long-run, bear markets like the so-called Lost Decade. Make no mistake—in the long run, a secular bear market can do as much or more damage to your portfolio as a cyclical bear market. Table 4.2 shows the changes in gold prices during the secular bear markets of the last fifty years. During the 1966–82 bear market, the S&P 500 yielded annualized returns of a mere 4.8 percent, but gold averaged 14.5 percent per year.

The second secular bear market stretched from March 2000 to at least March 2009.[33] It was (is?) one of the worst long-term bear markets of the past century, as evidenced by the 7 percent annualized loss produced by the S&P 500 over these years. But gold yielded annualized returns of 14 percent over the same nine years. As well as gold has performed as a hedge against *cyclical* bear markets, it has done even better during the most recent *secular* bear market.

Table 4.2. Average Annualized Returns of Gold and PME Mutual Funds during Past Secular Bear Markets

Time Period	S&P 500 Annualized Total Returns	Gold Price Annualized Returns	Average PME Fund Annualized Returns
Mar 2000–Mar 2009	−7.0%	+14.0%	+17.7%
Jan 1966–Aug 1982	+4.8%[a]	+14.5%[b]	+8.1%
Jan 1966–Dec 2013	+9.5%	+7.6%[b]	+6.5%

[a]Estimated for partial months based on monthly return data.
[b]Prior to 1971, the price of gold was fixed at approximately $35 per ounce.
Individual ownership of gold was illegal in the United States prior to 1975.
Sources: Developed by the author using data from www.morningstar.com. Gold returns based on London Gold Market Fixing prices.

Gold's Downside

Gold seems to be the perfect high-volatility hedge. It is viewed as a financial safe haven, and so it tends to go up when the stock market goes down. It has actually proven its hedging power time and again, over a very diverse range of economic conditions—the energy crisis and run-away inflation of the mid-1970s, the popping of the dot-com bubble and recession of the early 2000s, and the credit crunch and deflationary fears of the late 2000s. And it has performed even better over long-term bear markets.

It's almost too good to be true, isn't it? Well, I'm sorry to say, it *is* too good to be true. There is a problem with gold—and it's a big one. As Table 4.2 shows, over the forty-eight-year period stretching from 1966 through 2013, annualized gold returns trailed the S&P 500 by nearly 2 full percentage points. Although 2 percent may not seem like a huge difference, when compounded over nearly five decades, such a shortfall can have an enormous impact on your wealth. A $10,000 investment in gold made in January 1966 would have been worth $336,000 by December 2013. But that same $10,000 invested in the S&P 500 would have grown to $780,000—more than double the value of the gold investment.

And that's not all. Investors in gold can expect a very bumpy ride—even bumpier than the roller coaster that is the stock market. In fact, over the longer term, stock market volatility has been tame compared to the volatility in gold prices. Figure 4.1 shows the trend in gold prices versus the total returns of the S&P 500 between 1971 (the year the United States went off the gold standard) and 2010. The figure shows gold and stock returns in five-year increments (1971–75, 1976–80, etc.) to smooth out short-term volatility. Yet even when it is smoothed out in this way, the four-decade trend in gold prices looks very volatile. Gold suffered a horrendous twenty-year bear market between 1980 and 2000: from January 1, 1980, to January 1, 2001, the price of gold declined nearly 50 percent. Gold still hasn't fully recovered from that long downturn. If you had bought gold back on the January 21, 1980, high, by December 31, 2013, you would have earned a paltry 1.0 percent annualized return on your investment. That's less than the rate of inflation over the same period. That's right —over a thirty-four-year period, an investor in gold would not even have kept pace with inflation. So while someone who bought gold back in 1966 would have earned decent returns, someone unlucky enough to buy in early 1980 would have seen returns more like those of a passbook savings account—at a stingy bank.

Though stock returns often go down from one year to the next, when charted over longer five-year periods, they follow a relatively calm upward trend—as Figure 4.1 shows. That's why stocks have been such a great investment for the long term, buy-and-hold investor. Sure, you may lose money over a two- or even three-year period, but wait five years and you're almost sure to recover.[34] Gold, conversely, is very volatile even in the long run—when measured over five-year, and even ten- and twenty-year periods, the price of gold goes down as often as it goes up.

True, if you have a long enough time to wait, the price of gold will probably go up—but not by much. The fact is, over the long run, there is no particular reason to think that gold will do any better than keep pace with inflation.[35]

But wait a minute, how can gold possibly combine high volatility with low, inflation-like expected returns? Remember the ironclad rule of investing: all investments with high volatility have to have high returns to compensate investors for the risk they are taking. Don't they?

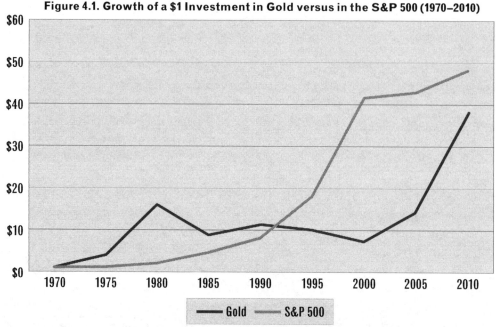

Figure 4.1. Growth of a $1 Investment in Gold versus in the S&P 500 (1970–2010)

Source: Developed by the author using data from "The 'New Math' of the Distribution Phase,"
American Funds Insights (Winter 2007). Gold returns based on London Gold Market Fixing prices.

Yes, they do, and this brings us to the fundamental problem with gold. Gold doesn't break the ironclad rule of investing because gold is not an investment. Or at least, it's not *purely* an investment. Most of the demand for gold comes from the jewelry market, not from investors. This means that gold is really more a commodity than an investment. This is why gold, like other commodities, such as crude oil, follows a boom and bust cycle. And it is why we should not expect gold to beat inflation in the long run. It is a commodity, and commodity prices generally follow the long-term trend in inflation. After all, it's the prices of commodities like wheat, corn, oil, and gasoline that help determine the rate of inflation.

The very same quality that makes gold such a good safe haven makes it a poor investment. As we have seen, unlike true investments, such as stocks or bonds, gold makes no promise of future returns—its value is entirely inherent. An investment in a stock represents an investment in an organization that has no other basic purpose than that of making money for its shareholders. It exists to produce profits. Gold has no such purpose, no raison d'être, no incentive for making you money. It does no work for you, and it doesn't care whether it makes you rich or poor. It just sits there, looking pretty.

It's true that gold has two of the three characteristics that make for a good high-volatility hedge: its price is highly volatile, and it does have low correlation with the stock market. But remember that a good high-volatility hedge should also generate high returns. If we don't get high returns, then we are compromising returns to reduce our portfolio's volatility. We simply cannot count on gold for high returns.

Gold as Insurance

Although I do not view gold as an ideal high-volatility hedge, I nonetheless include a *small* allocation to gold in the stock portion of my portfolio. I don't expect my gold allocation to generate returns similar to stocks, or even bonds. Why, then, own gold? Not as an *investment*, but as *insurance*. You don't buy insurance with the expectation that it's going to generate returns for you. You *pay* for insurance—it comes with a significant cost. The cost of buying gold is the returns you could have gotten by putting that money into stocks.

But as long as gold continues to be viewed as a safe haven, there is a reasonable chance that its price will go way up when the market goes way down. Hence a *little* bit of gold, though costly, just might go a long way toward reducing the pain of the next bear market. After all, as Table 4.1 shows, it's proven its worth time and again during past bear markets.

Because you must pay for gold without any expectation of earning a positive (inflation-beating) return, you cannot afford to put a lot of your investable money into gold. I allocate only 5 percent of the stock portion of my portfolio to gold. Any more than 5 percent, and I feel I am giving up too much in future returns to get the downside protection offered by gold.

The bottom line is that gold can, in small quantities, be used as an effective hedge —but one that requires compromising on returns. It should be viewed as insurance for your portfolio, not as an investment. But what if there were a way to buy gold that combined some part of its safe haven qualities with the promise of future earnings offered by stocks? There is—by investing in PME, or (because diversification is always our goal) mutual funds that invest in PME. An investment in a PME mutual fund is an investment in gold in the ground, *combined* with an investment in companies that are organized for the sole purpose of digging that gold out and selling it at a profit. With a PME fund, you get the benefits of owning gold—high volatility and low correlation with the stock market—coupled with the high expected returns of stocks.

Precious Metals Equities

Let's have another look at Table 4.1, which shows the average returns of PME funds and of gold during past market downturns. Your immediate reaction to the table might be, "Huh, what's so great about PME funds?" As the table shows, these funds had negative returns in six of the eight bear markets and corrections. This is the exact opposite of gold, which produced positive returns six out of eight times. The reason is simple: although the profits of gold mining companies will tend to increase along with the price of gold, gold mining stocks are also subject to the same factors that hammer the stocks of other companies when times are bad. These bearish factors include, for example, overcapacity, rising energy and supply costs, and high interest rates. In short, gold mining stocks are more closely correlated than gold with the broad stock market *because* they are stocks and share many of the characteristics of all stocks.

As Table 4.1 shows, PME funds have been far from perfect as a hedge. Nonetheless, there are four reasons to conclude that PME funds have been good, albeit imperfect, hedges over the past forty years.

Reason 1: The 1973–74 and 2000–2002 Bear Markets

First, regardless of how poorly PME funds may have performed during other market downturns, they worked beautifully during the 1973–74 and 2000–2002 bear markets. These were real killer bear markets. The 2000–2002 bear market was particularly devastating, and not only because the S&P 500 lost nearly half of its value. Of equal, if not greater, importance, this market downturn lasted for two and a half years—by far the longest-lived cyclical bear market of the past four decades. Market downturns that drag on and on are more dangerous than sharp but short-lived bear markets. This is especially true for retirees, who must continue to draw down on their portfolios to meet living expenses. The longer the bear market, the longer the time money must be withdrawn from a portfolio that is not earning any compensating returns. Although the 2000–2002 bear market was only the second worst of the past forty years when measured in terms of lost market value, when you take into account its length, it was, arguably, the worst.

Hence PME funds came through as hedges at the point of maximum danger —and they came through in a very big way. While the S&P 500 lost 47.4 percent of its value between 2000 and 2002, PME funds averaged a remarkable 46.6 percent *positive* return. During the 1973–74 bear market, they did even better: 57.5 percent. I'd gladly take these kinds of returns during the best of times, let alone during two of the worst bear markets of the past forty years. PME funds during the 1973–74 and 2000–2002 bear markets are an excellent example of the principle of correlation at work: a highly volatile asset class, with a low correlation to the broad stock market, can, when added to a stock portfolio, help to significantly reduce the volatility experienced during market downturns.

Reason 2: They Sort of Worked Even When They Didn't Work

Though it's true that PME funds generated negative returns during six of the eight big market declines, a closer look at Table 4.1 reveals that in most of these cases, they still outperformed the S&P 500. As long as a hedge loses less than the broader market, it will still help to reduce an investor's losses during downturns. In both the

1987 and 2007–9 bear markets, the losses incurred by PME funds were much less than the S&P 500's losses. In fact, as we saw in Chapter 2, PME funds moved *up* during the early and late stages of the 2007–9 bear market. It was only during the panic sell-off in the latter half of 2008 that these funds lost value.

The record of PME funds is spottier during the past four market corrections. Nonetheless during the two corrections when the price of gold rose (the 1990 and 2011 corrections), PME funds outperformed the S&P 500 (albeit only barely in 2011).

Reason 3: Secular Bear Markets

Table 4.1 shows PME fund performance during cyclical, or short-run, bear markets. But as we've already learned, an investor needs to look out for secular (long-run) as well as cyclical bear markets. Table 4.2 shows how PME funds performed during the two secular bear markets of the past half-century. During the 1966–82 bear, these funds performed well—not nearly as well as gold, but nonetheless significantly better than the S&P 500. However, during the more recent bear market, PME funds truly shone, generating an average annualized return of 17.7 percent. The average PME fund increased in value by more than 500 percent between 2000 and 2009. Are you beginning to understand why the Lost Decade is a myth to those investors who were using the principle of correlation to diversify their portfolios?

Reason 4: Nothing to Lose, and *Maybe* Much to Gain

Remember that, unlike low-volatility hedges (bonds), high-volatility hedges are supposed to work without forcing us to compromise by giving up returns. And this is exactly how PME funds have worked. In fact, adding a PME fund to your portfolio would have boosted your returns over the last five decades.

If you've been paying close attention, that last sentence should puzzle you. After all, Table 4.2 shows that from 1966 through 2013, the average PME fund generated annualized returns of only 6.5 percent. These returns were not only significantly less than the 9.5 percent returns produced by the S&P 500, they were even less than the 7.6 percent returns on gold.[36]

And they were less than the 8.8 percent annualized returns earned by the average large cap blend mutual fund. Therefore, we would expect that adding PME to a portfolio of large cap stocks would have reduced the portfolio's returns to less than 8.8 percent. For example, let's assume we had invested half of our money in a large cap blend fund and half in a PME fund on January 1, 1966. By 2013, we would expect the portfolio's returns to equal the average of the large cap fund's 8.8 percent returns and the PME fund's 6.5 percent returns—that is, 7.65 percent. Right?

Wrong. A portfolio split half and half between a large cap blend fund and a PME fund would have earned 9.3 percent annually between 1966 and 2013—*more* than the 8.8 percent earned by the large cap fund alone. How is this possible? Welcome to the mysteries of MPT. Remember, a well-diversified portfolio is like a gourmet meal: it is greater than the sum of its parts. Using the *principle of correlation*, you can combine two highly volatile investments into a portfolio that is less volatile than either of its components. Even more remarkably, that same less-volatile portfolio can *sometimes* produce higher returns than either of its constituent parts. That is exactly what happened for portfolios comprising large cap blend funds and PME funds over the last five decades. And, as we shall see, it happened for many other, more complex portfolios that included an investment in PME. Despite the relatively low returns of PME funds, adding these funds to well-diversified portfolios has often *increased* rather than reduced the portfolios' returns.

Now, I have a confession to make. I did add a little something—a secret sauce, if you will—to our 50 percent large cap/50 percent PME portfolio to get these remarkable results. This secret sauce *reduced* the portfolio's volatility over the long run, while *increasing* its returns from the expected 7.65 percent average to 9.3 percent.

So, what is this secret sauce? Sorry, but we are getting way ahead of ourselves. Before we can start adding sauces to our gourmet portfolio, we first need to learn much more about the basic ingredients—not only the large cap stocks and high-volatility hedges but also the low-volatility hedges and return boosters covered in the next two chapters. I promise that you will learn what the secret sauce is, and how it works, later. (For those who want a hint, take a close look at the table of contents.)

So let's review. PME funds were a superb hedge during the Lost Decade of 2000–2009. They were an excellent hedge against the 2000–2002 and 1973–74 cyclical bear markets. Although less effective during other cyclical market downturns, they still helped limit damage during the 1987 and 2007–9 bear markets. And they did all this while increasing the returns of well-diversified portfolios over the last five decades. Granted it's not a perfect record—but it's pretty darn good.

The Future Outlook for PME Funds

Will PME funds continue to work as well in the future? Ah, that's the million-dollar question. I don't know the answer, and neither does anyone else. But the fundamental characteristics that make these funds good hedges—low correlation with other stocks, high volatility, and the ability to generate high returns when included in a well-diversified portfolio—appear to remain in place.

And there is one other, very important point. Take one last peek at Table 4.1. Do you notice how, in every single market downturn that saw an increase in the price of gold, PME funds beat the S&P 500—usually by a wide margin? The reason for this is simple. Although PME may be hammered by the same forces that drive down all other stocks during a bear market, as long as the price of gold rises, gold mining companies will have at least one *unique* bullish factor working in their favor. And as Table 4.1 clearly shows, when stock prices decline, the price of gold usually rises.

If we think of gold as a safe harbor in a storm, then we might think of gold mining stocks as ships anchored in that harbor. These ships might still be buffeted and damaged by the wind and the waves, but they will be much safer than the other ships—the stocks of all other companies—out on the open seas. Gold mining stocks are not themselves safe havens, but they are anchored to one of the great safe havens of the financial universe. And this is not likely to change in our lifetime. As long as humans continue to look upon gold as a store of *intrinsic* value—as we have for thousands of years—we have reason to *hope* that the enterprises that mine this metal will hedge us against future bear markets.

But we should never *expect* that PME funds will always work like they did in 2000–2002 and during the Lost Decade. In investing, there are never any guarantees. Maybe during the next bear market they will fail as a hedge, like they did during the 1980–82 market correction (when, along with the price of gold, they declined even more sharply than the S&P 500).

It is because we cannot *count* on PME funds to work as a good hedge every time the market drops that we need to include other hedges in our portfolio. I am a big believer in diversification, and that includes diversification of our hedges. As long as we own a number of different hedges, including gold and a PME fund as well as an emerging-market bond fund, we increase our chances that at least one of these hedges will offset our losses when the bear returns (and return he will!).

Emerging-Market Bonds

So let's now consider the last of our high-volatility hedges. Emerging-market bonds are bonds issued by governments and corporations in emerging-market countries such as China, India, Turkey, Brazil, Mexico, and Poyais.

You may be wondering about that last one. If you've never heard of the Latin American nation of Poyais, that's because it doesn't exist. But that didn't stop British lenders from investing £200,000 in Poyaisian bonds in the 1820s.

Welcome to Poyais

Poyais was the invention of Gregor MacGregor, a former mercenary in Simon Bolivar's army. Bolivar led the revolution that ended Spanish rule throughout much of Latin America. In its wake, newly independent countries such as Peru, Argentina, and Chile, were opened to foreign investment for the first time. The rulers of these countries, desperate for funds to build their fledgling nations, combined with British bankers and investors dazzled by visions of the famed silver and gold mines of the New World. An emerging-market boom quickly ensued. Twenty-six new mining companies were registered on London's Royal Exchange by 1825, and Latin American governments raised £20 million via bonds issued in London.

With gold fever running rampant and so many new, exotic-sounding locales in which to bet their savings, British investors can perhaps be excused for becoming a bit confused. Enter MacGregor, the self-proclaimed Prince of Poyais, to exploit the confusion. Armed with a prospectus that sang the praises of Poyais's gold and timber resources and the "broad boulevards, colonnaded buildings, and ... splendid domed cathedral" of the capital city of Saint Joseph, MacGregor issued a Poyaisian bond through the London banks. He soon convinced many of his fellow Scots to invest in it.[37]

Perhaps in an effort to turn his fictitious princedom into a reality, MacGregor even persuaded some of his countrymen to emigrate to Poyais. In 1822 and 1823, the ships *Honduras Packet* and *Kennersley Castle* landed about 250 would-be Poyaisian settlers, including a banker and more than one doctor, on the coast of modern-day Honduras. Far from the broad boulevards MacGregor had promised, they found no port, town, or roads. Poorly organized, the settlers began to fight over rations. When the rainy season arrived, many of them became despondent. Eventually, a passing ship rescued them and brought them to Belize, but two-thirds of the settlers succumbed to malaria, yellow fever, and malnutrition.

Nonetheless, they served at least one of MacGregor's goals. Before the settlers left Britain, word of their planned emigration made Poyais appear all the more real and helped MacGregor sell his bonds.[38] The 6 percent interest rate was the same as that offered on the bonds of Buenos Aires, Peru, Chile, and Greater Columbia. That Poyaisian bond investors were willing to accept the same 6 percent rate indicates that they assessed the risk of a Poyaisian default as no different from that of these real governments.[39] The irony is that they were correct in this assessment. All of the latter governments defaulted on their foreign debts between 1826 and 1828, as, of course, did Poyais.[40]

I would like to be able to tell you that in the wake of these mass emerging-market defaults—not to mention MacGregor's scam—investors learned their lesson and were thenceforth much more careful and cautious when lending money to Latin America. But the record suggests otherwise. The defaults of 1826–28 constituted the first Latin American debt crisis, but it was far from the last. As just a few examples of the subsequent troubles, Argentina has defaulted on or rescheduled[41] its debt seven times (most recently in 2001), Brazil nine times, Chile nine times, Mexico eight times, and Venezuela ten times (most recently in 2004). A major debt crisis swept across the entire region in the early 1930s, and again in the 1980s and 1990s. And multiple defaults have not been limited to the emerging markets of Latin America. In Africa, Nigeria has defaulted on or rescheduled its debt five times since it gained independence in 1960, Morocco four times, and South Africa three times, while in Asia, Indonesia has defaulted or rescheduled its bond payments four times, India three times, and China twice.[42] It seems that once burned, investors in emerging-market bonds keep going back for more. (They have, though, become more adept at avoiding the bonds of nonexistent countries. Not that MacGregor stopped trying to "borrow" money for his fictitious nation. In 1826, in an attempted Ponzi scheme to pay off his previous investors, MacGregor tried to float a new Poyaisian bond, but this time investors weren't buying. To escape his creditors, he emigrated to Caracas, Venezuela, where he died in 1845.[43])

In short, emerging markets have a history of defaulting on their debt—over and over again. They default, in part, because they can get away with it. Investors in the bonds of domestic corporations have recourse to the bankruptcy courts in the event that the bond issuers fail to make payments. But when a foreign company or sovereign government proves unwilling or unable to repay its debt, bondholders have little or no legal remedy.

Fraudulent bonds, debt crises, serial defaulters—at this point you may be wondering why we're even considering emerging markets as a potential investment. Paradoxically, it is precisely the long history of defaults by emerging markets that makes their bonds an attractive high-volatility hedge. As we will see in the next chapter, most bonds are characterized by low volatility, reflecting the fact that they usually do not default. Emerging-market bonds are more volatile than most other types of bonds in part because many emerging markets have shown themselves to be serial defaulters. Emerging-market bonds are seen, rightly, as riskier than other types of bonds—even when they are issued by emerging markets in a relatively strong financial position. Just as British investors in the 1820s failed to distinguish the fake Poyais from real countries like Peru, modern investors have a tendency to lump emerging markets together—especially during a crisis. At the least sign of trouble in one country, they will often grab their money and flee not only the affected country but all of its neighbors. In this way, contagion often spreads rapidly from weak to strong emerging markets, with the result that emerging-market bonds tend to default across multiple countries in a cyclical pattern.

But as we have learned, with higher risk comes bigger rewards. Emerging-market bonds have higher expected returns than most other types of bonds. They also have relatively low correlation with stocks and U.S. bonds. And although they are much more volatile than other types of bonds, they have not been nearly as volatile as gold and PME funds (or, for that matter, stocks). Hence, in terms of volatility, emerging-market bonds are best viewed as lying somewhere in between the other high-volatility hedges and the low-volatility hedges represented by other types of bonds. As such, they tend to work on the principles of both correlation and compromise.

The Recent History of Emerging-Market Bonds

We can see emerging-market bonds at work as both correlation-principle and compromise-principle hedges in Table 4.3. Mutual funds specializing in emerging-market bonds are relatively new, so unfortunately there are no data on how such funds might have performed prior to the mid-1990s. However, from Table 4.3, we find that emerging-market bond funds posted double-digit gains during the long bear market of 2000–2002. In this bear market, emerging-market bonds worked like a high-volatility hedge, moving sharply upward while stocks plummeted. Conversely, during the 2007–9 bear market and the 2011 market correction, emerging-market bond funds failed to move in the opposite direction of stocks, although they did not lose nearly as much as the S&P 500. In both of these downturns their lower volatility, relative to equities, helped to reduce losses in portfolios hedged with emerging-market bonds.

Table 4.3. Average Returns of Emerging-Market Bond Mutual Funds during Past Bear Markets and Market Corrections

Time Period	S&P 500 Total Returns	Average Emerging-Market Bond Fund Returns
Bear Markets:		
Oct 2007–Mar 2009	−55.3%	−21.3%
Mar 2000–Oct 2002[a]	−47.4%	+15.5%
Jan 1973–Oct 1974	−44.8%[b]	NA
Aug 1987–Dec 1987	−32.9%[b]	NA
Corrections:		
Nov 1980–Aug 1982[c]	−20.0%[b]	NA
Jul 1990–Oct 1990	−19.2%	NA
Jul 1998–Aug 1998	−19.2%	−36.3%
Apr 2011–Oct 2011	−18.6%	−7.0%

[a]Combines the 2000–2001 and 2002 bear markets.
[b]Estimated for partial months based on monthly return data.
[c]Officially a bear market.
Source: Developed by the author using data from www.morningstar.com.

In 2000–2002, 2007–9, and 2011, emerging-market bonds worked well as either high-volatility or low-volatility hedges. But in 1998, they failed as a hedge, generating losses almost twice as large as those of the S&P 500. The 1998 market correction began as a currency crisis in Thailand, then spread to many other countries in Asia, and eventually caused Russia to default on its debt. Given its beginnings in emerging markets and its conclusion in a major emerging-market default, it is not surprising that emerging-market bonds fared even worse than the S&P 500 during the 1998 market correction. We should take this bit of history as fair warning—emerging-market bonds are *much* more volatile than other types of bonds. For this reason, I like Russell Wild's recommendation (in his excellent book *Bond Investing for Dummies*) that they be treated not as bonds but as stocks, and that they be placed in the *stock* portion of your portfolio.

Now let's look at the secular trends. From Table 4.4, we see that during the recent secular bear market, emerging-market bond funds averaged an impressive annualized return of 7.7 percent. Even more impressive, these funds have averaged 9.7 percent annualized returns over the last twenty years. This is 0.5 percent more than the S&P 500 and much more than other types of bond funds.

Since 1994, emerging-market bond funds have had negative returns in only three years:

- 1994 (the year the Mexican peso was devalued), when they lost an average 13.7 percent

- 1998 (the year of the Russian bond default), when they lost 24.2 percent for the year

- 2008 (the year of the global financial crisis), when they lost 18.1 percent for the year

Table 4.4. Average Annualized Returns of Emerging-Market Bond Mutual Funds during the Recent Secular Bear Market

Time Period	S&P 500 Annualized Total Returns	Average Emerging-Market Bond Fund Annualized Returns
Mar 2000–Mar 2009	−7.0%	+7.7%
Jan 1966–Aug 1982	+4.8%[a]	NA
Jan 1994–Dec 2013	+9.2%	+9.7%

[a]Estimated for partial months based on monthly return data.
Source: Developed by the author using data from www.morningstar.com.

The bottom line here is that emerging-market bond funds have been generating stock-like returns of nearly 10 percent, with volatility only about half that of stocks, ever since they were introduced back in the mid-1990s. This makes them an asset class with a very unusual, and enticing, risk-return profile.

The Outlook for Emerging-Market Bonds

Of course, the big question is, can emerging market bonds keep producing stock-like returns? There are two ways to answer this question, depending on the lessons one draws from history. First, there have unquestionably been enormous changes in the developing world over the past decade. For that reason, some may argue that the recent data are a misleading guide to the future. During the 1980s and 1990s, many emerging markets experienced financial crises brought on, in part, by an easing in the availability and cost of credit from the developed world. Emerging-market countries responded to loose credit by leveraging to the hilt, which in many cases led to asset class bubbles in their real estate and/or stock markets. When the bubbles burst, foreign investors reversed course, grabbed their money, and fled. The resulting depreciation in emerging-market currencies made it impossible for these countries to pay off their dollar-denominated foreign debts. On the basis of data in Reinhart and Rogoff's compendium and analysis of the history of financial crises, *This Time Is Different*, there have been no fewer than fifty-three external debt defaults or rescheduled payments by emerging-market governments between 1980 and 1999.[44] Countries defaulting or rescheduling their debts in these years included Algeria, Angola, Egypt, Kenya, Nigeria, Argentina, Bolivia, Brazil, Chile, Columbia, Costa Rica, Indonesia, the Philippines, Sri Lanka, Poland, Romania, Russia, and Turkey. Many emerging-market countries defaulted two or three times in these two decades.

The consequences for the economies of the defaulting countries were often devastating. With these events fresh in mind, the emerging markets have since "gotten religion" and instituted much more conservative, prudent economic policies. As a result, many emerging-market countries have gone from being net debtors to net creditors, and some, such as China, have built up enormous foreign currency reserves. At the same time, these countries have as a group doubled their share of world gross domestic product (GDP) since 1990. As of 2010, they accounted for 38 percent of world GDP, 50 percent of global exports and close to 50 percent of global imports, over 80 percent of foreign currency reserves, and nearly 40 percent of global stock market capitalization.[45] Their economic growth has been impressive, to say the least.

Hence the risk of default on emerging-market bonds is much lower today than it was back in the 1980s and 1990s. In fact, improvements in the credit ratings of many emerging-market bond issuers helped account for the outsized returns generated by this asset class over the past decade (bond prices rise when the bonds' credit ratings improve). Nowadays, many emerging-market countries seem more fiscally prudent than developed economies, and their bonds are starting to look safer than those issued by some European countries.

So the good news is that emerging-market bonds are not the dicey investments they once were. But as you know, with reduced risk comes reduced returns. At some point in the near future, we might expect that both the returns and the volatility of emerging-market bonds are going to become less stock-like and more like those of other types of bonds. Also, given the recent rise in their popularity among investors searching for yield in today's low-interest-rate environment, it is likely that correlations between emerging-market bonds and other asset classes will increase. Correlations will likely rise because the many investors new to these "risky" bonds will likely be tempted to sell them at the first sign of a downturn in the stock market. If and when correlations rise and returns fall, emerging-market bonds will continue to work as a hedge—but more as a low-volatility hedge based on the principle of compromise than as a high-volatility hedge working on the principle of correlation.

Here is where one's view of the lessons of history comes into play. If you believe that history in general—and economic history in particular—is a story of continual progress, then we would conclude that once the risks and returns of emerging-market bonds decline, and the correlations rise, they will never again return to the levels we've seen over the recent past.

But if you believe that history moves less in a straight line and more in cycles, there is reason to believe that at some point in the longer-term future, we will once again see the volatility and sovereign debt defaults that most recently characterized the 1990s. In fact, this is the conclusion that Reinhart and Rogoff reach based on their in-depth analysis of the historical data. One of the key points they draw from these data is that it is very difficult, and rare, for emerging markets to "graduate" from their status as serial defaulters to the status of financially responsible advanced economies. Graduation, they conclude, "is a very slow process, and congratulations are all too often premature."[46] They also point to the cyclical nature of emerging-market sovereign defaults, when they note that these defaults tend to cluster in certain periods (as in the 1980s and 1990s), separated by long lulls:

> Overall, one can see that default episodes, while recurrent, are far from continuous. This wide spacing no doubt reflects adjustments that debtors and creditors make in the wake of each default cycle. For example, today many emerging markets are following quite conservative macroeconomic policies. *Over time, though, this caution usually gives way to optimism and profligacy,* but only after a long lull.[47]

The italicized phrase explains why the cycle of emerging-market defaults tends to repeat itself. Quite simply, governments, like individuals, forget the lessons of history. As memories of the misery that accompanied the defaults of the 1980s and 1990s recede, and as foreign investors pour capital into emerging markets that now seem much safer, we are likely to see the familiar pattern of the past repeat itself:

> The problem is that crisis-prone countries, particularly serial defaulters, tend to overborrow in good times, leaving them vulnerable during the inevitable downturns. The pervasive view that "this time is different" is precisely why this time usually is *not* different and why catastrophe eventually strikes again.[48]

How long might the lull last before we see a new round of defaults? That, of course, is impossible to say, although based on data Reinhart and Rogoff present going back to 1800,[49] the lulls between major spikes in sovereign debt defaults appear to last anywhere from ten to forty years. About fifteen years have already passed since the last spike in defaults, so we might expect to see a new round of defaults any time between now and 2040. (But don't come looking for me in 2040 if this expectation proves wrong—it's just an educated guess.)

It is certainly possible that a few of the emerging-market countries will graduate from the debt default cycle. But it is less likely that emerging markets *as a group* will do so. And even if some countries do graduate, they may be replaced by new emerging-market nations that currently fall within the category of riskier, so-called frontier economies. In this way, risk within the group of emerging markets may continually replenish itself.

The bottom line here is that although returns from emerging-market bonds may well decline and correlations rise in the near term, in response to the current prudent policies of the countries issuing these bonds, over the longer run, emerging markets may continue to be risky, default-prone places to invest. Emerging markets would have to reward investors with high expected returns for shouldering these risks. And we might expect the current fad for investing in emerging-market bonds to end with a return of defaults and risk. An end to this fad could in turn lead to lower correlations between emerging-market bonds and stocks.

However, even if this time really is different, and the default risks associated with emerging markets permanently moderate, emerging-market bonds should still work as a hedge—a low-volatility, rather than high-volatility, hedge. Hence, regardless of what the future might hold for the emerging-market nations, we can have some confidence in the ability of their bonds to reduce our portfolios' volatility going forward.

Teamwork

So there you have it: three hedges—gold, PME funds, and emerging-market bond funds—at least two of which have the potential to reduce volatility without requiring too much sacrifice in returns. Which ones should you include in your portfolio? *All* of them. Each one has its own particular advantages and disadvantages, and its own unique role to play. Emerging-market bonds can be viewed as a bridge between high-volatility hedges and low-volatility hedges. Sometimes they work more like the former, and sometimes more like the latter.

PME funds lie somewhere between emerging-market bonds and gold. They have worked even better than emerging-market bonds as a hedge against *secular* bear markets, and they significantly outperformed emerging-market bonds during the 2000–2002 bear market. Conversely, they are much more volatile than emerging-market bonds.

And finally, gold is the ultimate portfolio insurance. It has proven to be a much more *reliable* hedge than the other two, having increased in value during six of the last eight major market downturns. Gold has also proven to be an exceptional hedge against secular bear markets. However, unlike either PME funds or emerging-market bonds, gold makes no promise of generating inflation-beating returns and should therefore be treated as portfolio insurance rather than as a true investment. A little bit of gold is good for your portfolio, but too much gold could be harmful to your long-run returns.

Always remember, high-volatility hedges are, as their name indicates, *highly volatile*. They are like medicine for your portfolio. In small doses they are therapeutic, but in larger doses they can be dangerous. This observation applies not only to gold but also to PME funds and emerging-market bond funds. In general, you should not devote more than about one-third of the stock portion of a portfolio to high-volatility hedges. And be sure to spread this money across all three hedges, to avoid a dangerous concentration of your wealth in a single asset class. As a rule, I do not devote more than 20 percent of the stock portion of my own portfolio to any one of the three high-volatility hedges—and in the case of gold, my rule is no more than 5 percent.

Not only does diversification across all three hedges reduce the chances of a dangerous drug overdose, it also helps to maximize the benefits of the correlation principle. Remember, each of the three hedges has its own unique strengths and weaknesses. It's often the case that when one hedge fails, another one comes to the rescue. A good example of this teamwork occurred during the 2000–2002 bear market. All three high-volatility hedges generated positive, double-digit returns over the entire two-and-a-half-year length of this bear market. But these positive returns were by no means spread evenly across time. On the contrary, some of the hedges performed relatively poorly during the early months of the downturn, whereas others underperformed in the latter months. Table 4.5 shows average returns for each of the three hedges broken down by year. Notice that between March 24, 2000, and December 31, 2000, emerging-market bond funds were the only hedge able to produce positive (albeit modest) returns. During calendar year 2001, both PME and emerging-market bond funds performed well, but gold lagged behind the other two hedges. It wasn't until 2002 that gold joined PME funds in posting double-digit returns. By that time, emerging-market bond funds, the best hedge in the early months of the bear market, had faded. An investment in any *single* hedge during the 2000–2002 bear market would have brought only temporary relief from the pain. Only by spreading your dollars across all three hedges could you have reduced your losses throughout the entire two-and-a-half-year period.

Table 4.5. Average Returns of High-Volatility Hedges during the 2000–2002 Bear Market

Asset Class	Time Period		
	Mar 24–Dec 31, 2000	Jan 1–Dec 31, 2001	Jan 1–Oct 9, 2002
Emerging-market bond funds	+2.8%	+12.5%	−0.2%
PME funds	−5.8%	+19.3%	+30.5%
Gold	−4.3%	+1.4%	+15.5%
S&P 500	−12.8%	−11.9%	−31.5%

Sources: Developed by the author using data from www.morningstar.com.
Gold returns based on London Gold Market Fixing prices.

Bear markets are painful and scary from beginning to end. By combining hedges, you can mitigate the pain and fear throughout these difficult downturns. This is one example of the ways in which hedges in a diversified portfolio can work together as a team.

Summary and Conclusions: Make Volatility Your Friend

Table 3.2 summarized the characteristics and roles played by U.S. and international large caps in a well-diversified portfolio. Table 4.6 extends Table 3.2 to include the characteristics and portfolio roles played by the high-volatility hedges—gold, PME, and emerging-market bonds.

Table 4.6. Summary of the Characteristics and Portfolio Roles Played by Large Caps and High-Volatility Hedges

Asset Class	Correlation with U.S. Large Caps	Volatility	Expected Returns	Role in Portfolio
Core Holdings:				
U.S. large caps	—	High	High	Core holding; produce high returns to beat inflation risk
International developed-market large caps	High	High	High	Long-run diversification benefits; currency diversification
Emerging-market large caps	High	High	High	Long-run diversification benefits; currency diversification
High-Volatility Hedges:				
Gold	Very low	Very high	Low	Insurance
PME	Low	Extremely high	Medium (but may increase portfolio returns when combined with secret sauce)	Applying principle of correlation
Emerging-market bonds	Low	Medium	Medium	Applying principle of correlation and/or compromise

As Table 4.6 shows, the one key characteristic shared in common by all three high-volatility hedges is low correlation with large caps. There is no doubt about it—large cap stocks are highly volatile investments. This volatility can threaten and even bankrupt a retiree's portfolio, as happened to John Stockman. But using black belt investing with high-volatility hedges, you can turn the stock market's volatility to your advantage. You can take the very market characteristic that strikes fear into the heart of investors *and use it against itself.* You can employ some of the most volatile investments in existence, like PME, to *reduce* your portfolio's volatility.

Volatility is the great enemy of stock investors everywhere. You cannot change the volatile nature of the stock market. But with the help of the high-volatility hedges, you can make volatility your friend.

CHAPTER 5

REDUCING PORTFOLIO VOLATILITY
WITH LOW-VOLATILITY HEDGES (BONDS)

ℒℯ

G old, PME funds, and emerging-market bonds are the investments that allow us to apply the principle of correlation to real-world portfolios. These asset classes have low correlation with the stock market and may go up when the market goes down. They are highly volatile, meaning that they have the potential to yield big, double-digit gains during market downturns. And finally, at least in the case of PME funds and emerging-market bonds, they don't require you to sacrifice much, if anything, in the way of returns. Reducing a portfolio's volatility without reducing its returns is the promise of the correlation principle. The high-volatility hedges help us to realize this promise.

Why We Need Low-Volatility Hedges

Unfortunately, there have been times (such as the 2007–9 financial crisis) when the high-volatility hedges haven't lived up to this promise as well as we would have liked. And on a few occasions, the high-volatility hedges have failed completely, and spectacularly. In 1980–82, both gold and PME funds lost more—much more—than the S&P 500. In 1998, both PME and emerging-market bond funds lost much more than the S&P 500.

The 1980–82 market correction is illustrative of a fundamental fact: no matter how well suited a particular asset class is as a hedge in a broad range of different market conditions, certain circumstances may arise to thwart the asset's hedging capabilities. As we learned in the last chapter, gold has performed well as a hedge in inflationary and deflationary environments (or at least environments characterized by the fear of deflation). However, it failed miserably during the 1980–82 market correction, losing 46 percent of its value. What went wrong? The 1970s saw a major bull market in gold, as investors sought to protect themselves from high levels of inflation. The price of gold finally topped out at $850 per ounce in January 1980—more than twenty-three times greater than the 1970 price of $36 per ounce. But in the early 1980s the Federal Reserve, under then chairman Paul Volcker, got serious about tackling inflation. Volcker tightened the money supply, causing interest rates to rise to double-digit levels, putting the economy into recession and sending the stock market tumbling. But as the Fed's bitter medicine of high interest rates began to work, inflation started to ease. In 1981, inflation stood at 8.9 percent; by 1982, it had dropped to 3.8 percent. Investors who had flocked to gold as a hedge against inflation now bolted for the exits, sending the price plummeting. The early 1980s were thus characterized neither by rising inflation nor fears of deflation but rather by a return from high to more normal levels of inflation. This environment of easing inflationary pressure proved a very difficult one for gold. As versatile as gold is as a hedge, it just won't work in certain economic conditions—in fact, it can actually work to *amplify* rather than dampen stock market losses. And when gold declines, it is usually a good bet that PME will follow—as happened during the 1980–82 correction.

What to do? At this point, it should be no surprise that my answer is to *diversify*. If, under certain market conditions, our high-volatility hedges may fail, then we need to hedge our hedges. We need to add *low-volatility* hedges to our portfolios.

Finding good high-volatility hedges is as difficult as finding a needle in a haystack. There just aren't many asset classes that combine low correlation to the stock market with high volatility and high expected returns. Fortunately, finding *low-volatility* hedges is much easier. You need look no further than *bonds*. Almost every type of bond in existence combines low correlation to stocks with low volatility.

Bonds work to hedge a stock portfolio in two ways. First, because they have little to no correlation with stocks, they often tend to go up when the stock market goes down. And second, even if they fail to go up, because they are much less volatile than stocks, they will not suffer the big losses that can hit the stock market. Because they work in both these ways, they tend to be more reliable than high-volatility hedges. The low volatility of bonds acts as a sort of fail-safe mechanism, ensuring that if they don't hedge your portfolio one way, they will still work the other way.

This point is illustrated in Table 5.1, which shows the average returns of investment-grade, intermediate-term bond funds during the last eight big bear markets and market corrections. These funds include a mix of both corporate and U.S. government bonds. For comparative purposes, the table also shows the returns of the S&P 500 and gold. As the table shows, bond returns increased during three of the four market corrections and during two of the four bear markets. Even in the three cases where bond returns failed to go up, they did not decline nearly as much as the

S&P 500. At no time did bond losses ever exceed, or even come close to, the losses sustained by the stock market—unlike the case for gold.

The low volatility of bonds is rooted in their very nature and is not likely to change in the future. A bond is a loan. The bond issuer is *contractually obligated* to repay this loan, with interest. In contrast, a publicly traded company is under no obligation to return principal to its shareholders. In the event of a bankruptcy, bondholders have legal priority over shareholders on claims to the bankrupted company's assets.

Furthermore, unlike stocks, bonds come with an expiration date. The principal or face value of a bond must be paid in full when the bond expires or matures. In other words, bondholders can expect to receive a known amount of money by a known date. Thus a bond's price, although subject to ups and downs, is ultimately anchored by the face value of the bond. Even if a bond suffers a significant price decline, as the bond approaches maturity, the price will tend to converge back toward the bond's face value. Short of a default, a bond's price cannot drift up or down *too far* from its face value without eventually being pulled back. Stocks, in contrast, have no such anchor. There is nothing in the *inherent* nature of a stock to prevent its price from drifting down to zero or up into the stratosphere. Given this inherent difference between bonds and stocks, we can reasonably expect that the former will continue to be much less volatile than the latter, in the future as in the past.

Table 5.1. Average Returns of Intermediate-Term Bond Mutual Funds during Past Bear Markets and Market Corrections

Time Period	S&P 500 Total Returns	Gold Price Returns	Average Intermediate-Term Bond Fund Returns
Bear Markets:			
Oct 2007–Mar 2009	−55.3%	+25.5%	−5.4%
Mar 2000–Oct 2002[a]	−47.4%	+12.1%	+22.7%
Jan 1973–Oct 1974	−44.8%[b]	+139.4%	−14.3%
Aug 1987–Dec 1987	−32.9%[b]	+6.2%	+1.1%
Corrections:			
Nov 1980–Aug 1982[c]	−20.0%[b]	−46.0%	+19.7%
Jul 1990–Oct 1990	−19.2%	+6.8%	−0.4%
Jul 1998–Aug 1998	−19.2%	−6.9%	+1.2%
Apr 2011–Oct 2011	−18.6%	+7.8%	+2.3%

[a] Combines the 2000–2001 and 2002 bear markets.
[b] Estimated for partial months based on monthly return data.
[c] Officially a bear market.
Sources: Developed by the author using data from www.morningstar.com. Gold returns based on London Gold Market Fixing prices.

More Teamwork

There is one other, very important point to be gleaned from Table 5.1. Take a look at the row representing the 1980–82 market correction. As we have seen, this correction was brought on by the Fed's decision to let interest rates rise to drive down inflation. The easing of inflationary pressures in turn caused gold prices to drop precipitously, thereby ruining gold's usefulness as a hedge against the stock market decline. But notice that while gold prices dropped, bonds produced double-digit returns. The environment was a very difficult one for gold, but the combination of high interest rates, high bond yields, and improving prospects for taming inflation was absolutely perfect for bonds. In fact, 1982 marked the beginning of the great bond bull market that only now, three decades later, shows signs of running out of steam.

In the previous chapter, we saw how three asset classes—gold, PME, and emerging-market bonds—worked together to limit losses throughout the entire length of the 2000–2002 bear market. The 1980–82 market correction provides another excellent example of teamwork between hedges—this time between gold and bonds. The same economic conditions that worked *against* gold worked *for* bonds. By hedging our hedges, we increase the chances that one hedge will work if the other fails.

Bonds combine excellent reliability as low-volatility hedges with a tendency to rise during periods of declining inflation, when gold and PME suffer. These are very good reasons to include them in our portfolios. Granted, we must accept the relatively low returns that come with bonds' low volatility. If the high-volatility hedges represented the vegetable side dishes to our gourmet portfolio, then bonds are the potatoes. Like potatoes, they are bland and unexciting—no triple-digit returns to be found here! But when the chips are down and our steak-like stock holdings have shrunk to the size of one of those mini-burgers, our "potatoey" bonds just might sustain us until the next bull market comes along.

Bonds in Their (Almost) Infinite Variety

So we're (I hope) agreed—let's buy some bonds. Just one quick question—what kinds of bonds should we buy? Let's see, there are corporate bonds, of course, and there are Treasury bonds—which are not to be confused with Treasury bills (or T-bills). There are junk bonds, and investment-grade bonds; long-term bonds, short-term bonds, *ultra* short-term bonds; agency bonds, mortgage-backed bonds ... oh, and don't forget municipal bonds. And then there are inflation-protected bonds ... and ...

OK, so I lied—the answer to the question of what kinds of bonds we should buy is not quick or simple. In fact, entire books are devoted to the subject. The fact is that bonds come in an almost infinite variety, each with its own esoteric characteristics, such as duration, callability, and credit rating.

Choosing bonds to buy can be very confusing, but we will cut through a lot of that confusion by focusing on just a few of the most important characteristics that determine a bond's risk–reward profile:

- Duration (and maturity)

- Credit quality

- Type of bond (corporate, Treasury, etc.)

Maturity and Duration

Bonds, unlike stocks, come with an expiration date. Not only is the bond issuer required to repay the loan, but it must be repaid in full by a specified date. The time between today's date and the date on which the principal must be repaid is referred to as the bond's maturity.

Maturity is a key determinant of the risk associated with any given bond. When you buy a bond, you expect (or at least hope) that everything will go off without a hitch. You expect to be paid your dividends in full and on time (twice a year, for most bonds), and you expect to get your principal paid in full when the bond matures. As long as everything goes according to plan, you will come out fine. You stand to lose money only if something goes wrong. And if you think about it, the longer the time until the bond matures, the greater the chances are that something could go wrong.

Let's take an example. Suppose you have two corporate bonds, one of which matures tomorrow, the other ten years from tomorrow. What can really go wrong with the first bond? The company issuing the bond is in business today; what are the odds that it will declare bankruptcy and default on its bonds in the next twenty-four hours? Pretty slim. Interest rates could suddenly skyrocket, sending bond prices plummeting. But even in this unlikely event, who cares? You're not going to sell the bond anyway, because you only have to wait one more day to get your principal back.

The odds of something going wrong within twenty-four hours are miniscule. Ah, but what about the other bond, which doesn't mature for ten more years? There's *plenty* of time for things to go drastically wrong with this bond. First off, you might run into some unanticipated expenses that force you to sell the bond before it matures. What if interest rates rose since you first bought the bond, and now the price you can get for it has dropped? Or maybe the company that issued the bond has hit a rough patch and doesn't look as solid as it did back when you bought it. This could cause the bond ratings agencies to lower the bond's credit rating. There's no way you're going to get the same price you paid for the bond if it now comes with a lower credit rating (i.e., an increased chance of defaulting).

Even if you don't need or want to sell the bond before it matures, there's still plenty that can go wrong. The rate of inflation could rise (the night thief again!), eating into the fixed payments you get from the bond. And of course, there's always the chance that the bond issuer could go bankrupt and default. The longer you have to wait until a bond matures, the greater the chances that something could go wrong.

Hence bond returns are more volatile for bonds with longer maturities than those with shorter maturities. A bond's *duration* is calculated based in part on its maturity, but duration also takes into account other factors, including the bond's price and coupon rate. Duration, like maturity, is measured in years, but duration is actually an estimate of the sensitivity of a bond's price to changes in interest rates or bond yields. For every 1 percentage point increase in a bond's yield, a bond's price will decline by an amount equal to the duration. For example, if the yield on a bond with a duration of five years increases by 2 percentage points, say, from 4 percent to 6 percent, then the bond's price will decline by approximately twice the duration, or $(2 \times 5) = 10$ percent. If the bond's yield instead *declines* from 4 percent to 2 percent, then the bond's price will *increase* by about 10 percent.

Don't worry too much about the mathematical details. The key point is that a bond's volatility increases more the longer the bond's maturity and duration. And as we've already learned, the greater an investment's volatility, the higher its expected returns. This is reflected in Table 5.2, which shows the average and worst returns for three types of bond funds—short-term, intermediate-term, and long-term U.S. government bond funds. As we would expect, average annualized returns and worst returns are largest for long-term bond funds and smallest for short-term funds.

Table 5.2. Average Returns and Volatility of U.S. Government Bond Funds, 1984–2013

Duration	Average Annualized Return	Worst Returns (and Time Period in Which They Occurred)
Short	5.8%	−3.3% (3 months in 1994)
Intermediate	6.4%	−6.5% (3 months in 1994)
Long	8.0%	−17.2% (17 months in 2012–13)

Source: Developed by the author using data from www.morningstar.com.

Duration versus hedging power. Which type of bond fund—short, intermediate, or long—provides the best hedge of stocks? Table 5.3 shows how bond funds of different durations performed during the worst stock market downturns of the past four decades. In general, no single fund type appears to significantly outperform the others as a hedge on a consistent basis. True, in the 2007–9 and 1973–74 bear markets, short-term bond funds performed a bit better than intermediate- or long-term funds. Short-term funds also did better during the 1980–82 market correction. But long-term funds did best during the 2011 market correction, and the differences in returns are quite small in the other four cases. On the basis of Table 5.3, we might give short-term funds a slight edge over intermediate- and long-term funds as a hedge against cyclical stock market downturns—but only a slight one.

Table 5.3. Average Returns of Short-, Intermediate-, and Long-Term
Bond Mutual Funds during Past Bear Markets and Market Corrections

Time Period	Long	Intermediate	Short
Bear Markets:			
Oct 2007–Mar 2009	−10.8%	−5.4%	−3.9%
Mar 2000–Oct 2002	+21.2%	+22.7%	+19.1%
Jan 1973–Oct 1974	−12.0%	−14.3%	−9.2%
Aug 1987–Dec 1987	+0.3%	+1.1%	+1.1%
Corrections:			
Nov 1980–Aug 1982	+19.3	+19.7	+23.2
Jul 1990–Oct 1990	−1.1%	−0.4%	+0.9%
Jul 1998–Aug 1998	+0.4%	+1.2%	+1.2%
Apr 2011–Oct 2011	+5.0%	+2.3%	−0.2%

Source: Developed by the author using data from www.morningstar.com.

So there is no clear-cut winner when it comes to protecting against *cyclical* stock market downturns. What about *secular* bear markets? Unfortunately, we do not have return data on short- and long-term bond funds all the way back to 1966, but we can go back as far as September 30, 1973, and see how bond funds performed during the second part of the 1966–82 secular bear market. The results for this past bear market, and the more recent secular bear market that began in March 2000, are shown in Table 5.4.

Table 5.4. Average Annualized Returns of Short-, Intermediate-,
and Long-Term Bond Mutual Funds during Past Secular Bear Markets

Time Period	Long-Term	Intermediate-Term	Short-Term
Mar 2000–Mar 2009	+3.9%	+3.9%	+3.1%
Sep 1973–Aug 1982	+6.4%	+5.7%	+6.8%
Sep 1973–Dec 2013	+8.0%	+7.1%	+6.3%

Source: Developed by the author using data from www.morningstar.com.

In the 1973–82 bear market, funds dedicated to short-duration bonds significantly outperformed intermediate- and long-term bond funds. But in the current secular bear market, short-term bond funds had the lowest returns. What explains this difference? Returns from bond funds come from two sources: dividends (or bond yields) and capital gains (changes in bond prices). Yields (dividends) are almost always higher for longer-duration bonds than for shorter-duration bonds. But long-duration bonds are much more sensitive to interest rate changes than short-duration bonds. They are also much more sensitive to unexpected inflation. Back in 1973–82, interest rates were rising and inflation was on a rampage. Together, these two factors forced long-term bond prices down. Although short-term bond prices were also affected, the magnitude of the impact was much smaller in their case. As illustrated in Figure 5.1, the larger dividends produced by long-term bond funds were more than offset by the decline in long-term bond prices, with the result that total returns for long-term bonds were less than total returns for short-term bonds.

In contrast, interest rates declined between 2000 and 2009, and inflation was tame. Hence long-term bond prices rose more than short-term prices. The resulting capital gains, combined with the larger dividends produced by long-term bonds, led to long-term bond fund returns that were larger than short-term bond fund returns (3.9 percent vs. 3.1 percent).

So, as in the case of cyclical bear markets, there is no one bond duration category—long, intermediate, or short—that we can count on to provide maximum protection during all secular bear markets. Depending on the specific economic conditions—rising or declining interest rates, low or high inflation—long-duration bonds may outperform or underperform shorter-duration bonds.

The problem with long-term bonds. This leaves us in a bit of quandary. Should we use long-term, intermediate-term, or short-term bond funds to hedge our portfolio? Because there is no clear winner when it comes to hedging power, perhaps we should simply select the bond fund that offers the highest yields and expected long-run returns going forward. Remember, bonds work in large part on the principle of compromise: they reduce a portfolio's volatility, but at the expense of the portfolio's returns. This compromise in turn exposes us to the possibility of not earning enough returns to outpace inflation—one of the two components of the retirement risk. And this inflation risk is all the greater today, given the historically low yields offered by bonds. To minimize this risk while still capturing the volatility-reducing power of bonds, it may make sense to select the bond duration category that offers the highest yields and expected returns: long-term bonds.

However, there is a problem with long-term bonds: they can significantly underperform for *decades*. During the thirty-five years between 1946 and 1981, long-term Treasuries yielded annualized returns of only 2 percent. This was nowhere near the 4.7 percent rate of inflation that we experienced during this period. Although it is true that shorter-maturity bonds also underperformed during this difficult period of rising inflation, they nonetheless did better than long-term bonds. Short-term Treasury bills produced annualized returns of 4.1 percent—more than double that of long-term Treasuries.[50]

Figure 5.1. Years 1973–82: Rising Interest Rates Cause Long-Term Bond Prices to Plunge More Sharply Than Short-Term Bond Prices

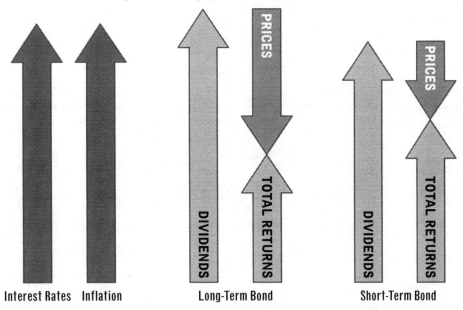

Interest Rates   Inflation   Long-Term Bond   Short-Term Bond

As the example of 1946–81 illustrates, long-term bonds are much more sensitive than shorter-duration bonds to the risk posed by high unexpected inflation. The inability of long-term Treasuries to keep pace with inflation over a *thirty-five-year* period indicates that, far from protecting a portfolio against the ravages of inflation, long-term bonds increase a portfolio's exposure to the risk of not earning enough returns to outpace inflation. And they do so during precisely those times when inflation exceeds expectations and poses an elevated risk to your nest egg. We will return to the question of what types of bonds you *should* include in your portfolio later, but for now we'll conclude that you should not rely on long-term bonds.

Duration and maturity are key determinants of a bond's risk–reward profile. Now we turn to another critical determinant: credit quality.

Credit Quality

A bond's credit quality is simply an assessment of the likelihood that the bond will default. The various bond rating agencies (including Standard & Poor's and Moody's) have come up with an alphabet soup of different grades to assess the risk of a bond's default, but we are going to keep this simple and consider only two classes of bonds: investment grade versus junk. An investment-grade bond is a bond with a low risk of default. A junk bond has an elevated default risk. Junk bonds are sometimes referred to as high-yield bonds, but the moniker "junk" may be more accurate, for reasons that will become apparent shortly.

Table 5.5 shows us how investment-grade and junk bond funds fared over past bear markets and market corrections. Let's take a look at the last column, showing junk bond returns.

Table 5.5. Average Returns of Investment-Grade and Junk Bond Mutual Funds during Past Bear Markets and Market Corrections

Time Period	S&P 500 Total Returns	Average Investment-Grade (Intermediate-Term) Bond Fund Returns	Average Junk Bond Fund Returns
Bear Markets:			
Oct 2007–Mar 2009	−55.3%	−5.4%	−29.8%
Mar 2000–Oct 2002[a]	−47.4%	+22.7%	−13.6%
Jan 1973–Oct 1974	−44.8%[b]	−14.3%	−28.1%
Aug 1987–Dec 1987	−32.9%[b]	+1.1%	−4.7%
Corrections:			
Nov 1980–Aug 1982[c]	−20.0%[b]	+19.7%	+19.9%
Jul 1990–Oct 1990	−19.2%	−0.4%	−10.4%
Jul 1998–Aug 1998	−19.2%	+1.2%	−7.2%
Apr 2011–Oct 2011	−18.6%	+2.3%	−8.3%

[a]Combines the 2000–2001 and 2002 bear markets.
[b]Estimated for partial months based on monthly return data.
[c]Officially a bear market.
Source: Developed by the author using data from www.morningstar.com.

Yikes! Junk bond funds managed to generate positive returns in only one of the last eight bear markets or market corrections. They did worse—and usually much worse—than investment-grade bonds in every stock market downturn except the 1980–82 correction. And even then, they only barely beat out investment-grade bonds.

What's going on here? Junk bonds are issued by companies that are in a weak financial condition. During normal times, these companies may do all right. But as soon as the economy tanks and the stock market plummets, these fragile companies are the first to fail. They default on their debt, and these defaults are reflected in the negative returns junk bond funds produce during market downturns.

When the stock market declines, junk bonds follow stocks downward. In other words, high-yield bonds are highly correlated with the stock market. Remember, the key characteristic of a good hedge is *low* correlation with the stock market. Junk bonds are *not* a good hedge, and they do *not* have a place in a well-diversified portfolio. As we discussed in the preceding chapter, the way to get high-yielding bonds into your portfolio is to buy an emerging-market bond fund. Avoid junk bonds. They are aptly named.

Types of Bonds

We have now covered most of the key determinants of a bond's risk–reward profile that we identified at the outset of this chapter—maturity, duration, and credit quality. There remains one more factor we need to consider: bond type.

There are many different types of bonds—corporate, municipals, mortgage backed, international—but again, we are going to keep this simple. We will focus specifically on Treasuries—that is, bonds issued by the U.S. Treasury Department—and contrast their performance with bond funds that hold a mix of bond types.

"Follow the money," part 2. Why Treasuries? Well, remember back in the last chapter when we "followed the money" during the panic selling that gripped the market in autumn 2008? The cash raised from all that selling had to be put somewhere, and when we followed the money, it led us to one of the market's great safe havens: gold. Gold was one of the only asset classes that managed to rise in value during the panic. Virtually everything else went down—including all kinds of bonds as well as stocks. But there was one other asset class that bucked the trend along with gold: U.S. government bonds. Between July and December 2008, yields on the ten-year Treasury note declined from 4 percent to 2.4 percent—and as we know, when bond yields go down, bond prices go up. That demand and prices for U.S. government bonds rose during the worst market plunge since the Great Depression confirms Treasuries' status as a true safe haven.

One summer's day. There is one other, even more telling bit of history that reveals the market's almost mystical faith in Treasuries. You may recall that back in summer 2011, congressional Republicans and President Obama went down to the wire before finally reaching an agreement to raise the U.S. debt ceiling. Because the government must borrow to meet its existing obligations, a failure to raise the debt ceiling would have meant a potential default on U.S. government debt. On Friday, August 5, 2011, after the markets closed, the bond rating agency Standard & Poor's responded to this political brinksmanship by lowering the U.S. government's credit rating from AAA to AA+. The downgrade signaled increased odds of a future default on Treasuries—a possibility that had for decades been unthinkable. *Trillions* of dollars in Treasuries are held by private investors and governments throughout the world, in part because they are—or at least were—believed to be an absolutely rock solid investment. The credit downgrade shook some of the market's most fundamental assumptions.

By waiting until after the markets closed on Friday to announce the downgrade, Standard & Poor's gave investors the weekend to ponder their next move. When the markets reopened Monday morning, the response was swift. By the end of the day, the S&P 500 had dropped 6.6 percent, the DJ Stoxx Index (for Europe) had declined 3.6 percent, and the Nikkei Index (Japan) was down 2.2 percent. And where did the cash raised from this global sell-off go? It went into … Treasuries! On August 8, the ten-year Treasury yield declined from 2.58 to 2.40 percent—a very large move by bond market standards, indicating a *rise* in Treasury prices and in demand for Treasuries. Treasuries served, in effect, as a safe haven from themselves. An investment that can hedge itself? Now *that's* a hedge!

Yes, the financial markets sometimes act like they've gone stark raving mad. But in this case, the market's reaction to the credit downgrade wasn't quite as schizophrenic as it might at first seem. True, the downgrade punctured the myth that Treasuries were somehow immune from the possibility of default. But Treasuries had, and still have, more going for them than a belief that the U.S. government will always repay its debts. Although not riskless, Treasuries are still viewed as *less risky* than virtually all other asset classes. And equally important, the market for Treasuries is so huge and liquid that it is the only market that can absorb the cash from major sell-offs like the one that occurred on August 8, 2011. A few assets may be less risky than Treasuries—Swiss bonds might be one example. But the available supply of Swiss bonds is simply not large enough to satisfy the demand for low-risk assets that can arise during a major sell-off. Not even gold, our other safe haven, can match the liquidity offered by Treasuries. Although the total value of all gold in the world is in the trillions of dollars, most of this gold is illiquid, either locked in the vaults of central banks or privately held in the form of jewelry that is not for sale. The Treasury market offers a unique combination of size and liquidity, which, when combined with the relatively low risk of Treasuries, makes them an almost perfect safe haven.

The record of Treasuries as a hedge. Table 5.6 shows just how well U.S. government bond funds have performed during past bear markets and market corrections. Table 5.6 compares intermediate-term government bond funds against intermediate-term funds that contain a mix of bond types (including, e.g., corporate bonds, municipal bonds, mortgage-backed securities, as well as Treasuries). In every stock market downturn, U.S. government bond funds beat mixed bond funds, in two cases (1973–74 and 2007–9) by a wide margin. Notice that government bonds lost money in only one downturn (the 1973–74 bear market), and even in that case, the loss was small.

Government bond funds also beat mixed bond funds during the most recent secular bear market—although as Table 5.7 shows, mixed funds had a slight edge during the 1970–82 bear market. More significant is the difference in returns over the entire forty-year period stretching from 1970 to 2010. A typical investor in government bond funds would have earned 6.5 percent per year—0.5 percent less than an investor in mixed bond funds.

Let's sum up what we've learned so far. Treasuries, like gold, are considered a safe haven by investors around the world. As such, they have offered better protection than other types of bonds in all of the cyclical stock market downturns of the past forty years. Clearly the bond portion of our portfolio should include a good helping of Treasuries.

Table 5.6. Average Returns of U.S. Government and Mixed Intermediate-Term Bond Mutual Funds during Past Bear Markets and Market Corrections

Time Period	S&P 500 Total Returns	Average U.S. Government Bond Fund Returns	Average Mixed Bond Fund Returns
Bear Markets:			
Oct 2007–Mar 2009	−55.3%	+7.9%	−5.4%
Mar 2000–Oct 2002[a]	−47.4%	+26.6%	+22.7%
Jan 1973–Oct 1974	−44.8%[b]	−1.2%	−14.3%
Aug 1987–Dec 1987	−32.9%[b]	+1.2%	+1.1%
Corrections:			
Nov 1980–Aug 1982[c]	−20.0%[b]	+20.7%	+19.7%
Jul 1990–Oct 1990	−19.2%	+0.4%	−0.4%
Jul 1998–Aug 1998	−19.2%	+2.0%	+1.2%
Apr 2011–Oct 2011	−18.6%	+4.8%	+2.3%

[a] Combines the 2000–2001 and 2002 bear markets.
[b] Estimated for partial months based on monthly return data.
[c] Officially a bear market.
Source: Developed by the author using data from www.morningstar.com.

Table 5.7. Average Annualized Returns of U.S. Government and Mixed Intermediate-Term Bond Mutual Funds during Past Secular Bear Markets

Time Period	Average Mixed Bond Fund Annualized Returns	Average U.S. Government Bond Fund Annualized Returns
Mar 2000–Mar 2009	+3.9%	+5.2%
Jan 1970–Aug 1982	+5.7%	+5.6%
Jan 1970–Dec 2013	+7.0%	+6.5%

Source: Developed by the author using data from www.morningstar.com.

But the protection offered by government bonds has come at the price of lower returns in the long run. Most mixed bond funds will provide you with adequate exposure to Treasuries while offering the prospect of higher returns relative to government-only funds. Mixed funds also provide the benefits that come with diversification across numerous bond issuers. Although the risk of default on U.S. Treasuries is certainly very low, after the 2011 debt ceiling debacle, Treasuries can no longer be considered riskless. For these reasons, I prefer mixed to Treasury-only bond funds. I obtain the superior hedging power offered by U.S. government bonds through a different vehicle—Treasury Inflation-Protected Securities.

Treasury Inflation-Protected Securities. In addition to its "regular" bonds, the U.S. Treasury issues a special kind of bond that is designed to protect the holder from inflation. These special bonds, called Treasury Inflation-Protected Securities, or TIPS for short, are an excellent addition to any portfolio. Because they are issued by the U.S. Treasury, TIPS exhibit the same safe haven characteristics that make Treasuries such a good hedge for stocks. But at the same time, TIPS are shielded from inflation.

Inflation—particularly unexpected inflation—wreaks havoc for bond investors. As fixed-income investments with relatively low yields, even a small increase in inflation can turn bonds into money losers. As I am writing this, the yield on the ten-year Treasury note is about 2.5 percent. If you buy a ten-year note today, you can expect to eek out a small gain in your purchasing power as long as inflation stays below 2.5 percent. But because past inflation has normally fallen in the 2 to 3 percent range, a 2.5 percent yield may merely match, not beat, inflation.

And inflation can put a double whammy on your bond investments, because when inflation goes up, interest rates often follow. In fact, the Federal Reserve fights inflation by raising interest rates. Rising interest rates in turn cause bond prices to drop, right at the same time that inflation is eating away at your meager bond dividends.

Stocks are also subject to the ravages of inflation, but not to the same degree as bonds. Unlike bond dividends, which are fixed, companies can increase the dividends they pay on their stock shares when inflation rises. Furthermore, stock prices, unlike bond prices, are not ultimately anchored and pulled back to a face value payable on maturity. Hence stock prices can and often do rise with inflation. Some types of stocks, such as energy stocks and Real Estate Investment Trusts, perform quite well in an inflationary environment. And as we've already seen, precious metals equities (PME) are good hedges against inflation. In contrast, bonds capable of hedging against inflation are almost entirely lacking—with the important exception of TIPS.

How are TIPS protected from inflation? Consider a Treasury note versus a TIPS note, both with a face value of $1,000. Whereas this original face value is fixed for the Treasury note, for TIPS, both the face value and the dividend are adjusted upward every six months based on the change in the Consumer Price Index (CPI). If, for example, the CPI rises 20 percent, then the TIPS note's face value will rise to $1,200, and the dividend will increase by 20 percent.

TIPS are a relatively new investment product, having first been issued in 1997. Nonetheless, we do have data on how inflation-protected bond funds[51] have performed since 1997. Over the longer term, TIPS funds have been outperforming Treasury funds. From 1998 through 2013, TIPS funds averaged 5.5 percent annualized returns, versus 4.4 percent for intermediate-term Treasury funds. During the recent secular bear market running from March 24, 2000, to March 9, 2009, TIPS funds averaged 5.6 percent annualized returns, versus 5.2 percent for intermediate-term Treasury funds.

Table 5.8 shows how TIPS did during the more recent cyclical bear markets and market corrections. For comparison, the table also shows return data for intermediate-term Treasury funds. In the two market corrections with data (1998 and 2011), average returns for TIPS funds were slightly less, but comparable to, returns of regular Treasury funds. In the 2000–2002 bear market, TIPS outperformed other Treasuries by a significant margin. In the 2007–9 bear market, the reverse was the case.

Table 5.8. Average Returns of Inflation-Protected and U.S. Government Intermediate-Term Bond Mutual Funds during Past Bear Markets and Market Corrections

Time Period	S&P 500 Total Returns	Average U.S. Government Bond Fund Returns	Average Inflation-Protected Bond Fund Returns
Bear Markets:			
Oct 2007–Mar 2009	−55.3%	+7.9%	−1.4%
Mar 2000–Oct 2002[a]	−47.4%	+26.6%	+32.8%
Jan 1973–Oct 1974	−44.8%[b]	−1.2%	N/A
Aug 1987–Dec 1987	−32.9%[b]	+1.2%	N/A
Corrections:			
Nov 1980–Aug 1982[c]	−20.0%[b]	+20.7%	N/A
Jul 1990–Oct 1990	−19.2%	+0.4%	N/A
Jul 1998–Aug 1998	−19.2%	+2.0%	+0.3%
Apr 2011–Oct 2011	−18.6%	+4.8%	+4.6%

[a]Combines the 2000-01 and 2002 bear markets.
[b]Estimated for partial months based on monthly return data.
[c]Officially a bear market.
Source: Developed by the author using data from www.morningstar.com.

It should not be too surprising that TIPS struggled a bit in 2007–9. The latter part of this bear market was characterized by deflation. Whereas TIPS will outperform other types of bonds during periods of unexpected inflation, they will lag other bonds in a deflationary environment. Just as the face values of TIPS *increase* when the CPI goes up, they *decrease* when the CPI drops owing to deflation.

However, the government has placed a limit on the extent to which the face value of TIPS can decline. Once the original face value is reached, there are no further adjustments owing to deflation. Hence the downside risk of owning TIPS during a deflationary period is limited. If you hold TIPS to maturity, you will, at a minimum, receive the original face value. In contrast, there is no limit to the downside risk of owning standard Treasuries during an *inflationary* period. Should hyperinflation set in, standard Treasury notes—as well as all other non-inflation-adjusted bonds—could quickly become worthless.

The potential for downward adjustments to their face value means that TIPS will not do as well as standard Treasuries if deflation occurs. No single asset class can guarantee superior returns in *all* economic conditions. This is why diversification —including diversification of your bond holdings—is so necessary and important. The bond portion of your portfolio should include a healthy dose of TIPS, but don't overdo it—you also want to hold regular, non-inflation-adjusted bonds as a hedge against deflation.

Savings bonds versus Treasuries/TIPS. In addition to Treasuries and TIPS, the government offers savings bonds. There are two types of savings bonds—EE Bonds, which have no inflation adjustment, and I Bonds, which are inflation adjusted. Both types of bonds must be purchased directly from the Treasury;[52] unlike Treasuries and TIPs, they cannot be accessed through broker accounts, mutual funds, or exchange traded funds (ETFs).

Normally, the yields on Treasuries and TIPS exceed savings bond yields. However, the current abnormally low interest rates have created an opportunity for investors willing to purchase their government bonds directly rather than through a mutual fund. First, EE Bonds are guaranteed to double in value if they are held for at least twenty years. This means that their twenty-year yield is effectively 3.5 percent. This yield *may* be a bit higher than yields on Treasuries with twenty-year maturities. For example, in May 2013, Treasuries selling on the secondary market and maturing in 2033 had yields averaging about 3.35 percent—0.15 percent less than the EE Bond yield. Keep in mind, though, that you would need to hold your EE Bonds for twenty years to capture this 0.15 percent difference in yields.

The current opportunity for I Bonds looks more interesting. Like TIPS, the overall yield on I Bonds includes two components: a fixed rate and an inflation rate set to the CPI. However, the fixed rate for I Bonds cannot go below zero. In contrast, the fixed rate for TIPS not only can go negative but *has* gone negative during some recent TIPS auctions. This does not mean that these recently auctioned TIPS are generating negative yields, as the (normally positive) inflation rate may more than offset the negative fixed rate. But it does mean that the yield on these particular TIPS will not keep pace with inflation.

If the fixed rate on TIPS remains below zero, you should consider I Bonds as an alternative. With a fixed rate that must be at least zero, I Bonds will, at a minimum, ensure that your returns will keep pace with inflation.

Table 5.9 summarizes the key characteristics of the two types of savings bonds and two types of Treasury bonds. As the table shows, there are some important differences between savings bonds and TIPS/Treasuries. First, Treasuries and TIPS can be bought and sold on the secondary bond market; savings bonds cannot. This in turn means that savings bonds, unlike TIPS/Treasuries, do not fluctuate in value. You can redeem a savings bond without penalty any time between five and thirty years after you purchase the bond. You can also choose to redeem the bond between one to five years after your purchase, but in this case you will lose the last three months of interest. Your ability to decide when to cash in a savings bond is a definite advantage over the fixed maturity of TIPS and Treasuries. If, for example, the yields on new issue bonds increase, you can redeem all of the savings bonds you have held for at least one year and replace them with the new, higher-yielding bonds. (You could in this same circumstance sell your Treasuries or TIPS, but if bond yields have risen over the course of the year, then the price you will receive will be less than the price you paid for the bonds.)

**Table 5.9. Key Characteristics
of U.S. Government Savings Bonds and TIPS/Treasuries**

Characteristic	Savings Bonds		TIPS/Treasuries	
	EE	I	Treasuries	TIPS
Can be bought or sold?	No	No	Yes	Yes
Value (price) fluctuates?	No (but penalty assessed if redeemed before 5 years)	No (but penalty assessed if redeemed before 5 years)	Yes	Yes
Dividends	Accrue until bond is redeemed	Accrue until bond is redeemed	Paid semi-annually	Paid semi-annually
Maturity when first issued?	30 years (but may be redeemed any time after 1 year)	30 years (but may be redeemed any time after 1 year)	Varies (30 years maximum)	Varies (30 years maximum)
Inflation protected?	No	Yes	No	Yes
Taxed?	When redeemed	When redeemed	Annually	Annually
Purchase limits?	$10,000 per year	$10,000 per year	None	None
Availability	Only direct through government	Only direct through government	Through brokers, mutual funds, and ETFs	Through brokers, mutual funds, and ETFs

Unlike TIPS and Treasuries, savings bonds do not generate semi-annual dividend payments. Instead, the interest on a savings bond accrues until you decide to redeem the bond. The interest compounds semi-annually. When you redeem the bond you will receive all of the interest the bond has returned plus the amount you paid for the bond (adjusted for inflation in the case of I Bonds).

A specific advantage of I Bonds is that, unlike TIPS, their value is never reduced during periods of deflation. Finally, both EE and I Bonds offer important tax advantages for investors who do not have enough room for bonds in a tax-deferred account. Although they must be held in a non-IRA TreasuryDirect account, the taxes on EE and I Bonds are deferred until they are redeemed. Hence they are effectively treated as if they are being held in a tax-deferred account.

However, an important disadvantage of EE and I Bonds is that the government limits the amount you can invest. In each calendar year, you are allowed to purchase a maximum of $10,000 worth of I Bonds and $10,000 worth of EE bonds via a TreasuryDirect[53] account. There are no limits to the amount of Treasuries and TIPS you can buy.

Building a Bond Portfolio

Let's sum up what we've learned so far. First, long-term bonds are particularly susceptible to inflation risk and should therefore be avoided. Second, we should avoid junk bonds and stick to investment-grade bonds. Third, we should include a good helping of Treasuries in our portfolio—but we can obtain an adequate exposure to Treasuries using mixed bond funds. And fourth, we should hold TIPS and/or I Bonds to protect our bond portfolio from inflation.

Meeting all those goals sounds like a tall order that would require many investments, but I'm going to suggest a simple way to do it that requires you to purchase only three bond funds in four easy steps:

- Step 1: Take the total amount of money you intend to invest in bonds and split it into three equal parts.

- Step 2: With the first third, buy an inflation-protected bond fund and/or I Bonds.

- Step 3: With the second third, buy a short-term bond fund with a mix of bond types (including a good helping of corporate bonds as well as Treasuries).

- Step 4: With the remaining third, buy an intermediate-term fund with a mix of bond types (including a good helping of corporate bonds as well as Treasuries).

The resulting portfolio will be hedged against the possibility of both inflation (via TIPS or I Bonds) and deflation; it will protect you from future market storms via the safe haven of government bonds; but at the same time, the inclusion of a mix of nongovernment bonds will reduce your exposure to the possibility of future U.S.

credit downgrades. The short-term fund will reduce the risk you face from rising interest rates; it should perform better than longer-duration funds in the event of high unexpected inflation; and it may outperform inflation-protected bonds in the event of deflation. The intermediate-term fund will help to offset the relatively low yields you must expect from the short-term fund.

The recommended approach uses TIPS as the primary means of gaining exposure to U.S. government bonds. Although inflation-protected bond funds will generally include some nongovernment bonds, according to data on Morningstar's website, these funds allocate, on average, 79 percent of their assets to TIPS. However, mixed bond funds also typically include significant holdings of Treasuries (19 percent, on average, in the case of short-term funds and 30 percent for intermediate-term funds[54]). Assuming typical allocations, the resulting portfolio will be split approximately 43 percent government bonds and 57 percent other bonds, with about 26 percent allocated to TIPS and approximately 17 percent to standard Treasuries. You can use Morningstar to check the allocations of specific bond funds. To do this, go to the Morningstar website and enter the ticker symbol of the fund in the "Quote" box at the top of the page. When the next page comes up, click on the word "Portfolio" in the gray-colored bar beneath the name of the fund. Scroll down to the section called "Sector Weightings"; the column labeled "% Bonds" will show you how the fund is allocated across Treasuries, TIPS, and other government bonds as well as corporate, securitized, municipal, cash, and other nongovernment bonds.

There is an alternative to the preceding bond allocation recommendations that can virtually eliminate the retirement risk—at least for a while. This alternative, the liability-matching bond portfolio (LMBP), makes use of the unique inflation-hedging characteristics of TIPS and I Bonds to meet retirees' financial needs. The LMBP approach is not for everyone, and it involves a significant amount of effort to implement and maintain. But for those who are willing to take on the additional work (or to hire a professional to do the work), it is a viable alternative well worth considering. We address this alternative in detail in Chapter 12.

Summary

Table 5.10 adds the low-volatility hedges to our ongoing summary of asset class characteristics and portfolio roles. The key characteristic shared by all the categories of bonds recommended herein is low volatility. It is this low volatility, rooted in the inherent nature of bonds, that makes them a very reliable means of hedging portfolios via the principle of compromise. In trying times, when the stock market is plummeting and your high-volatility hedges fail to work as hedges, an allocation to bonds will serve as a second line of defense, protecting you from sharing John Stockman's fate.

Table 5.10. Summary of the Characteristics and Portfolio Roles Played
by Large Caps, High-Volatility Hedges, and Low-Volatility Hedges

Asset Class	Correlation with U.S. Large Caps	Volatility	Expected Returns	Role in Portfolio
Core Holdings:				
U.S. large caps	—	High	High	Core holding; produce high returns to beat inflation risk
International developed-market large caps	High	High	High	Long-run diversification benefits; currency diversification
Emerging-market large caps	High	High	High	Long-run diversification benefits; currency diversification
High-Volatility Hedges:				
Gold	Very low	Very high	Low	Insurance
PME	Low	Extremely high	Medium (but may increase portfolio returns when combined with secret sauce)	Applying principle of correlation
Emerging-market bonds	Low	Medium	Medium	Applying principle of correlation and/or compromise
Low-Volatility Hedges:				
Intermediate-term mixed bonds	Low	Low	Low	Applying principle of compromise (and to a lesser extent correlation)
Short-term mixed bonds	Low	Very low	Very low	Applying principle of compromise
TIPS and I Bonds	Very low	Low (zero for I Bonds)	Low (but will keep pace with inflation)	Applying principle of compromise (and to a lesser extent correlation); Protecting bond portfolio from inflation

BEATING THE NIGHT THIEF: PROTECTING YOUR PORTFOLIO FROM INFLATION WITH RETURN BOOSTERS

I n the preceding two chapters, we focused on asset classes that can be used as hedges to protect your portfolio from negative stock market volatility. Whether high or low in volatility, the one characteristic all of these asset classes share is low correlation with large cap stocks. Now we are going to shift gears. Small cap stocks and value stocks—the two *return boosters* that will add spice to your gourmet portfolio—are highly correlated with the S&P 500. Therefore they are not good volatility hedges. When the stock market tanks, the return boosters usually follow the broad market down the tubes. In fact, losses in the return boosters have often exceeded overall market losses.

If the return boosters are not good hedges, then why do we want them in our portfolio? Let's go back and review our fundamental goal here. This book is all about reducing the retirement risk—the risk that you might outlive your money. There are *two* ways this can happen: too much volatility and not enough returns. So far, we have been focusing on asset classes designed to reduce volatility. By adding both high-volatility and low-volatility hedges to our portfolio, we can avoid the fate of John Stockman during the Depression.

But we don't want to wind up like Joe Bondsman, either. The second component of the retirement risk—not enough returns to outpace inflation—increases when we add bonds to our portfolio. And the risk posed by bonds is possibly even greater today than it was back in 1962, when Bondsman retired. In 1962, the yield on the ten-year Treasury note was a fairly low 4 percent. In early 2014, the yield on the ten-year Treasury note stood at around 2.7 percent—less than what it was in 1962. There is very little room left for yields to go lower or prices to go higher. Very low current yields and the prospect of falling prices: if anything, the outlook for bonds seems even worse today than it did back in 1962.

There is no question that we need to include low-volatility bonds in our portfolios if we want to avoid the fate of John Stockman. But with the outlook for bond returns so poor, we need to be especially concerned that, in using bonds to mitigate portfolio volatility, we don't drive down our overall portfolio's returns to levels incapable of keeping up with inflation. In short, today even more so than in the past, we face a delicate balancing act between avoiding too much volatility on one hand, and not enough returns on the other.

The return boosters can help us thread the needle between too much volatility and not enough returns. Small cap stocks and value stocks have produced higher returns over the long run than the S&P 500. By adding these two asset classes to our well-diversified portfolio, we may be able to boost our returns above what we could expect from large caps alone.

But won't the addition of high-volatility, high-return asset classes like small caps undo the volatility-reducing effects of bonds? No. First of all, we do not need to add large amounts of these relatively risky assets. They are the spices to our dish and are best used in moderation.

And second, the return boosters are not entirely without diversification benefits. It is true that they are highly correlated with the S&P 500, but they are not *perfectly* correlated with it. And even a highly correlated asset class provides some limited ability to smooth out volatility. As we shall see, the return boosters have not always followed the S&P 500 down during bear markets. During the 2000–2002 bear market, small cap value stock funds actually generated slightly *positive* returns. And during the Lost Decade, the return boosters outperformed the S&P 500 by a wide margin.

It is the combination of high returns plus some diversification benefits that enables the return boosters to increase portfolio returns without undoing the volatility-reducing effects of our low- and high-volatility hedges. Don't get me wrong—adding small caps and value stocks to your portfolio can increase your losses during cyclical bear markets. But history shows, time and again, that when used to spice up a portfolio of large cap stocks, high-volatility hedges, and low-volatility hedges, the return boosters have had only a limited negative impact on short-term portfolio volatility while significantly increasing long-term returns. The advantages of these asset classes far outweigh the disadvantages. Along with large caps, high-volatility hedges, and low-volatility hedges, return boosters are a key ingredient of any well-diversified portfolio.

Small Cap Stocks

Small capitalization (small cap) stocks are the stocks of small companies. As we learned in Chapter 3, Morningstar defines large cap stocks as the 70 percent of all publicly traded stocks with the largest market capitalizations. Morningstar defines small cap stocks as the 10 percent of all publicly traded companies with the smallest market capitalizations.

Small cap stocks qualify as return boosters because they have produced significantly higher returns than large caps over the long run. A number of academic studies have confirmed the existence of this *size premium*, but the definitive study was performed by Eugene Fama and Ken French in 1992.[55]

Why have small caps outperformed? Fama and French explained the higher returns as reward for the higher risks, or volatility, associated with small caps. Small companies tend to be less diverse than large companies; they may sell only a limited number of products, or their products may appeal to limited niche markets. During economic downturns, this lack of diversification increases the vulnerability of small companies relative to larger companies. Small companies also tend to be less financially secure than large companies, with limited access to capital. Potential creditors may gravitate more toward large companies with longer histories and well-established brands, especially during recessions and other times of elevated default risk.

Given the risks associated with small companies, it follows that the stocks of these companies should tend to be more volatile than large cap stocks. And according to the ironclad rule of investing, those who take on more risk must be rewarded with larger expected returns. The market perceives small cap stocks as relatively risky, and it discounts the prices of these stocks to reflect the elevated risks. When a small company takes advantage of its growth potential and becomes a large company, the investor who bought into the company's stock at the risk-discounted price is rewarded with outsized returns.

The Historical Record for Small Caps

The relatively high volatility of small caps is reflected in their performance during cyclical bear markets and market corrections. Table 6.1 shows average returns of small cap mutual funds during the eight big bear markets and market corrections of the last forty years. For comparison, the average returns of large cap funds are also shown. In five out of eight cases, small cap funds did worse than large cap funds. Interestingly, the differences between small and large caps are larger during the market corrections than during the bear markets. Of the four bear markets, small cap fund performance was worst relative to large cap funds during the 2007–9 financial crisis. Small cap funds did slightly better than large cap funds during the 1973–74 bear market and much better during the 2000–2002 downturn. The worst performance of small cap funds relative to large cap funds came during the 2011 market correction.

Table 6.1. Average Returns of Small Cap and Large Cap Mutual Funds during Past Bear Markets and Market Corrections

Time Period	S&P 500 Total Returns	Average Large Cap Blend Fund Returns	Average Small Cap Blend Fund Returns
Bear Markets:			
Oct 2007–Mar 2009	−55.3%	−54.7%	−59.0%
Mar 2000–Oct 2002[a]	−47.4%	−47.4%	−24.3%
Jan 1973–Oct 1974	−44.8%[b]	−43.5%	−39.6%
Aug 1987–Dec 1987	−32.9%[b]	−28.5%	−30.9%
Corrections:			
Nov 1980–Aug 1982[c]	−20.0%[b]	−7.6%	−7.4%
Jul 1990–Oct 1990	−19.2%	−18.3%	−25.2%
Jul 1998–Aug 1998	−19.2%	−19.7%	−26.2%
Apr 2011–Oct 2011	−18.6%	−20.9%	−28.6%

[a]Combines the 2000–2001 and 2002 bear markets.
[b]Estimated for partial months based on monthly return data.
[c]Officially a bear market.
Source: Developed by the author using data from www.morningstar.com.

As Table 6.2 shows, the rewards for accepting a bit more volatility in the short term can be substantial. First, notice that over the past forty-eight years, small cap funds have yielded average annualized returns of 10.2 percent per year—1.4 percent more than large cap funds. This might not seem like a big difference, but compounded over 48 years, it is substantial. If you had invested $10,000 in the average large cap fund on January 1, 1966, it would have been worth $585,000 by December 31, 2013. That same $10,000, invested in the average small cap fund, would have grown to $1,039,000—nearly double the growth of the large cap fund.[56]

Table 6.2. Average Annualized Returns of Small Cap and Large Cap Mutual Funds during Past Secular Bear Markets

Time Period	S&P 500 Annualized Total Returns	Average Large Cap Blend Fund Annualized Returns	Average Small Cap Blend Fund Annualized Returns
Mar 2000–Mar 2009	−7.0%	−7.3%	−2.2%
Jan 1966–Aug 1982	+4.8%*	+5.2%	+5.7%
Jan 1966–Dec 2013	+9.5%	+8.8%	+10.2%

Note: Estimated for partial months based on monthly return data.
Source: Developed by the author using data from www.morningstar.com.

However, better long-term returns are only part of the story. Remember that although small caps are highly correlated with large caps, they are not *perfectly* correlated. The addition of small caps to your portfolio will therefore bring some diversification benefits. These benefits are usually too limited to show up in the short run (though the 2000–2002 bear market is a notable exception). But the diversification benefits can prove to be substantial during *secular* bear markets. Consider the most recent secular bear market (2000–2009). The average large cap fund generated negative annualized returns of 7.3 percent. A $10,000 investment in a typical large cap fund made on March 24, 2000, would have shrunk to less than $5,100 by March 9, 2009. Losses for the average small cap fund, though still substantial, were much less than large cap losses. The same $10,000, invested in the average small cap fund, would have declined 2.2 percent per year, to $8,165 by March 2009.[57]

Although the differences weren't as significant, small cap funds beat out large caps during the 1966–82 secular bear market as well. We cannot assume that small caps will *always* outperform large caps during secular bear markets, but the historical record should give us some confidence that the diversification benefits of small caps are real and can be substantial.

Summing Up the Case for Small Caps

Investing for, and in, retirement is a marathon, not a sprint. You are in this for the long haul. It's inevitable that, over the years, you will encounter the occasional bear market. Adding a highly volatile return booster like a small cap fund to your portfolio might cause you to experience lower lows during the inevitable downturns. Conversely, though, the superior long-term returns generated by small cap funds can help you to avoid the other pitfall of the retirement risk—not earning enough returns to outpace inflation. And finally, the diversification benefits provided by small caps may help you increase your returns during *secular* bear markets.

Superior returns over the long run and diversification benefits that can help during secular bear markets? This is a winning combination. Be sure to cash in on these winnings, and make a place for small caps in your portfolio.

Value Stocks

In addition to small versus large caps, we can also draw a distinction between *growth* stocks and *value* stocks. Growth stocks are the stocks of companies that are expected to grow rapidly and outperform the market. Google and Amazon are examples of well-known growth stocks. Think of growth stocks as the popular stocks. Investors love them, flock to them—and bid up their prices.

Value stocks, conversely, are the stocks of companies that are expected to grow slowly, if at all. Think of value stocks as the unloved stocks. If the stock market was a department store, value stocks would end up in the bargain bin, ignored and un-wanted—except, perhaps, by the shrewdest shoppers, the bargain hunters.

A number of different methods have been devised to distinguish value stocks from growth stocks. For example, Eugene Fama and Ken French, in their previ-ously cited 1992 study, classified stocks as value or growth based on the ratio of a stock's price to its book value. The higher a stock's price relative to its book value, the more growth oriented the stock. Morningstar uses a number of different factors to categorize stocks and stock mutual funds as either value, growth, or blend (a category of stocks and funds that lies somewhere between value and growth), but the two most important factors Morningstar uses are price to projected earnings and long-term projected earnings growth.[58] Although differing in the details, these and other classification methods all come down to an attempt to measure the price of a stock relative to its underlying current, or expected future value.

Why does the distinction between value and growth matter? Because numerous studies have shown that, over the long run, value stocks have generated higher re-turns—a *value premium*—relative to growth stocks. The Fama and French study is the best known of the studies demonstrating the existence of the value premium, but their results have been confirmed by many others. Nor does the evidence sup-porting a value premium begin and end with academic studies. The principles of value investing were first expounded by Benjamin Graham back in the 1930s, in his classic book *Security Analysis*. Graham's protégé, Warren Buffet, put those principles to practice with great success. Buffet is the best known—and richest—value investor.

The existence of the value premium may seem counterintuitive. The stocks that have grown the fastest, and are expected to continue to outperform, generate *lower* returns than underperforming stocks? How can this be?

Fama and French originally explained the value premium the same way they explained the size premium—value stocks are riskier than growth stocks and hence have generated higher returns. As we have already seen, in the case of small caps, the data support this explanation. Do the data likewise support their view that value stocks are riskier than growth stocks? Let's take a look.

The Historical Record for Value Stock Funds

As Table 6.3 shows, large cap value stock funds have beaten not only large cap growth funds and large cap blend funds but also the S&P 500 over the 1966–2013 time frame. A $10,000 investment in the average large cap value fund made on January 1, 1966, would have been worth $906,000 by December 31, 2013. The same investment in the average large cap growth fund would have grown to $747,000—a difference of

$159,000.[59] Over the long run, the value premium has translated into big bucks for value investors.

Notice also, that value funds outperformed blend and growth funds (and the S&P 500) over both of the secular bear markets of the last forty-eight years (Table 6.3). In the 1966–82 bear market, the difference between value funds and growth funds was relatively small (0.4 percent per year). But in the more recent 2000–2009 bear market, value funds yielded annualized losses of 3.8 percent, while growth funds produced negative returns of 10.1 percent—a 6.3 percentage point difference.

Table 6.3. Average Annualized Returns of Large Cap Value, Blend, and Growth Mutual Funds during Past Secular Bear Markets

Time Period	S&P 500 Annualized Total Returns	Average Large Cap Value Fund Annualized Returns	Average Large Cap Blend Fund Annualized Returns	Average Large Cap Growth Fund Annualized Returns
Mar 2000 –Mar 2009	−7.0%	−3.8%	−7.3%	−10.1%
Jan 1966 –Aug 1982	+4.8%*	+7.3%	+5.2%	+6.9%
Jan 1966 –Dec 2013	+9.5%	+9.8%	+8.8%	+9.4%

Note: Estimated for partial months based on monthly return data.
Source: Developed by the author using data from www.morningstar.com.

The Exception That Proves the Rule?

Table 6.3 indicates that value stocks have outperformed growth stocks over the long run. What is surprising is that they have appeared to do this while exhibiting *less* volatility than growth stocks. As Table 6.4 shows, mutual funds investing in value stocks have lost less than growth funds in most of the bear markets and market corrections of the last forty years. In fact, the pattern the table shows is remarkably consistent—value funds beat blend funds, and blend funds in turn beat growth funds, in every down market, except the two most recent (the 2007–9 bear market and 2011 market correction). The relatively poor performance of value funds in these last two cases may be partly because the financial sector is weighted heavily toward value stocks. The financial sector was at the center of the 2008 stock market storm. And although the 2011 market correction was triggered mainly by the European debt crisis, it was once again banks—especially banks with a large exposure to Greek, Spanish, and Italian bonds—that were especially hard hit.

Table 6.4. Average Returns of Large Cap Value, Blend, and Growth Mutual Funds during Past Bear Markets and Market Corrections

Time Period	S&P 500 Total Returns	Average Large Cap Value Fund Returns	Average Large Cap Blend Fund Returns	Average Large Cap Growth Fund Returns
Bear Markets:				
Oct 2007 –Mar 2009	−55.3%	−57.2%	−54.7%	−53.0%
Mar 2000 –Oct 2002[a]	−47.4%	−28.1%	−47.4%	−59.8%
Jan 1973 –Oct 1974	−44.8%[b]	−36.7%	−43.5%	−54.0%
Aug 1987 –Dec 1987	−32.9%[b]	−26.1%	−28.5%	−32.1%
Corrections:				
Nov 1980 –Aug 1982[c]	−20.0%[b]	−4.9%	−7.6%	−10.9%
Jul 1990 –Oct 1990	−19.2%	−17.4%	−18.3%	−22.2%
Jul 1998 –Aug 1998	−19.2%	−18.5%	−19.7%	−22.0%
Apr 2011 –Oct 2011	−18.6%	−21.2%	−20.9%	−20.5%

[a] Combines the 2000–01 and 2002 bear markets.
[b] Estimated for partial months based on monthly return data.
[c] Officially a bear market.
Source: Developed by the author using data from www.morningstar.com.

The historical data present us with a big dilemma. If value stocks generate better returns with less volatility than growth stocks, then they break the ironclad rule of investing that bigger returns always come with bigger risks. There are some who believe that the lower observed volatility of value stocks indeed proves that they are an exception to the rule. There are others who insist that there can be no exceptions and that there must be hidden risks associated with value stocks that are not showing up in the data.

Many explanations of these risks have been proposed, but there is no general agreement as to just what they are. As just one example, value companies' heavy reliance on leverage has been hypothesized to be the hidden risk.[60] There is perhaps some evidence in the volatility data to support this view. While value stocks have outperformed growth stocks in *most* of the recent (post-1970) market downturns, the 2007–9 bear market is a notable exception. So, too, was the 1929 Crash. Not only were the losses value stocks incurred significantly greater than those of other stocks be-tween 1929 and 1932, they also failed to match the returns of growth stocks during the bubble that preceded the Crash.[61] In other words, a value investor would have earned relatively low returns in the years leading up to 1929 and then suffered larg-er losses in the years following 1929—a bad combination indeed.

The 2007–9 and 1929–32 bear markets share one unique feature in common. Unlike other U.S. bear markets since 1929, both were marked by major banking crises and a severe tightening of credit. Given that value companies tend to be high-ly leveraged, it would make sense that they are especially vulnerable to banking crises. Perhaps the data are telling us that value stocks are less volatile than growth stocks under normal credit market conditions but *more* volatile during a credit crunch. Fama and French hypothesized the existence of financial weaknesses in value stocks that only show up in periods of extreme stress, such as 1929–32.[62] In any event, the fact that value stocks have experienced larger losses than growth stocks during the two worst bear markets of the last nine decades does suggest that there might be a real, if infrequent, possibility of greater losses with these stocks.

The belief that the value premium reflects the higher, albeit hidden, risks as-sociated with value stocks is rooted in a theory: the efficient market hypothesis (EMH). According to this hypothesis, stock prices fully capture and reflect all avail-able information. Because an individual investor has no access to information that is not already reflected in a stock's price, it is impossible to gain an advantage in knowledge that would allow the investor to profit at the expense of other investors. In other words, the EMH holds that the market cannot be beaten through expert stock selection. The only way to achieve returns higher than average market returns is by investing in riskier stocks.

The EMH in turn is based on the assumption that investors as a group act rationally. Value stocks are riskier than growth stocks, and faced with this risk, rational investors demand a premium, in the form of a larger long-run return, for their investment in value stocks.

Yet, as we have seen, the historical data on the volatility of value versus growth stocks are at best ambiguous. Given the lack of clear evidence that value stocks re-ally are riskier, other non-risk-based explanations of the value premium have been proposed.

An Alternative Explanation of the Value Premium

The main alternative explanation of the value premium rests on the assumption that, contrary to the EMH, the market is not entirely rational but rather is subject to certain cognitive biases. Evidence of these biases has been found by psychologists working in the field of behavioral finance (including Richard Thaler, Daniel Kahne-man and Amos Tversky). Personally, I find the behavioral finance perspective to be pretty persuasive. But regardless of my personal views, it is important to consider this alternative explanation given its potential implications. If true, then the value premium can be captured without any added risk. The debate over the explanation for the value premium is a contentious one, and we are certainly not going to settle it here. But you should nonetheless be aware of both sides of the debate.

By all the usual metrics, growth *companies* outperform value *companies*. They grow their sales, their revenues, and their earnings faster than value companies. But fast-growing sales, revenues, and earnings do not necessarily translate into high stock returns. The returns you earn on a stock depend as much on the price you paid for the stock as on the stock's earnings per share. And the price you pay for a stock depends on the market's future expectations for the stock.

In fact, you can think of the stock market as a mechanism for pricing future expectations about earnings. Suppose there are two stocks, A and B. Stock A is a growth stock priced at $10 per share and with earnings last quarter of 50 cents per share (hence a current price to earnings, or P/E, ratio of 20:1). B is a value stock, priced at $10 per share and with earnings of $1 last quarter (for a P/E ratio of 10:1). The consensus among analysts is that stock A will see its earnings grow by 5 cents, to 55 cents per share, over the next quarter. Earnings per share for stock B are expected to decline 3 cents, to 97 cents per share. Given these earnings projections, would you be willing to pay the same $10 price for shares of B as for shares of A? Not likely, and neither would anyone else. As a result, the price of stock A would increase relative to the price of B. What matters to investors considering purchasing (or selling) a stock is not what has happened in the past, but what they expect will happen in the future. And because growth stocks are expected to grow earnings faster than value stocks, they will be priced higher (all else being equal).

In other words, future expectations are already built into stock prices. Stocks with high expectations—that is, growth stocks—come with high prices; value stocks come with lower expectations and are therefore relatively cheap. Furthermore, because future expectations are already built into stock prices, prices change only in response to a surprise. Returning to our example, let's suppose that instead of increasing by 5 cents per share, as the market was expecting, earnings for stock A only increase 2 cents per share. Let's also suppose that instead of declining 3 cents per share, earnings for stock B decline only 1 cent per share. Assuming nothing else has happened contrary to expectations, it is likely that the price for stock A will drop while that for B will rise. Even though earnings per share declined for B, what matters is that earnings didn't decline as much as the market expected. This is a good surprise, and the price of stock B will go up. Similarly, even though stock A increased its earnings, it failed to live up to expectations. This is a bad surprise, and A's price will decline.

Clearly Company A outperformed Company B during the quarter, but the shareholders of A's stock received no reward for this outperformance. For the shareholder, what matters isn't a company's performance; it's a company's performance *relative to the market's expectations.* Growth companies face high expectations; they must beat these expectations to generate returns for their shareholders. Value companies would have a very difficult time matching the sales, revenue, and earnings growth produced by growth companies, but they don't have to match growth company performance to produce good returns for their shareholders—all they have to do is beat the relatively low expectations the market has set for them.

This explains why rapid growth in a company's sales, revenues, and earnings doesn't necessarily translate into *higher* stock returns for the company's shareholders. But it doesn't explain why returns are actually *lower* for growth stocks than for value stocks. Shouldn't growth stocks have as much chance of beating the market's expectations as value stocks? They should—*if* the market is as realistic in setting expectations for growth stocks as it is for value stocks. But this is a very big "if." Remember, growth stocks are the popular stocks. They are the stocks that grab all the media attention, all the hype and hoopla. They are the ones your coworkers talk about around the water cooler. They made those lucky people who got in on them at the ground floor rich. And they're *still* growing like crazy.

And value stocks? Borrrrring. You never hear about those companies—except maybe when one of them declares bankruptcy.

So, which type of stock—growth or value—do you think is more likely to be overpriced? And which is more likely to be underpriced?

I will give you a hint. Warren Buffet made his billions by searching out stocks that were underpriced relative to their true value and then waiting for those stocks to beat the market's low expectations for them. And where did he look for these bargains? Among *value* stocks.

This is where cognitive biases come into play. Behavioral finance explains the market's perceived tendency to underprice value stocks and overprice growth stocks as being caused by these biases. For example, Chapter 2 mentioned the recency effect —the tendency humans have of putting more emphasis on recent events than on remote ones. Psychologists have also identified the existence of an "availability bias" —a human tendency to overemphasize events that are dramatic or that receive heavy media attention. When a growth stock enjoys a recent price run-up that is heavily covered by the media, both recency bias and availability bias may work to mislead investors into bidding up the stock's price beyond its true value.

Stock Market Bubble Protection

If the preceding alternative explanation based on cognitive biases is correct, the potential implication is that value stocks may generate *higher* returns with *less* risk. That there is at least a chance that value stocks are the single exception to the ironclad rule of risk and reward is one more reason—besides their history of yielding high returns—to include a good helping of value stocks in a well-diversified portfolio.

The debate on whether value stocks come with hidden risks is a contentious one. It is not an issue we can resolve here. However, I'll venture that there is at least *one* particularly dangerous risk that value stocks will *usually* do a better job of mitigating than growth stocks. That is the risk posed by stock market bubbles.

A bubble occurs when speculative fever grips the masses and causes them to bid up the price of a particular asset far beyond its true value. As the price rises, more and more people see a chance to get rich quick—thereby bidding the price up even higher, to crazy levels. Sooner or later, reason makes a return, the bubble bursts—and the speculators get burned.

History provides many examples of such market manias. One of the most famous and bizarre examples occurred in Holland in the seventeenth century, when a mania for tulip bulbs gripped the Dutch people. Tulip bulb prices reached astronomical levels until finally, at some point, a few of the speculators—perhaps realizing all along that this was a bubble and that a tulip was just a flower—came to their senses and sold their bulbs. The selling snowballed, panic replaced mania, and the bubble burst. Today tulips can be found all over Holland; they're a dime a dozen.

As we saw in Chapter 1, the Stock Market Crash of 1929 was a more recent example of a burst bubble. John Stockman and countless real people were caught up in the stock mania of the 1920s, upending their lives and going into debt to buy stocks on margin. Many were financially ruined when the bubble inevitably burst. A much more recent example occurred in the late 1990s—the dot-com bubble. The phenomenal growth of the Internet led first to interest in, then the hyping of, and finally a mania surrounding companies built to exploit the new technology for profit. Speculators (those who knowingly or otherwise try to ride a bubble to riches are speculators, not investors) weren't particularly choosy when it came to deciding where to put their money. Pretty much any company that had a licensed domain name on the Internet would do. As the bubble expanded, even companies that never turned a dime of profits saw their stock prices rise to astronomical levels. A few of the dot-com companies, such as Amazon, went on to become great success stories. Many more vanished without a trace when the bubble burst in 2000.

By definition, the dot-com companies that were swept up in the mania were growth companies. Even the ones that never produced any revenues or earnings (in fact, *especially* these ones) met the various definitions used to distinguish growth from value—they had sky-high P/E ratios or price to book value ratios, and the market had great expectations for their future earnings growth. In contrast, the value stocks of the late 1990s were the stocks that sat out the dot-com bubble. We might then expect to find that growth stocks far outpaced value stocks as the bubble expanded, and then fell far lower than value stocks when the bubble burst. And this is in fact what happened. Table 6.5 shows average annualized returns for large cap value funds, blend funds, and growth funds during and after the dot-com bubble. The first row shows returns as the bubble grew, from January 1, 1995, to when the market topped out on March 24, 2000. The results are exactly what we would expect to see as a stock market bubble expands. The average growth fund left the average value fund in the dust, as market expectations (and prices) for the dot-com growth stocks grew and grew beyond all rational bounds.

Table 6.5. Average Annualized Returns of Large Cap Value, Blend, and Growth Funds during the Internet Stock Bubble and Aftermath

Time Period	Average Large Cap Value Fund Annualized Returns	Average Large Cap Blend Fund Annualized Returns	Average Large Cap Growth Fund Annualized Returns
Bubble expands: Jan 1, 1995 –Mar 24, 2000	+18.3%	+24.8%	+31.3%
Bubble bursts: Mar 25, 2000 –Oct 9, 2002	−12.2%	−22.3%	−30.1%
Expansion and collapse: Jan 1, 1995 –Oct 9, 2002	+7.3%	+6.9%	+6.8%

Source: Developed by the author using data from www.morningstar.com.

The second row shows what happened when the bubble burst and the market plummeted during the long bear market that ran from March 2000 to October 2002. Growth funds averaged a whopping annual decline of 30.1 percent over these two and a half years as the speculators came to their senses and dumped their tech stocks. Value funds also declined, partly because the 2000–2002 bear market was not solely the result of the dot-com bubble. The collapse of Enron and the accounting scandals that followed added to the stock market's woes. There was also a recession lasting from March to November of 2001, and the 9/11 terrorist attacks occurred during this period. Nonetheless, the average value fund sustained losses less than half those of growth funds.

Finally, as the third row of the table shows, over the entire period covering both the bubble's expansion and its subsequent collapse, value funds outperformed growth funds by 0.5 percent annually.

Table 6.5 covers large cap funds. Many of the Internet companies were start-ups that fell within the small cap growth category, so the performance differences between value stocks and growth stocks might be expected to have been even larger for small cap funds. Table 6.6, which focuses on small caps, shows that this is the case. During the bubble's expansion, small cap growth funds produced annualized returns more than double that of small cap value funds (see the first row of the table). But the tables turned dramatically when the bubble burst. In fact, small cap value funds managed to eke out a small *positive* return of 0.3 percent per year during the

2000–2002 bear market, while small cap growth funds were losing 27.6 percent of their value annually. Over the entire bull and bear period from January 1, 1995, to October 9, 2002, small cap value funds beat small cap growth funds by a full 2 percentage points per year.

Table 6.6. Average Annualized Returns of Small Cap Value, Blend, and Growth Funds during the Internet Stock Bubble and Aftermath

Time Period	Average Small Cap Value Fund Annualized Returns	Average Small Cap Blend Fund Annualized Returns	Average Small Cap Growth Fund Annualized Returns
Bubble expands: Jan 1, 1995 –Mar 24, 2000	+14.1%	+19.5%	+30.1%
Bubble bursts: Mar 25, 2000 –Oct 9, 2002	+0.3%	−10.4%	−27.6%
Expansion and collapse: Jan 1, 1995 –Oct 9, 2002	+9.4%	+8.8%	+7.4%

Source: Developed by the author using data from www.morningstar.com.

By definition, growth stocks should be the focus of the euphoric buying that arises during a bubble. If the stocks that get swept up in a bubble were not growth stocks at the bubble's beginning, they will quickly become growth stocks as their prices rapidly inflate along with the bubble. Value stocks, conversely, are the least likely to be affected by a stock bubble. Hence avoiding growth funds, and tilting your portfolio toward value funds, should help you to avoid the booms and busts of most stock market bubbles.

But we must add a word of caution. When it comes to investing, the possibility always exists that exceptional events will cause asset classes to act in unexpected ways. The 1920s bubble and subsequent crash appear to have been one such exception. Although value stocks did not rise as high as growth stocks during the bubble's expansion, as we would expect, they unexpectedly fell further when the bubble burst. It is important to recognize that the Great Depression was much more than the bursting of a stock bubble. It began as a bursting bubble, but it became a banking crisis that led to a severe contraction in credit and a deflationary spiral. Imagine that the 2000–2002 dot-com collapse happened at the same time as the 2007–9 financial crisis and you can get some limited sense of what the 1929 Crash must have been like. As previously discussed, the poor showing of value stocks during the early years of the Depression may have been more a result of the credit crunch than the bursting bubble.

What's the takeaway from all this? Value stocks should mitigate the impact of *most* bursting bubbles. But never underestimate the stock market's ability to surprise and confound us, as it did in 1929. In investing, expect the unexpected, and never trust your hard-won savings to any single asset class or investment. Diversification is always the key to mitigating the retirement risk. Do not go overboard when allocating your savings to value stocks. A *moderate* allocation to the return boosters —small caps as well as value stocks—should help you to boost your returns without unduly increasing your portfolio's volatility. An *immoderate* allocation may be asking for trouble.

Small Caps + Value Stocks = Even Better Returns

If you can earn higher returns by investing in small caps and in value stocks, can you increase your returns even more by combining the two and investing in small cap value stocks? The answer is *yes.* From 1979 through 2010, the Russell 2000 Value Index (an index of small cap value stocks) produced annualized returns of 13.7 percent—4.4 percentage points more than the 9.3 percent returns produced by the Russell 2000 Growth Index. Combining value with small cap stocks is an excellent way to boost your portfolio's returns, even beyond what is possible using small caps and large cap value stocks separately.

You can also use small cap and value stocks to boost the returns of your international equity investments. A number of studies have confirmed that both the value and size premiums found in the U.S. stock market also occur across many other countries.[63] In fact, you may be able to reduce the correlations between your U.S. and international investments by tilting the latter toward small caps. Small companies tend to be less dependent on exports, and more reliant on local domestic markets, than large caps. As a result, international small caps are better insulated than larger companies from factors affecting the U.S. stock market.

Summary

Table 6.7 adds the return boosters to our ongoing summary of the characteristics and portfolio roles of the various asset classes you can use to create your gourmet, well-diversified portfolio. The return boosters all share one key characteristic: the potential to outperform large caps. By adding them to your portfolio, you stand to reduce the chances that you will not earn returns sufficient to outpace inflation. Furthermore, because they are not perfectly correlated with large caps or with each other, they will provide real, albeit limited, diversification benefits. Thus, to the extent that these assets are more volatile than other stocks (which, again, is in question in the case of value stocks), their diversification benefits will, at least to some extent, offset any resulting increase they cause in overall portfolio volatility. In short, when included in a well-diversified portfolio, their higher expected returns can be had without a commensurate increase in volatility.

Table 6.7. Summary of the Characteristics and Portfolio Roles Played by Large Caps, High-Volatility Hedges, Low-Volatility Hedges, and Return Boosters

Asset Class	Correlation with U.S. Large Caps	Volatility	Expected Returns	Role in Portfolio
Core Holdings:				
U.S. large caps	—	High	High	Core holding; produce high returns to beat inflation risk
International developed-market large caps	High	High	High	Long-run diversification benefits; currency diversification
Emerging-market large caps	High	High	High	Long-run diversification benefits; currency diversification
High-Volatility Hedges:				
Gold	Very low	Very high	Low	Insurance
PME	Low	Extremely high	Medium (but may increase portfolio returns when combined with secret sauce)	Applying principle of correlation
Emerging-market bonds	Low	Medium	Medium	Applying principle of correlation and/or compromise
Low-Volatility Hedges:				
Intermediate-term mixed bond funds	Low	Low	Low	Applying principle of compromise (and to a lesser extent correlation)
Short-term mixed bond funds	Low	Very low	Very low	Applying principle of compromise
TIPS and I Bonds	Very low	Low (zero for I Bonds)	Low (but will keep pace with inflation)	Applying principle of compromise (and to a lesser extent correlation); protecting bond portfolio from inflation

Table 6.7. Summary of the Characteristics and Portfolio Roles Played by
Large Caps, High-Volatility Hedges, Low-Volatility Hedges, and Return Boosters
(continued)

Asset Class	Correlation with U.S. Large Caps	Volatility	Expected Returns	Role in Portfolio
Return Boosters:				
Small caps (U.S. and international)	High	Very high	High	Increase portfolio returns to help beat inflation; add limited diversification
Large cap value stocks (U.S. and international)	High	High (but less than large cap growth?)	High	Increase portfolio returns to help beat inflation; add limited diversification
Small cap value stocks (U.S. and international)	High	Very high	Very high	Increase portfolio returns to help beat inflation; add limited diversification

CHAPTER 7

THE FOURTH ATTRIBUTE

History does not repeat itself, but it does rhyme.
—**Mark Twain**

W e have spent a lot of time in the last four chapters discussing history. We have reviewed the performance of the various asset classes during past bear and bull markets going back to the 1960s. We found that each asset class has usually done its job. The high-volatility hedges went up when the rest of the market went down—or if they didn't go up, they at least didn't go down as much as the broader market. The low-volatility hedges worked to reduce portfolio volatility in every bear market and market correction of the past forty years. And the return boosters have produced market-beating returns at least since the 1960s.

But investing is all about the *future*, not the past. The stock and bond markets often seem to be in a state of constant change. Sometimes the U.S. market moves in lockstep with emerging markets, but then the correlation breaks down. Sometimes U.S. stocks climb as the dollar strengthens; but sometimes the dollar and stocks move in opposite directions. Sometimes stocks and bonds move up together; sometimes they don't. Most ominously, the correlations between asset classes have been rising over time, especially with the increasing popularity of passive (index) investing and ETFs.

Previously we learned the three attributes that distinguish a good hedge: low correlation with large cap stocks, high returns similar to large caps, and high volatility. But these three attributes do us no good if they do not *persist* over time. Persistence of past behavior patterns is thus the fourth key attribute of a good hedge. It is also an essential attribute of a good return booster.

Therefore, it is time to circle back to a question I raised in Chapter 2: how do we know that the asset classes we plan to use will behave in the future as they have in the past? The key is to look for asset classes that have something *intrinsic* that either makes them behave the way they do or that touches something equally intrinsic in human nature. If the particular behaviors we value in our hedges and return boosters are rooted in the very nature of these assets, or in our own nature, then they are less likely to prove ephemeral.

Consider, for example, gold. It is by nature just a lump of metal with no potential (unlike stocks) to grow or produce dividends. But in dark times, when people lose faith in the promises of future gains offered by stocks and bonds, they turn to the one asset whose value depends on no such promises. It is precisely because gold is seen as intrinsically valuable that it serves as a financial safe haven when people flee paper assets. Furthermore, it is extremely unlikely that our belief in gold's intrinsic value will change. For thousands of years, and across vast cultural divides, human belief in the value of gold has persisted. There is something timeless in the attraction gold has exerted over us.

Not all of the asset classes we've covered owe their past performance to something intrinsic to their very nature, or to human nature. Consider Treasuries. Like gold, the markets have viewed Treasuries as a financial safe haven. But there is nothing *intrinsic* to the nature of Treasuries that makes them so. On the contrary, Treasuries are seen as nearly risk-free investments because the United States has earned the trust of investors around the world. The United States hasn't defaulted on its debt since 1790—more than 220 years ago.[64] But this doesn't mean we *couldn't* default in the future. The safe haven status of Treasuries rests on nothing other than a reservoir of earned trust, and trust is a fragile thing.

But Treasuries are an exception among the asset classes we've chosen as our hedges and return boosters. Like gold, most of these asset classes have something inherent in their nature that should justify our expectation that they will continue to perform in the future as they have in the past. Consider, for example, the low volatility of bonds. A bond's price is anchored by the bond's face value. The bond issuer is contractually obligated to pay the face value at maturity. Security price volatility reflects uncertainty about the future, but it is a fundamental, inherent characteristic of bonds that their future payoff is fixed and known with a relatively high degree of certainty. Although a bond's price can drift away from its face value for a while, as the bond approaches maturity, its price will tend to converge back toward its face value. This holds true for all types of bonds, including emerging-market bonds and Treasuries. Their safe haven status may not be an inherent feature of Treasuries, but their low volatility is.

Gold mining stocks make good high-volatility hedges because they are by their inherent nature tied inextricably to gold itself. By definition, gold mining companies produce gold. When the price of gold rises during times of trouble, the value of the reserves owned by these companies likewise rises, as does the companies' revenues per unit sold. Because gold mining stocks derive their value in large part from the safe haven that is gold, the attributes that have made these stocks good hedges in the past should probably persist as long as humans value the yellow metal.

Emerging-market bonds may or may not continue to yield high returns with relatively high volatility. But even if in the future they fail to work as high-volatility hedges, they should still provide portfolio protection as low-volatility bonds. Their status as a hedge to stocks should persist, one way or the other.

While gold, PME, and bonds all appear to possess intrinsic characteristics that should cause their past behavior to persist, what would happen if the ability of these assets to hedge a stock portfolio were to become widely known? Many a great investment idea has ceased to work once it has been discovered by the market. When a new idea becomes known, investors quickly jump on the bandwagon, causing the price of the recently discovered asset to rise. As the price rises, the dividends paid by the asset decline as a percentage of the price, and hence the asset's future returns decline. What is to prevent this from happening in the case of the low- and high-volatility hedges?

I wish I could claim to be the discoverer of the hedging capabilities of bonds, gold, and PME, but I can't. Bonds have been widely used for decades, by institutional investors such as pension funds as well as amateur investors, to protect portfolios from stock market volatility. Similarly, gold has been used as a safe haven investment —a hedge—at least as long as Treasuries have, and probably much, much longer. No doubt the market has also recognized the obvious connection between gold and PME that enables the latter to be used as a hedge. In fact, PME's relatively low long-run returns, which we noted in Chapter 4, probably reflect the widespread use of PME as a hedge. (Fortunately, these low returns have not dragged down the overall returns of portfolios that combine PME with the soon-to-be-revealed secret sauce.) In short, gold, bonds, and PME have been used as hedges for many years, and any impact this has had on the returns, correlations, or volatility of these assets should already be reflected in the historical data we reviewed in Chapters 4 and 5. There is little reason to expect that the future behavior of these assets will differ from their past behavior owing to a discovery of their hedging power that took place long ago.

★★★

Although there are strong reasons to believe that the high-volatility and low-volatility hedges will continue to work as hedges in the future, the situation for the return boosters is more complex. A debate rages over whether the value and size premiums will persist. Those on one side of this debate argue that because the existence of the premiums are now widely known, these premiums will be arbitraged away. Arbitrage is the process by which the mispricing of a security is identified, exploited, and thus corrected. Suppose, for example, that a stock is priced at $21.00 on the New York Stock Exchange (NYSE) and at the equivalent of $21.05 on the London Stock Exchange (LSE). Arbitrageurs, discovering this price anomaly, will buy the stock on the NYSE and sell it on the LSE, capturing the $0.05 difference as profit, and causing the New York price to rise and the London price to fall until the pricing discrepancy disappears.

The key point is that, for arbitrage to take place, a mispricing must exist. Therefore, those who argue that the value and size premiums will be eliminated through arbitrage are assuming, either explicitly or implicitly, that (1) the market has underpriced small caps and value stocks (making it possible for savvy investors to buy them on the cheap and realize superior returns when they revert to their true value) and (2) the market will recognize and arbitrage away this mispricing going forward. These assumptions in turn rest on a more basic implied assumption: that the value and size premiums are the result of cognitive biases. If, instead of a psychological explanation, the prices of value stocks and small caps are a rational reflection of some heightened risk (hidden or otherwise) associated with these stocks, then there is no mispricing for arbitrageurs to discover and eliminate. It makes no difference that the premiums, known to only a relative few in the past, are now common knowledge; if they are a reward for risk and not a consequence of cognitive biases, then the premium should persist as long as the risk persists.

As we saw in Chapter 6, the data indeed support the contention that small caps are riskier (i.e., more volatile) than large caps. To the extent that the risks small caps face—such as limited access to capital and heightened exposure to recessions—arise directly from their size, then these risks are intrinsic to small caps and should persist. And as long as the risks persist, so should the premiums that investors will demand to compensate for these risks.

However, the case for the value premium is less clear. Even assuming value stocks are riskier than growth stocks, these risks at best show up infrequently in the data. Value stocks suffered bigger losses than growth stocks during the extreme credit market conditions that prevailed in 1929–32 and 2007–9, but these special cases aside, value stocks have generally been less volatile than growth stocks. Investors will likely receive frequent reminders of the risky nature of small caps and can therefore be expected to price them appropriately in light of the risks. But the well-hidden nature of any risks associated with value stocks may tempt investors to bid up their prices in an effort to capture what may seem to them to be a riskless return premium. In this case, the value premium could disappear for extended periods of time—only to reappear when unusually severe bear markets rudely awaken investors to the hidden risks of value stocks. (In fact, both value and small cap stocks have underperformed over lengthy time frames in the past—only to catch up and then surpass the broader market.)

If, rather than a risk story, cognitive biases cause investors to underprice value stocks, as many contend, then as this mispricing becomes widely known, arbitrageurs should respond by selling growth stocks, buying value stocks, and hence eliminating the price anomaly—and, with it, the value premium. On the battleground between rationality and irrationality that is the stock market, correct reasoning should ultimately prevail over the faulty thinking that gave rise to the mispricing in the first place. Of course, it is possible that our psychological biases will prove more stubborn, and persistent, than this argument suggests. The fact is, Fama and French published their findings on the value and size premiums in 1992, yet globally, value stocks (along with small caps) have continued to outperform in the two decades since.[65] If the value premium is an arbitrage opportunity, it is apparently not an easily exploitable one.

Nonetheless, while there's good reason to expect the size premium to persist, the future of the value premium may be less assured. Value stocks do, however, offer at least a possibility of continued outperformance. For this reason, they remain a reasonable bet, albeit not a sure bet. Small cap value stocks in particular are an attractive option, because these stocks should continue to offer a size-based premium even if the value premium disappears.

★★★

To sum up, all of the hedges we have studied appear to share the crucial fourth attribute of a good hedge: persistence of past behavior patterns. So do small caps, and, perhaps, value stocks. By persistence, I do not mean that every hedge and return booster recommended herein will always work as we'd like. On the contrary, in the preceding chapters, we've already seen past examples where our hedges did not work as well as we would have liked. We've even seen a few examples where our hedges have suffered worse losses than the broader market. And while the return boosters have outperformed the market over the long run, there have been many shorter periods when they've underperformed. Persistence is not the same thing as perfection, and none of the hedges or return boosters is perfect. Rather, persistence means that *when conditions favor a particular hedge or return booster*, we can entertain a reasonable hope (not a certainty) that it will work more or less as well as it has under similar conditions in the past.

History's Broad Lesson

We have spent a lot of time studying the past behavior of each of the recommended return boosters and hedges *only* because there are good reasons to believe that their past behavior patterns will persist. As long as this holds true, a study of historical asset returns should shed light on how our hedges and return boosters can help us to navigate the retirement risk in the future.

There is, however, a broader lesson to be learned from the past: the boundless capacity of events to take us by surprise. Events that seem inevitable to us in retrospect surprised and often shocked those who lived through them. It seems obvious to us today that the stock market was in the grip of a mass delusion during the dot-com bubble of the late 1990s, but that was understood by relatively few at the time (hence the delusion). More recently, the exotic derivatives engineered by Wall Street—CDOs, CDSs, and so on—that blew up spectacularly in 2007–8 seem today to have obviously been built on a shaky foundation of bad loans. But at the time, the high risks inherent in these derivatives went unnoticed not only by the general public, but by the investment banks and insurance companies that created, bought, and sold them. AIG, Bear Stearns, Lehman Brothers, and the others didn't see the subprime mortgage meltdown coming—until it was too late.

And these are only the most recent examples. The stock market has always been, and to this day remains, prone to extreme events. Yet these events seem to take us by surprise every time.

Therefore, a wise investor will (1) at all times be prepared for the worst (while hoping for the best) and (2) above all be humble.

Given the volatility of the stock market and its unbounded capacity to surprise and shock us with negative events, you should maintain a well-hedged portfolio *at all times*. Do not give in to the temptation to sell your low-returning bonds and gold when the stock market does nothing but rise for years or even decades. During such good times, you may hear market mavens and so-called financial experts proclaim that "this time is different," that the economy has entered a "new era" in which the business cycle of boom and bust has finally been tamed, and the only direction the market can go is up. Do not be fooled by such talk! History teaches us that "this time" is almost never different and that these kinds of proclamations are most prevalent when, like in the late 1920s and late 1990s, a bubble is about to burst and the financial house of cards is about to tumble down.

In addition to preparing for the worst (while hoping for the best), we must also recognize and respect the ability of the financial markets to *humble* all investors. It seems at times, as Bernard Baruch once said, that "the main purpose of the stock market is to make fools of as many men as possible" (and, to update Baruch, let's include women as well). Baruch's observation applies just as forcefully to financial geniuses as to those of more modest intellectual endowments. Irving Fisher is a case in point. In Chapter 1, I mentioned his proclamation that "stock prices have reached what looks like a permanently high plateau." What I didn't mention is that he made this statement three days before the October 1929 Crash. Fisher was a brilliant economist, but his ill-timed stock market prediction irreparably damaged his reputation.

The proper attitude of an investor toward the financial markets is one of humility. Being humble means remembering at all times that we can neither predict the future nor devise an investment strategy that covers all potential contingencies. No matter how clever we might think ourselves to be, the possibility remains that all of our best-laid plans will be foiled by events. It is certainly possible that some new crisis may arise that completely thwarts the buy-and-hold, well-diversified portfolio's ability to protect our nest eggs. Because we must be humble and recognize this possibility, it is important to have a backup plan. Chapter 18 of this book provides information you can use to help you distinguish merely scary situations from circumstances that pose a significant danger to the survival of your portfolio, along with a set of possible actions you can take in the latter case. These actions include, as a last resort, abandoning the buy-and-hold approach to avoid a catastrophic, unrecoverable loss. Chapter 19 presents a market reentry plan, just in case you must avail yourself of this option of last resort.

William Bernstein, an expert on modern portfolio theory and author of *The Four Pillars of Investing* and *The Intelligent Asset Allocator*, admonishes all investors to read and learn about financial history. Nothing can impress upon the mind a better understanding of the inherent instabilities of the financial system, its proclivity toward great upheavals, and its unending capacity to surprise and humble us than a familiarity with its history. To this end, you will find a number of excellent books on financial history in the Recommended Reading section at the end of this book. All of the histories listed are fascinating reads not just for financial geeks but for the general public. Some deal with very recent history (the 2007–9 financial crisis), while others go further back in time. Read as many of them as you can, and learn their lessons well: expect the unexpected, at all times be prepared for the worst (while hoping for the best), and above all be humble in your attitude toward the markets and investing.

★★★

In Part III of this book, we continue to look to history for guidance by asking a series of what-if questions about past bull and bear markets. What if we had bought and held various well-diversified portfolios during the great cyclical and secular bull and bear markets of the last forty years? To answer these what-ifs, we run backtests on the selected portfolios and study the results in depth. The answers we find may pleasantly surprise you.

(And maybe, in Part III, you will learn the identity of the secret sauce that, when combined with PME, enhances portfolio returns. Or maybe that secret will be kept until later. Read on to find out.)

PART III

PUTTING WELL-DIVERSIFIED
PORTFOLIOS TO THE TEST

CHAPTER 8

BASIC PORTFOLIO PERFORMANCE, 1972–2013

~~

L et's quickly sum up what we've learned so far. We've learned that the retirement risk—the risk of outliving your money—can manifest itself in two ways. You can encounter too much (negative) market volatility (John Stockman's path to bankruptcy) or not earn enough returns to outpace inflation (Joe Bondsman's road to financial ruin). We've also learned about the two ways to diversify and reduce a portfolio's volatility. First, we can add low-volatility investments (bonds) to a portfolio of high-volatility investments (stocks). The resulting mix will be less volatile than a portfolio consisting of stocks alone, but it will produce lower returns than an all-stock portfolio. This approach to diversification is based on the principle of *compromise*: to reduce the risk of too much market volatility, you must take on some increased risk of earning returns insufficient to outpace inflation.

Black belt investing is the second way to reduce market volatility. It is based on the principle of *correlation*, and it works by turning volatility to your advantage. By mixing into your portfolio some *high-volatility* investments with *low correlation* to the broad stock market, you can reduce the portfolio's volatility without having to give up much, if anything, in the way of returns. Black belt investing using the correlation principle allows you to reduce your risk of winding up like John Stockman without increasing your risk of winding up like Joe Bondsman. However, the correlation principle is less reliable than the compromise principle. Under some conditions, it works quite well (as in the 2000–2002 bear market), but in other situations, it does not work as well (as in the 2007–9 financial crisis). For this reason, a portfolio constructed according to the principle of correlation should also make use of the principle of compromise, as a backup or fail-safe mechanism. Just as a nuclear power plant includes multiple layers of safeguards to prevent a meltdown, a well-diversified portfolio should make room for both high-volatility and low-volatility hedges to reduce the risk that you'll experience a financial meltdown.

We also learned about the asset classes that you can use to create a gourmet, well-diversified portfolio. We learned about both U.S. and international large cap stocks—the meaty core at the center of such a portfolio. We studied the vegetable side dishes—the high-volatility hedges (gold, precious metals equities [PME], and emerging-market bonds) that you can use to put the powerful principle of correlation to work in your portfolio. We studied the potatoes—the low-volatility bonds that, though bland and unexciting, just might sustain your portfolio when the stock market hits hard times. And we learned about the special spices—small caps and value stocks that can boost your returns and help keep you from following in Joe Bondsman's footsteps.

In Part II, we studied the behavior of each of these asset classes—the ingredients of a gourmet portfolio—during past bear markets and bull markets, of both the cyclical (short-term) and secular (long-term) variety. We saw how each asset class responded to various economic and market conditions, and we learned that each has its own unique advantages and disadvantages—its own flavors and textures—and its own job to perform in a well-diversified portfolio.

In Part II, we considered each asset class in isolation. However, we need to understand not only how the asset classes behave separately but how they behave when they are mixed together in a portfolio. And what better way to do that than to actually create some portfolios and see how they would have performed during past bull and bear markets? In this chapter, we create some simple, or basic, portfolios that include only a few asset classes. In the next chapter, we create some more sophisticated or advanced portfolios that make full use of all of the asset classes we studied in Part II. In both chapters, we mix in different amounts of bonds to create portfolios ranging from conservative to aggressive. Once you have a feel for how different well-diversified portfolios respond to different situations, you'll be ready for the job of creating the special portfolio that best suits your own tastes for risk. That's a job we'll tackle together in Part IV.

The Basic Portfolios

The Data Challenge

To put our portfolios to the test, we will need historical data. Unfortunately, data on mutual fund returns become spotty the further back in time we go. From the mid-1990s up to the present, we can obtain the data we need for all of the asset classes of interest to us. For the early 1990s, return data are available for most, but not quite all, of our asset classes. As we go further back in time, into the 1980s and especially the 1970s, the data cover fewer and fewer asset classes. Unfortunately, mutual funds for the more exotic investments, like emerging-market bonds and in-flation-protected bonds, did not exist back then. This limits our ability to backtest our portfolios, especially during the earlier market downturns like the 1973–74 bear market. (A backtest is like a forecast, except that it shows how a portfolio actually would have performed in the past rather than projecting how it might perform in the future.)

There is, however, a way around this problem. If we limit our portfolios to just a few of the more basic asset classes, we can obtain the return data we need all the way back to the early 1970s.

So here is what we will do. For the purpose of backtesting during *cyclical* (short-term) bear markets and market corrections, we will create a few basic portfolios comprising just a few asset classes. We will be able to get the return data we need to test these basic portfolios. Although the tests will not tell us how more sophisti-cated portfolios would have held up to the market strains of the 1970s and 1980s, they will still give us a good indication of diversification's potential for mitigating one of the two key components of the retirement risk: too much (negative) volatility.

In addition to testing the basic portfolios' performance during cyclical down-turns, we will also look at how they would have performed over the long run, from the 1970s up to the present. We will test the portfolios' returns and survivability for both a young person who does not need to draw down on her nest egg and a retiree who must make regular withdrawals to meet living expenses. This long-run test will tell us how well the portfolios mitigate the second key component of the retirement risk: not enough returns to keep up with inflation.

Then, in the next chapter, we will focus on the 1990–2011 period. Because data are available on almost all of our asset classes during this latter period, we will be able to construct and test more advanced portfolios and compare the results with the basic portfolios we create in this chapter. Our focus in Chapter 9 will be on the secular (long-term) bull market of the 1990s and the secular bear market of the 2000s, although we will also drill down into the results to see how the advanced portfolios would have held up during the cyclical downturns of the 1990s and 2000s—especially the big, bad bear markets of 2000–2002 and 2007–9.

In addition to getting around the data limitations, this approach has other ad-vantages. We will be able to "get our feet wet" by creating a few basic portfolios before we dive into the bigger challenge of constructing more advanced portfolios. And although a top-notch portfolio will take advantage of the hedging, diversification, and return-boosting benefits of *all* of the asset classes we studied in Part II, there is a limit to the number of investments that should or can be held by those with more modest retirement nest eggs. The basic portfolios we will study in this chapter rep-resent a good starting point for the construction of a personalized portfolio for those of more modest means, including young people who have just started saving. And as we shall see, these basic portfolios, though simple, are still very powerful tools for reducing volatility while maintaining good returns.

Four Steps to Portfolio Development

Whether it will be simple and basic or complex and sophisticated, the creation of a portfolio always involves the same four steps. We begin by picking the ingredients, or asset classes, that our gourmet portfolio will comprise.

Step 1: Picking the asset classes (or ingredients). In Part II, we divided the asset classes of interest into four main groups:

- *Large cap stocks* (including international developed-market and emerging-market stocks as well as U.S. large caps)

- *High-volatility hedges* (gold, PME funds, and emerging-market bond funds)

- *Low-volatility hedges* (U.S. government bond funds, TIPs funds, and investment-grade mixed bond funds)

- *Return boosters* (small cap funds and value stock funds)

Our goal, in this chapter, is to create a basic portfolio with just a few key ingredients. What could be simpler than a portfolio including one asset class from each of the preceding categories? For starters, let's consider the following:

- A U.S. large cap blend fund

- A PME fund (for our high-volatility hedge)

- A short-term, investment-grade mixed bond fund (for our low-volatility hedge)

- A small cap value fund (for our return booster)

This list of ingredients covers most of the bases of a well-diversified portfolio. The PME fund will provide the portfolio with some of the hedging benefits of gold, without weighing down returns as gold can do. Mixed bond funds generally include a good helping of Treasuries, so this portfolio will capture the hedging power of Treasuries while still providing the diversification benefits of other types of bonds. By including a small cap value fund, we'll get the return-boosting power of both small caps and value stocks. There is only one really significant, avoidable weakness in this portfolio: it does not include any foreign investments. Therefore, let's complicate our ingredient list just slightly by adding a fifth element to it: a foreign large cap blend fund.

Step 2: Deciding on the mix of stocks and bonds. The second step of creating a portfolio is also the most important—and the hardest. This is where we must decide how much of our money we will allocate to the stock portion of our portfolio and how much to the bond portion. Nothing will have a bigger impact on the volatility and returns of your own portfolio than this decision. We will consider the stock/bond allocation decision in depth in Part IV. But for now, we aren't going to limit ourselves to a single allocation—instead, we are going to create three separate portfolios, based on three separate stock/bond splits. This will allow us to test how different stock/bond allocations would have performed in the past and enable you to get a feel for the risks and returns associated with different allocations. We will consider a conservative stock/bond allocation, a moderate allocation, and an aggressive allocation, as follows:

- *Conservative portfolio*: 40 percent stocks, 60 percent bonds (40/60)

- *Moderate portfolio*: 60 percent stocks; 40 percent bonds (60/40)

- *Aggressive portfolio*: 80 percent stocks; 20 percent bonds (80/20)

Step 3: Allocating the stock portion of the portfolio. Once we've decided on our stock/bond mix, the next step is to measure out each individual ingredient in the appropriate amount. This is done separately for the stock and bond portions of the portfolio. Table 8.1 shows the percentage of our money that we will allocate to each asset class in the stock portion of the portfolio. Notice, first, that we will allocate 20 percent to our high-volatility hedge—the PME fund. Twenty percent is the maximum amount I feel comfortable investing in what is, after all, a very small and highly volatile niche of the global equities market. Should gold and PME suffer some sort of major crash, a 20 percent allocation will limit the impact on our portfolio's overall returns.

Table 8.1. Basic Portfolios Stock Allocation

Asset Type	Asset Class	Percentage Allocation
Large caps	U.S. large cap blend	30%
Large caps	Foreign (developed-market) large cap blend	30%
High-volatility hedge	PME	20%
Return booster	Small cap value	20%
Total		**100%**

We'll allocate an additional 20 percent of the portfolio to the small cap value fund. Small cap value stocks make up a mere 3 percent of the Dow Jones U.S. Total Market Index. We are significantly overweighting our investment in small cap value stocks to boost our returns.

After allocating 20 percent to small cap value stocks and another 20 percent to PME, we are left with 60 percent for large caps. We have split this amount equally (30 percent each) between U.S. and international large caps.

Step 4: Allocating the bond portion of the portfolio. Finally we need to allocate the bond portion of our portfolio to our asset classes. But because we are only going to include a single asset class (short-term, investment-grade bonds) in our bond portfolio, it follows that this single asset class will make up 100 percent of our allocation. So Step 4 is already done.

Applying the asset allocation. Let's assume we have $100,000 to invest. So now, we need to take this money and distribute it according to the percentage allocations we've already decided. First, we split it according to our stock/bond allocation, as follows:

- *Conservative (40/60) portfolio*: $40,000 stocks, $60,000 bonds

- *Moderate (60/40) portfolio*: $60,000 stocks; $40,000 bonds

- *Aggressive (80/20) portfolio*: $80,000 stocks; $20,000 bonds

Then, we take these stock/bond splits and split our money further in accordance with the percentage allocations in the stock and bond portions of our portfolios. The final results are shown in Tables 8.2–8.4.

Table 8.2. Basic Portfolio, Conservative Allocation

Asset Class	Percentage Allocation	Dollar Allocation
Stocks:		**$40,000**
U.S. large cap blend	30%	$12,000
Foreign large cap blend	30%	$12,000
PME	20%	$8,000
Small cap value	20%	$8,000
Bonds:		**$60,000**
Short-term investment-grade bonds	100%	$60,000
Total		**$100,000**

Table 8.3. Basic Portfolio, Moderate Allocation

Asset Class	Percentage Allocation	Dollar Allocation
Stocks:		**$60,000**
U.S. large cap blend	30%	$18,000
Foreign large cap blend	30%	$18,000
PME	20%	$12,000
Small cap value	20%	$12,000
Bonds:		**$40,000**
Short-term investment-grade bonds	100%	$40,000
Total		**$100,000**

Table 8.4. Basic Portfolio, Aggressive Allocation

Asset Class	Percentage Allocation	Dollar Allocation
Stocks:		**$80,000**
U.S. large cap blend	30%	$24,000
Foreign large cap blend	30%	$24,000
PME	20%	$16,000
Small cap value	20%	$16,000
Bonds:		**$20,000**
Short-term investment-grade bonds	100%	$20,000
Total		**$100,000**

Short-Term Bear Market Tests

Bear Market Depth Reduction

Using the portfolio allocations presented in Tables 8.2–8.4, along with average mutual fund return data for the five asset classes composing our portfolios, we can calculate total portfolio losses during each of the eight major bear markets and market corrections of the last four decades. I've assumed that we start at the beginning of each market downturn with our original $100,000. I've also assumed that we will rebalance our portfolios on an annual basis, at the beginning of January. Some of our investments will suffer larger bear market losses than others. When we rebalance, we sell a portion of the higher-returning (or lower-losing) investments and use the proceeds to buy more of the lower-returning investments—thereby returning our portfolios to their originally planned percentage allocations. By rebalancing on January 1, our results reflect this selling and buying process for those bear markets and market corrections that last through one or more Januaries.[66] We consider the subject of rebalancing in depth in Chapter 15.

Table 8.5 compares the losses suffered by our three basic portfolios with the S&P 500's losses for the eight major market downturns. The first column of the table shows the distribution of losses for the S&P 500. Reading down this column from top to bottom, we find that four of the eight market downturns produced S&P 500 losses falling in the 15 to 20 percent range (these were the four market corrections). The S&P 500's worst loss (which came during the 2007–9 financial crisis) fell in the 55 to 60 percent range.

The next three columns of the table show the losses our three basic portfolios would have incurred during the same eight market downturns. Let's take a look at the aggressive portfolio (in the second column). This portfolio managed to limit losses to less than 20 percent in six of the eight downturns. The worst loss incurred by the aggressive portfolio would have been 40 to 45 percent, as compared with the S&P 500's worst loss of 55 to 60 percent.

Table 8.5. Distribution of Losses Incurred by the Basic Portfolios and the S&P 500 over the Eight Major Bear Markets and Market Corrections of 1972–2013

Total Percentage Lost at Market Bottom	Number of Market Downturns by Loss Range			
	S&P 500	Aggressive Portfolio	Moderate Portfolio	Conservative Portfolio
5% to 10% **Gain**				1
0% to 5% **Gain**				1
0% to 5% Loss			1	
5% to 10% Loss		1	2	4
10% to 15% Loss		1	3	
15% to 20% Loss	4	4		1
20% to 25% Loss			1	1
25% to 30% Loss		1		
30% to 35% Loss	1		1	
35% to 40% Loss				
40% to 45% Loss	1	1		
45% to 50% Loss	1			
50% to 55% Loss				
55% to 60% Loss	1			
Total number of downturns	8	8	8	6

Source: Developed by the author using data from www.morningstar.com.

By including a larger helping of bonds, the moderate portfolio further reduced losses below 15 percent during six of the eight downturns. The worst loss incurred by the moderate portfolio fell in the 30 to 35 percent range.

Finally, the conservative portfolio kept losses in the single digits (less than 10 percent) during six of the eight bear markets and market corrections. Even more impressively, this portfolio managed to produce modest *gains* during two of these six downturns. One of these two gains (of 5.8 percent) was generated during the 1980–82 market correction, when the S&P 500 declined by 20.0 percent. The other gain was smaller (only 0.3 percent) but much more impressive because it came during the killer 2000–2002 bear market. The S&P 500 lost 47.4 percent of its value during this bear market.

The worst loss incurred by the conservative portfolio fell in the 20 to 25 percent range—less than half of the worst loss experienced by the S&P 500 (55 to 60 percent).

One of the most dangerous financial situations a person can face is to retire just before or during a bear market. This is what happened to John Stockman, who retired just a few months before the 1929 Crash. It's much more difficult to recover from a major loss when it occurs early in retirement rather than later (after you've had time to build up a larger nest egg). The basic portfolios we've created would have significantly reduced the odds of experiencing bear market–sized losses early in retirement. Remember that a bear market is defined as a loss of 20 percent or more and that we have had four bear markets since 1970. But even the aggressive portfolio would have reduced the number of times our losses exceeded 20 percent to only two. And the conservative portfolio would have reduced this number even further, to just a single occurrence. Instead of four chances of retiring into a bear market–sized loss over the past forty years, the basic portfolios would have reduced our chances to just one or two. Even a basic portfolio, containing only five investments but built on the principles of correlation and compromise, has the power to tame some of the fiercest bears we've ever encountered.

Table 8.5 shows losses in terms of percentages, but what happened to the $100,000 principal? After all, you can't spend percentages. Figure 8.1 presents the results of the backtests in the units we know and love—good old dollars. In this figure, the dark gray bars show how much money would have been left in an S&P 500 Index fund[67] on the day the market hit bottom during each of the past eight market corrections and bear markets. The light gray bars show the *additional* amount of money you would have saved had you been invested in the moderate portfolio instead of 100 percent in the S&P 500 fund. In all eight downturns, the reduction in losses achieved through diversification would have been significant, ranging from $4,525 (during the 2011 market correction) to a whopping $38,976 (during the 2000–2002 bear market). Interestingly, the savings are the largest for the four bear markets and the long-lived 1980–82 market correction. Loss reductions exceed $17,000 in all five of these downturns, while savings are less than $10,000 in the three short-lived (less than one year) market corrections. This is indeed a happy fact, as it is the bear markets and the long-lived market corrections that pose the greatest risk to retirement. At least over the last four decades, diversification has worked best when it's been most needed.

**Figure 8.1. Dollars Remaining at Market Bottoms
for the Moderate Portfolio and the S&P 500
over the Eight Major Bear Markets and Market Corrections of 1972–2012**

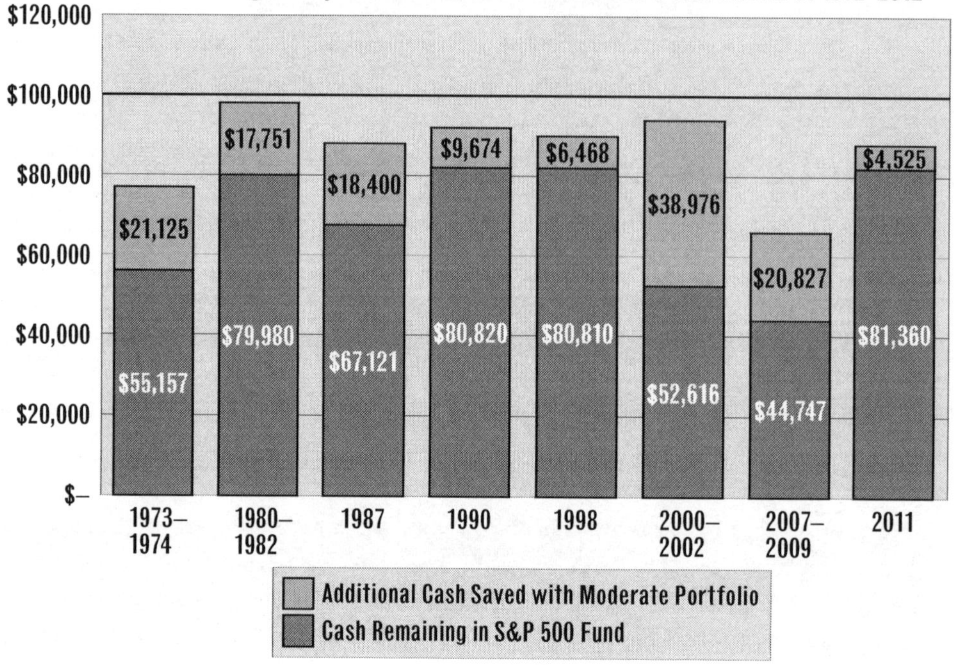

Source: Developed by the author using data from www.morningstar.com.

Now, I know what some of you are thinking. Some of you are fixated on the gaps between the $100,000 grid line and the tops of the light gray bars in the figure. Those gaps represent the amount of money you would have lost out of your $100,000 moderate portfolio. And yes, while those gaps are a lot smaller than the gaps between the $100,000 grid line and the S&P 500 (dark gray) bars, they are still substantial. A well-diversified portfolio is not a magic wand that will keep you from losing money in the stock market. It will *reduce* your occasional losses, not *eliminate* them. And sometimes those occasional losses will be enormous. Take the worst case: the 2007–9 bear market. The moderate portfolio would have reduced your losses by more than $20,000 relative to the S&P 500. But you would have still lost nearly $35,000. Even the conservative portfolio would have lost almost $25,000 during 2007–9.

And some of you—not all of you, but some of you—are thinking, "I don't want to lose that kind of money. Ever. *And if a well-diversified portfolio can't prevent losses like those, I'll be better off forgetting about diversification and just selling my investments before it ever gets that bad."*

I can empathize with the first part of that thought. Who *would* want to lose 25 or 35 percent of their money? But if the second part of that thought describes your thinking, please, *please* don't throw this book in the trash! At least not yet. In Part V, you will learn why you will probably wind up much worse off selling during downturns than holding a well-diversified portfolio through thick and thin. The details are all in Part V, but here's the quick synopsis: if you sell during a downturn, chances are you will turn a temporary loss into a permanent loss. The selling part is easy. It's the *buying back* into the market that's treacherous. Unless you are fully prepared, mentally and emotionally, to buy back into the market *when the future looks bleaker than it did when you sold*, you *will* wind up locking in your losses forever. If you wait to buy back until the future looks brighter (as most people who sell during bear markets do), you will wind up having sold low and bought high.

And one last point while we're on this subject: the market has recovered from every single one of the downturns shown in Figure 8.1. In investing, patience is rewarded. Panic is punished.

Bear Market Recovery Length Reduction

The history of market recoveries. But just how patient do you have to be? Wouldn't it take forever to recover from a 35 percent loss?

A few years ago, I accompanied my mother to a free dinner hosted by a man in the business of selling annuities. In attendance were about thirty people, mostly older. After dinner, he gave us his pitch. It was a very good pitch—if by "good" we mean successful in misleading a lot of people. To persuade us that an annuity is a much better investment than stocks, he talked about how the market lost almost half its value during 2000–2002. He stated (correctly) that if you lose half your money in a market downturn, you then have to *double* your remaining money just to get back to even. "How long," he asked, "would it take you to double your money? Wouldn't that take forever?"

He intended this question to be rhetorical, but I'm going to answer it here. It took four years. An investment in the S&P 500 made on March 24, 2000 (the beginning of the bear market) would have fully recovered by October 2006—four years after the October 2002 market bottom. (It took an additional year—five years total—for the S&P 500 to fully recover on an inflation-adjusted basis.) I'll add that the dinner took place *after October 2006*. The market had already fully recovered when our dinner host posed his question.

Let's take an even worse case. In the 2007–9 bear market, the S&P 500 lost 55 percent of its value. A $100,000 investment in the S&P 500 on October 9, 2007, would have been worth only $45,000 by March 9, 2009. The S&P 500 would have to return more than double—nearly 125 percent—of its March 9, 2009, value to recover from such a devastating loss. How long would *that* take?

As it turns out, it took less time than the recovery from the 2000–2002 bear market. Between March 2009 and September 2012, the S&P 500's total returns (dividends plus capital gains) surpassed 125 percent. That's three and a half years to more than double your money. (Full recovery in dollars adjusted for inflation took until March 2013, or four years.)

Now let's consider the Mother of All Worst Cases—the 1929 stock market crash and subsequent depression. The Dow Jones Industrial Average dropped *89 percent* between 1929 and 1932. Surely it would take decades, if not forever, to recover from that kind of a loss, no?

It's true that the Dow didn't reach its 1929 pre-Crash value until 1954. But the Dow does not account for dividends. And even after taking dividends into account, it provides a distorted image of the real recovery time, given that it includes a mere thirty stocks and is not adjusted for the deflation that occurred during the Great Depression. According to Ibbotson Associates, the deflation-adjusted total returns (dividends plus capital gains) of the *entire* U.S. stock market took a little less than five years to recover from the 1932 market bottom.[68]

To put these recovery times into perspective, between 1970 and 2012, the S&P 500 has taken, on average, roughly 7 years to double its value. The rallies from the 2000–2002 and 2007–9 bear markets cut this average doubling time in about half. The fact is that the rallies that follow bear markets happen *fast*. Why? The market can be counted on to overreact during a major sell-off. It's as if everyone suddenly believes that cartoon character walking around with the sign saying "The world is coming to an end." Panic sets in, investors sell everything that isn't nailed down, and the major indices plummet to incredible lows. On top of the general panic, hedge funds, Wall Street banks, and other institutions that leverage their stock positions are forced to sell to meet margin calls. Then investors wake up a few months later and, perhaps feeling a bit sheepish and embarrassed, find that the world has not come to an end after all. Oops. They also find that stocks are selling at ridiculously low, "end of the world" prices. The smarter investors start buying, prices rise, and soon enough greed replaces fear. It all happens very quickly, because the professional money managers who account for over 95 percent of the total trading volume on the New York Stock Exchange[69] know that once a rally begins, they *have* to move fast or miss out on those bargain-basement prices. I can't count the number of pros I heard on CNBC during the spring and summer of 2009, saying things like "I don't believe in this rally," "we're heading for a double-dip recession," and "I'm holding my nose while buying into this rally." But most of them, despite their own disbelief that the rally would last, said that they *were* buying—presumably because they felt they had to buy or be left behind in the dust. The market is governed by a herd mentality, and once the herd stampedes—be it during a panic sell-off or during the recovery rally that inevitably follows—the market will move at stampede speed.

So much for our annuity salesman.

But while three, four, or five years is a lot shorter than forever, it's still a very long time to have to wait when you've lost a lot of money and need to get it back. Can our basic portfolios speed up the recovery process? Let's take a look at what history has to tell us.

Turbocharge recovery rallies using the basic portfolios. Figure 8.2 shows the amount of time it would have taken for each of the three basic portfolios to fully recover their losses following the four bear markets that have occurred since 1970. The recovery time for the S&P 500 is also shown. With a single exception, the basic portfolios recovered faster than the S&P 500 following all four downturns. The single exception occurred after the 1987 bear market; as the figure shows, the aggressive portfolio was unable to improve upon the recovery time for the S&P 500. The improvements on recovery time from the 1987 downturn were relatively modest even for the moderate and conservative portfolios.

However, keep in mind that the 1987 bear market was much shorter and shallower than the other three bear markets shown in Figure 8.2. During the three worst bear markets, all three basic portfolios cut recovery times by nearly half or better. Following 1973–74, the S&P 500 took a little longer than one and a half years to recover; our three portfolios took between six and nine months to return to their original $100,000 value. After the 2007–9 bear market, the S&P 500 needed a little more than three years to fully recover; our portfolios cut this time to about eighteen months.

But the most stunning achievement came in the wake of the 2000–2002 bear market. It took the S&P 500 a little longer than four years to recover from this downturn—by far the longest recovery of the four bear markets. The aggressive portfolio reduced this time to between six and nine months, and the moderate portfolio fully recovered its losses in fewer than three months. The recovery time for the conservative portfolio does not appear in Figure 8.2, because that portfolio did not sustain any losses in 2000–2002; instead, it yielded slight gains.

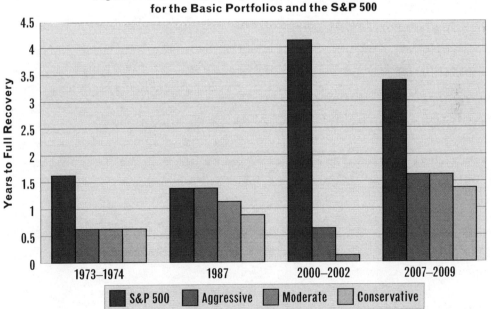

Figure 8.2. Recovery Times from the Last Four Bear Markets for the Basic Portfolios and the S&P 500

Source: Developed by the author using data from www.morningstar.com.

Time is money. The longer a bear market and subsequent rally take before your losses are recovered, the longer you must endure without any portfolio growth. Waiting years just to recover your losses can be frustrating for a younger person still in the workforce. But it can be devastating for a retiree who must continually withdraw funds from her portfolio to meet living expenses. The reductions in bear market recovery times achievable by well-diversified portfolios could mean the difference between beating the retirement risk and being beaten by it.

Market corrections. Figure 8.2 shows only bear markets, that is, market downturns that exceeded a 20 percent loss. What about the four major market corrections that have occurred since 1970? Paradoxically, our portfolios tended to recover more slowly than the broader market from these more limited (less than 20 percent) downturns.[70]

Why would our portfolios, which proved so effective at speeding up recoveries after bear markets, slow recovery down after market corrections? The answer is that these portfolios reduce recovery times not by speeding up the recovery process but by reducing the size of the losses that need to be recovered. In fact, because all three of our portfolios include a sizeable helping of low-volatility, low-returning bonds, they actually rise in value *at a slower rate* than the stock market during recovery rallies. However, following major bear markets like 1973–74 and the downturns of the 2000s, the S&P 500 had a much longer hill to climb than our portfolios to get out of the hole and back to even. In all three cases, the recovery rallies started out very strong but sputtered and slowed down before the S&P 500 could finish this long, hard climb. Our portfolios, having a much shorter hill to climb, were able to fully recover their losses before the market ran out of steam. If you think of a recovery rally as an uphill race, then after the worst bear markets, that race is a marathon for the S&P 500 but a middle-distance run for our portfolios; the market tires out long before it can catch up to us.

In the case of market corrections, conversely, the S&P 500 has a much shorter distance to climb to get out of the hole, the recoveries still start out strong, and hence the S&P 500 has been able to complete the climb in a matter of months, not years. Furthermore, diversification with high-volatility and low-volatility hedges has proven less effective at reducing losses during market corrections than during bear markets. Our basic portfolios, weighed down by bonds and with a shorter lead, get passed and fall behind the stock market during the short sprints to recovery that follow market corrections.

Bonds are thus a double-edged sword. They reduce the *size* of losses during market downturns, but they also slow down the *pace* of recovery. However, while our basic portfolios increased the length of time needed to recover from past market corrections by a few months, they have successfully reduced bear market recovery times by *years*. And of course, bear markets pose a much greater danger to your nest egg than market corrections. We can accept some lengthening of recovery times for market corrections to significantly reduce recovery times for major bear markets.

Long-Run Tests

So far we have tested our portfolios over short-term, cyclical events: bear markets, market corrections, and recovery rallies. We have learned that they can significantly reduce both the depth of bear markets and the time needed to recover from these downturns. In short, they can significantly mitigate the impact of market volatility, the bane of John Stockman, and one of the two key components of the retirement risk.

But the question remains, how do our portfolios stack up against the other key piece of the retirement risk: not enough returns to keep up with inflation (the undoing of Joe Bondsman)? Our portfolios use both of the principles we learned about in Chapter 2 to reduce volatility—*correlation* and *compromise*. The latter principle, com-promise, involves adding low-volatility assets to reduce a portfolio's overall volatility. In our portfolios, we used a short-term bond fund to implement this principle of compromise. And it worked—in every single bear market and major market correc-tion, the conservative portfolio (containing 60 percent bonds) sustained lower losses than the moderate portfolio (40 percent bonds), and the moderate portfolio incurred fewer losses than the aggressive portfolio (20 percent bonds). The more bonds we add to our portfolio, the lower the resulting volatility.

But we achieved this volatility reduction by accepting the lower returns that come with bonds. This is the principle of compromise. By using bonds to reduce volatility, did we wind up reducing *returns* to the point where they could not keep up with inflation? Are we simply trading John Stockman's fate for Joe Bondsman's? To answer this question, we must shift our focus from the short run to the long run and test our portfolios' ability to generate inflation-beating returns.

The Initial Test

Return data on all five of our asset classes are available back to 1972. Therefore, as a first test, let's see how our basic portfolios would have performed assuming that we invested our $100,000 on January 1, 1972. We will rebalance each portfolio at the beginning of each subsequent year, but other than for rebalancing, we will not do any buying or selling of assets for the entire forty-two years between 1972 and 2013. *Buy and hold* is our strategy, so we will *buy* in 1972 and then *hold* for the next forty-two years. Furthermore, for this initial step, we will assume no withdrawals from the portfolio to meet expenses or savings added to the portfolio. We can imagine a twenty-three-year-old who is a knowledgeable investor but on a limited income with no potential for savings. Let's call her Anne. Anne comes into a $100,000 inheritance in 1972, puts it in a retirement account, and does not touch it (except to rebalance it) until she is ready to retire at age sixty-five. What kind of retirement can she expect?

As Table 8.6 shows, buying and holding any one of our three basic portfolios would have made Anne a millionaire at retirement. But the investment in the bond fund does come at a price. The conservative portfolio, with a 60 percent allocation to bonds, yields $2.44 million at retirement, while the aggressive portfolio grows to $4.14 million. None of our basic portfolios can match a 100 percent investment in the stock market. As measured by the S&P 500, a 100 percent stock portfolio would have grown to $6.56 million.

Table 8.6. Growth and Annualized Returns of the Basic Portfolios, 1972–2013

Performance Metric	S&P 500	Portfolio		
		Aggressive	Moderate	Conservative
Total value in 2013	$6.56 million	$4.14 million	$3.23 million	$2.44 million
Annualized returns, 1972–2013	10.5%	9.3%	8.6%	7.9%

Source: Developed by the author using data from www.morningstar.com.

Still, even the $2.44 million produced by the conservative portfolio isn't bad, no? This portfolio generated annualized returns of 7.9 percent—2.6 percentage points less than the S&P 500's 10.5 percent returns. To put these numbers in perspective, the average compound annual rate of inflation between 1972 and 2013 was 4.2 percent. Just to keep pace with inflation, the conservative portfolio would have to have grown to $563,000 by 2013. But although the conservative portfolio's returns of 7.9 percent were less than double the rate of inflation, this portfolio more than *quadrupled* the purchasing power of the original investment from $563,000 to $2.44 million. *This* is the power of compounding. The night thief, inflation, uses this power for evil. But Anne has put this power on her side, earning investment returns that far surpass inflation. And if the conservative portfolio beat inflation, so, too, did the much higher-returning moderate and aggressive portfolios.

The Stress Test

How to devise a test from hell. But we have not yet put the portfolios to a true test of their endurance. The real test of any portfolio is its ability to survive not before but during retirement, when it must generate returns sufficient to cover the retiree's living expenses.

So, let's now suppose that instead of a twenty-three-year-old with no need to withdraw from the portfolio, our investor is instead a sixty-five-year-old widower, Bob, on the verge of retirement. And to make this a really good test, we will suppose that, instead of in 1972, Bob retires on January 1, 1973. This is just eleven days before the beginning of the killer 1973–74 bear market, when the S&P 500 lost nearly half of its value. Nothing could be unluckier than retiring right when the market takes a major dive.

But Bob is indeed unlucky, because he retired during the high-inflation years of the 1970s and early 1980s. Between 1973 and 1982, inflation averaged nearly 8.7 percent per year. In contrast, inflation ran just under 3 percent per year between 1983 and 2013. We will therefore assume that Bob increases his annual withdrawals by 8.7 percent between 1973 and 1982, before reducing the inflation adjustment to 3 percent for the remainder of his retirement. Assuming he starts his retirement in 1973 by withdrawing 4 percent of his portfolio's value (or $4,000), by 1983 his required annual withdrawal would have more than doubled to $8,729. Had inflation remained at a more normal 3 percent per year, Bob's withdrawal in 1983 would have been only $5,376. The stagflation of the 1970s and 1980s increased his living expenses by more than $3,000. By 2013, Bob would need to withdraw $21,188 to keep pace with inflation—more than five times his original $4,000 withdrawal.

Retiring at the beginning of a major bear market *and* a lengthy period of high inflation puts a double whammy on Bob's portfolio. He is due for some good luck, so we will now imagine that he has a very long, healthy life. He dies on December 31, 2013, at the ripe old age of 106. But although this is good luck in many ways, it is *bad* luck financially. It means that his retirement portfolio must survive not for twenty, or even thirty, years but for a very long forty-one years. Financially, the combination of the bear market at the start of retirement, the abnormally high inflation, and Bob's longevity constitutes a *triple* whammy.

I'm not piling one financial misfortune on top of another to be cruel to Bob. My purpose is to devise the most difficult portfolio stress test possible. If our basic portfolios can survive the test of a 1973 retirement that lasts up to the present, then we can safely assume that they could have survived anything else that happened between 1973 and 2013 (*except* perhaps a retirement that begins in the Lost Decade of the 2000s—that is a test we will save for the next chapter). We will use Bob's woes to try to break our portfolios to see just how strong they really are.

Stress test results. Like Anne, Bob makes no trades after his original investments in 1973, other than to rebalance his portfolio at the beginning of each year. Figure 8.3 shows the amount of money that would remain in each of our three basic portfolios on December 31, 2013, the day of Bob's death. For comparison, we also show how Bob would have fared had he invested the entire $100,000 in the S&P 500.

What a difference between pre-retirement and retirement! Instead of being left with millions, like Anne, Bob is left with $427,434 if he went with the aggressive portfolio, and even less if he used one of the other portfolios. Clearly the test we devised proved a difficult one.

Nonetheless, all the portfolios would have seen Bob through to his final days—although the conservative portfolio just barely squeaks by. In 2014, had he lived, Bob would have needed to withdraw $21,824 from the $15,838 remaining in the conservative portfolio. He almost certainly would have been bankrupt by the end of 2014. This may be cutting things a little too close for comfort.

In contrast, the moderate and aggressive portfolios finished with more than enough money to spare.

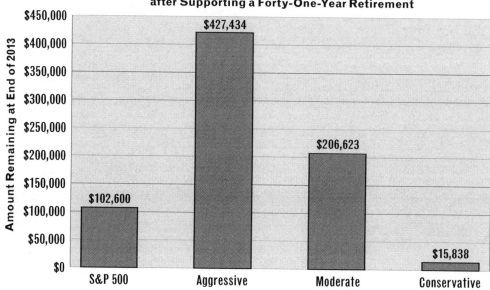

Figure 8.3. Value of the Basic Portfolios on December 31, 2013, after Supporting a Forty-One-Year Retirement

Source: Developed by the author using data from www.morningstar.com.

The Goldilocks portfolios. In Figure 8.3, we have a dramatic illustration of the two sides of the retirement risk. The two portfolios in the middle proved the safest; the two at the extreme left and right less so.

Although the 100 percent S&P 500 portfolio survived and kept its initial value intact, it was nonetheless weakened by volatility. We know it was volatility, not lack of returns, that hurt this portfolio because we know it produced the best long-run average returns of all four portfolios (as shown in Table 8.6). Figure 8.4 shows the trajectory of the S&P 500 portfolio over the course of Bob's retirement; for comparison, we also show the conservative portfolio's trajectory. This figure illustrates just how much damage volatility can do to a retiree's portfolio. From 1995 through 2009, the S&P 500 portfolio traces out a roller-coaster ride of exhilarating highs and stomach-churning free falls. It is the trajectory of a portfolio subject to too much market volatility.

Contrast the steep mountains and deep valleys of the S&P 500 portfolio's trajectory with the long, gentle hill the conservative portfolio climbs and then descends. This is the trajectory of a portfolio that has minimized volatility but that, in its latter years, is not generating returns sufficient to outpace inflation. It is significant that the portfolio peaks not at the beginning of a major bear market (in 2000, like the

S&P 500 portfolio), but right in the middle of the great stock and bond *bull* market of 1982–99. There were no major stock market downturns near the conservative portfolio's 1993 peak, and not even the outsized stock returns of the late 1990s—the dot-com bubble years—prove sufficient to reverse the portfolio's declining trend. That the portfolio began its decline in the midst of a calm, secular bull market is evidence that it simply ran out of steam. Bob's withdrawals slowly grow with inflation and eventually overtake returns. By 1998, the required annual withdrawal reached 7.6 percent of the portfolio's value—which is nearly equal to the 7.7 percent annualized return the portfolio generated between 1973 and 2013. As withdrawals continued to increase 3 percent per year beyond 1998, the point of no return was passed. The conservative portfolio was severely weakened by the second component of the retirement risk—not enough returns to outpace inflation.

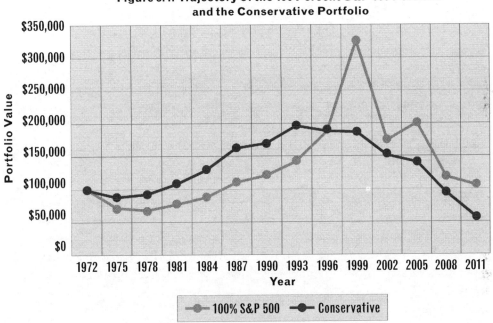

Figure 8.4. Trajectory of the 100 Percent S&P 500 Portfolio and the Conservative Portfolio

Source: Developed by the author using data from www.morningstar.com.

Either the S&P 500 portfolio or the conservative portfolio would have seen Bob through to the end of his life—but not without some anxious days and sleepless nights. Bob might have found the S&P 500 portfolio a little too hot and the conservative portfolio a little too cold.

In contrast, at least for the conditions prevailing in 1973–2013, the moderate and aggressive portfolios were just right. Both followed a bumpier trajectory than the conservative portfolio. Their losses were larger during the downturns of 1973–74, 2000–2002, and, most especially, 2007–9. Yet paradoxically, they proved to be *less risky* than the conservative portfolio. They struck a better *balance* between the two components of the retirement risk, keeping volatility in check without compromising returns too much in the process. Call them the Goldilocks portfolios.

The key takeaways. Too many investors are frightened by the risk of *temporary* stock market losses into relying too heavily on bonds. Our stress test shows that, in highly inflationary conditions, a portfolio weighted too heavily toward bonds can be as dangerous—or even more dangerous—than one weighted too heavily toward stocks. We have not thus far considered a basic portfolio comprising 80 percent bonds and 20 percent stocks, but I have put just such a very conservative portfolio to the same stress test and found that it would have run out of money by the end of 2007—six years too soon for Bob. A 100 percent bond portfolio would obviously have done even worse.

The high inflation of the 1970s and early 1980s wreaked havoc on bonds. Can such inflation recur in the future? Of course it can. Will it? I don't have a crystal ball, and neither does anyone else. There are many smart, knowledgeable economists who believe that the Federal Reserve has been pursuing highly inflationary policies. There are many other smart, knowledgeable economists who believe the Fed's recent actions helped prevent *deflation* and can be unwound before they lead to future inflation. We don't know what the future will bring. The best we can do is prepare for as many possible futures as we can, including the possibility of high inflation. To do that, add bonds to your portfolio *in moderation*. Make this one of your key takeaways from the stress test: in building a portfolio, all things in moderation.

And make this your other key takeaway: all three of our basic portfolios survived the toughest historical test we could devise. All lasted through a very long, nearly forty-one-year retirement that began with a major stock market loss and a ten-year period of abnormally high inflation and ended with the turmoil of the Lost Decade. The chances that you will face a forty-one-year retirement are low, and the odds that such a long retirement would begin with the double whammy of a major bear market and a long bout of inflation are even lower. But isn't it good to know that if you are as unlucky as Bob, you still have a very good chance of enjoying a long, comfortable retirement?

Assuming, of course, that, like Bob, you diligently apply the principles of correlation and compromise, and stick with a buy-and-hold investment strategy through thick and thin?

CHAPTER 9

ADVANCED PORTFOLIO PERFORMANCE, 1990–2013

∾

n the last chapter, we created a few basic, five-asset portfolios. We then ran them through each of the eight worst market downturns since 1972. In every case, our portfolios significantly reduced losses compared to the broader market, as measured by the S&P 500. Following the four worst bear markets, our portfolios also reduced recovery times, in most cases by a year or more.

Then, after these short-term tests, we came up with a devilishly difficult long-term stress test. We imagined Bob, a sixty-five-year-old who retired on January 1, 1973, right at the beginning of a major bear market *and* a ten-year period of abnormally high inflation. All three of our portfolios managed to outlast Bob's forty-one-year retirement, extending all the way through 2013.

These tests demonstrate the ability of well-diversified portfolios to significantly reduce volatility while maintaining long-run returns at a level sufficient to outpace inflation. Even basic portfolios, containing only five investments but diversified based on the twin principles of *correlation* and *compromise*, demonstrated their power to defeat the retirement risk under some of the toughest scenarios recent history could throw at us.

If basic portfolios with only five investments can stand up to the test of time this well, what might we expect of more advanced portfolios with double the number of investments? In this chapter, we answer this question. We create some more advanced portfolios using *all* of the asset classes we studied in Part II. We then put them to a variety of tests. We compare the results with the performance of the basic portfolios, and we drill down into the results to gain a deeper insight into how low-volatility hedges, high-volatility hedges, and return boosters can all work together to protect you from the retirement risk.

The Advanced Portfolios

We begin by creating three portfolios. By now, you're already familiar with the four-step process to portfolio creation, so we'll skip the details and get right to the results. As was the case for our basic portfolios, our advanced portfolios will be defined by adjusting the allocation between stocks and bonds as follows:

- *Conservative portfolio*: 40 percent stocks, 60 percent bonds (40/60)

- *Moderate portfolio*: 60 percent stocks; 40 percent bonds (60/40)

    70/30

- *Aggressive portfolio*: 80 percent stocks; 20 percent bonds (80/20)

Within the stock portion of the portfolios, the allocation to the various asset classes will be the same across all three portfolios. Table 9.1 shows the stock allocations. We have included two different large cap asset classes, all three of the high-volatility hedges we studied in Part II, and three return boosters. We have included emerging-market bonds in the *stock* portion of our portfolios because, as we saw in Chapter 4, the volatility of emerging-market bonds lies somewhere between stocks and other types of bonds. Therefore we are treating this asset class as if it is a high-volatility stock investment rather than a low-volatility bond investment. Also, because return data on emerging-market bond funds are not available prior to 1994, in the backtests that follow, we will zero out our allocation to this asset class during the 1990–93 period. For the years 1994 through 2013, we will increase the allocation to emerging-market bonds to 15 percent (and reduce the allocation to U.S. large caps by a corresponding amount).

Table 9.1. Advanced Portfolios Stock Allocation

Asset Type	Asset Class	Percentage Allocation
Large caps	U.S. large cap blend	10% (25%[a])
Large caps	Emerging-market large caps	10%
High-volatility hedge	Emerging-market bonds	15% (0%[a])
High-volatility hedge	Precious metals equities (PME)	15%
High-volatility hedge	Gold	5%
Return booster	U.S. large cap value	10%
Return booster	U.S. small cap value	15%
Return booster	Foreign (developed-market) small cap blend	20%
Total		**100%**

[a]For the period 1990–93, data on emerging-market bond fund returns are lacking. Therefore the allocation to emerging-market bonds is held at zero until 1994, when 15 percent of the U.S. large cap allocation is shifted to emerging-market bonds.

The stock portion of the portfolios has been split between large caps (30 percent of the total[71]), high-volatility hedges (35 percent), and return boosters (45 percent). As was the case for the basic portfolios, the total allocation to international equities is 30 percent, but with two-thirds of this total assigned to small caps to take advantage of the greater diversification benefits offered by international small caps.[72] The inclusion of two new hedges (emerging-market bonds and gold) has allowed us to increase the total allocation to high-volatility hedges from 20 percent in the basic portfolios to 35 percent in the advanced portfolios. The allocation to gold has been limited to 5 percent, reflecting our belief that gold should be viewed more as insurance than as a high-returning investment.

The inclusion of multiple small cap and value stock investments has allowed us to increase the total allocation to the return boosters from 20 percent in the basic portfolios to 45 percent. The increased allocations to high-volatility hedges and return boosters should help to reduce portfolio volatility and increase returns, without over-exposing the portfolios to the risks associated with too great a concentration in any single asset class.

Table 9.2 shows the allocation within the bond portion of the portfolios. This allocation is the same one recommended in Chapter 5, and it provides the same advantages noted in that chapter, including a hedge against inflation and rising interest rates, partial capture of the larger yields offered by intermediate-term bonds, and the added protection from stock market declines provided by the safe haven of TIPS and Treasuries.

Table 9.2. Advanced Portfolios Bond Allocation

Asset Type	Asset Class	Percentage Allocation
Low-volatility hedge	Inflation-protected bonds (TIPS)	34%
Low-volatility hedge	Short-term mixed bond fund	33%
Low-volatility hedge	Intermediate-term mixed bond fund	33%
Total		**100%**

All that's left now is to take our $100,000 and allocate it according to the percentage allocations in Tables 9.1 and 9.2. As an example, I've done this for the moderate portfolio in Table 9.3.

Table 9.3. Advanced Portfolio, Moderate Allocation

Asset Class	Percentage Allocation	Dollar Allocation
Stocks:		**$60,000**
U.S. large cap blend	10% (25%[a])	$6,000 ($15,000[a])
Emerging-market large caps	10%	$6,000

Table 9.3. Advanced Portfolio, Moderate Allocation *(continued)*

Asset Class	Percentage Allocation	Dollar Allocation
Emerging-market bonds	15% (0%)[a]	$9,000 ($0[a])
PME	15%	$9,000
Gold	5%	$3,000
U.S. large cap value	10%	$6,000
U.S. small cap value	15%	$9,000
Foreign small cap blend	20%	$12,000
Bonds:		**$40,000**
Inflation-protected bonds (TIPS)	34%	$13,600
Short-term investment-grade bonds	33%	$13,200
Intermediate-term investment-grade bonds	33%	$13,200
Total		**$100,000**

[a]Years 1990–1993.

The Advanced versus the Basic Portfolios, 1990–2013

As our first test, let's see how the advanced portfolios would have stacked up against the basic portfolios for the years 1990–2013. This period provides a great test, because it includes both the raging bull market of the 1990s and the long bear market of the 2000s. So we get to see our portfolios in action during both good times and bad.

We will start by investing $100,000 in each portfolio on January 1, 1990, and we will run the test through December 31, 2013. As in all our tests, we will use the buy-and-hold investment strategy and make no changes to our portfolios, except to rebalance them at the beginning of each year. For this initial test, we assume no withdrawals will be made from the portfolios and no additional savings will be added to them. As usual, the test will be conducted using average total return data for mutual funds from the Morningstar website.[73]

Figure 9.1 shows the growth of each advanced portfolio, along with the corresponding basic portfolio, over the years 1990–2013. The growth of a $100,000 investment in the S&P 500 is also shown. For each of the three risk levels—aggressive, moderate, and conservative—the advanced portfolios have significantly outperformed the basic portfolios. In the case of the conservative portfolios, the advanced version winds up nearly $119,000 ahead of the basic version by December 31, 2013. The gap between the advanced and basic portfolios increases as we move to higher risk levels.

The higher returns earned by the advanced portfolios reflect the impact of the return boosters. Forty-five percent of the stock portions of the advanced portfolios have been allocated to a combination of small caps and value stocks, as compared with only 20 percent for the basic portfolios.

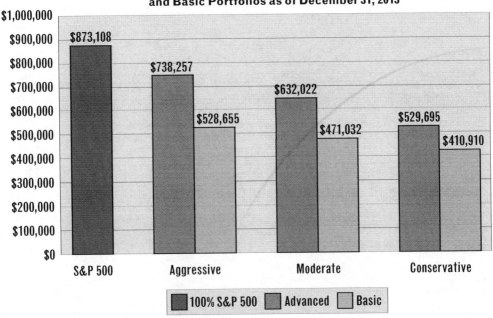

Figure 9.1. Money Remaining in the Advanced Portfolios and Basic Portfolios as of December 31, 2013

Source: Developed by the author using data from www.morningstar.com.
Gold returns based on London Gold Market Fixing prices.

Secular Bulls and Bears

It's not surprising that the advanced portfolios' increased allocation to return boosters leads to higher returns. What *is* surprising is that these increased returns do not come at the expense of greater volatility. Consider Table 9.4, which shows the average annual returns of each portfolio during two distinct time periods: the bull market of the 1990s and the Lost Decade of the 2000s. Notice first, that for all three risk levels, the advanced portfolio beats out the corresponding basic portfolio during *both* the bull market and the bear market. Yet the *differences* between bull market and bear market returns are much smaller for the advanced than for the basic portfolios. For example, at the aggressive level, the basic portfolio averaged 8.6 percent annualized returns during the 1990s bull market and 5.8 percent annualized returns during the 2000s bear market—nearly a 3 percentage point difference. In contrast, the advanced portfolio yielded 9.2 percent returns during the 1990s and 8.8 percent returns during the 2000s—a mere 0.4 percentage point difference. The advanced portfolio produced higher returns than the basic portfolio, but with significantly *less* volatility measured over ten-year periods. Keep in mind that, within the aggressive risk level, both portfolios have the same (20 percent) allocation to low-volatility bonds. Differences in the size of the bond allocation therefore do not account for the volatility differences. Rather, the volatility differences are mainly the result of differences in the allocations to the high-volatility hedges. The basic portfolio includes a 20 percent allocation to a precious metals equity (PME) fund, whereas the advanced portfolio allocates nearly twice this amount (35 percent) across three different high-volatility hedges.

By increasing our allocation to a diverse set of high-volatility hedges, we have reduced long-term portfolio volatility without reducing returns. In fact, we have increased returns by loading up on return boosters.

Table 9.4. Annualized Returns during the 1990s Bull Market and the Lost Decade of the 2000s

Portfolio Risk Level	Portfolio	Annualized Returns 1990–1999	Annualized Returns 2000–2009
Aggressive	Basic	8.6%	5.8%
	Advanced	9.2%	8.8%
Moderate	Basic	8.1%	5.5%
	Advanced	8.5%	8.1%
Conservative	Basic	7.5%	5.1%
	Advanced	7.8%	7.3%
Highly aggressive	100% S&P 500	18.2%	−1.0%

Sources: Developed by the author using data from www.morningstar.com.
Gold returns based on London Gold Market Fixing prices.

The advanced portfolios are clearly superior to the basic portfolios. By adding additional asset classes, we have lowered long-term volatility and increased returns, while avoiding a dangerous concentration in any single asset class.

Slaying Secular Bears

Still, like the advanced portfolios, the basic portfolios have the ability to generate good returns with much less volatility than the broader stock market. The last row of Table 9.4 shows just how volatile the S&P 500 has been over the long run. After yielding annualized returns of over 18 percent in the 1990s, S&P 500 returns plummeted to *negative* 1 percent in the 2000s. This is the kind of volatility that can give an investor whiplash! The three basic portfolios provided a much smoother ride—and the advanced portfolios did even better.

Those poor post-2000 returns from the 100 percent S&P 500 portfolio spell danger, especially for those unfortunate enough to have retired near the turn of the century. You may have noticed that we have been using a 4 percent withdrawal rate for our retiree backtests. We even started Joe Bondsman's retirement with a 4 percent withdrawal rate. As we discuss in Chapter 11, historical analyses have shown that if you begin your retirement with a withdrawal rate of 4 percent or less, chances are very good that you will never run out of money.

But compare that 4 percent withdrawal rate with the S&P 500's annualized returns of −1 percent from 2000 through 2009. Clearly, if you withdraw 4 percent from a portfolio *shrinking* at an average annual rate of 1 percent, then a lot of money will be draining out of the portfolio while no new money is coming in. This is a situation that can be weathered if it lasts for a few months, or even a few years. But the S&P 500 averaged −1 percent returns for *ten years*. Withdrawing 4 percent per year from a portfolio with negative returns over such a long period is dangerous. True, the S&P 500 has produced 9.5 percent returns over the long run (1966–2013). But as the 2000–2009 Lost Decade proves, the stock market's volatility is such that it can return less than 4 percent—much less—over very long periods of time. Long-run returns of 9.5 percent wouldn't have helped someone unlucky enough to have retired in or near 2000 with a 100 percent S&P 500 portfolio.

As we first noted back in Chapter 2, it is the *length*, not the *depth*, of a bear market that often poses the greatest risk to a retiree's portfolio. *Cyclical* bear markets are deep but relatively short-lived. During such events, the amount of time over which a retiree must withdraw money from her portfolio without earning compensating returns is typically no longer than two to three years. A retiree's portfolio can usually survive such short-lived drawdowns. *Secular* bear markets are shallow but long-lived; they typically last more than a decade. If, over such a long period of time, the withdrawal rate exceeds a portfolio's average returns, the portfolio is likely to either be bankrupted or at least severely weakened. But if, conversely, average returns exceed the withdrawal rate, the portfolio will probably be safe. As Table 9.4 shows, between 2000 and 2009, all of our portfolios, whether basic or advanced, yielded average returns in excess of a 4 percent withdrawal rate. The Lost Decade would not have been lost to a retiree using one of our portfolios. It is a well-diversified portfolio's ability to make *secular* bear markets effectively disappear that offers retirees safety from the most dangerous financial storms: the ones that drag on for many years.

This safety, however, comes with a catch. (There's always a catch, isn't there?) To enjoy the market-beating returns of the 2000s offered by our portfolios, a buy-and-hold investor would have had to give up those huge, 18-plus percent stock market returns of the 1990s. To mitigate the retirement risk and enjoy good returns during hard times, you must be prepared to give up even better returns during good times. And to do this, you must be able to control your emotions—to not give in to greed when the market is going gangbusters, and to not give in to fear when the market is in free fall. In Part V, we tackle the subject of controlling the strong emotions evoked by bull and bear markets.

The Cyclical Bear Markets of the 2000s

The return data in Table 9.4 demonstrate the ability of the advanced portfolios to produce superior returns with low volatility across long-term (secular) bull and bear markets. But can these portfolios also reduce short-term volatility during cyclical bear markets?

They can, and they have. Figure 9.2 shows the amount of money that would remain in each of our basic and advanced portfolios on October 9, 2002 (the bottom of the 2000–2002 bear market), assuming we started with $100,000 at the beginning of the bear market (March 24, 2000). As the figure shows, at every risk level, the advanced portfolios do a better job of protecting savings than the basic portfolios. The advanced moderate portfolio actually generates a small *positive* return ($274, or 0.3 percent), while the advanced conservative portfolio yields an even more significant gain of $8,115 (8.1 percent). Quite impressive results, given the S&P 500 portfolio's *loss* of $47,384.

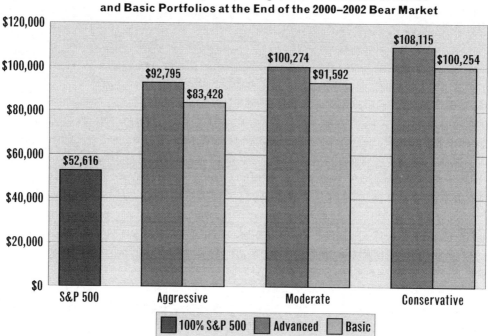

Figure 9.2. Money Remaining in the Advanced Portfolios and Basic Portfolios at the End of the 2000–2002 Bear Market

Source: Developed by the author using data from www.morningstar.com.
Gold returns based on London Gold Market Fixing prices.

The advanced portfolios also outperform the basic portfolios during the 2007–9 financial crisis, although by a smaller margin than in 2000–2002 (Figure 9.3). Over the short as well as the long term, the advanced portfolios reduce volatility while delivering returns superior to the returns of the basic portfolios.

Just how do our advanced portfolios manage to reduce the risk posed by market volatility without significantly increasing the risk posed by not enough returns? We are now going to spend some time answering this question. We are going to drill down into the backtest results, take the portfolios apart, and put them back together again to see how each component contributes to the portfolios' overall performance.

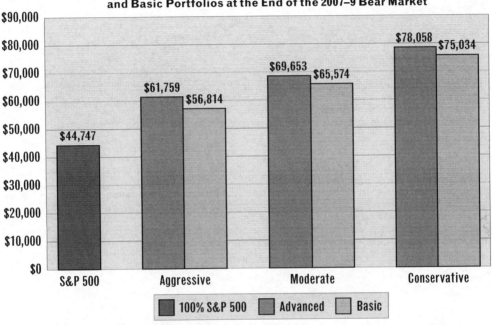

Figure 9.3. Money Remaining in the Advanced Portfolios and Basic Portfolios at the End of the 2007–9 Bear Market

Source: Developed by the author using data from www.morningstar.com.
Gold returns based on London Gold Market Fixing prices.

Drilling Down into a Well-Diversified Portfolio

Table 9.5 shows the results of this process. In the first row, we start with a portfolio that has been stripped of all return boosters and hedges. The money allocated to the return boosters and hedges is instead allocated to the U.S. large cap blend fund. We are left, in this first row, with a 100 percent stock portfolio. Ninety percent of our funds have been allocated to U.S. large caps, with the remaining 10 percent allocated to our other large cap asset class: emerging-market stocks.

In the second row, we add back in the return boosters: the small cap value fund, the international small cap blend fund, and the U.S. large cap value fund. In the third row, we add back in the high-volatility hedges: gold, the PME fund, and the emerging-market bond fund. At this point we are back to the stock allocations shown in Table 9.1. However, we have not yet added in the low-volatility hedges (bonds). In the last row of the table, we add in the bonds (Table 9.2) in the amount of 40 percent. This gets us back to our advanced moderate portfolio.

Table 9.5. Gradual Build-Up of the Advanced Moderate Portfolio

Asset Type Included	COLUMN 1 Annualized Returns, 1990–2013	Secular Bulls and Bears		Cyclical Bears	
		COLUMN 2 Bull Market Annualized Returns, 1990–1999	COLUMN 3 Bear Market Annualized Returns, 2000–2009	COLUMN 4 Cumulative Returns, Mar 2000 –Oct 2002	COLUMN 5 Cumulative Returns, Oct 2007 –Mar 2009
Large caps only	+8.5%	+15.8%	+0.0%	−47.0%	−55.2%
+ Return boosters	+9.3%	+14.3%	+3.0%	−38.7%	−57.2%
+ High-volatility hedges	+9.3%	+9.8%	+9.4%	−14.3%	−45.6%
+ Low-volatility hedges	+8.0%	+8.5%	+8.1%	+0.3%	−30.3%

Sources: Developed by the author using data from www.morningstar.com.
Gold returns based on London Gold Market Fixing prices.

The columns show the returns we would get at each step of the process for different time periods. Column 1 shows the overall annualized returns for the entire 1990–2013 time frame. The second column shows annualized returns for the 1990s bull market, and the third column shows annualized returns for the Lost Decade of the 2000s. The fourth column shows total cumulative returns for the 2000–2002 bear market, and the last column shows total cumulative returns for the 2007–9 bear market. Let's drill into these results and see what they can tell us.

We'll start in the first row. As column 1 shows us, a portfolio consisting of nothing but large cap stock funds would have yielded annualized returns of 8.5 percent from 1990 through 2013. These returns would have proved highly volatile, dropping from 15.8 percent in the 1990s (column 2) to 0.0 percent in the first decade of the new century (column 3). The 100 percent large caps portfolio would have lost about half of its value in each of the two big bear markets of the 2000s (columns 4 and 5).

The second row shows what happens when we add return boosters to the large caps. Notice, first, that our overall returns for 1990 to 2013 increase from 8.5 percent to 9.3 percent (column 1). For those of you more interested in dollars than in percentages (and who isn't?), the portfolio with return boosters grows from $100,000 in 1990 to $842,933 in 2013. The 100 percent large cap portfolio grows to only $708,389.

Interestingly, we get this additional $134,544 with slightly *lower* long-run volatility. Comparing the second and third columns, returns for the portfolio with return boosters drop by 11.3 percentage points (from 14.3 to 3.0 percent) between the 1990s and the 2000s, versus a 15.8 percentage point drop for the large-cap-only portfolio. Adding return boosters to the large caps also significantly reduces our losses during the 2000–2002 bear market, from 47 to 38.7 percent (column 4).

Clearly, although they are far less effective than true hedges in reducing volatility, the return boosters do add some diversification benefits to the portfolio. In particular, the inclusion of a significant allocation to value stocks helps to moderate volatility. Recall, from Chapter 6, that value stocks were less affected by the dot-com bubble of the late 1990s than growth stocks. This helps explain why the portfolio with the return boosters yields lower returns in the 1990s than the large-cap-only portfolio (14.3 vs. 15.8 percent). It also explains why the addition of value stocks to our portfolio reduced losses in 2000–2002. This reduction in turn helped to raise returns from 0.0 percent to 3.0 percent over the 2000–2009 time frame (column 3). The addition of the return boosters did increase losses during the 2007–9 financial crisis (column 5), but the increase (from 55.2 to 57.2 percent) was relatively small. I would be more than happy to accept this slight increase in losses to secure that additional $134,544 in long-run returns.

Now let's take a look at the third row of the table. Adding the high-volatility hedges—gold, PME, and emerging-market bond funds—to our portfolio of large caps and return boosters has a major effect on volatility. As a comparison of the second with the third column of the table shows, once we add in our high-volatility hedges, returns drop by only 0.4 percentage points (from 9.8 to 9.4 percent) between the 1990s bull market and the 2000s bear market. Furthermore, our losses in 2000–2002 (column 4) drop from deep bear market territory (38.7 percent) to only 14.3 percent. And these reductions in both short- and long-term volatility come at no cost to long-term (1990–2013) returns, which remain at 9.3 percent (column 1). This is the principle of *correlation* at work—the high-volatility hedges enable you to significantly reduce your portfolio's volatility without requiring you to give up returns.

There is only one major blemish in the third row of the table: the returns in the last column (for the 2007–9 bear market). Although adding the high-volatility hedges to our portfolio reduces our 2007–9 losses somewhat, the loss reduction is nowhere near what we would like to see. Even after the addition of the high-volatility hedges, we face a crushing loss of nearly half of the portfolio's value. As we learned all the way back in Chapter 2, the correlation principle is by no means perfect. Sometimes it works beautifully (think 2000–2002), sometimes not so well.

So, to reduce our losses when the principle of correlation fails, we fall back on the principle of compromise. We add some low-volatility hedges, to reduce overall portfolio volatility at the cost of some returns. This is what we have done in the last row of the table. By adding the finishing touch—bonds—to our gourmet portfolio, we are finally able to turn the huge market losses of 2000–2002 into a modest gain (column 4). We are also able to maintain the difference in returns between the 1990s and the 2000s at 0.4 percentage points (column 2 vs. column 3). And finally, we get our losses in 2007–9 down from nearly one-half to less than one-third (30.3 percent). This is still a deep loss, but it is a lot better than where we started with the 100 percent large cap portfolio. The loss could be reduced further by adding more bonds. The conservative portfolio, with a 60 percent allocation to bonds, limits the loss to 21.9 percent.

All this volatility reduction does come at a cost to returns—as the principle of compromise requires. Overall annualized 1990–2013 returns drop from 9.3 percent to 8.0 percent with the addition of the low-volatility hedges (column 1). Still, these returns are not far off the 8.5 percent returns produced by the portfolio consisting of large caps only (first row of table). For those keeping count of the dollars, our final portfolio, including low-volatility bonds along with high-volatility hedges, return boosters, and large caps, would grow from $100,000 in 1990 to $632,022 by the end of 2013. This is more than a sixfold increase—not bad for a twenty-four-year period, including the so-called Lost Decade.

The Holistic Approach to Investing

We took the advanced moderate portfolio apart and put it back together again so you could see how beautifully all the pieces fit together. The return boosters significantly increased returns without greatly increasing volatility. They provide modest diversification benefits that actually reduced volatility in some conditions. The high-volatility hedges turned the 2000–2002 bear market into a market correction. Even more importantly, they reduced long-term volatility by raising returns during the secular bear market of 2000–2009 to a level nearly equal to the portfolio's returns during the 1990s bull market. Finally, the low-volatility hedges reduced short-term volatility, completely eliminating the 2000–2002 downturn and helping to lower the pain threshold in 2007–9. And while they cost us some in long-run returns, by combining them with the return boosters and high-volatility hedges, we still wound up with returns not that much lower than those offered by large cap stocks alone.

So take one last good, long look at Table 9.5. My hope is that, having now seen how the various pieces of a well-diversified portfolio can add up to good returns with low volatility, you will never be tempted to remove, ditch, or otherwise replace any of the pieces composing your buy-and-hold portfolio. Yes, sometimes some of the pieces will reduce your returns or increase your losses. During bull markets, gold prices may go down instead of up. *Don't worry, be happy.* Gold and PME funds are *supposed* to go down when your stock investments are going up. This means they are doing their job and stand a very good chance of going up when the stock market goes down. *Don't sell them.* You will need them when the market tops out and the bear returns (and return he always will).

During bear markets, your large caps and return boosters will, temporarily, cost you gobs of money. *Don't sell them.* You need them to generate good, inflation-beating returns so you can recover your losses quickly and go on to new highs when the bull returns (and return he, too, always will).

Like a great gourmet meal, a well-diversified portfolio is a beautiful meshing of various ingredients to form a whole that is greater than the sum of its parts. You should always view your gourmet portfolio holistically. Each ingredient is integral to the whole. As long as you keep all the ingredients together, your portfolio should do a great job of protecting you from the retirement risk.

More Stress Tests

Stress Test 2

In Chapter 8, we put the basic portfolios to a diabolical test. We imagined a sixty-five-year-old, Bob, who had the financial misfortune to retire on January 1, 1973. To make matters worse, we imagined that Bob's portfolio would need to sustain him throughout a very long, forty-one-year retirement—all the way to December 31, 2013.

By starting the test on January 1, 1973, we ensured it would be as tough as possible, because it included the 1973–74 bear market *and* the ten-year period of high inflation right at the outset. A test that had started in, say, 1974 would have been easier because Bob would have missed the first year of the 1973–74 bear market. A test that began *after* 1974 but before 1982 would have been easier still because it would have entirely dodged not only the 1973–74 bear market but also the early years of the high-inflation period. And finally, any test that began after 1982 and before the late 1990s would have been a cakewalk for our portfolios, because 1982 marked the beginning of the great bull market of the 1980s to 1990s and a period of tame inflation. We picked January 1, 1973 as Bob's retirement date because this date put our portfolios up to the toughest test we could devise.

The toughest, at least, up until the late 1990s. But what if we now imagine someone—let's call her Mary—who retired on January 1, 2000. This is only three months before the 2000–2002 bear market—a downturn that was even deeper than the 1973–74 bear market. Furthermore, 2000–2002 was followed by a second, and worse yet, downturn—the 2007–9 financial crisis. True, Bob lived through these two bear markets. But in his case, he had the entire 1983–99 bull market to recover from the financial effects of the 1970s and early 1980s. By the time Bob turned ninety-one, in 1999, most of the portfolios we tested for him had not only recovered but soared to new heights (the basic conservative portfolio was, you will recall, an exception).

Mary, conversely, would be starting her retirement right at the beginning of the Lost Decade. Unlike Bob, she would have no opportunity to build up a cushion in her nest egg. True, she would not have to go through a period of high inflation. But she would experience greater volatility than Bob right when volatility poses the greatest threat to a retiree's finances: at the beginning of retirement. She would be facing, in rapid succession, two of the worst bear markets in modern history right out of the gate. If Bob's retirement posed the most diabolical test of our portfolios between the early 1970s and the late 1990s, then Mary's presents one of the most daunting tests the market has devised since 1999.

This time, we will put the advanced portfolios to the test. Once again, we will assume that our retiree—Mary—will begin her retirement with a $100,000 nest egg. She will withdraw $4,000 (corresponding to a 4 percent withdrawal rate) from her portfolio to support herself in the first year of retirement, and after that she will increase her withdrawals by 3 percent per year to account for inflation. (Actual inflation between 2000 and 2013 averaged only 2.4 percent, but by using a 3 percent rate, we will make Mary's test tougher.) Like Bob, she will follow a strict buy-and-hold investment strategy and make no changes to her investments other than to rebalance her portfolio at the beginning of each year.

Test 2 results. Figure 9.4 shows the amount of money that would remain in each of the advanced portfolios, and a 100 percent S&P 500 portfolio, as of December 31, 2013. Every one of the advanced portfolios grows in value from the $100,000 starting point. The conservative portfolio grows by over 42 percent, to $142,405, whereas the aggressive portfolio grows more than 81 percent, to $181,609. With the 3 percent inflation adjustments, Mary's original $4,000 withdrawal would need to grow to $6,050 in 2014 to continue to support Mary's lifestyle. A $6,050 withdrawal corresponds to 4.25 percent of the $142,405 remaining in the conservative portfolio, 3.72 percent of the $162,659 in the moderate portfolio, and only 3.33 percent of the $181,609 in the aggressive portfolio. In other words, with the exception of the conservative portfolio, the required withdrawal rates have actually declined below the original 4 percent rate. This indicates that the moderate and aggressive portfolios have grown safer with the passage of time. When a portfolio can stand up to two major bear markets in the space of 14 years, support a person in retirement, and still grow significantly, it has passed a very challenging stress test with flying colors.

The 100 percent S&P 500 portfolio, conversely, has not done so well. Had Mary chosen this portfolio, she would have lost more than half of her initial nest egg only fourteen years into her retirement. Because we don't know the future, we can't say how much longer this portfolio would last. However, the $6,050 amount Mary must withdraw in 2014 is equal to 14.4 percent of the portfolio's $42,129 remaining value. Mary's withdrawal rate has more than tripled from the original 4 percent—a very bad sign. Unless, going forward, the S&P 500 yields the kind of double-digit returns it produced back in the 1990s, this portfolio is on a path to bankruptcy.

Still, it could take a while to completely run out of money. Even if the stock market yields zero returns, the remaining $42,129 would support Mary for close to five and a half years. It's possible she could make it to the end of her life without running out of money.

But imagine yourself in Mary's position. Would you sleep better having a nest egg that has grown by 42 percent (the conservative portfolio), 62 percent (the moderate portfolio), or 81 percent (the aggressive portfolio) since you retired, or one that has lost nearly 58 percent of its value (the 100 percent S&P 500 portfolio)?

The last fourteen years demonstrate just how volatile the stock market can be, and how dangerous that volatility is to a person unlucky enough to retire at the wrong time. But the answer is not to flee stocks entirely and invest in bonds. This merely substitutes one component of the retirement risk (too much volatility) for the other (not enough returns). The answer is to buy a set of investments similar to the advanced portfolios and hold them through thick and thin.

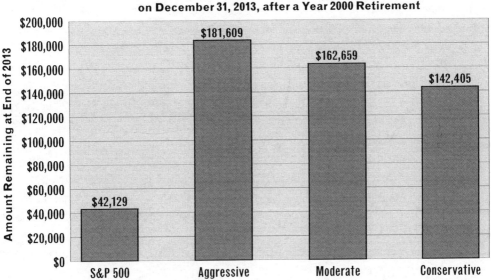

Figure 9.4. Value of the Advanced Portfolios on December 31, 2013, after a Year 2000 Retirement

Source: Developed by the author using data from www.morningstar.com. Gold returns based on London Gold Market Fixing prices.

Stress Test 3

The preceding stress test was among the most diabolical the market has come up with, at least since the early 1970s. Our advanced portfolios passed this test with flying colors. But we did have a bit of an advantage going into this test: we knew beforehand that black belt investing was particularly effective during the 2000–2002 bear market. In fact, you'll recall that two of the advanced portfolios (the conservative and moderate portfolios) produced *positive* returns during 2000–2002 (recall Figure 9.2). It is probable that the correlation principle worked as well as it did in 2000–2002 because this bear market was, in part, a response to a stock bubble. The dot-com mania of the late 1990s inflated the prices of some stocks beyond all reason, while leaving other stocks (including, for example, gold mining stocks) in the dust. When the bubble burst, our hedges, and even some of our return boosters, escaped much of the damage because they hadn't participated in the bubble. Well-diversified portfolios should be especially effective at reducing losses during the bear markets that follow stock bubbles, because the high degree of diversification at the heart of these portfolios keeps at least some of the portfolios' investments from inflating during the bubbles' expansionary stages. This is good news indeed for investors using well-diversified portfolios, because there have been many stock market bubbles in the past, and there are sure to be many in the future. In his book *A Random Walk Down Wall Street*, Burton Malkiel gives an excellent, and very entertaining, history of stock market bubbles. As just a few examples, back in the early 1960s, the market went through the tronics boom, when a mania developed for new issue stocks that included "tronics" (as in electronics) somewhere in their name—regardless of whether they had anything to do with electronics. (You can't make this stuff up.) In the mid- to late 1960s, the rage was all for conglomerates formed through mergers. In the early 1970s, a bubble formed around the "Nifty Fifty," a group of large cap growth stocks including IBM, Xerox, and McDonald's. In the 1980s, it was biotechnology stocks. And on, and on, and on. If we can count on one thing, it's that the stock market will keep right on blowing bubbles as long as people dream of striking it rich and forget (or never learn) history.

All of these earlier bubbles, like the much bigger, badder dot-com bubble, have one thing in common: they affected some asset classes while leaving others relatively untouched. As long as this selectivity remains a characteristic of future stock bubbles, a well-diversified portfolio is likely to include investments that escape the damage when the bubbles burst—just as our advanced portfolios avoided most of the fallout from the dot-com bubble.

The 2007–9 financial crisis was quite a different story. Although this bear market originated in a bubble, this time the bubble formed outside the stock market (in the housing sector). When this bubble burst, it brought down the *entire* stock market with it, not just some stocks or sectors. Virtually all asset classes dropped through the floor, with the exception of the safest of safe havens (gold and Treasuries). It is fortunate for us that financial crises like 2007–9 are rarer events than stock market bubbles, because the principle of correlation is less effective in dealing with such events. Black belt investing can soften the blow of such a widespread debacle, but it can't eliminate the damage.

We know from the preceding stress test that all our portfolios met the challenge of a retirement beginning at the start of the 2000–2002 bear market. By the time 2007 rolled around, all three advanced portfolios had built up a very sizeable cushion against what was the much more difficult challenge of 2007–9. For example, the moderate portfolio had grown in value by nearly 50 percent, to $148,876, by the beginning of 2007. What would have happened, though, if Mary had retired in 2007 rather than 2000, leaving her no time to grow her nest egg beyond the original $100,000?

To make this third and last test as difficult as possible, we'll suppose Mary retired on October 9, 2007—the day the market reached its top. We'll make all the usual assumptions: a 4 percent withdrawal rate, increased by 3 percent per year, and annual rebalancing. How much would she have left on December 31, 2013?

Test 3 results. The answer is given in Figure 9.5. Even a quick comparison of these results with the results from Stress Test 2 (Figure 9.4) makes one thing clear: an October 2007 retirement does indeed make for a more difficult test. Unlike the case in Stress Test 2, none of our advanced portfolios have fully recovered by December 31, 2013.

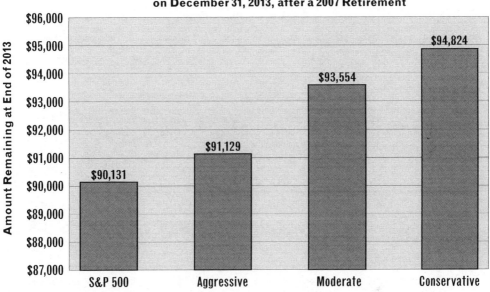

Figure 9.5. Value of the Advanced Portfolios on December 31, 2013, after a 2007 Retirement

Source: Developed by the author using data from www.morningstar.com.
Gold returns based on London Gold Market Fixing prices.

This should not be surprising. As we learned in the last chapter, it would have taken the basic portfolios around one and a half years to recover from the 2007–9 bear market, and this recovery time assumes no withdrawals for living expenses. With a 4 percent withdrawal rate, the recovery time lengthens. Some of our portfolios actually do manage to recover by early 2011—only to be pulled back under by the market correction that began in April of that year.

Table 9.6 shows some key data describing where the portfolios stand at the beginning of 2014. Column 1 of the table shows Mary's required withdrawal for 2014. Her original $4,000 annual withdrawal, representing 4 percent of the $100,000 starting value, has grown to $4,919 by January 2014 owing to the 3 percent annual inflation adjustment. Column 2 shows the amount of money remaining in each portfolio on January 1, 2014. Column 3 calculates the withdrawal rate for 2014 by dividing the required withdrawal (from the first column) by the amount of money remaining in the portfolio (second column).

Table 9.6. Portfolio Size, Withdrawals, and Withdrawal Rates
for Mary's Portfolios at the Beginning of 2014

Portfolio	COLUMN 1 Required Withdrawal in 2014 (Dollars)	COLUMN 2 Amount Remaining in Portfolio at the Beginning of 2014 (Dollars)	COLUMN 3 Withdrawal Rate at the Beginning of 2014 (Percent)
Conservative	$4,919	$94,824	5.19%
Moderate	$4,919	$93,554	5.26%
Aggressive	$4,919	$91,129	5.40%
100% S&P 500	$4,919	$90,131	5.46%

Sources: Developed by the author using data from www.morningstar.com.
Gold returns based on London Gold Market Fixing prices.

As you can see, all of the withdrawal rates in column 3 are larger than the 4 percent withdrawal rate she used at the beginning of her retirement. Because 4 percent is considered to be the *maximum* safe withdrawal rate based on historical analysis, should we not conclude that all of the portfolios are headed for disaster? Not at all. The 4 percent value represents the maximum withdrawal rate you should use *for the first year* of your retirement. It is understood that *after* the first year, the withdrawal rate will fluctuate, owing both to the inflation adjustment and to your investments' gains and losses. When you lose money, especially early in retirement, your withdrawal rate may well increase above 4 percent. If, like Mary, you retire at the beginning of a major bear market, your withdrawal rate will most definitely skyrocket well above 4 percent. But this possibility has already been taken into account in the historical backtests that first established 4 percent as a safe *initial* withdrawal rate. These backtests will be discussed in more detail in Chapter 11, but briefly, they are based on historical stock and bond market return data going all the way back to 1926. The backtests indicate that as long as you *start* with a 4 percent withdrawal rate, the odds are good (though not *certain*) that you will beat the retirement risk even if you encounter a major bear market at the beginning of your retirement that causes your withdrawal rate to rise above 4 percent. The portfolios in Table 9.6 encountered a major bear market right at the beginning of Mary's retirement, followed only a few years later by a market correction. It is to be expected that the withdrawal rates for her portfolios would exceed 4 percent following these two events. The key question we need to address is not whether the withdrawal rates as of January 2013 exceed the original 4 percent rate but rather whether those withdrawal rates have become too large to allow Mary's portfolios to survive the remainder of her retirement.

Groundhog Day. But how can we answer this question, given that we don't know what the future will bring? We cannot, in fact, arrive at a definitive answer. The best we can do is look to the past as a *rough, imperfect* guide.

Perhaps you've seen the movie *Groundhog Day*. In that film, the protagonist, a Pittsburgh weatherman (played by Bill Murray) woke up each new morning only to find that it *wasn't* a new morning. Instead, he was trapped in an endless repetition of the same day (Groundhog Day), with the same events and outcomes. Let's imagine that Mary somehow gets trapped in a similar situation. December 31, 2013 is followed by January 1, *1990*, and the next twenty-four years of market returns are an exact repetition of the returns produced in 1990 through 2013. I've done this backtest, and all three of the advanced portfolios would survive this test (or retest), despite that they begin 1990 with the reduced amounts and higher withdrawal rates shown in Table 9.6.

Let's imagine that Mary, like Bob from the last chapter, faces a forty-one-year retirement. Adding the twenty-four years of repetition (from 1990 through 2013) to the original six and a quarter years of her retirement (from October 2007 through 2013) yields thirty and a quarter years—well short of forty-one years. So, we will have to send her back to January 1, 1990 a second time, *à la Groundhog Day*—this time using the withdrawal rates and portfolio amounts at the end of her *second* December 31, 2013. All three advanced portfolios (as well as the 100 percent S&P 500 portfolio) survive a second run from 1990 through 2000—forty-one years total, with an additional quarter year for good measure.

To survive this test, all of the advanced portfolios had to make it through the 2007–9 financial crisis not once, but *twice*. They also passed through the 2000–2002 bear market once. However, by beginning Mary's *Groundhog Day* experience in 1990, we did give her a significant advantage. She had the decade-long 1990s bull market to recover from the financial crisis, before she had to face the Lost Decade of the 2000s (including a replay of the crisis).

Groundhog Day 2. They didn't make a sequel to the movie *Groundhog Day*. Perhaps a sequel of a movie about endless repetition would have been too repetitive? But we are going to make our own little sequel to Mary's test. This time, instead of having Mary's portfolios repeat 1990–2013 and then 1990–2000, let's imagine that they must instead repeat 2008 through 2013 ad infinitum. In other words, fewer than five years after the market bottomed in March 2009, Mary's portfolios must repeat the worst of the financial crisis (the portion stretching from January 1, 2008, through March 9, 2009). In this sequel to Mary's *Groundhog Day*, the portfolios do not have the benefit of a long bull market before they must face the financial crisis again. After putting the portfolios through 2008–13 a second time, they will continue to repeat 2008–13 until they are bankrupted.

The sequel to *Groundhog Day* does indeed prove to be a much tougher test than the original. The 100 percent S&P 500 portfolio survives two repeats of the financial crisis, but fails during the third repeat, for a total of twenty-three years. The three advanced portfolios survive *three* repeats of 2008. The aggressive (80/20) portfolio survives for twenty-five years, while both the moderate and conservative portfolios last twenty-six years.

The *Groundhog Day* test and its sequel should not be considered realistic. However, the sequel in particular does provide a *high-stress* test of the portfolios' survivability. Three replays of the financial crisis, fewer than five years after the end of the original version of the crisis, represents a very high level of volatility. This high volatility makes for a robust if unrealistic test of the portfolios. And although the advanced portfolios do not quite make it to thirty (let alone forty) years, their ability to withstand a total of *four* financial crises (the original and three repetitions) is nonetheless impressive.

The sweet spot? On the basis of the test results, the conservative portfolio appears to be the most likely to survive a period of high volatility, followed by the moderate portfolio, and then the aggressive portfolio. This is the exact opposite of the results of the stress test we gave the basic portfolios in the last chapter. In that test, the aggressive portfolio did the best, followed by the moderate portfolio, and then the conservative portfolio.

The differences in the results between these two tests are easy to explain. Bob's retirement was primarily a test of the ability of the portfolios to generate returns sufficient to keep up with the high inflation of the 1970s and early 1980s. Not surprisingly, the conservative portfolio, with its heavy allocation to bonds, had the most difficulty generating the inflation-beating returns needed to pass this test. A very conservative 20/80 portfolio was also tested, as you may recall, and this portfolio performed even worse than the conservative portfolio, failing to survive the full length of Bob's forty-one-year retirement.

Mary's sequel to the *Groundhog Day* retirement, conversely, was primarily a test of the portfolios' ability to weather extreme volatility encompassing the entire stock market. The aggressive portfolio, with its heavy allocation to stocks, had the most difficulty on this test—although the differences in the performance of the three portfolios were much less pronounced than the differences that emerged from Bob's test. The performance differences between our three advanced portfolios (which survived twenty-five to twenty-six years) and the 100 percent S&P 500 portfolio (which survived only twenty-three years) were more significant, indicating that all-stock portfolios do indeed exhibit elevated risk during periods of extreme market volatility.

So let's sum up. Well-diversified portfolios that have an allocation to low-volatility bonds somewhere in the 20 percent to 60 percent range performed relatively well in just about all of our tests. But once we go beyond this range to either extreme —less than 20 percent or more than 60 percent bonds—we start to run into more significant levels of risk. Is a bond allocation falling somewhere between 20 and 60 percent in a "sweet spot" that allows us to avoid too much negative volatility without giving up too much in returns? Perhaps. Let's make a note of this question. We will return to it in Part IV, when we consider the all-important issue of how to divvy up your own personal portfolio between stocks and bonds.

Conclusions

In this and the last chapter, we created some experimental gourmet portfolios out of the ingredients we learned about in Part II: large cap stocks, high-volatility hedges, low-volatility hedges, and return boosters. We then put our gourmet creations to the worst tests the markets have thrown at investors over the last four decades. We put our three basic portfolios to the test of a retirement beginning in 1973. All three portfolios survived a rocky forty-one years that included the 1973–74 bear market, the 2000–2002 bear market, and the 2007–9 financial crisis, as well as the stagflation of 1973–82. We put our three advanced portfolios to the test of a 2000 retirement. All three portfolios not only recovered from the 2000–2002 and 2007–9 bear markets, but grew substantially by 2013 — despite the low stock market returns of the so-called Lost Decade. Finally, we put the three advanced portfolios to the test of an October 9, 2007, retirement — right at the beginning of the 2007–9 financial crisis. Although the jury is still out on this third test, all three portfolios survived the lengthy forty-one-year *Groundhog Day* version of this test, and even managed to last for at least twenty-five years during the extremely volatile *Groundhog Day* sequel test.

What can we conclude? Buying and holding well-diversified portfolios has withstood the test of recent history: the Lost Decade, the bursting bubbles, the recessions, the oil embargoes, 9/11, the financial crisis, stagflation—all of it. We cannot be certain that a well-diversified, buy-and-hold portfolio will survive anything and everything the *future* might have in store. When it comes to the future, there can be no certainty. It is entirely possible that the financial markets will think up new tests in the next forty years that will be worse than anything and everything we've encountered in the last forty. But, reflecting on our stress tests, we *can* be certain that our well-diversified portfolios have demonstrated great resilience in the face of a wide variety of market misbehaviors. My hope is that you can take confidence in this demonstration of resiliency — and that you are now ready to commit to a buy-and-hold investment strategy using your *own* well-diversified portfolio.

If so, read on. In the last two parts of this book, you will learn how to create and maintain the gourmet portfolio that best suits your own unique tastes. After some preliminaries described in Chapter 10, Chapter 11 will help you to develop an asset allocation for your portfolio, taking into account your means, the asset classes available to you, and your tolerance for volatility. In Chapter 12, we will cover an alternative approach to allocating the bond portion of your portfolio that can virtually eliminate the retirement risk—at least for a while. In Chapter 13, you will learn how to choose the specific investments—the mutual funds or exchange traded funds—to buy and hold. Chapters 14 and 15 will cover various techniques that you can use to improve your portfolio's performance, including dollar cost averaging, tax loss harvesting, and rebalancing. Chapter 16 will explain why buy and hold is a better strategy for the amateur investor than market timing, performance chasing, and all other strategies that require frequent trading. Chapter 17 discusses the emotional aspects of investing and explains how to stick with a buy-and-hold strategy through thick and thin. And finally, in Chapters 18 and 19, you will learn how to take your portfolio's temperature, to distinguish situations that pose a real danger to your financial health from those that may merely seem scary. These last two chapters will also provide a hierarchy of actions you can take in the former case, up to and including selling (or buying) stocks.

(And don't forget about the secret sauce first mentioned in Chapter 4. In one of these upcoming chapters, the secret will finally be revealed.)

HOW TO BUY

CHAPTER 10

SAVING FOR RETIREMENT, CALCULATING A WITHDRAWAL RATE, AND OTHER PRELIMINARIES

M y hope is that in Parts I through III, I've convinced you *why* combining the principles of correlation and compromise is an excellent way to build a portfolio that reduces the risk of too much volatility without significantly increasing the risk of not enough returns. It is time now to shift gears and turn from the question of "why diversify?" to the question of "how?" How can *you* create an asset allocation plan that meets your unique needs and fits your circumstances? How should you go about choosing the specific mutual funds or exchange traded funds (ETFs) you will need to implement this plan? How should you maintain your portfolio of funds/ETFs so that it will grow at a decent pace until you are ready to retire, and then provide a secure, comfortable retirement for the remainder of your life? These are the questions that we address in Part IV. And there is good news: as we seek an answer to these questions, we will discover other solutions to the retirement risk. We will eventually combine these solutions with the principles of correlation and compromise to form a powerful, *defense in depth* approach to protecting your nest egg.

In the next chapter, you will learn how to apply the basic four-step process to asset allocation that we first introduced in Chapter 8. But before we can begin this process, there are a few preliminary steps you need to complete. These preliminary steps include making sure that you and your family have adequate insurance, establishing an emergency fund, developing and implementing a retirement savings plan (if you are still working), and calculating your withdrawal rate (if you are retired or close to retirement). To understand why these preliminary steps are important, we need to briefly revisit the retirement risk.

Retirement Risk Redux

Up until this point, we have focused relentlessly on two sides, or components, of the retirement risk: too much volatility and not enough returns to outpace inflation. This formulation has served us well thus far, but it is a bit of an oversimplification. A more accurate statement is that these two components represent the *investment-related* risks to your retirement. There are three other noninvestment risks that are just as important. In the preceding chapters, we were focused exclusively on investing, so we had no need to consider the noninvestment aspects of the retirement risk. But we have reached the point where, at the risk of complicating matters, we must come to a full and complete understanding of the retirement risk in all its glory.

To fully comprehend *all* aspects of the retirement risk, both investment and noninvestment related, it will help to visualize your retirement account(s) as a kitchen sink. But instead of water, this sink flows with money. Once you retire, the sink will (we hope) be partially full with the money you have saved during your working life. The sink has a faucet, and new money is pouring in from this faucet. The faucet represents the market, and the money coming out of it is the earnings — both capital gains and dividends — on your investments. Depending on how the market is doing, sometimes the money from the faucet floods into the sink, and sometimes it just drips. And unfortunately, during bear markets, the faucet reverses flow and sucks money out of the sink.

This isn't the only way money in the sink gets lost. The basin of the sink is completely open, making it a tempting target for burglars. Remember inflation, the night thief? Every night while you're asleep, he shows up and helps himself to a bit of the money in your sink.

Now, as long as the faucet is flowing nice, strong, and steady, the sink will fill up with money more quickly than the night thief can empty it, and you will have nothing to worry about. But clearly you face two risks of loss. First is the risk that the faucet will reverse itself and suck up money from the sink. Depending on the amount of money lost, as well as the frequency and timing of the faucet reversals, the result can be bankruptcy. The magnitude, frequency, and timing of faucet reversals together constitute the risk posed by negative market volatility.

And second, the night thief may steal money from the sink faster than the faucet can replenish it. This is the risk of not earning enough returns to keep pace with inflation.

Of course, by now, you are thoroughly familiar with these two risks. But as you know, kitchen sinks come not only with a basin and a faucet but also with a drain. When you are working, you will (or at least you *should*) keep a stopper in the drain. This prevents the drain from posing any risks to you. But once you retire, you will need to occasionally use some of the money in the sink to meet your living expenses. You do this by removing the stopper and letting some of the money drain out of the basin. Thus, while the faucet represents the market in our sink metaphor, the drain is your living expenses. (More precisely, it is that portion of your expenses not covered by Social Security and other non–investment income sources like pensions.)

So far, we have focused on the risks posed by the two-way faucet (negative market volatility) and the open basin (such a tempting target for inflation). But the drain also comes with its own three uncertainties, or risks. First, if you drain money out of the basin too quickly, the faucet (market) will not be able to replenish the money fast enough to keep pace with the drain. Suppose, for example, that you are withdrawing 10 percent of the money in the basin each year but the market is replenishing the money at a rate of only 5 percent annually. If this situation is allowed to continue, then eventually the basin will be completely emptied—and you will be bankrupt. Conversely, if you withdraw only 5 percent of the money per year and the market (faucet) returns 10 percent per year, the money in the basin will grow, and you will never go broke (assuming that the night thief keeps his pilfering to less than 5 percent per year).

The rate at which you drain money out of the basin to meet your everyday expenses (for groceries, utilities, and the like) is referred to as the *withdrawal rate*. We have touched on the concept of the withdrawal rate in prior chapters. You may recall that Joe Bondsman, as well as Bob and Mary from Chapters 8 and 9, all began their retirements using a 4 percent withdrawal rate. We will have much more to say about the withdrawal rate later in this chapter, and throughout the remainder of the book. But for now, let's simply note that the higher your withdrawal rate, the greater is the risk of outliving your money.

The second drain-related risk is the uncertainty posed by *time*. You don't know for how long you'll need to keep pulling out the stopper and draining money from the sink. You may need to drain money for only a short while, or you may need to keep draining money much longer than most people. In the latter case, you run the risk of eventually emptying the basin. We touched on this risk, *longevity risk*, in Chapter 8. You may recall that Bob's financially challenging retirement was made all the more difficult by its length. The longer you live, the greater the chances are that you will run out of money before you die. It stands to reason that if you keep opening and closing the drain for forty years, you're more likely to empty the basin than if you do this for only ten years. The extent of the longevity risk you face depends mainly on your health, not your investment portfolio. But because a long life increases the odds of running out of money, the longevity risk is properly seen as a fourth, non-investment-related component of the retirement risk. Short of eating more junk food and exercising less—which I don't recommend—longevity risk is not easy to mitigate.[74] But as advances in medicine continue to increase life expectancies, you should build your retirement plan on the assumption that you will live a long life—unless, of course, the prospect of being a ninety-nine-year-old greeter at Wal-Mart appeals to you. This is why we gave Bob such a long life—to make sure that our portfolios could stand up to the added stress of a very long retirement. Buying and holding a durable, well-diversified portfolio is one of the best ways to guard against longevity risk. Another way to reduce this risk is by delaying claiming your Social Security benefits. We will discuss this option in more detail later.

In addition to the withdrawal rate and longevity risk, the drain at the bottom of your sink comes with a third uncertainty or risk. You do not know, in advance, how much money you will need to drain out of the sink each time you pull the stopper. You can, of course, come up with a good estimate of the amount of money you need to meet your everyday expenses—things like food, electricity to heat and cool your home, gasoline to run your car, and so on. As we will see, it is these everyday *expected* expenses that you will use to estimate your withdrawal rate. But there is always the possibility that you will encounter *unexpected* expenses. Being unexpected, these expenses cannot be included in the withdrawal rate you plan to use in retirement. Therefore they constitute a risk factor that is separate and distinct from the risk posed by a too-high withdrawal rate. Especially when these expenses are large, they may cause you to empty your sink. Maybe your adult children will move back in with you to save money (their money, not yours). Maybe your idiot neighbor down the street will sue you for everything you own. Maybe the house that nice real estate agent sold you will turn out to be a money pit. Yes, you can and should make a budget for your retirement. But life is what happens while you're planning for it.

Fortunately, unlike longevity risk, there are two simple steps you can take to reduce (though not eliminate) the risk posed by unexpected expenses. These steps are (1) buy insurance and (2) create an emergency or rainy day fund, separate from your retirement savings. As these two steps may require you to set aside some money that might otherwise have gone into your retirement account(s), they should be completed before you begin the four-step asset allocation process. Let's briefly consider these preliminary steps.

Insurance

Many types of large, unexpected, and potentially catastrophic expenses can be addressed in advance through insurance. In addition to the more common insurance products that you may (or should) already have, such as medical insurance, life insurance, automobile insurance, and homeowner's insurance, there are some other less common types that you can use to significantly reduce the risks posed by unexpected expenses. For example, you should consider purchasing liability or umbrella insurance to protect your nest egg from lawsuits and claims that may not be covered, or that may exceed the coverage limits of your other policies. If you are still working and do not receive disability insurance through your employer, you should consider purchasing your own policy.

Most importantly, you should purchase a good long-term care policy. Health care expenses are one of the biggest unknown risks you will face in retirement. At some point, you and/or your significant other stand a good chance of needing either part-time or full-time care. Depending on your needs, the cost of this care can easily force you to draw down the principal in your retirement accounts. To make up for the losses you might need to chase higher returns by increasing your allocation to stocks—at the expense of greater volatility and added stress that could in turn further damage your health. Long-term care insurance can help you to avoid these problems. The time to buy long-term care insurance, if you don't already have it, is now. The younger you are when you buy your policy, the lower your premiums will be. Be sure to look for a policy that includes coverage for in-home care, as you will probably want to remain in your home for as long as possible should you need help.

A detailed discussion of insurance is beyond the scope of this book, but there is one bit of advice too important not to mention. Especially when it comes to insurance products such as life and long-term care, which may not pay off for many years, be sure to buy from well-established, sound insurance companies. You want to have some confidence that your insurer(s) will still be in business when you need them. Look for a company with an excellent credit rating—and that might be considered "too big to fail."[75] A lesson we should take from the 2007–9 financial crisis is that we can't trust even major, well-established insurance companies from engaging in reckless behavior that puts their own survival—and your insurance policies—at risk. But if, like AIG, your insurance company is considered too big to fail, there is at least a chance that the government might step in to save the company from itself. When looking for an insurer, bigger is better.

Emergency Fund

In addition to insuring yourself and your family, you should also establish an emergency or rainy day fund to cover unexpected contingencies, like the loss of your job or, if you are retired, a large medical bill. A long-standing rule of thumb suggests that you should save three to six months' worth of your salary in your emergency fund. While this may be a good starting point, it is important to take your own employment situation into account when deciding on how large an emergency fund you need. While three to six months' of salary may suffice for someone with a stable job, such as a federal government employee, a tenured teacher, or a physician with an established practice, for many others, it may not be enough. The recent deep recession and still-ongoing recovery have highlighted the difficulty of finding a job during a weak economy. The government was forced to extend unemployment benefits, more than once, for the many who found themselves unemployed for *years* rather than months. Given this recent experience, most people would probably be better served by an emergency fund capable of covering their expenses for a year. And if your current employment situation is particularly uncertain, you may even want to save one and a half to two years' worth of salary in your emergency fund.

The one thing you do *not* want is to be forced to dip into your retirement accounts in the event of a layoff or other emergency. This is especially true given that layoffs often occur at the same time the stock market takes a dive—and you shouldn't be raiding your retirement accounts when they've already been weakened by stock market losses. Rather, you should treat your retirement savings as off limits for all purposes other than funding your retirement. By building up a sizeable emergency fund, you will not only be protecting yourself and your family from the risk posed by a lengthy period of unemployment; you will also be protecting your retirement nest egg. Alternatively, relying on an inadequate emergency fund may someday force you to rob your future to meet present expenses.

Because the money in your emergency fund has to be there when you need it, you should put this money in cash investments that will protect the principal and that will give you full access to your funds at all times. An FDIC-insured bank savings account is a safe place for an emergency fund. You may be able to earn a slightly higher interest rate by opening an Internet savings account instead of an account at your local brick-and-mortar bank; just be sure that the account is FDIC insured. You can do an Internet search on "online savings rates" to find the Internet banks offering the highest rates.

FDIC-insured CDs can also be a good option for emergency savings. It is true that you may have to pay a penalty to withdraw money from a CD before it matures; however, the penalty you would face during an emergency may be relatively small (e.g., three or six months' worth of interest) and could be more than offset by the relatively high interest rate you would typically earn from a CD.[76]

A money market fund or account is a possible alternative to a savings account or CD, but keep in mind that it is possible (albeit unlikely) to lose principal with a money market.

You should treat your emergency fund as being entirely separate from your retirement portfolio. This means that when calculating your withdrawal rate, you should not include the money in your emergency fund in the calculation. An emergency fund is for *unexpected* expenses. Your estimated withdrawal rate should equal your *expected* living expenses in retirement divided by the money you have saved to meet those *expected* expenses.

Establishing a Safe Withdrawal Rate

This takes us to the last preliminary (I promise) before we can begin the four-step asset allocation process. Buying insurance and saving money in an emergency fund can help reduce one key noninvestment aspect of the retirement risk: the risk that you might encounter large unexpected expenses. But as we saw earlier, expected expenses—the kinds of everyday expenses that you can anticipate and should include in a budget—also pose a bankruptcy risk if they are too high. It is these expected expenses that you will use to estimate your withdrawal rate.

As we saw earlier in our kitchen sink analogy, if your withdrawal rate—the rate at which you drain money from the basin—exceeds the rate at which the faucet (i.e., the market) replenishes the money in the basin, then you will face a significant risk of outliving your money. But fortunately, unlike the other investment- and non-investment-related components of the retirement risk, reducing the risk posed by the withdrawal rate is straightforward. If a high withdrawal rate presents a threat of bankruptcy, then simply by lowering your withdrawal rate, you can reduce this threat. In fact, your withdrawal rate represents, not only a risk, but a tremendous risk-reducing opportunity. You can mitigate *all* aspects of the retirement risk, both investment and noninvestment related, by establishing a low, safe withdrawal rate. Reducing your withdrawal rate is one of the most important risk-reduction measures you have at your disposal, quite apart from the principles of correlation and compromise.

Although establishing a safe withdrawal rate for retirement might seem like a step that applies only to people in or near retirement, as we shall see, by far the most effective way to accomplish this goal is by implementing a good retirement savings plan when you are young. If you begin saving for retirement in your twenties, the power of compounding will have decades to work to your advantage. If you put off saving for retirement until later in life, you run the significant risk that you will either have to postpone retirement, accept a lower standard of living, or use a withdrawal rate that significantly increases your chances of bankruptcy. In this section, we address the withdrawal rate issue from the perspective of both young savers and retirees.

The Relationship between Your Withdrawal Rate and the Retirement Risk

As we have seen, the investment-related components of the retirement risk are typically at odds with one another. If you seek to reduce the risk posed by too much market volatility the obvious way, by increasing your allocation to low-volatility investments like bonds, then you will wind up increasing the risk of not earning enough returns to outpace inflation. The principle of correlation is the only way out of this dilemma. And as we have seen, this principle cannot be relied on to work as well as you would like under all circumstances. For this reason, we must also employ the more reliable principle of compromise and accept the risk posed by lower returns to reduce the risk presented by market volatility.

The beauty of reducing risk by lowering your withdrawal rate is that it requires no such compromise. When you reduce your withdrawal rate, you reduce the risks posed by market volatility, low returns, longevity, and large unexpected expenses. It is true that, unlike the correlation principle, lowering your withdrawal rate will not actually reduce the volatility in returns earned by your portfolio. However, it will reduce the total deductions (market losses plus withdrawals) you experience during bear markets. More importantly, it will reduce the possibility that negative market volatility might lead to bankruptcy. In other words, rather than working directly on volatility itself, reducing your withdrawal rate reduces the impact that volatility can have on the long-term survival of your portfolio.

Furthermore, lowering your withdrawal rate is a much more reliable way of reducing risk than the correlation principle. *Nothing* is more effective at reducing the retirement risk than minimizing your withdrawal rate.

Consider the risk posed by market volatility. Suppose we have two retirees, Malcolm and Denise, with the same well-diversified portfolio. Malcolm has a withdrawal rate of 2 percent, while Denise has a 6 percent rate. If a market downturn reduces the size of each retiree's nest egg by half, then Malcolm's withdrawal rate will double from 2 to 4 percent—a level that is still likely to be less than the returns Malcolm earns from his investments. But Denise's withdrawal rate will double to 12 percent. It is unlikely that Denise will be able to earn consistent returns larger than her new withdrawal rate, and as a result, she will need to draw down on her principal to fund her living expenses. This is an unsustainable situation. The lower the withdrawal rate, the less likely it is that market volatility will push that rate to unsafe, unsustainable levels.

But a lower withdrawal rate also reduces the risk of earning insufficient returns. Instead of a short, sharp downturn, let's suppose that Malcolm and Denise instead encounter a lengthy, twenty-year secular bear market. Both Malcolm and Denise achieve average returns of 3 percent per year over this period. For the sake of simplicity, we will assume the inflation rate averages zero. Because Malcolm's withdrawal rate is only 2 percent per year, he will be able to fund his living expenses entirely out of his investment earnings—and his portfolio will continue to grow. But Denise's withdrawal rate of 6 percent exceeds her average 3 percent returns, and hence she will need to draw down on her principal to cover part of her expenses. After twenty years of low returns, her portfolio will have shrunk to only 15 percent of its original size.[77]

If you can combine a low withdrawal rate with the principle of *correlation*, this combination will not only reduce the retirement risk; it will also give you much more flexibility when deciding how much to rely on the principle of *compromise* (i.e., on low-volatility hedges). For example, a risk-averse person can afford to make a larger allocation to bonds if she has a relatively low withdrawal rate, because she will not need to earn as much in returns to support her limited withdrawals. By the same token, a risk-tolerant person with a low withdrawal rate can afford to limit her allocation to bonds and reach for higher returns with stocks, because negative market volatility is less likely to elevate her withdrawal rate to a dangerous level. In fact, the initial withdrawal rate (the rate in the first year of retirement) is *the most important factor* a retiree must consider when making the crucial decision of how much to allocate to bonds versus equities. To help you in this decision, we will look at the relationship between withdrawal rates and asset allocation in the next chapter.

How to Calculate a Withdrawal Rate

For now, the good news is that most people should be able to exert a significant degree of control over their withdrawal rate. The formula for calculating your withdrawal rate in retirement is simple:

(handwritten: 114.3)

> Withdrawal rate = 100% × (Annual living expenses − Noninvestment retirement income)/Total money in retirement accounts

(handwritten: Emgene = 300K)

(handwritten: 125 − 7.5/2500 = 2% ↓50% 4%   105 − 61 = 44/2500 = 1.8% ↓50% 3.6%)

As an example of how to use the formula, let's consider a married couple, Ed and Alice. Both are sixty-four years old and planning to retire in one year. First, they estimate their total annual living expenses, or household budget, in retirement as $75,000. This estimate includes taxes—income taxes, property taxes, and taxes on dividends, interest, capital gains, and withdrawals from 401(k)s and IRAs.

Next, they estimate their retirement income. Ed expects to receive $25,000 per year from Social Security as well as a $5,000 per year pension. Alice's Social Security benefits are estimated at $20,000 per year. They estimate their dividend and interest income at $2,000 per year.

Finally, they calculate the size of their investment nest egg. In addition to $50,000 in a savings account, which Ed and Alice maintain as their emergency fund, they have a jointly owned brokerage account with $100,000. Alice has a $350,000 401(k), while Ed has $200,000 in an IRA.

Here's how Ed and Alice would calculate their withdrawal rate:

Living expenses = $75,000

Noninvestment income = $25,000 + $5,000 + $20,000 = $50,000

Total money in retirement accounts = $100,000 + $350,000 + $200,000 = $650,000

Withdrawal rate = 100% × ($75,000 − $50,000)/$650,000 = 3.85%

Notice that Ed and Alice did not include the $2,000 income from their investments (i.e., dividend and interest income) in the calculation of their retirement income. While investment income goes toward meeting withdrawals, it does not reduce the withdrawal rate and cannot be included in the calculation of the withdrawal rate. Note also that Ed and Alice did not include their $50,000 emergency fund in their calculations. Again, the emergency fund is money you set aside for unexpected expenses. It should not be included in the money available to cover your regular, expected household expenses.

★★★

The goal here is to reduce the retirement risk by reducing your withdrawal rate to as low a level as possible, while still enabling a comfortable, enjoyable retirement. Given the preceding formula, there are three basic ways to reduce your withdrawal rate to a safe level:

- Increase the total amount of money in your retirement nest egg

- Reduce your living expenses

- Increase your noninvestment retirement income

Let's take a look at each of these options.

Increasing the Size of Your Retirement Nest Egg: A Guide to Saving for Retirement

Whereas the second and third options apply to retirees, the first option is for those still working and saving. In general, younger workers have a much better opportunity than older workers when it comes to this first option. Not only do younger workers have more time to save for retirement, but compounding can work wonders on these savings. If your employer offers a 401(k), 403(b), or similar investment vehicle with matching contributions, you can even add years or decades of "free money" to your own savings. Saving and investing to increase the size of your retirement nest egg is the best way for young workers to reduce their future withdrawal rates.

Just how much will you need to save to pay for your retirement? Previously we learned how a (nearly) retired couple, Ed and Alice, can calculate their withdrawal rate based on their savings, expected expenses, and income in retirement. If you are still working and nowhere near retirement, you can use the same formula to estimate the size of the nest egg you will need to support your retirement. For this purpose, the withdrawal rate formula can be rearranged as follows:

Total amount needed for retirement = (Living expenses − Retirement income)/(Desired withdrawal rate/100%)

Let's consider another example to illustrate how to use this rearranged formula. Mark and Betsy are twenty-six-year-olds celebrating their second wedding anniversary. Both of them have the option of diverting a portion of their paychecks to their employer-sponsored 401(k)s. To get a sense of how much they should be saving, they would like to estimate the size of the nest egg they will need in retirement. The first step in this process is to estimate current living expenses. For those who have a household budget (and who adhere to that budget), this step is already done. But we'll assume Mark and Betsy don't live by a budget. In this case, there are two possible ways to approach the estimation task: bottom up and top down. In the bottom-up approach, a detailed, itemized household estimate is developed. One way to do this is by saving all of your bills (for utilities, insurance, and credit cards), detailed checking account statements, and any and all receipts paid in cash (for gas, groceries, restaurants, hotels, etc.) over at least one year and preferably two or three years. Then, using these records, create a list of all of your budget items (be sure to include taxes) and add up the total amount you spent on each item. If this total represents two (or three) years of expenses, divide the result by 2 (or 3) to obtain an annual cost estimate. This approach obviously requires a significant effort, but for those who are nearing retirement, that effort may well prove worthwhile. The key advantage provided by the bottom-up approach is that it will allow older persons to develop a better estimate of how their expenses might change in retirement. (For example, if a worker spends $2,000 per year on gasoline but estimates that half of this amount is used commuting to and from work, then gasoline expenses in retirement might be estimated at $1,000.)

However, for a young couple like Mark and Betsy, the bottom-up approach may well be overkill. They are so far from retirement that it is difficult, if not impossible, to address such basic questions as where they will be living and how their standard of living might change as they age. They therefore opt for the much simpler top-down approach. In this approach, total expenses are estimated simply by adding up total net income (from pay stubs) and subtracting total savings (from bank and brokerage statements). Again, the calculation should cover at least one year; because Mark and Betsy have been together two years, they estimate a two-year total and divide it by 2. The result is an estimated $40,000 per year for living expenses. Without any clear idea of how this amount might change over their working lives, let alone in retirement, they will simply assume that it will remain constant.

Next, based on the Social Security Administration's online benefits calculator, they estimate they will receive a total of $25,000 in retirement income from Social Security. To solve the preceding equation, they must also specify the withdrawal rate they would like to have in retirement. As we saw in the previous chapter, 4 percent is generally considered to be the *maximum* safe initial withdrawal rate in retirement. The 4 percent rate is based on historical backtests indicating that a 75 percent stock/25 percent bond portfolio using this rate would have survived all possible thirty-year retirements starting in any year stretching back to 1926.[78] The tested 75/25 portfolio even survived the Great Depression and the stagflation of the 1970s and early 1980s. However, there is no guarantee that, in the future, we will not encounter situations even worse than those of the past century. For this reason, I would suggest targeting a 3 to 3.5 percent withdrawal rate to improve your odds of beating the retirement risk. If you plan to retire early (before age sixty-five), you should definitely limit your withdrawal rate to 3 percent or less.

Using a 3.5 percent withdrawal rate, estimated annual expenses of $40,000 per year, and Social Security benefits of $25,000 per year, Mark and Betsy estimate the size of the nest egg they need to retire as follows:

Total amount needed for retirement = ($40,000 − $25,000)/(0.035) = $428,571

However, there is one very important wrinkle Mark and Betsy have not yet considered: to determine your living expenses and income in retirement, you must take inflation into account. This holds true for those near retirement who are using the formula to calculate their future retirement withdrawal rate. But it *especially* applies to younger workers using the formula to calculate the total size of the nest egg they need for retirement.[79] The formula for calculating the impact of inflation is a bit complicated.[80] But assuming the future inflation rate is similar to the 3 percent rate that we have averaged over the long run (from 1913 to 2013), I've calculated the results of the inflation formula for you in Table 10.1.

Table 10.1. Inflation Multipliers Based on an Assumed 3-Percent Inflation Rate

Number of Years until Retirement	Calculated Inflation Factor
1	1.03
2	1.06
3	1.09
4	1.13
5	1.16
10	1.34
15	1.56
20	1.81
25	2.09
30	2.43
35	2.81
40	3.26
45	3.78

Suppose, for example, that you are twenty-one years away from retiring and want to calculate the size of the nest egg you will need. In this case, you would multiply your estimates of both living expenses and Social Security income by the inflation multiplier of 1.81, from the twenty-year row in Table 10.1 (since 21 is closest to 20[81]).

Returning to our previous example, Mark and Betsy estimated their annual living expenses and Social Security income *in today's dollars*. Because they are currently twenty-six years old and are hoping to retire in approximately forty years, they need to multiply their expenses and Social Security income[82] by 3.26, the inflation multiplier for forty years from Table 10.1. This adjustment would yield the following results:

Living expenses in retirement = 3.26 × $40,000 = $130,400

Social Security income = 3.26 × $25,000 = $81,500

Total amount needed for retirement = ($130,400 − $81,500)/(0.035) = $1,397,143

Yikes! As you can see by comparing this result with the $428,571 we estimated earlier, inflation has a *huge* impact on the required size of the nest egg. Hence, it is very important to account for inflation using the appropriate inflation multiplier from Table 10.1.

The broader implications of these results, especially for younger readers, are clear—meeting the goal of a secure retirement is a very expensive proposition. For Mark and Betsy, saving $1.4 million might seem impossible. But it isn't, because time is on their side. The key for Mark and Betsy, and for you, is to begin saving for retirement as soon as possible. Table 10.2 shows how various savings amounts build wealth over time. In this table, we assume a worker starts by saving the amount shown in the first column and then increases this amount by 4 percent per year. (For example, the first row of the table corresponds to saving $2,000 in Year 1, $2,080 in Year 2, $2,136.20 in Year 3, etc.). A 4 percent annual increase in the amount you save should be doable, assuming that your income rises slightly faster than the 3 percent long-term rate of inflation. Columns 2–5 of the table show the final value of the amount saved after ten, twenty, thirty, and forty years. Mark and Betsy need to save a total of $1.4 million and have forty years to meet this goal. Reading down column 5 (the forty-year column) to the first number that exceeds $1.4 million, and then across to the first column, we find that Mark and Betsy can start out by saving $6,000 in their first year. But if they had only twenty years instead of forty years until retirement, they would need to increase their initial savings rate to nearly $30,000 to meet their $1.4 million goal (found by reading down column 3 to the first estimate that exceeds $1.4 million, and then across to the starting amount in column 1). And if they had only ten years until retirement, they would need to start out by saving $90,000 (see rows shaded in gray in Table 10.2). The sooner you start saving, the easier it will be to meet your retirement goal.

You can use Table 10.2 in this same way to get a rough idea of how much you need to be saving to meet your own retirement goal. This table assumes that you will earn a 5 percent annual average return on your retirement portfolio. This assumption may seem too conservative for someone using a moderate 60/40 portfolio, at least relative to historical returns. But given current market valuations and dividend yields, there is reason to believe that both stock and bond returns will underperform historical averages going forward. And in any event, there is less harm erring on the pessimistic than on the optimistic side. This way, at worst, you will exceed your savings goal and wind up with a bigger nest egg than you originally targeted. The alternative, of using an overly optimistic estimate of your future returns, could cause you to fall short of your savings goal.

Table 10.2. Estimated Growth of Annual Savings for a Moderate 60/40 Portfolio

COLUMN 1	COLUMN 2	COLUMN 3	COLUMN 4	COLUMN 5
Starting Amount Saved in Year 1	Total Amount Accumulated after 10 Years	Total Amount Accumulated after 20 Years	Total Amount Accumulated after 30 Years	Total Amount Accumulated after 40 Years
$2,000	$31,000	$97,000	$226,000	$470,000
$4,000	$62,000	$194,000	$453,000	$940,000
$6,000	$94,000	$291,000	$679,000	$1,411,000
$8,000	$125,000	$388,000	$906,000	$1,880,000
$10,000	$156,000	$485,000	$1,132,000	$2,351,000
$12,500	$195,000	$607,000	$1,416,000	$2,939,000
$15,000	$234,000	$728,000	$1,699,000	$3,526,000
$17,500	$273,000	$849,000	$1,982,000	$4,114,000
$20,000	$312,000	$971,000	$2,265,000	$4,702,000
$25,000	$390,000	$1,213,000	$2,831,000	$5,877,000
$30,000	$468,000	$1,456,000	$3,397,000	$7,053,000
$35,000	$546,000	$1,698,000	$3,964,000	$8,228,000
$40,000	$624,000	$1,941,000	$4,530,000	$9,404,000
$45,000	$702,000	$2,184,000	$5,096,000	$10,579,000
$50,000	$780,000	$2,426,000	$5,662,000	$11,755,000
$60,000	$936,000	$2,912,000	$6,795,000	$14,105,000
$70,000	$1,093,000	$3,397,000	$7,927,000	$16,456,000
$80,000	$1,249,000	$3,882,000	$9,060,000	$18,807,000
$90,000	$1,405,000	$4,368,000	$10,192,000	$21,158,000
$100,000	$1,561,000	$4,853,000	$11,325,000	$23,509,000

Table 10.3 is similar to Table 10.2, except that it assumes a 6 percent average return on investments. This table is more appropriate for someone using an aggressive, 80/20 portfolio. Table 10.4 assumes a 4 percent average return and should be used by those adopting a conservative, 40/60 mix of stocks and bonds.

Table 10.3. Estimated Growth of Annual Savings for an Aggressive 80/20 Portfolio

COLUMN 1	COLUMN 2	COLUMN 3	COLUMN 4	COLUMN 5
Starting Amount Saved in Year 1	Total Amount Accumulated after 10 Years	Total Amount Accumulated after 20 Years	Total Amount Accumulated after 30 Years	Total Amount Accumulated after 40 Years
$2,000	$33,000	$108,000	$265,000	$581,000
$4,000	$66,000	$215,000	$530,000	$1,163,000
$6,000	$99,000	$323,000	$795,000	$1,744,000
$8,000	$132,000	$431,000	$1,060,000	$2,326,000
$10,000	$165,000	$538,000	$1,325,000	$2,907,000
$12,500	$206,000	$673,000	$1,656,000	$3,634,000
$15,000	$247,000	$808,000	$1,988,000	$4,360,000
$17,500	$288,000	$942,000	$2,319,000	$5,087,000
$20,000	$329,000	$1,077,000	$2,650,000	$5,814,000
$25,000	$412,000	$1,346,000	$3,313,000	$7,267,000
$30,000	$494,000	$1,615,000	$3,975,000	$8,721,000
$35,000	$576,000	$1,885,000	$4,638,000	$10,174,000
$40,000	$658,000	$2,154,000	$5,300,000	$11,628,000
$45,000	$741,000	$2,423,000	$5,963,000	$13,081,000
$50,000	$823,000	$2,692,000	$6,625,000	$14,534,000
$60,000	$988,000	$3,231,000	$7,950,000	$17,441,000
$70,000	$1,152,000	$3,769,000	$9,275,000	$20,348,000
$80,000	$1,317,000	$4,308,000	$10,600,000	$23,255,000
$90,000	$1,482,000	$4,846,000	$11,925,000	$26,126,000
$100,000	$1,646,000	$5,385,000	$13,250,000	$29,069,000

Table 10.4. Estimated Growth of Annual Savings for a Conservative 40/60 Portfolio

COLUMN 1	COLUMN 2	COLUMN 3	COLUMN 4	COLUMN 5
Starting Amount Saved in Year 1	Total Amount Accumulated after 10 Years	Total Amount Accumulated after 20 Years	Total Amount Accumulated after 30 Years	Total Amount Accumulated after 40 Years
$2,000	$30,000	$88,000	$195,000	$384,000
$4,000	$59,000	$175,000	$389,000	$768,000
$6,000	$89,000	$263,000	$584,000	$1,152,000
$8,000	$118,000	$351,000	$778,000	$1,536,000
$10,000	$148,000	$438,000	$973,000	$1,920,000
$12,500	$185,000	$548,000	$1,216,000	$2,401,000
$15,000	$222,000	$657,000	$1,460,000	$2,881,000
$17,500	$259,000	$767,000	$1,703,000	$3,361,000
$20,000	$296,000	$876,000	$1,946,000	$3,841,000
$25,000	$370,000	$1,096,000	$2,433,000	$4,801,000
$30,000	$444,000	$1,315,000	$2,919,000	$5,761,000
$35,000	$518,000	$1,534,000	$3,406,000	$6,721,000
$40,000	$592,000	$1,753,000	$3,892,000	$7,682,000
$45,000	$666,000	$1,972,000	$4,379,000	$8,642,000
$50,000	$740,000	$2,191,000	$4,865,000	$9,602,000
$60,000	$888,000	$2,629,000	$5,838,000	$11,522,000
$70,000	$1,036,000	$3,068,000	$6,811,000	$13,443,000
$80,000	$1,184,000	$3,506,000	$7,784,000	$15,363,000
$90,000	$1,332,000	$3,944,000	$8,757,000	$17,284,000
$100,000	$1,480,000	$4,382,000	$9,730,000	$19,204,000

Mark and Betsy are a young couple, just starting their life together, and as yet have no significant savings. But what if you've already accumulated a nest egg, and rather than calculating the total amount you need to save before retirement, you need instead to estimate the additional amount to be saved to meet your goal? Table 10.5 shows how the lump sum savings you have already accumulated will grow over time, using the same return assumptions underlying Tables 10.2–10.4. For example, if you are using an aggressive 80/20 portfolio, any savings you have accumulated so far should multiply by 1.79 times in 10 years, 3.21 times in 20 years, 5.74 times in 30 years, and 10.29 times in 40 years. Keep in mind that the more you are able to save in tax-advantaged accounts like IRAs and 401(k)s, the more likely it is that you will be able to meet, and even exceed, the accumulation amounts shown in the tables.

Table 10.5. Estimated Growth Multipliers
for Lump Sum Savings Using Various Portfolios

COLUMN 1	COLUMN 2	COLUMN 3	COLUMN 4	COLUMN 5
Portfolio	Multiplier After 10 Years	Multiplier After 20 Years	Multiplier After 30 Years	Multiplier After 40 Years
Aggressive (80/20)	1.79	3.21	5.74	10.29
Moderate (60/40)	1.63	2.65	4.32	7.04
Conservative (40/60)	1.48	2.19	3.24	4.80

Let's consider an example illustrating how to use Table 10.5 in combination with Tables 10.2–10.4. Cindy and Stewart are a married couple in their early forties, with two children. They have already saved $200,000 in their retirement accounts. Using the same formula we used for Mark and Betsy, Cindy has estimated that they will need $1.5 million upon retirement. They both plan to retire in twenty-two years and are using a 75/25 mix of stocks and bonds. They want to know how much they should be saving per year to meet their $1.5 million goal.

As a first step, Cindy calculates the expected growth of the $200,000 in existing savings using Table 10.5. Since their 75/25 allocation is closest to the aggressive 80/20 stock/bond mix, and they have approximately twenty years to retirement, the most appropriate multiplier from Table 10.5 is 3.21.[83] Multiplying $200,000 by 3.21, Cindy estimates that their current nest egg will grow to $642,000 by the time she and Stewart are ready to retire. Subtracting this amount from their $1.5 million goal leaves them with an additional $858,000 they still need to save. Turning next to Table 10.3 (the table for an 80/20 portfolio), and reading down column 3 (for a retirement in twenty years), the first value that exceeds $858,000 is $942,000. Reading across to column 1, $942,000 corresponds to an initial savings amount of $17,500. If Cindy and Stewart save $17,500 in the current year, and increase their savings amount by 4 percent each and every subsequent year, by the time they are ready to retire, they stand a good chance of reaching their $1.5 million goal.

★★★

Tables 10.2–10.5 will give you a *rough* idea of how much you should be saving to get ready for retirement, but you will need to revisit and adjust your savings plan periodically to stay on track. Estimating your needed savings is fraught with uncertainty. What will your expenses look like in retirement? Will taxes increase, decrease, or stay the same? How much will Social Security pay you twenty, thirty, or forty years from now? What returns will you earn on your investments? Will inflation remain relatively tame or go on a rampage? These are just a few of the questions that defy easy answers. However, as you get closer to retirement, your answers to these and other key questions should become clearer. By periodically estimating your living expenses in retirement, the total size of the nest egg you will need, and the amount you should be saving annually, your estimates will gradually become more accurate.

You can use Tables 10.2–10.5 not only to develop your savings plan but also to periodically check if you're still on track to meeting your goal. If, for example, you started saving $6,000 toward a $1.1 million goal using a 40/60 conservative portfolio forty years before your expected retirement, then Table 10.4 indicates that you should have $89,000 saved after ten years, $263,000 after twenty years, and $584,000 after thirty years (see gray-shaded row in Table 10.4). If you find yourself falling behind (for example, you've saved only $50,000 after ten years), you can use Tables 10.2–10.5 to estimate the needed increase in your savings amount. If you close in on your retirement goal faster than expected, you can use the tables to estimate a reduction in your annual savings amount.

Although your savings plan will need to be adjusted as circumstances change, don't let this stop you from implementing your plan as soon as possible. Even if you can't save the entire amount recommended for you in the tables, start by saving an amount you can handle. The most important thing is not the *amount* you save but to start saving *now*. And if you need to start out small, you may be able to catch up later by increasing the 4 percent annual step-up in your savings rate. (This approach should work particularly well if your income rises faster than the rate of inflation.) Though a buy-and-hold, black belt investment strategy can help you get to your retirement goal, it is even more important to implement a good savings plan as soon as possible. Remember, as we learned from Joe Bondsman, the effects of inflation compound over time. The best way to combat this pernicious effect is to put the power of compounding on your side by implementing your savings and investment program at as young an age as possible.

★★★

If you are an older worker nearing retirement, it becomes more difficult, though not impossible, to reduce your withdrawal rate by increasing your nest egg size. One option, of course, is to increase your savings rate, being sure to take full advantage of tax-free (Roth) and tax-deferred retirement accounts. Another possibility is to delay your retirement. If you are nearing retirement age and you estimate that your initial withdrawal rate will exceed 4 percent, you should definitely consider a delayed retirement. This will give you more time to grow your nest egg and to benefit from compounding.

Alternatively, you might consider the other two options for establishing a safe withdrawal rate—reducing your living expenses and/or increasing your retirement income.

Reducing Your Expenses

I would never advocate reducing your retirement budget to a bare-bones minimum. On the contrary, include in your budget those luxury items that you can afford without going over a 4 percent initial withdrawal rate. If you have always wanted to travel more when you retire, then include travel in your budget. If you want to play more golf, or pursue some new hobby, include the costs in your budget. You should enjoy these and other luxuries not only because they will make for a happier retirement but also because they will give you more flexibility to cut expenses if and when necessary. A bare-bones budget cannot be reduced when market conditions necessitate reductions. But you can always put off a trip overseas or a new set of golf clubs for a year or two when a bear market takes a bite out of your nest egg.

Although you shouldn't skimp on the good things, many people will have expenses that they can reduce without significantly sacrificing their quality of life. Empty nesters, for example, might consider downsizing to a smaller house. Few if any actions will provide greater budget savings. In addition, you might be able to add some of the equity in your current house to your retirement accounts. You might also consider a less expensive automobile when it comes time to buy a new vehicle.

Taxes are an area where you may be able to achieve significant savings without making any sacrifices at all. In Chapter 13 we discuss how to select the most tax-efficient investments for your portfolio, and in Chapter 14 we cover a technique that can further reduce your tax bill. One of the most effective ways you can reduce your future tax bill is to put at least some of your retirement savings in a Roth account (IRA or 401(k)). The "retired you" will thank the "young you" for doing so every time you make a tax-free withdrawal from your Roth account.

If you do decide to downsize and are not tied to your current area, there are a number of states that offer tax incentives for retirees as well as a low cost of living. In addition to states without income taxes (including, for example, Wyoming, Florida, and Alaska), there are states without sales taxes (including New Hampshire, Delaware, and Alaska), states that do not tax Social Security or pension income, and two states (Pennsylvania and Mississippi) that do not tax *any* retirement income (including withdrawals from IRAs and 401(k)s). If you are seriously considering moving to another state to reduce your taxes and other living expenses, you should consult a tax professional before making a move. State tax policies can be complicated, with low taxes on, say, income being offset by higher taxes on property or consumption. You will want to make sure that your move will reduce your total tax bill, not just one or two taxes.

Increasing Your Retirement Income

Here again, I would never recommend taking a job if you neither want nor need to work in retirement. However, for those who would like to continue working—or for those who need more income to get their initial withdrawal level below 4 percent —part-time work is an option to consider.

You can also increase your retirement income by delaying collecting your Social Security benefits. For every year you delay, up to age seventy, your benefits will increase by 7 to 8 percent. But there is a price to pay for delaying. Although you will receive a larger check once you begin collecting, you will in the meantime be forgoing a source of income.

Those of a certain age may recall the cartoon character Popeye. It was 1932 when Popeye's friend Wimpy first said, "I'll gladly pay you Tuesday for a hamburger today." Wimpy understood the time value of money—and hamburgers. It may seem like the Social Security Administration (SSA) is trying to sell you the *opposite* of the deal Wimpy wanted. They are asking you to pay *today* (by giving up your Social Security check) for a reward (bigger Social Security checks) *tomorrow*. Shouldn't we learn from Wimpy and grab the money due us as soon as we can?

In most cases, the answer is no. There is an important difference between the SSA's offer and Wimpy's. The SSA is offering you a *bigger* reward if you wait. A 7 to 8 percent benefit increase per year is huge. For example, for those born in 1960 or later, it adds up to a 43 percent increase in Social Security income just for waiting five years instead of collecting at the traditional age of sixty-five. For those tempted to start collecting at the earliest possible age—sixty-two—waiting until age seventy will increase the size of your Social Security checks by about seventy-seven percent.

There are a number of ways to assess the cost–benefit trade-offs of delaying Social Security. Some researchers, noting that delaying is similar to purchasing an investment like an annuity, have compared this "investment" to various other low-risk investments. They have found delaying Social Security to provide higher returns with less risk.[84] Another way to assess the trade-offs is by comparing the total amount of lifetime benefits[85] that the Social Security recipient is likely to receive by delaying versus the total amount accruing from claiming benefits earlier. This approach was taken in an actuarial analysis by Shoven and Slavov of the National Bureau of Economic Research.[86] They found that delaying benefits is advantageous for many individuals and married couples, particularly when real interest rates are less than 3.5 percent (as is the case today).

While these studies are informative, they probably *understate* the full benefits of delay. Delaying Social Security will not only probably, eventually, make you richer; it will also almost certainly make your retirement more *secure*—by increasing your retirement income and reducing your withdrawal rate. And it will do this immediately once you begin to collect those fatter checks. In other words, if you view delaying as similar to taking the Social Security income you forgo and investing it in an annuity, this investment will not only produce higher returns than comparable investments, *it will also reduce your retirement risk*. An "investment" that can increase returns *and* reduce risks is a win-win unlike any real investment. It is too good a deal to pass up.

I'm not necessarily suggesting that you delay your *retirement* until seventy to get these bigger checks. If you do not need Social Security income to get your initial withdrawal rate to 4 percent or less, there is no reason you cannot retire at an earlier age while still deferring your benefits until seventy. In fact, a study published in the *Journal of Financial Planning* shows that portfolios will last longer (thereby reducing longevity risk) if you delay collecting Social Security and instead fund the first years of retirement from savings.[87] This approach involves accepting higher withdrawal rates in your sixties to get lower withdrawal rates in your seventies and beyond. The long-term risk-reduction benefits of this approach outweigh the added risks in your sixties, in part because you can always change your mind and claim your benefits before you reach seventy. For this reason, there really are no short-term risks. In Chapter 18, you will learn how to "take the temperature" of your portfolio. If you delay collecting benefits and then find that your portfolio is either too hot or too cold, one of the temperature-regulating options still open to you in your sixties will be to claim your Social Security benefits before reaching seventy. This way, you will still have gained a portion of the advantages of delaying without having put your portfolio at any additional risk.

An example will help to illustrate the risk-reduction advantages of delaying your benefits. Suppose that at age sixty-two, you have a $1 million nest egg and annual living expenses of $35,000. Let's further suppose that your Social Security income will be $10,000 if you begin collecting at sixty-two but $17,700 (77 percent higher) if you wait to seventy. You decide to retire at sixty-two but delay collecting benefits, because your low, 3.5 percent withdrawal rate ($35,000/$1,000,000) should keep your portfolio safe until age seventy. To keep this simple, let's assume that over the next eight years, your investment returns match your 3.5 percent withdrawal rate. In this case, you will be able to fund your $35,000 in annual expenses entirely from your returns without dipping into principal, and your nest egg will still be worth $1 million at age seventy. This is a very lucky result, as your withdrawal rate has remained steady at a low 3.5 percent. Furthermore, by applying for your delayed benefits, you will now be able to cut that rate in half to 1.73 percent (since the $17,700 you will receive in income is about half of your $35,000 in expenses). (For simplicity, we're assuming zero inflation in this example, but in any event, the amount you will receive at seventy will increase with inflation.) Had you instead started collecting Social Security at sixty-two, it is true that you would have received $80,000 in income ($10,000 per year for eight years), and with your 3.5 percent investment returns, this additional income would have grown to $93,685. But at seventy, your withdrawal rate would then be 2.29 percent ([$35,000 − $10,000]/$1,093,685)—significantly higher than the 1.73 percent rate you would have attained by waiting to collect your benefits.

Now let's suppose that instead of good luck, immediately upon retiring at sixty-two, you encounter a bear market that reduces your nest egg to $500,000 and causes your withdrawal rate to skyrocket to 7 percent by the time you reach sixty-four. Because your decision to wait until age seventy can be revoked at any time, and you now have a dangerously elevated withdrawal rate, you decide to begin collecting Social Security at sixty-four to cool down your portfolio. Because your Social Security income rises about 7 percent for every year you wait, by waiting to sixty-four, your income will increase to $11,450, and your withdrawal rate will now be 4.71 percent ([$35,000 − $11,450]/$500,000). Had you instead chosen to begin collecting at sixty-two, you would have earned an extra $20,000 ($10,000 for two years) from Social Security, raising the value of your nest egg to $520,000. But your withdrawal rate at sixty-seven would be 4.81 percent ([$35,000 − $10,000]/$520,000)—slightly higher than it would have been had you waited to collect Social Security. And this calculation doesn't even take into account the losses you would have incurred on the $20,000 in Social Security income during the bear market.

As this example shows, regardless of whether your luck is good or bad, by waiting, you reduce your long-term withdrawal rate (and therefore the retirement risk) while still retaining the full flexibility to respond to an unlucky event (such as a bear market) that could raise your withdrawal rate to a dangerous level.[88]

The rules governing Social Security benefits become more complicated, and the options more numerous, if you are married or divorced. Before making any final decisions, be sure to read and understand the rules and options that apply to your particular situation. AARP is a good place to start to learn more about this subject.[89]

Summary

The retirement risk comes not only with the two investment-related components we first learned about in Chapter 1, but also with with three noninvestment components: longevity risk, the risk posed by a high withdrawal rate, and the risk of large, unexpected expenses. In this chapter, we covered three ways to reduce the retirement risk understood in this fuller sense. First, to mitigate the risk posed by large, unexpected expenses, you can make sure you and your family have adequate insurance coverage. Second, you can build an emergency fund. Like insurance, such a fund will help you to mitigate the risk posed by large, unexpected expenses.

Finally, and most importantly, you can work to establish a low initial withdrawal rate in retirement. A low withdrawal rate is the single most effective, reliable step you can take for mitigating all aspects of the retirement risk—both investment and noninvestment related. This step is not just for those near retirement. If you are still working—and especially if you are young and have many years ahead of you before retirement—then you should start working *now* on establishing a low withdrawal rate. You can do this by estimating the amount of money you will need in retirement and the amount you need to save to reach this goal, and then implementing a plan to save the needed amount. If you are nearing retirement or already retired, you should calculate your withdrawal rate. If it is above the safe 4 percent level, you should consider options for reducing it, including increasing your retirement income and lowering your living expenses.

Making sure you have adequate insurance coverage, establishing an emergency fund, calculating your withdrawal rate (if you are in or near retirement), and implementing a good savings plan (if you are not yet retired) are all critically important preliminaries to the main subject of Part IV: creating and maintaining a well-diversified portfolio. Assuming you have addressed these preliminaries, we can now return to that subject.

CHAPTER 11

ASSET ALLOCATION

I f you've insured yourself against life's little surprises, built up an emergency fund, developed a good retirement savings plan, and taken the other steps necessary to minimize and (if you are in or near retirement) calculate your withdrawal rate, you're now ready for the main event: developing an asset allocation plan for your portfolio. This plan will specify the percentage of your total nest egg that you will invest in each of the asset classes composing your portfolio.

Throughout this book, I have likened a well-diversified portfolio to a gourmet meal. This metaphor was selected carefully. Not only is a gourmet meal, like a well-diversified portfolio, greater than the sum of its parts. But the master chef is as much, if not more, an artist as a scientist. Similarly, the creation of a well-diversified portfolio is as much an art as a science.

Yes, a well-diversified portfolio is based in part on the scientific principle of correlation. But once the specific asset classes that tend to exhibit low correlation have been identified, the scientist's work is done. It is possible to calculate, scientifically, an optimum percentage allocation for each asset class based on asset class correlations, returns, and standard deviations. In fact, modern portfolio theory (MPT) is at its core a technique for calculating optimum portfolio allocations. MPT, you may recall from Chapter 2, is the Nobel Prize–winning theory based in large part on the principle of correlation. But while we have focused heavily on this principle, we have considered MPT only in passing. In effect, we have borrowed the principle underlying MPT while ignoring the optimization mathematics built on this principle. This was done for good reason: the principle is useful, but the math is not. The problem with trying to use the MPT to calculate optimum allocations is that the returns, correlation coefficients, and volatility data used as inputs to the calculations are constantly changing in unpredictable ways. If we use historical data as our inputs, the result will be excellent estimates of optimal asset allocations *in the past*. But such a solution is optimal only for the past and will likely be nowhere even remotely close to the optimum solution for the future. Alternatively, if we use forecasted data as our inputs, the results will be only as good as the forecasts—and the forecasts are likely to be very poor, given the unpredictability of correlation coefficients and other factors. MPT is an elegant theory, but from a practical standpoint, there is no way to use it to calculate an optimum asset allocation.

Furthermore, any scientific attempt at developing an optimal, one-size-fits-all portfolio ignores the many subjective elements that must be taken into account. As we shall see, the portfolio that is right for *you* depends on a whole host of specific circumstances: whether you're still working or retired, your withdrawal rate, whether you have a 401(k) or 403(b), and your tolerance for risk.

If you've watched the master chefs on TV, then you know they don't work with a cookbook in front of them. Instead of carefully measuring out ingredients according to a recipe, they use a pinch of this, a dash of that. And the value of their work, like a work of art, is in the eye (or the taste buds) of the beholder.

So it is with a retirement portfolio. The remainder of this chapter will guide you step by step through the art of asset allocation. The factors you need to consider in developing your own gourmet portfolio will be explained. Guidelines you can use in the portfolio construction process will be provided. We will also consider some example portfolios, all or parts of which you may be able to apply to meet your own needs. But the ultimate decisions you make will need to be your own, based on your specific circumstances and taste for risk.

We have already covered the science of asset allocation in Parts I–III. Time now for the artiste, the master chef—you—to step up and create a portfolio that will provide for a long, secure, and comfortable retirement.

Step 1: Selecting the Asset Classes

As we learned in Chapter 8, the first step in the asset allocation process is to select the specific asset classes that will be included in your portfolio. You may, of course, use the same asset classes we used in our basic or advanced experimental portfolios. However, those portfolios did not cover the full range of possibilities, especially with respect to the return boosters. And there are at least two reasons you may want to consider some of the alternatives to the asset classes we used. First, you may have a personal preference for some asset classes over others. And second, you may not be able to access some of the asset classes we used in Part III, particularly if you have all or most of your investable money in a 401(k) plan. Unfortunately, most 401(k)s severely limit their investment offerings, both in number and in type. You can determine which asset class each of the mutual funds in your 401(k) covers by going to Morningstar's website and entering the fund's ticker symbol in the "Quote" box at the top of the page. On the next page, look under the word "Category" to find the fund's asset class. You can obtain more detailed information on the fund's investments by clicking on the word "Portfolio" in the gray bar.

Table 11.1 provides a wide variety of asset choices in each of the four main asset groupings: large caps, return boosters, low-volatility hedges, and high-volatility hedges. The first column in the table lists those asset classes that will best meet the needs of a robust, well-diversified portfolio. Those asset classes we used in the basic or advanced portfolios are shown in bold. The second column lists possible substitutes for the asset classes in the first column. These substitutes are not ideal, but they may be used if you cannot access any of the preferred asset classes in the first column.

Table 11.1. Asset Class Options

Primary Asset Classes	Possible Substitutes (to Be Used Only if None of the Primary Asset Classes Are Available to You)
LARGE CAPS	
• **U.S. large blend** • **Foreign (developed-market) large blend** • World large blend (includes U.S.) • **Emerging-markets large blend** • Total U.S. stock market fund (includes some mid and small caps) • Total international stock fund (includes some mid and small caps)	None necessary
RETURN BOOSTERS	
Large Cap Value: • **U.S. large cap value** • Foreign (developed-market) large cap value • World large cap value (includes U.S.) • Emerging-markets large cap value	None
Small Cap Blend: • U.S. small cap blend • **Foreign small cap blend** • World small cap blend (includes U.S.) • Emerging-markets small cap blend	• U.S. mid cap blend • Foreign mid cap blend • World mid cap blend • Emerging-markets mid cap blend
Small Cap Value: • **U.S. small cap value** • Foreign small cap value • World small cap value (includes U.S.) • Emerging-markets small cap value	• U.S. mid cap value • Foreign small cap value • World small cap value • Emerging-markets small cap value

Table 11.1. Asset Class Options *(continued)*

Primary Asset Classes	Possible Substitutes (to Be Used Only If None of the Primary Asset Classes Are Available to You)
LOW-VOLATILITY ASSETS	
• Short-term bond • Intermediate-term bond	None
• Inflation-protected bond	• U.S. government short-term bond
HIGH-VOLATILITY ASSETS	
• Precious metals equities • Emerging market bond • Gold	None

Large Caps

The first (top) section of Table 11.1 shows the main choices available for the large cap asset type. Two or three of these asset classes should be sufficient to diversify your own portfolio. Substitute asset classes are not given for large caps because you shouldn't have any trouble finding at least one U.S. large cap blend fund in your 401(k). Most 401(k)s should also include at least one international large cap blend fund.

In addition to the asset classes listed in the table, it is possible to invest in funds that specialize in specific regions (such as Asia/Pacific) or countries (such as China or India). However, when it comes to international investing, you are better off selecting geographically diversified foreign and emerging-market funds rather than trying to pick regional or country "winners." Also, whether you are selecting a U.S. or non-U.S. large cap, you should stick with blend funds and avoid growth funds (large cap *value* funds are considered return boosters).

Return Boosters

Although return boosters can be a bit harder to find than large caps in some 401(k)s, the good news is that there are many different asset classes that fit the bill. Table 11.1 lists the various return boosters. These have been subdivided into three main categories: (1) large cap value; (2) small cap blend; and (3) small cap value. As possible substitutes for the latter two groupings, mid caps (stocks that lie between small and large caps in size) are included in the second column of the table. Given the numerous primary choices and potential substitutes listed in the table, you should be able to find at least one or two return boosters in your 401(k) to include in your own portfolio. We used three different return boosters in our experimental advanced portfolios; there is no need to include more than three in your own portfolio.

Low-Volatility Asset Classes

You should not have too much difficulty accessing low-volatility asset classes in your 401(k), with the possible exception of inflation-protected bonds (i.e., TIPS). If your 401(k) does not offer a TIPS fund, and you cannot make room for such a fund in an IRA or other account, a potential alternative is a U.S. government (Treasury) short-term bond fund. Although not protected from inflation, short-term bond funds are less exposed to the risks of unexpected inflation than longer-duration funds. And by using a government bond fund as your TIPS substitute, you can still gain the safe haven advantages offered by TIPS. If your 401(k) does not offer a short-term government bond fund, you can use a mixed short-term bond fund as your substitute.

Remember to avoid high-yield junk bonds—limit all of your bond selections to investment-grade bonds only.

High-Volatility Asset Classes

The last (bottom) section of Table 11.1 presents the high-volatility asset classes. These are the asset classes that you are likely to find most difficult to access. In general, they are *not* offered by 401(k)s or other defined-contribution plans, and unfortunately there are no substitutes for any of them. What to do? If you have most of your money in your employer's 401(k) plan, then you need to use your other accounts —IRAs and taxable accounts—to hold your high-volatility hedges. In effect, you will be using these other accounts to hedge the main part of your portfolio in your 401(k). Fitting high-volatility hedges into your portfolio can be a real challenge, so we'll take a look at an example illustrating how to do it later in this chapter.

Step 2: Deciding on the Right Mix of Stocks and Bonds

Step 2 of the asset allocation process presents the most difficult, and most important, asset allocation decision you must make. How much of your nest egg should you invest in low-volatility hedges—that is, bonds? It's a crucial and difficult decision because, unlike the case with high-volatility hedges, it involves making a major trade-off between the competing components of the retirement risk. If you invest too little in bonds, your portfolio will be subject to excessive volatility. In a worst case, you could wind up like John Stockman. If you overdo it and put too much money in bonds, you may not be able to earn returns sufficient to outpace inflation. At worst, you might join Joe Bondsman at the poorhouse.

To avoid both Stockman's and Bondsman's fates, you must find a safe balance between stocks and bonds. You will need to consider a number of factors to find this balance, but none are more important than whether you are currently working or in (or near) retirement. As we shall see, the entire decision process is different for someone who's working than for a retiree. In this section, we'll first tackle the decision for those who are still working. Then we will turn to those who are already retired or who are within five years of retiring.

Current Workers

If you are working and retirement is still far off (more than five years away), then your *current* withdrawal rate is zero. (I am assuming here that you are not withdrawing any money from your retirement nest egg to cover current expenses.) The retirement risk still applies, but its meaning is different for you than for a retiree. First, you still run the risk of not earning enough returns, but because you are not withdrawing any money from your portfolio, there is no danger that you will go broke. Rather, the risk is that you will not earn returns sufficient to grow your portfolio to the size needed to support a secure, comfortable retirement.

Similarly, you still run the risk of too much volatility. But as long as you are not withdrawing any money from your portfolio, there is no *practical* danger that you will go broke during a bear market. This statement may not seem obvious, so let me explain. John Stockman was bankrupted in the 1929 Crash because he was withdrawing money from his all-stock portfolio to meet his living expenses. Although his investments declined 90 percent in value, this still left him with 10 percent. He would have recovered had he not been withdrawing money from the remaining 10 percent. As long as your withdrawal rate is zero, the value of all your investments would have to drop not 90 percent, or 95 percent, or even 99 percent, but 100 percent, to bankrupt you. Since you are going to be purchasing a well-diversified portfolio of U.S. and international stocks and bonds, to lose 100 percent of your money, the global stock and bond markets would essentially have to drop to zero. In other words, the hundreds of millions of investors, speculators, and traders composing the financial markets would need to reach a consensus that the entire universe of publicly traded corporations is worthless and that all issuers of corporate and government bonds will default on their legal obligations to repay their loans.

What would it take for the world to conclude that the entire stock and bond market—and by implication, the global economy itself—is worthless? It would take more than an economic calamity. Such an event would likely signal something much worse—some sort of global collapse of civilization. Is this possible? It's not very likely, at least in our own short lifetimes. But yes, it is possible. Anything is possible. History provides numerous examples of past civilizational collapses: Rome, the Mayans, Easter Island. It's easy to imagine nightmare scenarios that could end civilization as we know it, including nuclear war, catastrophic climate change, drug-resistant pandemics, and even an asteroid striking the earth. (Think these things can't happen? Just ask the next dinosaur you meet about that last one.)

But should we worry about protecting our portfolios and our retirement from such nightmares? No, we shouldn't. We are talking here about the sort of scenario that would likely render money itself useless and force us back to a preindustrial barter economy. Should this happen, you needn't be worried about your retirement. No one will be retiring. And you will have much bigger things to worry about. If asteroids and pandemics are what keep you awake at night, I'm afraid this book won't help you. You need a survivalist guide instead.

So, as stated previously, if you are still working and not withdrawing any money from your retirement nest egg, there is no *practical* danger (i.e., danger of the sort worth worrying about) that negative market volatility will bankrupt you.

But as previously noted, you still run the risk of too much volatility. If volatility can't bankrupt you, and for all practical purposes you can count on a full recovery, then what is the risk? Let me show you. I'd like you to head to the nearest mirror. If you're married, bring your spouse with you. Now, take a good, long look in the mirror.

That's right. *You* (and your spouse) are the risk. To be more precise, too much negative volatility may cause you to panic and sell when the market is in a tailspin and stock prices are at rock bottom. If you succumb to the fear, and then wait to buy back into the market until the recovery rally is well advanced, you will wind up having sold low and bought high. Do this a few times over a series of bear markets, and you will wreck your chances of saving enough money for a secure, comfortable retirement. It's not the market's volatility itself that presents the risk; it's your potential reaction to the volatility. (We will tackle ways to mitigate this risk in Chapter 17.)

Let's sum up. Younger people who are not yet near retirement still face the two components of the retirement risk. But these components have a different meaning for workers than for retirees. Too much volatility means running the risk that you will abandon the buy-and-hold approach and sell in the midst of market downturns —the absolute *worst* time to sell. *This risk is psychological.* Not earning enough returns means running the risk of building a nest egg that will be too small to support you when you reach retirement age. *This risk is real.*

If I were writing this book for robots, my advice would be very simple. I would advise those robots who are not yet near retirement to put all of their money into stocks. Because robots lack emotions, I could count on them to hold their stock investments through the inevitable ups and downs of the market. The *psychological* risk of selling during a market downturn would not exist for my robot readers, and hence the retirement risk would have only one component for them—the *real* risk of not earning enough returns to keep pace with inflation. This risk can be minimized by holding a 100 percent stock portfolio.

But this advice will not do for us emotional humans. We must balance the real risk posed by not earning enough returns against the psychological risk posed by too much market volatility. To minimize the real risk without triggering the psychological risk, *put as much money into stocks as you can stomach.* If you are extremely risk tolerant and will be able to adhere to the buy-and-hold approach through the worst market storms, you might not need any bonds at all. But if, like most of us, you would not be able to bear the loss of half or more of your savings without selling—or suffering many sleepless nights—then you will need some bonds to dampen your bear market losses. Ideally, you want your bond allocation to be just large enough to reduce your bear market losses to a level that you can live with—and not one iota larger.

Of course, this advice is a lot easier for me to give than for you to implement. For one, no one knows just how bad the bear markets of the future will be. Are we talking about downturns like 2000–2002, when the market lost nearly half of its value but the high-volatility hedges reduced the losses of well-diversified portfolios to less than 20 percent? Or 2007–9, when the market lost more than half of its value, and the high-volatility hedges were nowhere near as effective as in 2000–2002? Or are we talking 1929–32, when the Dow dropped 89 percent? Unfortunately, there's just no way to know what the future might hold.

What's more, you can't know in advance how you'll react to some future unknown event. But here, at least, you can gain some insight from past downturns, especially if you experienced these downturns as an investor. So to get some kind of handle on the right mix of bonds and stocks for *your* risk tolerance level, ask yourself the following questions: Were you invested in the stock market during the 2007–9 bear market? If yes, how much of your retirement savings was invested in stocks or stock funds, and how much in bonds? How did you react to the downturn? Did you sell all or a portion of your stocks? Did you lose a lot of sleep worrying about your losses? If you answer yes to either of these last two questions, this is an indication that you probably had too much money allocated to stocks going into the downturn. If, for example, you had 60 percent allocated to stocks and 40 percent to bonds, you might want to set your new allocation going forward to 50 percent stocks and 50 percent bonds, or even (if your memories of 2008 are particularly painful) 40 percent stocks and 60 percent bonds. If, conversely, you were never tempted to sell your stocks during the crisis, and you slept like a baby, you may have had too much of your money in bonds and not enough in stocks.

If you were not invested in the stock market back in 2008, you will have to base your stock/bond allocation decision on imagination rather than experience. In Chapter 9 (see Figure 9.3), we tested how well our advanced and basic portfolios would have held up during the 2007–9 financial crisis, assuming a withdrawal rate of zero. Table 11.2 summarizes the results of that test. As the table shows, a working person using an aggressive allocation (80 percent stocks and 20 percent bonds) would have experienced a total loss of 38 to 43 percent of his nest egg. Someone using the moderate allocation (60 percent stocks and 40 percent bonds) would have lost 30 to 34 percent, whereas someone relying on the conservative allocation (40 percent stocks and 60 percent bonds) would have experienced a loss of 22 to 25 percent. It is very difficult to do, but try to imagine how you might react to losses in each of these ranges and then pick your allocation accordingly. If, for example, you don't think you could live with a 40 percent loss but might be able to handle a 30 percent loss, then you might try the advanced moderate 60/40 stock/bond allocation.

Before making your final decision, be sure to read the rest of this book. My hope is that some of the material in Part V may help you to reduce your anxiety level during the occasional shocks the market tosses our way. The better prepared you are, both mentally and emotionally, for the market's inevitable ups and downs, the less you may need to rely on bonds and the compromises they require you to make.

Table 11.2. Total Losses Experienced by the Basic and Advanced Portfolios during the 2007–9 Bear Market

Portfolio	Total Percentage Loss
Aggressive (80% Stocks/20% Bonds):	
Advanced	38%
Basic	43%
Moderate (60% Stocks/40% Bonds):	
Advanced	30%
Basic	34%
Conservative (40% Stocks/60% Bonds):	
Advanced	22%
Basic	25%

Sources: Developed by the author using data from www.morningstar.com.
Gold returns based on London Gold Market Fixing prices.

Whether you can use past experience or have to rely more on imagination, there is a lot of guesswork involved in selecting a stock/bond mix that is appropriate for you. But understand that if you don't get the mix quite right at first, you can always adjust your allocation. In Chapter 14, we discuss the best way to make changes to your portfolio if needed. And in Chapter 19, you'll learn how to recover and reenter the market if you allocate too much to stocks and sell during a downturn. Finding the mix that best suits your own tolerance for volatility may require some trial and error—so don't sweat the initial stock/bond decision too much.

Current and Near-Term Future Retirees

If you're nowhere near retiring, your psychological tolerance for volatility is the only factor you need to consider when deciding on an appropriate stock/bond split. But the decision process is more complex if you are already retired or within five years of retiring. Unlike a worker, a retiree faces a real danger of going broke if he encounters either too much volatility or not enough returns to outpace inflation. And a person within five years of retirement faces the danger of a drastic reduction in her nest egg, with no time to recover, if she is unfortunate enough to experience a major bear market before her retirement date. For retirees and those nearing retirement, nothing about the retirement risk is purely psychological—it is 100 percent real.

How, then, should a retiree, or near-retiree, approach the stock/bond allocation decision? The key factor determining the decision should be your withdrawal rate. As we mentioned in Chapter 10, the lower your withdrawal rate, the more flexibility you should have in selecting a stock/bond allocation. To understand why this is the case, we need to revisit someone we first met in Part III. You may recall Bob, who retired in 1973 using a basic portfolio and an initial withdrawal rate of 4 percent (which he increased each subsequent year to account for inflation). Bob faced the triple whammy of a deep bear market beginning immediately upon his retirement, a lengthy period of high inflation, and a very long forty-one-year retirement (longevity risk). We now need to ask what would have happened had Bob retired using various alternative initial withdrawal rates?

Table 11.3 gives us the answers for the aggressive (80/20), moderate (60/40), and conservative (40/60) basic portfolios that we looked at in Chapter 8, as well as for a very conservative portfolio consisting of 20 percent stocks and 80 percent bonds.

Combinations of withdrawal rates and portfolios that led to bankruptcy before 2013 are highlighted in the table in dark gray (indicating danger). For these dark gray combinations, the table shows the number of years the portfolio survived. For example, at a 4.5 percent initial withdrawal rate, the table indicates that the conservative (40/60) portfolio would have lasted for thirty-one years (from 1973 until 2004).

Table 11.3. Performance of the Basic Portfolios for Bob's Retirement, at Alternative Initial Withdrawal Rates

Initial Withdrawal Rate	Portfolios			
	Aggressive (80/20)	Moderate (60/40)	Conservative (40/60)	Very Conservative (20/80)
High Withdrawal Rates:				
6.0%	18 years	17 years	16 years	16 years
5.5%	22 years	21 years	20 years	18 years
5.0%	29 years	26 years	24 years	22 years
4.5%	Survives	36 years	31 years	27 years
Low Withdrawal Rates:				
4.0%	Survives	Survives	Survives	35 years
3.5%	Survives	Survives	Survives	Survives
3.0%	Survives	Survives	Survives	Survives
2.5%	Survives	Survives	Survives	Survives
2.0%	Survives	Survives	Survives	Survives

Sources: Developed by the author using data from www.morningstar.com.
Gold returns based on London Gold Market Fixing prices.

Those combinations of a withdrawal rate and portfolio that would have survived until December 2013 are shown in Table 11.3 in white (indicating safety), with two exceptions. These two exceptions—the aggressive (80/20) portfolio, at a 4.5 percent withdrawal rate, and the conservative (40/60) portfolio, at a 4 percent withdrawal rate—are highlighted in lighter gray (indicating caution), because these portfolio/withdrawal rate combinations only barely made it through Bob's retirement. They probably would not have survived another year beyond 2013.

There are two critical points to be gleaned from Table 11.3. Notice, first, that at withdrawal rates of 3.5 percent or less, all of the portfolios would have survived. However, at withdrawal rates in excess of 4 percent, virtually all of the portfolios would have been bankrupted before 2013.

The second key point to be gleaned from Table 11.3 is that the portfolios weighted heavily toward stocks proved to be less risky than those weighted toward bonds, *regardless* of the initial withdrawal rate. Though Bob experienced a lot of volatility during his long retirement—including the big 1973–74, 2000–2002, and 2007–9 bear markets—the main risk to his portfolio came from the high inflation and low bond returns of the 1970s and early 1980s. Since 1983, we have enjoyed *high* bond returns and *low, stable* inflation. Unfortunately, many people—investment professionals and financial advisors included—have short memories. They have been lulled by the great bond bull market of the past three decades and have forgotten the ravages a long bond bear market and high inflation can inflict on a portfolio weighted too heavily toward bonds. But we have experienced high inflation in the past, and we might well see a return of high inflation in the future. And far from being a thing of the past, low bond returns are our likely fate, at least for the next few years.

The Trinity Study. On the basis of Table 11.3, we can draw a few tentative conclusions. At withdrawal rates above 4 percent, the risk of bankruptcy is high, but the safest portfolios are those weighted heavily toward stocks. At a 4 percent withdrawal rate, it becomes possible to avoid bankruptcy with a wider selection of stock/bond mixes, although as the bond allocation is increased to 60 percent and higher, the risk of running out of money increases. At lower withdrawal rates (3.5 percent and less), virtually any stock/bond mix should offer a high degree of safety.

These conclusions must, however, be viewed as tentative, because they are based on a limited amount of historical data. Though the 1973 to 2013 period provides an excellent test of a portfolio's ability to withstand high inflation *and* significant volatility (including four major bear markets), it is not necessarily the absolute worst case in the historical record. For example, a retirement that began in 1929 and continued through the Great Depression would have been subjected to volatility even worse than that experienced by Bob. And we cannot ultimately know how a retirement beginning with the 2007–9 financial crisis—like Mary's in Chapter 9—will work out, because we don't know what the next three decades will bring.

Fortunately, retirement withdrawal rates have been extensively studied. One of the best known and most influential of these studies was conducted in the 1990s by three professors, Philip L. Cooley, Carl M. Hubbard, and Daniel T. Walz, at Trinity University in San Antonio, Texas. The Trinity Study, as it has come to be known, was updated by the three professors and published in the *Journal of Financial Planning* in 2011.[90] The updated version used historical data on stock and bond returns from 1926 through 2009 to test portfolio survivability for five different stock/bond allocations, ranging from 100 percent stocks to 100 percent bonds. The study's authors considered retirements of fifteen, twenty, twenty-five, and thirty years. For each of these retirement lengths, they looked at retirements beginning on January 1 of each calendar year. For example, for retirements lasting thirty years, they considered a person retiring on January 1, 1926, and surviving until December 31, 1955; a person retiring on January 1, 1927, and surviving until December 31, 1956; and similarly all the way up to a person retiring on January 1, 1980, and surviving until December 31, 2009. This gave them a total of fifty-five different thirty-year retirements to test, spanning from 1926 to 2009. The Trinity authors determined the percentage of these fifty-five retirements that succeeded for different withdrawal rates and stock/bond mixes, with a successful retirement defined as one that did not end in bankruptcy before the thirty years were up. Initial withdrawal rates were adjusted for inflation in each subsequent year.

The Trinity Study and its update have some limitations. First, the authors constructed their portfolios using only two asset classes: large company stocks (represented by the S&P 500) and corporate bonds (represented by Salomon Brothers Long-Term High-Grade Bond Index). Furthermore, the returns data they used do not take mutual fund fees and expenses into account (although, assuming that low-cost index funds would be used, this should not make a big difference in their results).

These weaknesses aside, the great strength of the Trinity Study update is that it covers eighty-four years of market history, *including* the 1929 Crash and Great Depression as well as the stagflation of the late 1970s and early 1980s. Interestingly, stagflation may have posed the worst-case scenario for retirees over this time span —even worse than the Depression. The Trinity authors note that for a thirty-year retirement with a 5 percent initial withdrawal rate and a 50/50 split between stocks and bonds, bankruptcy occurred in a total of eighteen of the fifty-five time spans tested. And all but one of these eighteen failures occurred for retirements spanning the late 1970s.[91] If we can infer from this bit of information that stagflation was the biggest danger to retirees' portfolios over the past eighty-four years, then Bob's 1973 retirement is in fact a very good (or rather diabolical) test of portfolio survivability. Not surprisingly, given the preeminent risks posed by the late 1970s, the updated Trinity Study results tend to confirm our tentative conclusions based on Bob's retirement. For example, at a 4 percent withdrawal rate, the 75 percent stock/25 percent bond portfolio performed best, achieving a 100 percent survival rate for a thirty-year retirement. The 50 percent stock/50 percent bond portfolio in the updated Trinity Study achieved a 96 percent survival rate for a thirty-year retirement. However, the 25 percent stock/75 percent bond portfolio was successful only 80 percent of the time.[92] In other words, this portfolio would have failed one out of five times between

1926 and 2009 — a failure rate that confirms the dark gray (danger) color we gave to the very conservative (20/80) portfolio at a 4 percent withdrawal rate in Table 11.3.

The conclusions we can draw from the Trinity Study update are similar to the conclusions we drew from Table 11.3. At withdrawal rates below 4 percent, most asset allocations (excepting 100 percent bonds) would have survived the worst of the past eighty-four years. At a 4 percent initial withdrawal rate, the safest portfolios are those with at least a 50 percent allocation to stocks. And at withdrawal rates of 5 percent or greater, none of the portfolios offer a high degree of safety, although the least risky are those that are weighted heavily toward stocks. At such high withdrawal rates, the long-term returns of bond-heavy portfolios may fall below the withdrawal rate — especially during periods of high inflation, when withdrawals can increase rapidly above their initial levels. Don't forget, bonds work on the principle of *compromise*. Adding bonds to your portfolio will reduce its volatility, but this benefit comes with an increased risk of insufficient returns. At high withdrawal rates, this risk outweighs the benefits of lower portfolio volatility.

This is one of the reasons why it is important to keep your initial withdrawal rate low: 4 percent or less. Not only does a low withdrawal rate significantly improve your odds of beating the retirement risk, it also enables you to *safely* add bonds to your portfolio. There are probably very few people who can withstand the volatility of a 100 percent stock portfolio without selling during market downturns — or suffering severe insomnia. This goes especially for retirees, who must depend on their portfolios to meet their living expenses. Yet, at withdrawal rates of 6 percent or more, the Trinity Study update shows that adding bonds to an all-stock portfolio *reduces* its chances of survival. You do not want to be in a position of having to (1) forgo bonds and suffer the emotional consequences or (2) invest in bonds and risk a high chance of bankruptcy. Fortunately, as long as you keep your initial withdrawal rate at or (better yet) below the recommended 4 percent maximum, you will not have to sacrifice the peace of mind an allocation to bonds can bring.

Guidance for retirees in their sixties, and near-retirees in their fifties and sixties. The Trinity Study update provides a solid basis for guidelines on selecting an appropriate stock/bond mix. For those in their sixties just beginning retirement, as well as those in their late fifties and early sixties within five years of retiring, I used the Trinity results for a thirty-year retirement, supplemented with Table 11.3, to develop the following guidelines:

- *For those with initial withdrawal rates*[93] *of 3.5 percent or less,* any stock allocation ranging from 20 to 100 percent should provide a high degree of safety from the retirement risk. The selection of a specific allocation within this broad range should be based on your own personal comfort level and goals. Those who are risk averse might consider the conservative (40/60) or very conservative (20/80) portfolios. Alternatively, risk-tolerant investors may prefer the moderate (60/40) or even aggressive (80/20) portfolios — choices that may increase your long-term returns and eventually allow you to spend more in retirement.

- *For those with withdrawal rates in the 3.5 to 4 percent range,* stock allocations ranging from 50 to 100 percent offer the lowest risk of bankruptcy. Again, the choice of a specific allocation within this range should be made based on your risk tolerance.

Again, withdrawal rates above 4 percent are not recommended. However, some retirees may not be able to get their withdrawal rate down to the 4 percent level. In addition, some retirees may prefer to accept a higher risk of bankruptcy to enjoy a higher living standard. As long as you understand the risks, the following guidelines may be used by those with withdrawal rates above 4 percent:

- *For withdrawal rates between 4 and 6.5 percent,* a stock allocation ranging from 75 to 100 percent provides the lowest risk of bankruptcy.

- *For withdrawal rates exceeding 6.5 percent,* a 100 percent stock allocation offers the best chance of avoiding the retirement risk.

The updated Trinity Study results indicate that 100 percent stock allocations offer a lower risk of bankruptcy than other allocations at *most* withdrawal rates. However, I would avoid using a 100 percent stock allocation unless your withdrawal rate exceeds 6.5 percent, for two reasons. First, very few retirees are likely to be able to withstand the volatility of a 100 percent stock portfolio. Second, the possibility always exists that we could see more frequent, or deeper, bear markets in the future than we have in the past, in which case the risks of bankruptcy associated with stock-heavy portfolios may prove greater than suggested by the Trinity Study results.

Of course, the possibility of a future worse than the past applies not only to stock downturns but to bond returns and inflation. Therefore, *if you have the necessary risk tolerance*, it may make sense to avoid the low ends of the stock allocation ranges presented earlier, as well as the high ends. For example, for withdrawal rates between 3.5 and 4 percent, the highest degree of safety from future as well as past market misbehavior may lie not with a 50/50 portfolio or an all-stock portfolio but rather toward the middle ground provided by the moderate (60/40) and aggressive (80/20) portfolios. This is where the sweet spot we first sought back in Chapter 9 appears to lie.

Yet it is well to remember that the future remains unknown, and all of our efforts to plan for it by selecting a stock/bond mix that proved safe in the past may come to naught. Therefore, you must ultimately be prepared to alter your withdrawal rate or your asset allocation—or both—as the future unfolds. In the last two chapters, we tackle the subjects of when, and how, to make mid-course corrections in your asset allocation plan when circumstances warrant.

Guidance for your seventies and eighties. The preceding guidelines are for those in their late fifties and sixties who are just entering their retirement years. But as you age, one of the key non-investment-related components of the retirement risk, namely, longevity risk, declines. As a result, the chances of bankruptcy associated with all stock/bond mixes likewise decline.

Therefore, risk-averse retirees may want to increase their allocation to bonds as they age. To address this possibility, I developed additional guidelines based on the results for twenty-five-year-long and fifteen-year-long retirements from the updated Trinity Study. These older-retiree guidelines, along with the guidance provided earlier for younger retirees, are presented in Table 11.4. As this table indicates, the range of low-risk stock allocations widens significantly as you age. For example, a retiree in her seventies with a current withdrawal rate of 4 percent could choose to allocate 75 percent of her portfolio to bonds, while an eighty-year-old with the same withdrawal rate could use an 80 percent bond allocation. (Again though, you may want to avoid the extreme low and high ends of these stock allocation ranges, in case future market crashes or inflation prove worse than what we have experienced in the past.)

Table 11.4. Guidance on Lower-Risk Stock Allocations for Retirees

Current Withdrawal Rate	Lower-Risk Stock Allocation Ranges for Retirees in Their		
	Sixties and Younger	Seventies	Eighties and Beyond
3.5% and less	20% to 100%	20% to 100%	20% to 100%
3.51% to 4%	50% to 100%	25% to 100%	20% to 100%
4.01% to 5.5%	75% to 100%	50% to 100%	20% to 100%
5.51% to 6.5%	75% to 100%	75% to 100%	25% to 100%
6.51% to 7.5%	100%	75% to 100%	50% to 100%
7.51% to 8.5%	100%	100%	50% to 100%
8.51% to 9.5%	100%	100%	75% to 100%
Greater than 9.5%	100%	100%	100%

You do not have to change your stock/bond mix as you age. Table 11.4 should be used only if you want to reduce your portfolio's volatility by increasing your allocation to bonds. *Do not use Table 11.4 to reduce your allocation to bonds*, unless you are doing so following the specific guidance given in Chapter 18. Retirees should never reduce their bond allocation except under the very specific conditions of portfolio hypothermia discussed in that chapter.

To use Table 11.4, you will need your *current* withdrawal rate, not your initial withdrawal rate. (The initial withdrawal rate is used only in conjunction with the guidance for new retirees in their sixties and near-retirees in their fifties or sixties.) For example, if your initial withdrawal rate was 5 percent when you retired at sixty-five, but your current withdrawal rate at age seventy is 3.2 percent, you would use the first (3.5 percent and less) row in Table 11.4 to guide your selection of a new stock/bond mix. If your withdrawal rate has increased, for example, to 8 percent, and Table 11.4 indicates that you should *reduce* your allocation to bonds, again, *do not change your allocation* unless you are following the Chapter 18 guidance.

If you delay your retirement until your seventies, you should use the second (Seventies) column of Table 11.4 to select your *initial* stock/bond mix, based on your initial withdrawal rate at retirement.

Not your father's asset allocation advice. You may have heard or read asset allocation advice quite different from the preceding guidelines. The guidance most commonly offered is that you should hold your age in bonds. For example, if you are thirty years old, you should allocate 30 percent of your portfolio to bonds; if you are seventy, then hold 70 percent of your nest egg in bonds. Though simple, this advice is fundamentally flawed. It ignores the critical relationship between the withdrawal rate and the retirement risk. A sixty-five-year-old retiree with a 5 percent withdrawal rate faces a much larger risk of running out of money than a sixty-five-year-old with a 3 percent withdrawal rate. The former will likely be safer using an *aggressive*, 80 percent stocks/20 percent bonds portfolio than the conservative 35/65 allocation implied by the "hold your age in bonds" formula. The latter retiree (with a 3 percent withdrawal rate) should be safe from bankruptcy with a 35/65 or even a 20/80 portfolio and should simply choose the stock/bond mix that best fits her comfort level.

The "hold your age in bonds" advice is an example of a solution based on a flawed conception of the problem. The critical problem we all face is the retirement risk—the risk that we will outlive our money. There are *two* ways this could happen: too much negative volatility and not enough returns to outpace inflation. It is true that by increasing your allocation to bonds as you age, you will reduce the volatility of your portfolio. But you will also *increase* the risk of not earning enough returns to outpace inflation. The "hold your age in bonds" formula ignores the latter risk.

A good asset allocation plan must address both components of the retirement risk. The stock/bond allocation guidelines presented in Table 11.4 have been tested, and found to perform well, under extreme historic conditions of both high stock market volatility (including the 1929 Crash) and high inflation (including the stagflation of the late 1970s and early 1980s). You should use these guidelines to help you make your stock/bond allocation decision. Ignore the simplistic age-based formula.

Step 3: Allocating the Stock Portion of Your Portfolio

Choosing the right stock/bond allocation is admittedly hard to do. But now that you know how to do it, the remaining process is much easier. We just need to make sure that we (1) allocate enough money to high-volatility hedges to cushion our portfolios from bear markets, (2) allocate enough to return boosters to ensure that we earn returns sufficient to beat inflation, and (3) spread our money around enough to avoid a dangerous concentration in any single asset class.

Allocating to the Three Main Asset Types

To accomplish these three goals, first decide how much of the stock portion of your portfolio you want to allocate to each of the three main equity asset types: large caps (both U.S. and international), high-volatility hedges (gold, precious metals equities [PME], and emerging-market bonds), and return boosters (small caps and value stocks). Table 11.5 presents my own rough, subjective guidelines to help you make this decision.

Table 11.5. Rough Guidelines for Allocating the Stock Portion of Your Portfolio to the Three Main Equity Asset Types

Asset Type	Recommended Percentage Allocations	
	Recommended Minimum	Recommended Maximum
High-volatility hedges	20%	35%
Return boosters	20%	50%
Large caps	15%	60%

High-volatility hedges. I start by recommending an allocation of somewhere between 20 and 35 percent to the high-volatility hedges. You want to allocate enough money to these hedges to ensure that they will significantly reduce your portfolio's volatility—I put the minimum level at roughly 20 percent. But conversely, you want to remember that they are *hedges*. You should keep your allocation to them well below 50 percent so as to leave sufficient room for your core holdings.

How do you decide on a specific number within the 20 to 35 percent range? It depends on your tolerance for risk and your attitude toward financial loss and gain. Most people will probably want to lean toward the high end of the range. I say this because most people fear losing money more than they regret missing out on opportunities to gain money. (Many psychological experiments have confirmed this loss-aversion bias.) In general, you will minimize your losses during bear markets by choosing an allocation at or near the 35 percent recommended maximum.

However, if you are an unusually risk-tolerant individual, *and* someone who relishes big gains during bull markets, you may be better off choosing an allocation at or near the minimum recommended 20 percent level. High-volatility hedges are likely to underperform the broader market and weigh down your portfolio's returns during bull markets. If the thought of making 10 percent returns when your friends and neighbors are earning 20 percent drives you crazy and you're willing to accept steep losses when the market nosedives, consider a minimum allocation to high-volatility hedges.

Return boosters. For the return boosters, I recommend an allocation somewhere between 20 and 50 percent. Most people should pick a percentage at or near the high end of this range. In general, a large allocation to return boosters will improve your returns more than they will increase your volatility. And, in any event, volatility is best minimized by increasing your allocation to bonds and high-volatility hedges, not by limiting your allocation to return boosters.

However, although small caps and value stocks tend to outperform the broader stock market in the long run, they can nonetheless underperform for long periods of time. If you are the type of person who is less likely to stick to a buy-and-hold strategy if you underperform the market for years, you may want to limit your return booster allocation to the low end of the recommended range.

Large caps. Once you've decided on the size of your allocation to high-volatility hedges and return boosters, your large cap allocation is simply the remainder. For example, if you choose to allocate 30 percent of the stock portion of your portfolio to high-volatility hedges and 50 percent to return boosters, that leaves you 20 percent for large caps. Simple, right?

Allocating to Individual Asset Classes within the Three Main Asset Types

Once you've decided on an overall percentage allocation to the three asset types, it is a relatively straightforward matter to divvy up these percentages to the specific asset classes you selected in Step 1 of the asset allocation process (see Table 11.1). Here my general guidance is simple. For the high-volatility hedges and small caps, try to keep the amount of money you allocate to any specific asset class to 20 percent or less (5 percent or less in the case of gold) of the total stock portion of your portfolio. For large caps (including large cap value stocks), you can consider increasing the allocation up to 50 percent. Again, these percentages are based on my subjective judgment and are offered as rough guidelines only.

Let's consider how we might apply these rough guidelines in a bit more detail.

High-volatility hedges: Gold, PME, and emerging-market bonds. For most people (including all retirees and near-retirees), I recommend a small, 5 percent allocation to gold, and an approximately equal allocation of the amount remaining between a PME fund and an emerging-market bond fund. For example, if you are planning to allocate 35 percent of the stock portion of your portfolio to the high-volatility hedges, you could split this amount into a 5 percent allocation to gold, a 15 percent allocation to a PME fund, and a 15 percent allocation to an emerging-market bond fund.

However, if you are a younger person nowhere near retiring, *and* are risk tolerant, you might consider increasing your allocation to the PME fund and doing away with gold altogether, as a way of increasing your long-run returns. For example, if you are using a 35 percent high-volatility hedge allocation, you might allocate 20 percent to PME and 15 percent to emerging-market bonds. Then, as you approach retirement, you can shift 5 percent of your allocation from the precious metals mining fund to gold.

If you are planning to use a basic (five investment or less) portfolio rather than an advanced portfolio, and have room for only one high-volatility hedge, my recommendation is to make that one hedge a PME fund. In this case, I would limit the allocation to 20 percent to avoid an overconcentration in a single asset class.

Return boosters: Small caps and value stocks. If you are planning a large allocation (at or near 50 percent) to return boosters, you should plan on including two or three individual asset classes (from Table 11.1) in your portfolio. You should then choose an allocation plan that avoids an over-concentration in any single asset class. For example, you might allocate 30 percent to a large cap value fund and 20 percent to a small cap value fund. Or alternatively, if you want to include three return boosters in your portfolio, you might allocate 20 percent to a large cap value fund, 10 percent to a small cap blend fund, and 20 percent to a small cap value fund. These allocations are just suggestions, and you may want to weight your portfolio more heavily toward small caps or value stocks, depending on your personal preferences. (For example, if you believe those who contend that value stocks are the single exception to the ironclad rule of risk and reward, you may want to tilt your portfolio more toward value stocks than small caps.)

If you are planning to limit your return booster allocation to around 20 percent, you may need only one asset class. Small cap value stocks may be your best choice in this case, as they will provide exposure to both the size and value premiums.

Large caps: U.S., international, and emerging market. As with the return boosters, the key consideration in allocating among the different large cap asset classes is to avoid an overconcentration in any one asset class. However, because large caps compose the majority (70 percent) of the stock market, you can allocate much more than 20 percent of your money to a single large cap asset class without running the risk of overconcentration. Conceivably, you could get away with choosing a single large cap asset class rather than two or three. However, you want to make sure your portfolio is diversified not only by size (small vs. large caps) and style (value vs. blend) but also by geography. I recommend a 20 to 40 percent allocation to non-U.S. stocks, which should include both developed markets (Europe and Japan) and emerging markets. I would recommend leaning toward the high end of this range to ensure adequate currency as well as geographic diversification. You may be able to use return boosters to gain some or all of your needed exposure to international equities, but whether through return boosters, large caps, or both, don't forget to make room for a significant allocation to foreign stocks in your portfolio.

Summary of guidelines for allocating your stock portfolio. The preceding guidelines can be summarized as follows:

- *Guideline 1: High-volatility hedges.* Total allocation across all high-volatility hedges should be between 20 and 35 percent of the stock portion of the portfolio. Of this total, gold should be limited to 5 percent maximum (and might not be needed at all by young, risk-tolerant individuals). PME and emerging-market bond funds should each be limited to no more than 20 percent.

- *Guideline 2: Return boosters.* Total allocation across all return boosters should be between 20 and 50 percent of the stock portion of the portfolio. Most people should lean toward the high end of this range. Limit allocation to individual small cap asset classes to no more than 20 percent. Allocations to large cap value asset classes should not exceed 50 percent.

- *Guideline 3: Large cap blend funds.* Total allocation across all large cap blend funds should be between 15 and 60 percent of the stock portion of the portfolio. Allocations to individual large cap blend asset classes should not exceed 50 percent.

- *Guideline 4: Foreign stocks.* Total allocation across all foreign asset classes should be between 20 and 40 percent of the stock portion of the portfolio. Preferably you should lean toward the high end of this range.

Keep in mind that these guidelines are only my suggestions, based on my subjective opinions of what should work best for most people. There is no optimum asset allocation plan, and one size does *not* fit all. If you are a financial Evel Knievel and want to ride the stock market roller coaster for all it's worth, you may want to load up on return boosters and cut back on gold and the other high-volatility hedges. If you believe strongly that emerging-market stocks will outperform the U.S. market over time, you may want to exceed the 40 percent maximum for foreign stocks. Use the preceding suggestions as guidelines, not hard-and-fast rules, and build the gourmet portfolio that best suits your personal tastes. Remember, asset allocation is as much an art as a science, and you are the master chef of your portfolio.

Step 4: Allocating the Bond Portion of Your Portfolio

We'll keep this last step short and simple. For many people, the advice I offered back in Chapter 5 still applies: allocate the bond portion of your portfolio one-third to a short-term bond fund, one-third to an intermediate-term bond fund, and one-third to an inflation-protected bond fund (or a substitute fund; see Table 11.1). However, if you are planning to allocate more than 50 percent of your portfolio to bonds, you may want to increase the allocation to the inflation-protected fund. The greater your reliance on bonds, the greater your risk of not earning enough returns to outpace inflation. TIPS and I Bonds protect you from this risk. For those using a conservative (40/60) portfolio, a 50 percent allocation to inflation-protected bonds is warranted. And those using a very conservative (20/80) portfolio might want to increase this allocation to 75 percent.

That's all there is to Step 4. (For those willing to take on a significant amount of additional effort, Chapter 12 presents an alternative to these simple bond allocations that has the potential to virtually eliminate the retirement risk—at least for a while.)

Write It Down

Finally, after developing your asset allocation plan, it is a very good idea to write the plan down. By committing your asset allocation to ink and paper in the form of an investment plan, you will be less likely to fudge or otherwise stray from your planned allocation. Exhibit 11.1 provides an example of an investment plan for a retired couple using one of the basic portfolios we studied in Chapter 8.

Notice that in addition to an asset allocation, Exhibit 11.1 also specifies a process for rebalancing and a maximum actionable withdrawal rate (MAWR) for the portfolio. We delve into rebalancing in Chapter 15, and we describe how to select a MAWR in Chapter 18. (A person or couple not yet retired should also write down their savings plan; see Chapter 10.)

Practical Asset Allocation Examples

Asset allocation can be a challenging, tricky process, especially when you have to deal with real-world constraints such as the limited investment choices provided by most 401(k)s. To help you better understand the process and how to apply the various tables and guidelines presented in this chapter, let's work through a few hypothetical examples for investors at various stages in their lives. For each of our fictional investors, we'll describe the investor's financial situation, present a suggested asset allocation plan, and then go over the plan to explain it and make sure it adheres to the various guidelines. We'll start with Steve, single and fresh out of college, with a new job and a newly opened IRA.

Exhibit 11.1. Example Investment Plan for a Retired Couple

INVESTMENT PLAN

Overall Asset Allocation: 60% stocks, 40% bonds

Allocation of Stock Portion of Portfolio (with fund ticker symbols and account locations in parentheses):

U.S. Large Cap Blend (VFINX in taxable account):	30%
Foreign Large Cap Blend (VEA in taxable account):	30%
Precious Metals Mining (GDX in taxable account):	20%
U.S. Small Cap Value (VBR in taxable account):	20%

Allocation of Bond Portion of Portfolio:

Short-Term Investment Grade (VBSSX in IRA):	100%

Rebalancing:

Rebalancing to return the portfolio to the above target allocations will be done in all tax-deferred and tax-free accounts in January of each year. Rebalancing in taxable accounts will be done, to the extent possible, on a continual basis by withdrawing living expenses from outperforming assets. If further rebalancing is required to bring the taxable accounts in line with the target allocations, a decision will be made in January whether or not to pursue rebalancing or defer it to avoid incurring capital gains taxes.

Maximum Actionable Withdrawal Rate (MAWR) during Market Declines:

Based on Chapter 18 of *The Death of Buy and Hold*, a maximum actionable withdrawal rate (MAWR) of six percent has been established for our portfolio. Should the current withdrawal rate rise to the MAWR during a market downturn, efforts will first be made to reduce the withdrawal rate by reducing living expenses (specifically cutting luxury items from the budget), or increasing noninvestment income. If these efforts prove insufficient to keep the current withdrawal rate from rising again to the MAWR, we will undertake to sell all stock funds. We will then follow the guidance in Chapter 19 of *The Death of Buy and Hold* to time our reentry into the stock market.

Changes to Plan:

We will review this plan each January when we rebalance, and whenever there are substantial changes to our financial situation. When warranted we will make changes to the plan to take advantage of new opportunities (as explained in Chapter 14 of *The Death of Buy and Hold*), or to reflect changed life circumstances. As recommended in Chapter 14, we will not implement plan changes during bear markets, but will wait to implement changes until the market has begun to recover. During bull markets we will implement plan changes promptly.

Steve: Starting Out with a Basic Portfolio

In addition to $5,000 in a bank savings account (his rainy day fund), Steve has managed to put away a total of $1,000 in his IRA. However, he has a large amount of student debt and, at least until he's been on the job a few more years, does not expect to be able to add to his savings. His brokerage company charges a commission of $10 per trade, which means he would have to spend 1 percent of his total IRA savings for every ETF he purchases. This is too much to spend on brokerage costs, so Steve, like all investors with small nest eggs, should stick to mutual funds. (Unlike ETFs, mutual funds can be purchased without paying a commission.)

Because Steve's savings are in an IRA, he does not face the limited fund choices offered by 401(k)s. However, most of the mutual funds offered by his broker have minimum purchase amount requirements. To meet these requirements, Steve will need to limit his investments to a maximum of four funds. As his salary increases, his debts are repaid, and his retirement savings grow, Steve will be able to expand his portfolio to include more asset classes. But for the time being, he'll need to stick with a basic portfolio (similar to those we constructed in Chapter 8).

One last key bit of information: Steve is not what you would call a thrill seeker, but he is relatively risk tolerant when it comes to money.

Table 11.6 presents a possible asset allocation plan for Steve. Notice, first, that he plans to use an aggressive portfolio, split 80 percent stocks and 20 percent bonds. As a worker who still has many years ahead of himself before retirement, Steve should put as much of his savings into stocks as his nerves will allow. For a young person like Steve with no prior investment experience, knowing just how much to allocate to bonds is very difficult. But his 80/20 mix is a reasonable first guess for someone who is risk tolerant. He can always adjust this mix to better match his tolerance for losses, as he gains firsthand experience with bear markets.

Table 11.6. Steve's Asset Allocation Plan

Asset Type	Asset Class	Percentage Allocation	Dollar Allocation
Stocks:			**$800**
Large cap	Foreign large cap blend	30%	$240
High-volatility hedge	PME	20%	$160
Return booster	U.S. large cap value	50%	$400
Bonds:			**$200**
Low-volatility hedge	Short-term investment grade bonds	100%	$200
Total:			**$1,000**

Notice that even though Steve's portfolio includes only four asset classes, he has nonetheless been able to meet every one of my four guidelines for the stock portion of his portfolio. His 20 percent allocation to high-volatility hedges falls within my recommended 20 to 35 percent range (Guideline 1 above), without exceeding 20 percent for the single asset class he has chosen (PME). His 50 percent allocation to return boosters falls within the 20 to 50 percent recommended range, and because he has chosen a large cap value fund rather than a small cap fund, he can allocate 50 percent to this single asset class without exceeding my recommended maximum allocation (Guideline 2). His 30 percent allocation to the large cap blend fund falls within the 15 to 60 percent recommended range (Guideline 3). And because this is a foreign stock fund, he has met Guideline 4, which specifies a 20 to 40 percent allocation to foreign stocks. It should be noted that PME funds generally include a good helping of foreign as well as U.S. stocks (in gold mining countries such as Canada, South Africa, and Australia), so Steve's total allocation to foreign stocks is likely closer to the 40 percent maximum than to 30 percent.

With only $200 available to allocate to bonds, Steve cannot split the bond portion of his portfolio three ways and still meet the minimum purchase requirements of the various bond funds available through his broker. However, he has found a short-term bond fund with a zero minimum purchase requirement. Although Steve might have also considered an inflation-protected bond fund, the short-term fund will limit his exposure to inflation, while at the same time broadening his bond holdings to include a good helping of corporate and U.S. government issuers.

Linda and Tom: Mid-Thirties Married Couple

Linda and Tom have been married for two years and have total savings between them of $140,000. Of this total, $40,000 is in a joint savings account at the bank; this is the couple's emergency fund. Of their remaining savings, $95,000 is in Linda's 401(k) plan at work, and $5,000 is in Tom's IRA. Let's see how they plan to allocate the money in these two retirement accounts.

Because most of the couple's savings is in Linda's 401(k) plan, they will need to build their portfolio based mainly on the investment choices provided in that plan. Unfortunately, those choices are limited. Using the Morningstar website, Linda has identified the mutual funds in her plan that could be used to build a well-diversified portfolio. Those choices are listed in Table 11.7. Notice, first, that Linda's 401(k) does not offer any high-volatility hedges, nor does it offer an inflation-protected bond fund. It does offer two bond funds that can be used as low-volatility hedges. But to build a truly well-hedged portfolio, the couple will in effect need to use Tom's IRA to hedge the investments in Linda's 401(k).

Table 11.7. Asset Classes in Linda's 401(k) Plan

Asset Types	Asset Classes
Large cap blend	U.S. large cap blend
	Foreign developed-market large cap blend
	Emerging-market large cap blend
Return boosters	U.S. large cap value
	U.S. small cap blend
Low-volatility hedges	Intermediate-term bonds
	Short-term bonds

Tom was not invested in the stock market back in 2008, but Linda was. At that time, Linda (then single) had her portfolio split 70 percent stocks and 30 percent bonds. She found it difficult to sleep at night during the height of the financial crisis and wound up selling all her stock funds and going 100 percent to bonds. This is a clear indication that a 70/30 portfolio may be too volatile for Linda. Therefore, the couple decides to use a more conservative, 50/50 portfolio.

Table 11.8 shows Linda and Tom's asset allocation plan, along with the account that will hold each asset class (Linda's 401(k) or Tom's IRA). To make the distinction clearer, the asset classes to be held in Tom's IRA are shaded in the table.

Notice, first, that Linda has included all of the relevant asset classes from her 401(k) in the couple's portfolio. She has allocated 40 percent of the stock portion of the portfolio to return boosters, split half and half between the large cap value fund and the small cap blend fund. She has limited the allocation to foreign stocks to the low end of the recommended 20 to 40 percent range. Linda checks the market indices frequently and in the past has found it difficult to stick with a buy-and-hold approach when her portfolio underperforms the market. Although in the long run, foreign stock returns should be similar to U.S. stock returns, the former can underperform the U.S. market for long periods of time. Linda and Tom may therefore be more comfortable limiting their foreign stock holdings to the recommended minimum level.

Tom has invested the entire amount in his IRA—$5,000 total—to the three high-volatility hedges. This brings Linda and Tom's total allocation to high-volatility hedges up to 10 percent of the stock portion of their portfolio—well below the recommended 20 percent minimum. They both understand that these hedges tend to dampen losses during bear markets and would prefer to allocate a larger amount to them. But given that Linda's 401(k) does not offer these investment choices, and all of the money available in Tom's IRA has already been allocated, they will have to make due with a less than ideal 10 percent allocation. As Tom makes new contributions to his IRA, the couple plans to increase their allocation to the high-volatility hedges.

Table 11.8. Linda and Tom's Asset Allocation Plan

Asset Type	Asset Class	Account	Percentage Allocation	Dollar Allocation
Stocks:				**$50,000**
Large caps	U.S. large cap blend	Linda's 401(k)	30%	$15,000
	Foreign developed-market large cap blend	Linda's 401(k)	10%	$5,000
	Emerging-market large cap blend	Linda's 401(k)	10%	$5,000
Return boosters	U.S. large cap value	Linda's 401(k)	20%	$10,000
	U.S. small cap blend	Linda's 401(k)	20%	$10,000
High-volatility hedges	Emerging-market bond	Tom's IRA	5%	$2,500
	PME	Tom's IRA	2.5%	$1,250
	Gold	Tom's IRA	2.5%	$1,250
Bonds:				**$50,000**
Low-volatility hedges	Short-term investment-grade bonds	Linda's 401(k)	70%	$35,000
	Intermediate-term investment-grade bonds	Linda's 401(k)	30%	$15,000
Total:				**$100,000**

After allocating all of his savings to the high-volatility hedges, there is no room left in Tom's IRA for an inflation-protected bond fund. The closest substitute in Linda's 401(k) is the short-term bond fund. While such funds do not generally include TIPS, they are less exposed to the impact of unexpectedly high inflation than longer-term bond funds. Therefore, Linda and Tom have chosen to weight their bond allocation heavily toward the short-term bond fund. In effect, they have followed my recommendation to allocate one-third of their bond portfolio to a short-term bond fund and, on top of this, have allocated an additional one-third to the same fund as a substitute for an inflation-protected bond fund. In the longer-term future, after they have increased their allocation to the high-volatility hedges, they plan to use any additional money in Tom's IRA to purchase an inflation-protected bond fund.

Although not ideal, the asset allocation plan in Table 11.8 does a good job of accommodating Linda and Tom's attitudes toward risk, within the constraints imposed by Linda's 401(k). As new savings flow into Tom's IRA, they will be able to move more toward their ideal asset allocation, with an increased weighting to PME and emerging-market bonds, and a shift out of the short-term bond fund and into an inflation-protected bond fund.

Patrick and Sandra: Approaching Retirement

Patrick and Sandra Smith are empty nesters who have been married for thirty-five years. Patrick is sixty years old and planning to retire in five years. He has saved $400,000 in his 401(k). Sandra, who is fifty-eight, worked in the early years of their marriage but has spent the last twenty-five years raising their children and seeing them off to college. Together, Patrick and Sandra also have $100,000 in a bank savings account.

Both Patrick and Sandra are highly risk averse. Currently they are using a very conservative allocation of 20 percent stocks and 80 percent bonds. Because Patrick is only five years away from retirement, it is time for him and Sandra to work out a new asset allocation plan based on their expected initial withdrawal rate at retirement. They estimate this withdrawal rate at 3.9 percent—higher than they would like, but they have done everything they can to reduce it. Patrick and Sandra refer to the guidelines in Table 11.4 for those in their late fifties and sixties and receive a nasty surprise: their 20 percent allocation to stocks falls well outside the low-risk range of 50 to 100 percent for withdrawal rates in the 3.5 percent to 4 percent range.

This poses a major dilemma for the Smiths. Going into fall 2008, they had 50 percent of their savings invested in stocks. When the stock market crashed in mid-September, they tried to maintain this allocation, knowing that selling during a downturn could lock in their losses forever. The result was a health scare. Not only did Sandra develop a severe case of insomnia, but Patrick suffered a minor heart attack. Although there is no way to be certain, the stress caused by their stock losses was a likely contributor to both of their health issues. In mid-October 2008, they sold most of their stock mutual funds and moved to their current 20/80 allocation.

After their experience in 2008, they are sure that, emotionally if not physically, they cannot handle the volatility of a 50/50 portfolio. Yet they understand that their 20/80 portfolio, while much less volatile than a 50/50 portfolio, could actually put them at *increased* risk of running out of money. What, they wonder, should they do?

There are three key points that should help the Smiths to resolve their dilemma. First, nothing is worth risking your health. Second, when it comes to making a stock/bond allocation decision, there can only be rough *guidelines*, not one-size-fits-all, hard-and-fast rules. And third, referring back to Table 11.3, at a 4 percent withdrawal rate, the very conservative (20/80) portfolio actually survived for thirty-five years following Bob's extremely difficult 1973 retirement. While not as safe as the other, more aggressive portfolios we tested, this is still a pretty good result. Assuming Patrick follows through on his plans to retire at age sixty-five, a thirty-five-year retirement would take him to age one hundred and Sandra to age ninety-eight.

Taking all three of these key points into account, Patrick and Sandra decide on a reasonable compromise. They will increase their stock allocation from 20 percent to 30 percent. They are prepared to make this compromise in part because they will also be adding high-volatility hedges to their portfolio. In effect, they are substituting high-volatility hedges for a portion of their bond holdings. This will help to keep their overall portfolio volatility low, while at the same time increasing their expected returns. They will be sure to take the temperature of this new portfolio on a regular basis, watching out especially for the signs of portfolio hypothermia that are discussed in Chapter 18. They will increase their allocation to stocks if these signs indicate that they are in danger of not earning enough returns to outpace inflation.

While Patrick and Sandra's stock/bond split is not the best for most people, it is the best *for them*, given their limited tolerance for short-term losses. From an objective standpoint, at a 4 percent withdrawal rate, the updated Trinity Study indicates that a 50/50 portfolio has done a better job than a 25/75 portfolio of mitigating *both* components of the retirement risk over the past eight decades. But of course, the Trinity Study cannot take into account your subjective response to volatility. If you are a relatively risk-tolerant person with a low withdrawal rate (4 percent or less), you will likely be able to follow the guidance based on the Trinity Study. But if, like Patrick and Sandra, you are highly loss averse, you may need to consider portfolios outside the lowest-risk ranges to find a solution that will allow you to sleep at night. It is more important to choose a portfolio you can live with than a portfolio that falls within the lowest risk range. (That said, an even better approach is to try to reduce your withdrawal rate to 3.5 percent or less so as to widen the range of low-risk portfolios that will be available to you.)

Patrick's 401(k) provides the same asset class choices as Linda's (see Table 11.7), with one exception—it also includes an inflation-protected bond fund. This means that, like Linda and Tom, Patrick and Sandra face constraints in accessing the three high-volatility hedges. However, unlike Tom, Patrick and Sandra do not have an IRA that would provide more flexible access to these hedges. But they do have a bank account with $100,000 in savings. Given that Patrick's current take-home pay is $50,000 per year, this bank account provides them with enough funds to cover two years' worth of income in the event of an emergency. Considering that Patrick has a stable job and will be retiring in five years, and that the interest Patrick and Sandra are earning on this money won't even cover inflation, they need to lighten up on their emergency fund. Given their aversion to risk, they want to keep more than just six months' worth of income in their emergency fund. But they decide that they can live with a $50,000 fund if it will allow them to purchase the high-volatility hedges that will likely reduce their losses in future bear markets. Therefore, Patrick and Sandra open a new account at a brokerage firm and move half of the money in their bank account into the brokerage account. This provides them with a total of $450,000 outside their emergency fund, which, when split 30/70, gives them $135,000 to invest in stocks and $315,000 for bonds.

Table 11.9 shows Patrick and Sandra's asset allocation plan. Notice, first, that they are able to allocate the maximum recommended amount (35 percent) to the high-volatility hedges using the $50,000 in their new brokerage account. In fact, they have $2,750 remaining in this account after purchasing all three high-volatility hedges. They apply this left-over amount to a foreign large cap blend fund, to bolster their allocation to this asset class.

Table 11.9. Patrick and Sandra's Asset Allocation Plan

Asset Type	Asset Class	Account	Percentage Allocation	Dollar Allocation
Stocks:				**$135,000**
Large caps	Foreign developed-market large cap blend	Patrick's 401(k) (PLUS $2,750 from the brokerage account)	20%	$27,000
	Emerging-market large cap blend	Patrick's 401(k)	5%	$6,750
Return boosters	U.S. large cap value	Patrick's 401(k)	30%	$40,500
	U.S. small cap blend	Patrick's 401(k)	10%	$13,500
High-volatility hedges	Emerging-market bonds	Brokerage account	10%	$13,500
	PME	Brokerage account	20%	$27,000
	Gold	Brokerage account	5%	$6,750
Bonds:				**$315,000**
Low-volatility hedges	Short-term investment-grade bonds	Patrick's 401(k)	25%	$78,750
	Intermediate-term investment-grade bonds	Patrick's 401(k)	25%	$78,750
	Inflation-protected bonds	Patrick's 401(k)	50%	$157,500
Total:				**$450,000**

Within the brokerage account, Patrick and Sandra have weighted their allocation more heavily toward PME than toward emerging-market bonds. This choice reflects tax considerations. Ideally, bonds and bond funds should be held in 401(k)s or IRAs, because the dividends from these funds are taxed at your marginal tax rate rather than the lower rate applied to "qualified" dividends and capital gains. However, Patrick does not have access to an emerging-market bond fund through his 401(k). Because Patrick and Sandra want to be sure that their allocation to high-volatility hedges matches the 35 percent recommended maximum *without* exceeding the 20 percent suggested maximum for the PME fund, they decide to allocate 10 percent of the funds in the brokerage account to an emerging-market bond fund. Although they will have to pay high taxes on the dividends from this fund, they are willing to forgo some after-tax returns to gain the hedging potential provided by emerging-market bonds. The same logic has entered into their decision to allocate 5 percent of their stock portfolio to gold. (Returns on gold are taxed at the 28 percent rate applied to collectibles.)

This is by no means an ideal arrangement (except perhaps for the IRS). However, recall that Patrick and Sandra are in effect using the high-volatility hedges to replace 10 percent of their allocation to low-volatility bonds (which will be reduced from 80 percent to 70 percent). Although their returns on these hedges will be significantly reduced by taxes, they will still likely be higher than the returns they would have earned on the low-volatility bonds. This is especially true in the short- to mid-term, given the current low yields on domestic bonds. In effect, Patrick and Sandra are using the principle of *correlation* to reduce their (still heavy) reliance on the principle of *compromise*. Once Patrick has retired, he plans to roll over his 401(k) into an IRA. At this point, they will be able to move all of their bond and gold investments into the tax-sheltered IRA. This example illustrates the kinds of difficult trade-off decisions that must often be made when developing an asset allocation plan. The bottom line here is that you should try to place your investments in gold and emerging-market bonds in an IRA, 401(k), or other tax-sheltered account. But if that is not possible, you *might* still want to include an allocation to these assets in a taxable account, particularly if, like Patrick and Sandra, you plan to use them to replace a portion of your allocation to low-volatility hedges.

Like Linda and Tom, Patrick and Sandra have allocated 40 percent of the stock portion of their portfolio to return boosters. Notice, however, that they have weighted their allocation much more heavily toward large cap value stocks than toward small caps. This allocation reflects a personal preference on Patrick's part. He likes the idea, discussed in Chapter 6, that value stocks may offer superior protection from stock market bubbles. Furthermore, he has taken notice of the debate as to whether value stocks are an exception to the ironclad rule that higher expected returns mean higher risk. He and Sandra believe that if there is even a chance that value stocks *are* the exception that proves the rule, then there is good reason for a risk-averse couple to prefer value stocks over small caps.

Patrick and Sandra have decided to allocate 50 percent of the bond portion of their portfolio to inflation-protected bonds, with the remaining 50 percent split equally between short-term and intermediate-term bonds. They realize that their use of a less-than-optimal portfolio, weighted heavily toward bonds, has put them at increased risk of not earning enough returns to outpace inflation. By weighting their bond portfolio toward TIPS, they have taken a sensible step to limit the impact an unexpected rise in inflation could have on their bond returns.

Other than their decision to go with a 30/70 stock/bond split, Patrick and Sandra have followed all the recommended guidelines in this chapter. The result is an asset allocation plan that, while not ideal from a purely objective standpoint, nonetheless provides a reasonable compromise between the objective risk factors and the couple's subjective needs.

Patrick and Sandra: Twelve Years Further Down the Road

Let's now imagine that twelve years have elapsed. Patrick is now seventy-two, and Sandra is seventy. Patrick is retired, and he and Sandra are enjoying their new freedom and leisure time together. Fortunately, the markets have treated them kindly. As a result, their retirement portfolio has grown from $450,000 to $600,000. All of this growth has occurred in Patrick's tax-deferred account (originally his 401(k), which he rolled over into an IRA when he retired). In fact, the money in the taxable brokerage account has by this time been exhausted and the account closed. The high-volatility hedges that were originally placed in this account are now in Patrick's IRA, where they are shielded from high tax rates. With the increase in the size of their nest egg, the couple's withdrawal rate has declined from 3.9 to 2.9 percent.

At this point, Patrick and Sandra can use Table 11.4 (for retirees in their seventies) as a guide for increasing their allocation to bonds, if they so choose. And now the news is good: the low-risk stock allocations for a 2.9 percent withdrawal rate cover a wide range of possibilities from 80 percent all the way down to 20 percent. Patrick and Sandra therefore decide to move from the 30/70 allocation they selected twelve years ago to a more comfortable (for them) 20/80 allocation. The only other change they have made to their portfolio is a shift of 5 percent of their stock allocation, from the PME fund to the emerging-market bonds fund. Tax considerations were behind their original PME/emerging-market bonds allocation. Now that all of their investments are in an IRA, the tax issue is no longer relevant, and they have split their allocation to each of these two high-volatility hedges equally (15 percent each). Table 11.10 shows their new percentage and dollar allocation, reflecting the new stock/bond split, the new high-volatility hedge allocation, and the growth in their total savings to $600,000.

Table 11.10. Patrick and Sandra's New Asset Allocation Plan (for Their Seventies)

Asset Type	Asset Class	Account	Percentage Allocation	Dollar Allocation
Stocks:				**$120,000**
Large caps	Foreign developed-market large cap blend	Patrick's IRA	20%	$24,000
	Emerging-market large cap blend	Patrick's IRA	5%	$6,000
Return boosters	U.S. large cap value	Patrick's IRA	30%	$36,000
	U.S. small cap blend	Patrick's IRA	10%	$12,000
High-volatility hedges	Emerging-market bond	Patrick's IRA	15%	$18,000
	PME	Patrick's IRA	15%	$18,000
	Gold	Patrick's IRA	5%	$6,000
Bonds:				**$480,000**
Low-volatility hedges	Short-term investment-grade bonds	Patrick's IRA	25%	$120,000
	Intermediate-term investment-grade bonds	Patrick's IRA	25%	$120,000
	Inflation-protected bonds	Patrick's IRA	50%	$240,000
Total:				**$600,000**

Summary

As the preceding examples illustrate, there is no such thing as an optimum, one-size-fits-all portfolio. What works best for you will not work best for me, or for Joe at the office, or for that odd couple who lives down the street. *Your* best portfolio depends on a whole host of factors specific to your circumstances, including the size of your nest egg, whether you are in or near retirement, your withdrawal rate, the fund choices available in your 401(k), tax considerations, your emotional and physical tolerance for temporary losses, and your tolerance for underperforming the market over long stretches. If it all seems complicated, well, it is. I have tried to simplify things as much as possible by giving you a set of guidelines for each of the four steps of the asset allocation process. These guidelines can be summarized as follows.

Step 1: Selecting the Asset Classes

- Choose the asset classes that will compose your portfolio from among those listed in Table 11.1. In general, you should include all three high-volatility hedges, two or three return boosters, at least one large cap (which might also be a return booster), one or two foreign stock asset classes (which might be the same as your return boosters or large caps), and three bond asset classes. If you have a small nest egg ($5,000 or less), you may need to limit the number of asset classes you choose to as few as four (one for each of the four asset types).

Step 2: Deciding on the Right Mix of Stocks and Bonds

- If you are more than five years away from retiring, allocate as much of your nest egg as you can stomach to stocks.

- If you are retired or within five years of retiring, use the guidelines presented for different withdrawal rates in Table 11.4 to find the safest portfolios.

Step 3: Allocating the Stock Portion of Your Portfolio

- Your total allocation across all high-volatility hedges should be between 20 and 35 percent of the stock portion of your portfolio. Of this total, gold should be limited to 5 percent maximum (and might not be needed at all by young, risk-tolerant individuals). PME and emerging-market bonds should each be limited to no more than 20 percent.

- Your total allocation across all return boosters should be between 20 and 50 percent of the stock portion of your portfolio (but most people should lean toward the high end of this range). Limit your allocation to individual small cap asset classes to no more than 20 percent. Allocations to large cap value asset classes should not exceed 50 percent.

- Your total allocation across all large cap blend funds should be between 15 and 60 percent of the stock portion of your portfolio. Allocations to individual large cap blend asset classes should not exceed 50 percent.

- Your total allocation across all foreign asset classes should be between 20 and 40 percent of the stock portion of the portfolio. Preferably you should lean toward the high end of this range.

Step 4: Allocating the Bond Portion of Your Portfolio

- Allocate the bond portion of your portfolio one-third to a short-term bond fund, one-third to an intermediate-term bond fund, and one-third to an inflation-protected bond fund (or a substitute fund; see Table 11.1). If you are planning to allocate most of your nest egg to bonds, increase your allocation to TIPS or I Bonds to 50 percent (for a 40/60 portfolio) or 75 percent (for a 20/80 portfolio).

Keep in mind that these are only guidelines, not hard-and-fast rules. You can—and like Patrick and Sandra, may need to—ignore some or all of the rules, in order to build a portfolio that fits your circumstances and comfort level.

Finally, if it all seems too complicated, you can simply use one of the advanced or basic portfolios presented in Chapters 8 and 9 or one of the example portfolios in this chapter. There is no right or wrong answer when it comes to asset allocation. As long as you follow the two basic principles of *correlation* and *compromise*, and make sure that your gourmet portfolio includes at least one ingredient from each of the four main asset types (high-volatility hedges, low-volatility hedges, return boosters, and large caps), you will put the power of diversification to work for you.

CHAPTER 12

THE LMBP:
AN ALTERNATIVE ASSET ALLOCATION
FOR YOUR BOND PORTFOLIO

O nce you've developed an asset allocation plan using the procedures and guidance in Chapter 11, you will have taken a giant step toward balancing and minimizing both aspects of the retirement risk: too much negative market volatility and not enough returns to outpace inflation. But there is an alternative approach to allocating the bond portion of your portfolio that will nearly eliminate both of these risk factors—at least for a while. This approach involves matching the future value of your bond investments to your future expenses, using a *liability-matching bond portfolio* (or LMBP). As we shall see, this alternative is not for everyone. But depending on your circumstances, an LMBP just might suit you better than the bond portfolio recommended in Chapter 11. In this chapter, we explore what an LMBP is, how it works to reduce various components of the retirement risk, who might benefit from it, and how to implement and maintain it.

An example will show how the LMBP works. Dave is a seventy-year-old who has just retired with a $1 million nest egg and annual expenses of $60,000. He will receive $20,000 annually in Social Security benefits and must therefore fund the remaining $40,000 from his retirement portfolio. Hence his initial withdrawal rate is $40,000 divided by $1,000,000, or 4 percent. On the basis of Table 11.4 for retirees in their seventies, Dave can minimize the retirement risk using any stock allocation from 25 percent to 100 percent. Being highly risk averse, Dave chooses to allocate 25 percent of his portfolio, or $250,000 to stocks, and the remaining $750,000 to bonds. He allocates the $250,000 stock portion of his portfolio using the guidance provided in the preceding chapter. But as an alternative to the bond allocation guidance in Chapter 11, Dave invests his entire bond portfolio in a TIPS bond ladder. A bond ladder is a portfolio of individual bonds (*not* bond funds) diversified across a

221

wide range of maturities. Because Dave has expected expenses of $40,000 per year, he buys $40,000 worth of TIPS maturing in one year, $40,000 worth of two-year TIPS, $40,000 worth of three-year TIPS, and so on. He will hold the TIPS on each rung of his ladder until they mature. In one year, he will be paid the principal on his one-year TIPS, which he will use to meet his living expenses. Similarly, when his two-year TIPS mature, he will use his principal payment to meet his living expenses in the second year of his retirement. Because he is relying on his bond and not his stock holdings to meet his expenses, he is protected from the risk posed by stock market volatility. Furthermore, because he is holding his TIPS to maturity, fluctuations in TIPS prices will not matter to him. Barring a default by the U.S. Treasury, he is guaranteed to receive the principal on his TIPS when they mature. The risk to Dave's portfolio posed by stock and bond market volatility has been eliminated. Also, because the principal in Dave's bonds is automatically adjusted for inflation, the risk posed by not earning enough returns to keep pace with inflation has also been eliminated. If, for example, inflation causes Dave's expenses to rise by 10 percent, to $44,000, by the time he is seventy-five, the principal in his five-year TIPS will likewise rise from $40,000 to $44,000. The future value of his bonds has been matched to his future liabilities—hence the name "liability-matching bond portfolio."

The high degree of safety offered by the LMBP is made possible only by the existence of an investment that is guaranteed to keep pace with inflation and that comes with the full faith and credit of the U.S. government. The key is the inflation adjustment, a feature that is unique to TIPS and I Bonds. There are no equally safe alternatives to these bonds for retirees interested in building an LMBP. The alternative most often mentioned is an inflation-adjusted annuity, but if you buy such an annuity, you are exposed to the possibility that the insurance company will go out of business. How big is this risk? Consider that in the sixteen years between 1991 and 2007, eight insurance companies folded, and fifty-five[94] required assistance from state guarantee associations to meet their contractual obligations.[95] In 2008, American International Group Inc. was saved from bankruptcy at the last minute by the federal government. The experience of AIG is a reminder that in a financial crisis, even large, seemingly rock-solid insurers can very quickly lose the trust of their creditors and face ruin. The odds are much better that the U.S. government will still be in business, and meeting its obligations to bondholders, thirty years from now than any particular insurance company. Furthermore, the effective fees charged by insurance companies for annuities makes them fairly expensive products. In contrast, there are ways to buy TIPS that completely eliminate all trading costs and fees.

To eliminate the risk of market volatility and ensure that your investments will match your liabilities, an LMBP must comprise individual TIPS, not a mutual fund or exchange-traded fund (ETF) that invests in TIPS. Mutual funds are required to "mark to market," meaning that the share price of a fund must be calculated based on the *market prices*, not the face values, of the individual bonds held by the fund.[96]

The fund's value fluctuates up or down with the prices of the bonds held by the fund. By holding individual TIPS rather than a fund invested in TIPS, you ensure that you will receive the face value of each bond, not the market price.

The LMBP Delays, but Does Not Eliminate, the Retirement Risk

An LMBP might seem, at first glance, like the perfect solution to the retirement risk. After all, if it eliminates the risk of too much negative market volatility and not enough returns to keep pace with inflation, doesn't it therefore eliminate the retirement risk itself? Unfortunately, the answer is no. An LMBP *shifts* the retirement risk to a later time period. As long as you are able to withdraw your expenses from your TIPS ladder, your standard of living is protected from market volatility and inflation. But once the maturity date of the longest-dated bond in your ladder is reached, the retirement risk returns.

That said, if you can extend your bond ladder far enough out in time, the return of the retirement risk won't matter to you—because you'll be dead. A key question, therefore, is how far out can we build a TIPS ladder?

The maximum possible length is thirty years. Thirty years is the longest-dated TIPS bond or I Bond issued by the U.S. Treasury. However, thirty years is a theoretical maximum only. The actual length of an LMBP bond ladder will depend on a retiree's withdrawal rate and bond allocation. Returning to our previous example, Dave has a $750,000 bond portfolio and annual expenses of $40,000 per year. Buying $40,000 worth of each maturity, Dave can extend his ladder for 18.75 years. (This is calculated by dividing $750,000 by $40,000.) Because Dave is currently seventy, his original TIPS ladder will be exhausted by the time he is eighty-nine. This might seem like more than enough time to virtually eliminate longevity risk. But based on actuarial data published by the Social Security Administration,[97] a seventy-year-old American male has a greater than one in four chance of living to age eighty-nine or longer. And if we now suppose that Dave is going to wed Sharon, also seventy years old, the odds that at least one of them will live to eighty-nine or longer are greater than 50/50. Dave and Sharon can eliminate the retirement risk for the first 18.75 years of their life together, but there is a very good chance that at least one of them will still be alive when the retirement risk returns in about nineteen years.

To truly minimize the chances of the retirement risk returning while you're still alive, you will need to combine a very low withdrawal rate with a delayed retirement. For example, a person retiring at age seventy can extend her TIPS ladder to age one hundred if she uses a 25/75 stock/bond mix and a withdrawal rate of 2.5 percent or less. Only a fortunate few will be able to retire with such a low withdrawal rate.

However, there is another way to extend a TIPS ladder to thirty years and even beyond, and that is by doing it in stages. First, TIPS pay dividends twice a year, which can and should be reinvested in more TIPS. By reinvesting the dividends in TIPS with maturities beyond the end date of your ladder, you will be able to extend your ladder over time. The number of additional years you can add to your ladder will depend on the original length of your ladder (longer is better) and the fixed (noninflation) component of the yield you earn on your TIPS (more is better). Returning to our previous example, Dave and Sharon would be able to extend their TIPS ladder slightly more than two years if they earn a 1 percent fixed yield, and close to five years if they earn 2 percent. Unfortunately, with bond yields at historic lows, the current potential for extending a TIPS ladder by reinvesting dividends is more limited than these examples suggest.

But there are other ways to accomplish this goal. By *rebalancing* your portfolio, you will more than likely be able to transfer the gains you realize in the stock portion of your portfolio to your bond portfolio. These gains can then be used to extend your TIPS ladder. Rebalancing is a subject we tackle in depth in Chapter 15, but briefly, the purpose of rebalancing is to keep your portfolio from drifting away from your planned asset allocation. Over the long run, your portfolio will tend to shift away from bonds and toward stocks, because stocks usually outperform bonds. In the case of a retiree using an LMBP, this shift toward stocks will be even more pronounced because all of the withdrawals for living expenses will be taken from the bond portfolio, while the stock portfolio is left untouched. A retiree with a 25/75 portfolio may therefore see the portfolio gradually shift to 30/70, 40/60, and so on, if he does not rebalance the portfolio back to 25/75 on a regular schedule. Rebalancing in this case would be accomplished by selling a portion of the portfolio's stock investments and using the proceeds to buy long-dated TIPS.

In addition to rebalancing, a retiree *may* be able to reduce her percentage allocation to stocks, and increase her bond allocation, as she ages. In general, if the retiree's withdrawal rate declines or holds steady, a shift away from stocks and toward bonds may become possible. (See Table 11.4 and accompanying discussion for more details.) If circumstances permit such a shift, the retiree will be able to use the proceeds from the sale of her stock funds to extend her bond ladder.

Extending a TIPS ladder by reinvesting dividends is a sure thing (as long as the fixed yield on your TIPS is greater than zero), but the additional number of years you can buy using this approach is fairly limited. In contrast, your ability to shift funds from your stock portfolio to your TIPS ladder is uncertain and will depend on how well your stock investments perform and what happens to your withdrawal rate. But with a little bit of luck, you should be able to build a sizeable extension to your ladder using this approach.

By extending a TIPS ladder over time using the preceding techniques, you should *eventually* reach the point at which the risks posed by too much volatility and not enough returns have been pushed so far out in the future that they will no longer matter. But until your bond ladder has finally been extended beyond your lifetime, the risk of bankruptcy will still be lurking out there, just beyond the longest-dated bond in your ladder. And of course, because no one knows how long he will live or precisely how much he must spend to meet his future expenses, you can never be certain that all your needs can be met by a TIPS ladder for the rest of your life. An LMBP cannot truly *eliminate* the retirement risk, including both the non-investment-related and investment-related components of this risk. Nothing can ever eliminate the risk of outliving your money. Still, an LMBP can help you minimize the investment-related components of this risk, if you are fortunate enough to be able to build a TIPS ladder that extends far into the future. And even if you cannot at present construct a TIPS ladder that extends beyond your life expectancy, you may nonetheless want to consider an LMBP, not so much for its real impact on the retirement risk as for the psychological benefits it might bring you. Knowing that you have, say, ten or fifteen years of living expenses covered with an extremely safe investment may give you the peace of mind you need to sleep at night and to stick with a buy-and-hold strategy through thick and thin.

Going 100 Percent Bonds to Extend Your TIPS Ladder: A Major Mistake

You might be wondering, if the goal is to push the end of your LMBP TIPS ladder as far into the future as possible, why not allocate *all* of your nest egg to the ladder rather than holding a portion back in stocks? For example, if Dave allocated 100 percent, rather than 75 percent, of his $1 million nest egg to TIPS, he would be able to extend his ladder out 25 years instead of just 18.75 ($1,000,000 divided by $40,000 annual withdrawal is 25). Then, by reinvesting his dividends, he could potentially extend his ladder out even further to age ninety-seven, ninety-eight, even one hundred, depending on his fixed yield.

This solution might seem tempting, but there is a big problem with it. As we learned in Chapter 10, in addition to the two *investment-related* components of the retirement risk (too much negative market volatility and not enough returns to outpace inflation), this risk also comes with *noninvestment* components. And while a 100 percent allocation to an LMBP will essentially eliminate your investment-related risks (at least temporarily), it will also ratchet up your noninvestment risks. Consider *longevity risk*: the risk that you will live a longer-than-average life. Let's suppose that Dave and Sharon invest their entire $1 million in a TIPS ladder, and by reinvesting their dividends, they are able to extend this ladder twenty-seven years, to age ninety-seven. Do you think they've beaten the longevity risk? Not quite. The chances that at least one half of a seventy-year-old couple will live to ninety-eight or older are 9 percent—nearly one in ten. And if Dave and/or Sharon *do* live this long, they will have completely exhausted their life savings.

Granted, it is true that longevity risk declines rapidly as you approach and exceed age one hundred. But longevity risk is not the only noninvestment component of the retirement risk. The really big risk to an LMBP is the one posed by large, unexpected expenses. Allocating 100 percent of your nest egg to an LMBP assumes that you know what your expenses will be far into the future. You do *not* know this. In fact, the probability that you will incur major medical or long-term care expenses increases dramatically as you age. In particular, end-of-life expenses can be huge. Insurance will help you cover a portion of these costs, but the portion you will have to pay out of pocket can easily overwhelm your emergency fund. In fact, because medical costs are rising faster than the rate of inflation,[98] your TIPS investments may not keep pace with these costs—let alone the money market funds and savings accounts you use to hold your emergency fund. Stocks, and stocks alone, provide the best chance of keeping pace with rapidly rising health care costs.

If your health care or other expenses rise above your planned budget, and you have no stock investments outside your TIPS ladder, you may be forced to sell TIPS that you planned to use for future expenses to meet your present needs. You may or may not receive a price commensurate with the principal in your TIPS. What's worse, as you sell TIPS, your ladder will become shorter and your longevity risk will rise. In contrast, if you invest at least a portion of your nest egg in stocks, your stock portfolio will most likely grow significantly as you spend down your TIPS ladder. This will provide you with a sizeable reserve fund from which to pay medical, long-term care, and other unanticipated expenses. The problem with a 100 percent allocation to an LMBP is that it does not provide a fast-growing reserve for liabilities above and beyond those you can anticipate.

LMBPs are sometimes presented as an alternative to, rather than a component of, a well-diversified portfolio. This is unfortunate, because diversification—especially diversification into both stocks and bonds—is the key to minimizing all components of the retirement risk. An LMBP can help you to push the investment-related components of the retirement risk into the future—possibly so far into the future that they will be addressed by your heirs, not you. But if you attempt to accomplish this with a 100 percent TIPS portfolio, you will only wind up replacing these investment risks with the noninvestment components of the retirement risk—specifically, longevity risk and the risk of large unexpected expenses. An LMBP will help you to minimize all aspects of the retirement risk only if you implement it as part of a well-diversified portfolio.

So remember, the alternative asset allocation being suggested in this chapter applies *only to the bond portion of your portfolio*. Regardless of whether you choose to use an LMBP, you should select your stock/bond mix *solely* on the basis of the guidance presented in Chapter 11. Do *not* increase your allocation to bonds beyond the safe ranges presented in Table 11.4 for the sake of adding a few years to an LMBP ladder. Nor should your decision to use a TIPS ladder have any bearing whatsoever on how you allocate the *stock* portion of your portfolio. Use the guidance in Chapter 11 to determine your stock allocation. Consider using the guidance in this chapter only as a possible alternative to the bond allocation guidance given Chapter 11.

An LMBP is not a suitable alternative for all investors. In the next section, we consider which types of investors may benefit from an LMBP and which ones might be better off sticking with the bond portfolio guidance in Chapter 11. We also consider some of the other practical issues involved in purchasing and maintaining an LMBP bond ladder.

Before You Decide on an LMBP: Practical Considerations

Who Benefits from an LMBP?

An LMBP is not for everyone. First, younger workers who will not be making withdrawals from their retirement portfolio for many years do not face liabilities and therefore do not need a liability-matching portfolio. (Although it is worth mentioning that LMBPs are very well suited to meeting other financial goals, including saving for the down payment on a house or a college education for the kids.)

For those in or near retirement, key factors to consider before committing to an LMBP include your withdrawal rate, your planned date of retirement, and your health status and family medical history. As we have already seen, retirees with low withdrawal rates—no more than 3 percent and preferably less—will be more likely to benefit from the risk-reduction potential of an LMBP than those with higher withdrawals. To this consideration, it must be added that those with such low withdrawal rates will already have a low risk of running out of money regardless of whether they choose to use an LMBP.

Early retirees, as well as retirees in good health from families that have shown a propensity toward long lives, will have more difficulty building a TIPS ladder that extends beyond their life expectancy than those who delay their retirement and/or suffer from poor health.

A key question anyone considering an LMBP must address is whether he is willing to take on a significant amount of work to purchase and maintain a bond ladder. Unlike the bond portfolio recommendations in the preceding chapter—which can be easily implemented using mutual funds or ETFs—an LMBP requires you to buy a portfolio of *individual bonds*. These bonds must be diversified by maturity and closely matched to your forecasts of future expenses. Furthermore, once you have set up your bond ladder, you will need to reinvest the dividends you receive into more bonds. When you purchase a bond fund, this work is done for you by the fund manager. When you purchase a portfolio of individual bonds, *you* become the manager. You could hire a financial advisor to do this work for you, but this option does not come cheap, and you will need to make room in your budget for the advisor's fees.

The extra work—or extra expense—of an LMBP is more likely to be judged worth it by risk-averse retirees than those with a high tolerance for risk. Retirees who plan to weight their portfolios heavily toward stocks will probably not be able to extend a TIPS ladder far enough into the future to gain any real risk reduction. However, for risk-averse retirees, even a short TIPS ladder may offer enough psychological benefits to make the added effort worth it. In fact, for many, the main advantage of the LMBP alternative is likely to be the peace of mind it brings. Knowing that you have the next ten, twenty, or more years of living expenses covered should help you to sleep soundly. This knowledge may also help you to stick with the buy-and-hold approach during market crashes.

From a tax standpoint, TIPS come with a unique problem. Although the inflation component of the yield is added to the principal and not paid until maturity, this component is nonetheless taxed in the year it is accrued. In other words, with TIPS, you are taxed today for income you will not receive until the future. You will receive payments for the fixed (noninflation) component of the yield twice each year, but these dividend payments may not be sufficient to cover the taxes on your TIPS when they come due. Given this tax issue, TIPS should be held in an IRA, 401(k), or other tax-advantaged account. Retirees who hold all or most of their savings in taxable accounts will be severely limited in their ability to use TIPS in an LMBP. I Bonds can be used as a viable alternative to TIPS in this situation. The taxes on I Bonds are deferred until they mature or are redeemed. However, while retirees with modest nest eggs may be able to build an LMBP using I Bonds in place of TIPS, the $10,000 annual limit on the purchase of I Bonds will make it difficult for retirees with larger nest eggs to build an I Bond ladder.

Although I advocate using an LMBP *only* as a component of a diversified stock/bond portfolio, it is nonetheless true that the *bond portion* of this portfolio will lack diversification. Though the default risk for Treasuries and TIPS is viewed by the financial markets as miniscule, these investments are not riskless. And unfortunately, the "full faith and credit" of the United States is more and more frequently being used as a bargaining chip by politicians pursuing their own agendas. Presumably our political leaders will never actually trigger a default, but we have to consider the distinct possibility that they may continue to raise the *prospect* of defaulting as a means of winning political concessions. Especially for the risk-averse investors most likely to be interested in using an LMBP, the possibility that a U.S. default may be threatened every few years needs to be carefully considered. Ask yourself, will you lose sleep at night if you are sitting on an undiversified portfolio of government bonds and Congress periodically debates whether to raise the debt ceiling? Also, if such debates go down to the wire, as they did in summer 2011 and again in autumn 2013, will you be tempted to sell your TIPS? If your answer to either question is yes, the benefits you will realize from an LMBP may be outweighed by the psychological and real costs.

Finally, the LMBP is a relatively new concept in retirement planning. Although the concept is certainly sound in theory, the devil may lie in the practical details. And as we shall see, setting up and maintaining an LMBP bond ladder poses many devilish details. If the thought of pioneering a new approach to retirement makes you a bit nervous, an LMBP may not be for you.

Setting Up an LMBP

Bond portfolio allocation. If you do decide to use an LMBP, how should you go about building your bond ladder? You will first need to determine your percentage split between stocks and bonds using the guidance in Chapter 11. Once you have determined how much money to allocate to bonds, you will next need to split this amount between your TIPS or I Bond ladder and your other bond holdings. Thus far we have been assuming that 100 percent of the bond portfolio will be dedicated to the TIPS/I Bond ladder. But for rebalancing purposes, you should allocate a small percentage to a short-term bond fund. Although you will usually rebalance by shifting money out of your stock portfolio and into your bond portfolio, on occasion—particularly when you suffer large stock losses—you will need to move funds from bonds to stocks. By keeping a portion of your bond portfolio in a short-term bond fund, you will be able to rebalance into stocks without having to sell part of your bond ladder. If you are using a very conservative 20/80 or 25/75 stock/bond portfolio, you should allocate about 10 percent of the bond portion of your portfolio to a short-term fund. This percentage should be increased, up to 25 percent, as you move toward a more moderate stock/bond allocation (in the 50/50 to 60/40 range). Because your ladder will be invested 100 percent in government bonds, you can gain some limited diversification benefits by purchasing a short-term corporate bond fund.

Building your bond ladder. Once you have decided how much to allocate to a short-term fund and how much to your ladder, you will be able to calculate the length of your ladder as follows:

> Number of years = Total dollars allocated to ladder/Estimated yearly withdrawals for expenses

For example, if you are allocating a total of $220,000 to your bond ladder and you plan to withdraw $10,000 per year to meet your living expenses in retirement, then you will be able to extend your ladder out twenty-two years ($220,000 divided by $10,000 equals 22).

The calculation becomes more complicated if you expect your expenses to change significantly over time. For example, suppose you decide to retire at sixty-two but defer Social Security until age seventy. Suppose, furthermore, that you are allocating $400,000 to your ladder; that you estimate your total annual expenses as $30,000; and that your Social Security income, starting at age seventy, will be $20,000. In this case, you will need 8 times $30,000, or $240,000, to cover your expenses from age sixty-two to seventy. This will leave you with $400,000 minus $240,000, or $160,000, to cover your expenses after age seventy. Because these expenses will total $10,000 per year ($30,000 minus your $20,000 income from Social Security), you will be able to extend your ladder an additional sixteen years ($160,000 divided by $10,000) beyond age seventy. The total length of your ladder will be eight years plus sixteen years, or twenty-four years.

Buying your bonds. In this example, you would need to buy $30,000 worth of TIPS (and/or I Bonds) for each of the first eight years of your ladder and $10,000 for each of the remaining sixteen years. You could purchase all twenty-four years' worth of TIPS at the same time on the secondary bond market, but this is not recommended. The markups charged on the secondary bond market are hidden in the price quote you will receive—making it difficult to know whether you are getting a fair deal.

Instead, to the extent possible, you should buy your TIPS when they are first issued, during Treasury auctions. Not only are trading costs more transparent when you buy during auctions but, depending on your broker, you may be able to completely avoid these costs. Some brokers will place buy orders for you during auctions without charging a commission. Check with your broker to see if this option is open to you. (You can also avoid trading costs by purchasing direct from the Treasury, but this option does not allow you to hold your TIPS in an IRA—a major drawback.)

Unfortunately, because TIPS are issued for limited maturities of five, ten, and thirty years, you will not be able to build a complete ladder all at once if you buy during Treasury auctions. Instead, you should try to piece together your TIPS ladder gradually, before you reach retirement age, by slowly converting your bond portfolio to an LMBP. Ideally, the sooner you get started, the more TIPS you will be able to buy during Treasury auctions, and the less you will need to buy on the secondary market to fill in the holes in your ladder. However, the "sooner is better" strategy has a major flaw: the further you are from retirement, the less predictable your living expenses and nest egg size will be. Ultimately, you may need to wait to begin your bond purchases until you can form a good idea of how many TIPS you will need in each year. Once you can develop reasonable estimates of your expenses and the length of your ladder, you can begin making purchases during Treasury auctions. You probably won't be able to fill in every wrung on your ladder by the time you retire, but you will have reduced the extent to which you need to rely on the secondary market. (As another alternative to the secondary market, you could buy a TIPS mutual fund when you retire and then sell shares of the fund and use the proceeds to fill in the holes in your ladder during Treasury auctions. This approach will leave you exposed to fluctuations in the share price of your TIPS fund, but the volatility should be relatively limited.)

If you are building all or part of your ladder using I Bonds, you will in some ways have more flexibility and in other ways less. Although all I Bonds mature in thirty years, you can redeem them at any time after five years without penalty. This means that, in effect, you can assign each I Bond you purchase a specific date of redemption on your ladder. You are not limited by a fixed maturity date. However, because the maximum allowed purchase is only $10,000 per year, you may need to start buying your I Bonds long before your retirement date.

The difficulties associated with buying a TIPS ladder and the work involved in maintaining the ladder (i.e., reinvesting the dividends) combine to make the LMBP alternative a challenging prospect for the do-it-yourself investor. If you are seriously considering this alternative, you may want to consider working with a financial planner experienced in the implementation of liability-matching strategies.

Conclusions

As an alternative approach to allocating your bond portfolio, an LMBP offers the potential to virtually eliminate the investment-related components of the retirement risk—at least for a while. That said, an LMBP isn't for everyone. But if you are willing to take on the significant extra effort involved in setting up and maintaining a bond ladder, the LMBP alternative is well worth considering. Just remember that to be truly effective in reducing the retirement risk, an LMBP should be implemented as part of a well-diversified portfolio including stocks as well as bonds.

[Handwritten annotations:]

Cash
2017 ?
2018 ?
2019 ?

TIPS
2020 10,000
2021 10,000
2022 10,000
2023 10,000
2024 10,000
2025 10,000
_____
60,000

2015 10,000
2016
2017
2018
2019
2020 10,000
_____
60,000

10,000
10,000
_____
66,000
10,000
10,000
10,000
10,000
10,000
_____
50,000

2021 10,000
2022 10,000
2023 10,000
2024 10,000
2025 10,000
_____
50,000

2026 10,0000
2027 10,0000
2028 10,000
2029 10,000
2030 10,000
_____
50,000

INVESTING IN MUTUAL FUNDS AND ETFS

F or me, and, I hope at least a little bit for you, learning about investing is fun. But learning is never as fun as *doing*. The really fun part comes when you actually get to *execute trades*. Even though I've been doing it for many years, I still get a little jolt of excitement every time I click the "buy" or "sell" button on my broker's website. Maybe it's a modern-day vestige of the adrenaline rush our hunter-gatherer ancestors must have felt when they aimed and released their arrows. They hoped to bag mastodons. I hope for bags of money.

Maybe you will experience that same little jolt, or maybe I'm just weird that way. In any event, you are about to find out. At this point, you should have an asset allocation plan that meets your specific goals, needs, and circumstances. And you are now *almost* ready to implement your plan by taking aim with your arrow (cursor) and clicking on the "buy" button. But first, you need to address three final questions:

- *What* specific funds should I buy?

- *Where* (in what accounts) should I hold those funds?

- *When* should I buy those funds?

What, where, and when—these are the three questions we address in this chapter. Once you have answered them, you will be ready to turn your plan into a *real* portfolio.

What to Buy?

As complicated as tailoring an asset allocation plan to fit your specific needs might be, it seems like selecting the specific *investments* you should buy will be even more complicated. After all, there are thousands of different mutual funds and exchange-traded funds (ETFs) from which to choose and a whole host of criteria you might need to consider. Possible criteria include past returns, the volatility of those returns, the fund managers' age and experience, and how well each fund has performed relative to other similar funds.

But in fact, you don't need to worry about any of this stuff. There's really only one key criterion on which you need to focus—how expensive is it to buy and hold the fund? You want to own the least expensive fund (or ETF) in each asset class. And in most, if not all cases, the least expensive fund will be an *index fund*. The best way to maximize your returns and minimize your risk of being outpaced by inflation, is to buy a portfolio of low-cost index funds and ETFs.

The good news is that index mutual funds and ETFs (most of which are index based) have grown enormously in popularity over recent years. If you are one of the many converts to index investing, and need no further convincing that low-cost index funds are the way to go, you can give yourself a pat on the back *and skip ahead to the next section* (on "Where to Buy?").

Active versus Passive Management

For those of you who are not familiar with index investing, or not yet convinced of its benefits, no worries—we will cover what you need to know. Let's begin by explaining the difference between index, or *passive*, fund management and *active* management. An actively managed mutual fund or ETF seeks to *outperform* the broader market through skilled selection of stocks or bonds. In contrast, a passively managed fund, also known as an index fund, seeks to *match* the performance of an index like the S&P 500 by buying and holding all of the stocks or bonds in the index.

Because index funds involve no security selection skill on the part of the fund manager, and do not even attempt to beat the market, it stands to reason that they will underperform actively managed funds, right? Wrong! Like so many aspects of investing, the counterintuitive strategy is the better strategy. The vast majority of the studies that have been done on this topic—and there are many—have confirmed that most actively managed funds underperform comparable index funds. One of the most recent of these studies was published by the mutual fund giant Vanguard in April 2013.[99] Using data from both Morningstar and Vanguard, the study's authors compared returns for actively managed funds with average returns for low-cost index funds.[100] The five asset classes considered in the study were U.S. large cap blend, U.S. small cap blend, foreign large cap blend, emerging-market stocks, and intermediate-term bonds. For periods of five years, ten years, and fifteen years,[101] the average low-cost index fund beat *at least* 60 percent, and in many cases 80 percent, of the corresponding active funds in each asset class.[102]

How is it that the majority of fund managers are getting beaten by funds that simply ape a broad market index, like the S&P 500, the Russell 2000 (for small caps), or the Barclay's U.S. Aggregate Bond Index? Part of the answer is that they can't beat the market, because they *are* the market. The vast majority of the trades on the world's stock and bond markets are made by professionals: investment bankers, pension fund managers, hedge fund managers—and mutual fund managers. These professionals are trading against each other. When one of them is on the winning side of a trade, another is on the losing side. It stands to reason, therefore, that at most about half of mutual fund managers can be expected to best the market over any given time period.

Still, this doesn't explain why 60 to 80 percent of active managers are getting beaten by index funds. The other part of the explanation is costs. We would expect about half of active mutual fund managers to outperform the market and half to underperform it, *before taking costs into account.* But *all* mutual funds—the outperformers and the underperformers—incur costs. These costs reduce the returns of the winners and the losers. Suppose, for the sake of example, that all large cap active funds incur costs of 1 percent of assets under management each year. Suppose, furthermore, that of the 50 percent of mutual fund managers that beat the S&P 500 in a given year before considering costs, 10 percent beat it by less than 1 percent. Once costs are taken into account, the managers in this group will have earned less than the index. Only the 40 percent of funds that beat the S&P 500 by more than 1 percentage point will still wind up with market-beating returns after accounting for costs.

Of course index funds also incur costs. But these costs are, on average, much lower than those of actively managed funds. This statement holds true both for the costs that are reported in a fund's prospectus and for the hidden costs that aren't reported but that reduce *your* returns just as surely as the reported costs. We need to review the various cost items incurred by mutual funds to understand why this is the case.

Expense ratios. Let's start with the costs that are reported as "expense ratios" in each fund's prospectus. A fund with an expense ratio of, say, 1.2 percent will take 1.2 percent of the money you have invested in the fund each and every year. If the fund earns 10 percent in the market, you will see 8.8 percent returns (10 minus 1.2). If the fund loses 10 percent in the market, you will be out 11.2 percent. Rain or shine, you pay the fund 1.2 percent per year.

Where exactly does this money go? First, it goes toward the salary of the fund manager. In the case of an index fund, this is relatively low, because the manager is not responsible for deciding which stocks to buy or sell. But in the case of an actively managed fund, the manager is generally quite well paid. After all, he or she is a highly skilled, professional investor (who nonetheless usually gets beaten by the lowly index fund manager).

Next, there are the salaries and benefits of the research analysts who help the manager make the fund's stock or bond selections—unless, of course, we're talking about an index fund, which doesn't have to pay for research analysts it doesn't need. Then, of course, there are the travel expenses incurred by the fund manager, who will jet around to meet the top executives at the companies being considered as "buys." The index fund manager doesn't need to do much travelling.

Add in salaries and benefits for support staff, rent for office space (think big corner offices for active managers), office equipment, and the all-important fee for the mutual fund management company, and that should pretty much cover it. According to the Vanguard study mentioned previously, as of December 31, 2012, expense ratios averaged 0.82 percent for actively managed large cap funds versus 0.11 percent for large cap index funds and 0.14 percent for large cap ETFs. Actively managed government bond funds charged 0.50 percent, versus 0.15 percent for government bond index funds and ETFs.[103] These actively managed expense ratios might not seem that bad. After all, what's a measly 0.5 percent, especially if it's buying you the investing skills of some hotshot bond market genius? There are just two small problems with this line of reasoning. First, with yields on the ten-year Treasury note currently running around 2.5 percent, a 0.5 percent expense ratio will reduce your returns by about *20 percent* (0.5 percent divided by 2.5 percent is 20 percent). In other words, expense ratios *seem* small because they are quoted as a percentage of *assets invested* in a fund. But compared to what really matters—*returns*—they are much larger.

And the second small problem? Chances are your hotshot bond fund manager will get beaten by an index fund charging only 0.15 percent.

Trading costs. But the news gets worse. The costs included in the expense ratio are only part of the costs your fund, and you, incur. Trading costs will take another big bite out of your returns. Mutual fund managers must pay the same transaction costs for buying and selling stocks and bonds that individual investors pay. For example, they must pay commissions to the brokers that handle their trades. In addition, like all traders, they must pay the bid/ask spread. Stocks and bonds come with two prices: the bid price paid by buyers and the ask price paid to sellers. The bid price is always higher than the ask price, with the difference going to the market maker—a specialized middleman responsible for ensuring the market's efficient operation by buying shares of a particular stock or bond from sellers and selling shares to buyers. The bid/ask spread is usually only a small fraction of 1 percent for liquid investments like Treasuries and large cap stocks. However, for thinly traded securities, such as small cap stocks and many types of bonds, the bid/ask spread can easily rise to as much as 1 to 2 percent of the price.

In addition to broker commissions and bid/ask spreads, fund managers responsible for large pools of assets face an important additional cost that does *not* apply to the average individual investor. When you or I place an order for 100 or 1,000 shares of stock, the order is too small to impact the share price. But the manager of a large mutual fund routinely buys and sells *millions* of shares. To reduce the impact a major buy order can have on a stock's price, the manager may break the order up into smaller units and spread it out over time. But even so, if a large fund is seeking to take a major position in a stock, the initial purchases can drive up the stock's price, making the remaining purchases more expensive. The same process works in reverse to reduce the price active managers may receive when they sell a large position.

The resulting *market impact costs* are particularly important, because they can torpedo the early success of active fund managers. Managers who, either through skill or luck, outperform their benchmark indices will typically attract new investors to their funds. As the amount of money under management increases, so does the size of the trades the successful manager must make. And as the size of the trades increases, so does the likelihood that the fund will incur major market impact costs. These costs are partly responsible for the inconsistency in the performance of actively managed funds that has been observed in many studies (including the recent Vanguard study discussed earlier). Funds that outperform the market in their early years have a tendency to underperform once their early success attracts more assets. Paradoxically, when it comes to active funds, early success often leads to eventual failure. And the investors who pile into funds based on those early successes wind up getting burned.

Compared to active funds, index funds incur much smaller market impact costs —and much smaller trading costs in general. Index fund managers trade much less frequently than active managers. Index funds simply buy and hold all of the stocks or bonds in a market index. They make trades only when a stock or bond enters or leaves the index. In contrast, active funds tend to be much more, well, active. It is not unusual for an actively managed fund to turn over its entire portfolio over the course of a year.

Opportunity costs. Mutual funds that invest in stocks or bonds also include an allocation to cash or cash equivalents, such as money markets and T-bills. In the case of index funds, this cash allocation is kept small at all times. But active managers tend to allocate significantly larger percentages of their investors' money to cash. The reasons for this vary from fund to fund. Some managers like to keep a sizeable amount of cash on hand so that they can respond quickly to "buy" opportunities when they arise. Other managers, trying to time the market, will "go to cash" by selling off their holdings when they think stocks are about to tank (or worse, after they've already tanked).

But regardless of the reason, over the long haul the allocation to cash reduces mutual fund returns. Money market funds, T-bills, and other forms of cash yield significantly lower returns than stocks or bonds. In fact, at present, the yield on cash investments is essentially *zero*. The greater a fund's allocation to cash, the lower its long-run returns will be. Unlike many actively managed funds, index funds keep these *opportunity costs* low by minimizing their allocation to cash.

Your purpose in buying a stock mutual fund is to invest in *stocks*, not a combination of stocks and cash. The same logic holds for bond funds. Keep your cash investments limited as much as possible to your emergency fund by buying index funds for your retirement accounts.

Load funds. There is yet another cost item charged by *some* actively managed funds. This is the sales commission or load used to compensate brokers that sell the funds. A sales load may be charged up front when you buy the fund, or at the back end when you sell it. Purchasers of up-front load funds have the distinct privilege of seeing their principal reduced by as much as 5 percent right off the bat. This means that you will earn only 95 percent of the returns you would otherwise have earned in a comparable no-load fund. That's 5 percent less returns, each and every year, for as long as you own the fund. This comes on top of the 5 percent reduction in your principal. If you buy a deferred-load fund, you at least will have the illusion that your money is intact—until you sell the fund and once again must pay some percentage of your proceeds to the fund management company.

That load funds continue to exist is somewhat amazing, because there are many no-load funds from which to choose. Do a good deed, and help to kill off the remaining load funds by shunning them. *Never, ever* consider buying a load fund.

Taxes. Finally, in addition to higher expense ratios, trading costs, opportunity costs, and in some cases sales loads, actively managed funds generate significantly larger taxable distributions than index funds. When a mutual fund sells a stock or bond at a higher price than the original purchase price, it realizes a capital gain. If the capital gains realized by the fund are not offset by corresponding capital losses, then the fund must pass those gains on to you, the fund investor, in the form of capital gain distributions. You must pay taxes on these distributions. Actively managed funds generate larger capital gain distributions than index funds for the same reason that they incur larger trading costs. Frequent selling of stocks and bonds by active managers results in the frequent realization of capital gains. And active managers sometimes incur *short-term capital gains,* which are taxed at your marginal rate rather than the lower rate applied to long-term capital gains. Index funds sell much less frequently and hence keep most of their capital gains unrealized.

The tax consequences of frequent trading will not affect you if you keep your actively managed funds in an IRA or 401(k). But taxes can be a major drag on the returns of funds held in taxable accounts. And unlike expense ratios, trading costs, and opportunity costs, the impact of taxes will not show up in the fund returns advertised by mutual fund management companies. Your active fund manager may send you frequent reports about the wonderful trades she's been making on your behalf. But when the taxman comes to the door, your fund manager will be nowhere to be found. *You* get to pay the taxes on all those wonderful trades. Most especially for taxable accounts, index funds beat active funds hands down.

Four-Leaf Clovers

Expense ratios, broker commissions, bid/ask spreads, market impact costs, opportunity costs, front-end loads, deferred loads, capital gain taxes—it's quite a list, and low-cost index funds charge you less, much less, than active funds on every item. So let's pause for a moment and have some sympathy for the active fund manager, who must beat the market by a wide margin just to offset all these costs and match that slacker, the index fund manager.

Still, even though most active managers fail at this difficult task, some succeed, don't they? If, as the Vanguard study cited previously found, about 60 to 80 percent of active funds get beaten by passive funds, that still leaves 20 to 40 percent that are winners. While the majority of active funds might not measure up, who cares as long as we can find a few active managers who do outperform the indices?

I am not one of those investors who believe that there are *no* supremely skilled professionals capable of outsmarting the market. It seems unlikely that Warren Buffet's decades of success in the stock market are the result of luck and not skill. If he can do it, might there not be others?

I think there must be. But they are very few and far between. For although 20 to 40 percent of actively managed funds beat index funds in any particular time period, the funds that outperform in one period tend to underperform in the next. Numerous studies have shown that while outperformance is fairly common, *consistent* outperformance is rare. In fact, many of the top-performing active managers in one period wind up at the bottom in the next period. As just one example, the previously cited Vanguard study looked at the top 20 percent of all U.S. stock funds over the 2003–7 period and asked how these same funds performed in the subsequent (2008–12) five-year period. Only 15 percent of the funds remained in the top 20 percent—*less* than would be expected from a purely random result. This means that only 3 percent of all U.S. stock funds (15 percent of 20 percent) managed to stay at the top in both 2003–7 and 2008–12. What's worse, a much larger 24 percent of the top performers in 2003–7 wound up in the bottom 20 percent in 2008–12.[104] How would you like to find a fund with a stellar record and invest in the fund, only to wind up with returns far below average? This is exactly what happens to many mutual fund investors who chase performance, constantly trading to get in on the latest hot fund. By the time they buy in, the fund's no longer hot. Like greyhounds at the track, performance chasers never catch the rabbit.

Why do fund managers have such difficulty sustaining good performance? There are a number of reasons. First, some funds' outperformance is the result of luck, not skill. You might think that if a fund manages to beat the market five years in a row, that couldn't possibly be due to luck. If you believe this, try a little experiment. Flip a coin five times and see if you can get it to come up heads every time. If you don't get five heads on your first try, repeat the coin toss ninety-nine times. The odds are high that you will get five heads in a row at least once. If you repeat the experiment one thousand times, you should get five heads in a row approximately thirty times. Now consider that that there are thousands of actively managed mutual funds. It stands to reason that some of those funds will be able to beat the market five years in a row through pure luck.

Some fund managers use the ironclad rule of risk and reward to rack up market-beating returns—for a while. A fund manager might, for example, show a preference for volatile stocks. Because these stocks come with higher expected returns, a risk-taking manager can be expected to outperform during bull markets. But bull markets are *always* followed by bear markets, and managers who outperform in the former by piling on risk will underperform in the latter. This no doubt partly explains why, in the Vanguard study, many of the top performers during the 2003–7 bull market did so poorly during 2008–12 (which included the worst of the 2007–9 bear market as well as the 2011 market correction). The same logic applies in reverse to conservative managers who avoid riskier investments. They may outperform during bear markets but underperform in bull markets. Simply taking on more or less risk to get market-beating returns *part* of the time won't buy you *consistent* outperformance.

So of those active funds that manage to outperform index funds over any given time period, many, if not most, are managed by the lucky, the risk takers, and the risk averse. How, then, do you find the few managers who possess the supreme skills and self-confidence needed to *consistently* beat the index funds, in both bull and bear markets? And how many of these skilled managers will *still* be able to outperform when their reputation for success causes new money to flood into their funds, making it harder and harder for them to avoid large market impact costs?

I used Morningstar's premium fund screener in an attempt to answer these questions. First, I selected the granddaddy of the index funds—Vanguard's 500 Index fund (VFINX)—as the fund to beat. VFINX was the first successful index fund, launched in 1976, and with an expense ratio of 0.17 percent, it is still one of the least expensive funds tracking the S&P 500. I then compared the annualized returns for VFINX with the corresponding returns for actively managed funds in the U.S. large cap blend asset class. My criterion was simple—I looked for funds that beat VFINX over the last five years, ten years, fifteen years, and twenty years. In other words, I looked for funds with a long track record of consistent outperformance.

According to the Morningstar fund screener, there are 1,698 actively managed mutual funds in the U.S. large cap blend asset class. After screening out load funds, funds closed to new investment, and funds requiring a high (more than $10,000) minimum purchase, I was left with 290 funds. And out of these remaining funds, how many *consistently* beat VFINX over five, ten, fifteen, and twenty years? A grand total of seven. And three of these seven barely beat VFINX (by 0.3 percent per year or less) over the twenty-year period. Only four funds demonstrated long-term, significant, consistent outperformance over a low-cost index fund.

Searching for truly skilled fund managers is like trying to find a few needles in a haystack. Simply buying a low-cost index fund like VFINX avoids all the hard work and difficulties, while enabling you to beat the vast majority of actively managed funds. And most important, a portfolio of low-cost index funds will reduce your risk of not earning enough returns to outpace inflation, without exposing you to additional volatility. In other words, index funds, like black-belt investing using the correlation principle, enable you to reduce one component of the retirement risk without increasing the other component.

All this said, I'm guessing there are a few readers who still want to try their hand at active management. I get that. When I was a kid, I decided that I was going to find a four-leaf clover. And after hours and hours of searching, spread out over a few weeks, I finally did find one. (I also once balanced four golf balls on top of each other. I was a strange, but patient, kid.) If you're bound and determined to find your own four-leaf active fund manager, then for whichever asset class you're interested in, you should *start* your search as I did, by identifying a low-cost index fund in that same asset class. Then look for actively managed funds that have *consistently* beaten the index fund under a wide variety of conditions and over a lengthy time period. In addition to five-, ten-, fifteen-, and twenty-year periods, look at how any potential candidate funds performed during the 2000–2002 and 2007–9 bear markets; the 1990s, 2002–7, and 2009–13 bull markets; and the 1998 and 2011 market corrections. Seek active funds with low turnover and lower than average expense ratios. There may really be a few—a *very* few—true gems to be discovered, but you won't uncover them without doing a lot of homework.

And one last point: understand that any outsized returns you might be able to earn *will* come at the expense of increased risk. When you invest in a fund that simply tracks a broad market index, you are investing in the consensus opinions of *millions* of market participants. In fact, an investment in an index fund is an investment in the market itself. When you invest in an actively managed fund, you are placing a bet on the opinions of a *single, fallible* human (or maybe at most, two or three humans in the case of comanaged funds). No matter how good those opinions may have been in the past, there is no guarantee they will continue to prove successful in the future. Like everyone else, fund managers are subject to the ravages of time, to changes in their attitudes toward risk as they age, and to illnesses and personal crises that can affect their judgment. They are also subject to the pitfalls of success—not only market impact costs that grow with assets under management, but also the hubris that tends to grow particularly well on Wall Street and that has undone many a success story. When you buy an active fund, you are in effect investing in the life of a stranger. It's a bit like marrying a mail-order bride. You must be willing to accept all the risks and uncertainties that come with such an investment. (I'm talking here about the fund manager. You're on your own as far as mail-order brides go.)

Choosing Index Funds

Assuming I've convinced you to choose index funds over actively managed funds, the next question is, which index funds should you buy? The answer is simple. Look for funds with low expense ratios and low turnover. The lower the management expenses and trading costs incurred by an index fund, the closer the fund should come to matching the index's performance.

You can compare the expense ratios of different funds using Morningstar's fund screening tools. Morningstar's basic fund screener is available to anyone who signs up for a free membership to the website. The screener allows you to select any asset class in which you are interested, and obtain a list of the funds in that class that meet your criteria. To use the screener, select "no-load funds only" for the asset class of interest, and choose a minimum purchase level appropriate for your situation. Although the screener does not differentiate between index and active funds, you can eliminate most of the latter by selecting only those funds with an expense ratio less than 0.5 and annual turnover less than 25 percent. (Using Morningstar's premium fund screener, available to those who purchase a premium membership to the website, it is possible to screen out all active funds.) The resulting list may include some active funds as well as index funds, but the latter will typically include the word "index" somewhere in their name. Before you actually purchase a fund, you should read the fund's prospectus and make sure that it is in fact an index fund.

One-stop shopping. There are many low-cost index funds to choose from in the large cap blend category. However, the options thin out fairly quickly as you move to other asset classes. Three companies in particular stand out as offering the widest selection of index funds: Vanguard, Fidelity, and Schwab. If you are planning to use mutual funds (as opposed to ETFs) to build your portfolio, and your broker does not provide free access to the funds offered by at least one of these companies, you should seriously consider switching brokers. You can check out the websites of these companies to find out more about them and their fund offerings.

High-volatility hedges. Vanguard, Fidelity, and Schwab offer low-cost index fund options for the vast majority of the large cap, return booster, and low-volatility asset classes. However, index fund offerings are entirely lacking for the high-volatility hedges. Here you have two choices—either go with a low-cost (low expense ratio and low turnover) active mutual fund or buy an ETF. We take a look at ETFs in the next section.

401(k)s. While some 401(k)s offer a good selection of low-cost index funds, unfortunately many do not. If you have a 401(k) from a former employer with few or no index fund choices, you might consider rolling over the account to an IRA, preferably at one of the three companies mentioned earlier. However, you should be aware that in some states, 401(k)s are superior to IRAs in the protection they provide both from creditors and liability claimants. The legal protections vary from state to state. You may want to speak to a financial advisor or lawyer in your home state before committing to an IRA rollover, particularly if you have large assets to protect and are a professional subject to malpractice claims.

If your 401(k) is with your current employer, an IRA rollover is not an option. You will need to make the best of the situation by choosing the lowest-cost active funds (lowest expense ratios and lowest turnover) if index funds aren't available.

Exchange-Traded Funds

So far we have focused exclusively on mutual funds, but today there is an excellent alternative to this traditional investment: the ETF. ETFs are similar in many ways to mutual funds. Their key distinguishing characteristic is that they are bought and sold on an exchange, like a stock, rather than through a mutual fund management company. ETFs can be bought and sold throughout the day, whereas mutual fund purchases and sales are transacted only after the market closes. Of course this particular feature of ETFs is of no significant advantage to buy-and-hold investors (in fact, it can be an unwanted temptation to frequent trading). However, ETFs have other features to recommend themselves. Most importantly, ETFs were initially conceived as low-cost index funds. Although actively managed ETFs are now being brought to market, most ETFs available today are index funds. Furthermore, ETFs are available across a very wide range of asset classes, including precious metals equities (PME) and emerging-market bonds. ETFs thus provide good, low-cost investment options where few such options would otherwise exist. Also, because they are traded on exchanges and not through mutual fund companies, the entire universe of ETFs is available to you through your broker. In contrast, most brokers limit the selection of mutual funds they offer to their clients.

There is one other important advantage of ETFs. Because of the way they are structured, they generate lower taxable distributions than index mutual funds. For this reason, ETFs may be a particularly attractive option for taxable accounts.

There are, however, a couple of disadvantages to ETFs, which make them unsuitable for some investors. Because they are traded on exchanges, you must pay both a broker's commission and the bid/ask spread when you buy or sell an ETF. Depending on the amount of money you plan to invest in a fund, these trading costs can be prohibitive. Furthermore, the trading costs make ETFs an inappropriate investment vehicle if you plan to make frequent share purchases as part of a regular savings strategy. As a rough rule of thumb, try to keep the annual broker's commissions you pay on an ETF to less than 0.1 percent of the amount of money you have in the ETF. For example, if you pay a $10 commission on every trade, and you expect to place a total of about ten orders per year for a particular fund (as would be the case if you are investing your savings on a monthly basis), then you are looking at total annual commission costs of about $100 per year. You will need to hold about $100,000 in the ETF to keep these costs to 0.1 percent per year. In this particular example, if you were contemplating an investment of less than $100,000, you might instead consider an index mutual fund. (Another alternative would be to buy the ETF along with a mutual fund in the same asset class and limit your frequent purchases to the mutual fund.)

Some brokers offer commission-free trades on some ETFs, which can help to open the option of ETF investments to savers and those with smaller nest eggs. However, keep in mind that you still need to consider bid/ask spreads when choosing a particular ETF. Bid/ask spreads are very small and can be safely ignored for heavily traded ETFs such as the SPDR S&P 500 (ticker symbol SPY). However, they can become quite large for thinly traded ETFs. Partly for this reason, you should avoid new or unpopular ETFs that have not attracted a large amount of assets. (Another reason to avoid these ETFs is that they might not survive.) You can check the current bid/ask spread on an ETF by entering its ticker symbol in the "Quote" box on Morningstar's website.

Morningstar also provides an ETF screener, available to free as well as premium members, which you can use to compare expense ratios (that portion of ETF costs that includes manager and staff salaries, overhead, office rent, and the like, and is reported in the prospectus) for ETFs in any particular asset class. Once you have selected a few low-cost ETFs for further consideration, you can then learn more about each of your selections by entering the ticker symbols in the "Quote" box.

One word of warning: steer clear of ETFs that use leverage to try to double or triple returns from an index (or the inverse of an index). These ETFs will track the index (times two or three) only in the short term. Over periods of more than a day or a week, they may bear no relationship whatsoever to their benchmark index. Leveraged ETFs are for short-term traders only, not buy-and-hold investors.

Emerging-market bond ETFs. As previously mentioned, ETFs are the *only* option available for those who want to index their high-volatility hedges. There are quite a few emerging-market bond ETFs with expense ratios of 0.65 or less. But emerging-market bonds are one example—and there are many others—where ETF providers have perhaps gone too far in slicing and dicing asset classes into smaller and smaller niches. A number of the emerging-market bond ETFs concentrate on one region or even one country (China, in particular). Avoid these offerings and choose from diversified ETFs that cover all of the emerging-market regions. (This same advice applies to ETFs for foreign stocks.) Emerging-market defaults are a real possibility, and you do not want to concentrate your holdings in a particular country or small group of countries that may default. Diversification across the entire universe of emerging markets should significantly reduce any losses you experience due to defaults.

There is another important distinction among emerging-market bond ETFs (and mutual funds). Some of these ETFs invest in bonds that are denominated in dollars (i.e., the bond issuers are obligated to repay their debts in dollars) and some in bonds denominated in the local currency. The latter ETFs are usually distinguished from the former by the word "local" in their names (as in Wisdom Tree Emerging Markets Local Debt) or the name of the particular currency in which they invest (as in Market Vectors Renminbi Bond ETF). Usually local currency bonds will be more volatile than dollar-denominated bonds, because returns on the former will fluctuate with exchange rates. However, be aware that when emerging markets experience currency crashes (a frequent past occurrence), dollar-denominated bonds may not offer better safety than local currency bonds. When the local currency collapses, it becomes extremely expensive for an emerging market to convert its currency to dollars, thereby leading to defaults on its dollar-denominated debt. This is less of a risk today than it was in the past, as many emerging markets have built up sizable dollar reserves. But in the financial markets, what's past is prologue, and as I've mentioned before, emerging markets have found it very difficult to escape the cycle of currency crashes and defaults.

In fact, returns on dollar-denominated bonds have been shown to be correlated with currency fluctuations.[105] The bottom line here is that you should not necessarily prefer dollar-denominated bonds over local currency bonds on the basis of the latter's perceived higher risk. Furthermore, buying a local currency ETF may be a good way to improve the currency diversification of your portfolio. One option you might want to consider is to split your emerging-market bond allocation between a dollar-denominated ETF and a local currency ETF.

Buying and Selling Gold

Among all of the asset classes we've considered, gold is a special case. You can, of course, choose to buy and hold the physical substance. Gold can be purchased in the form of gold bars and gold coins, such as the Krugerrand, American Eagle, and Canadian Maple Leaf. The gold content of the latter two coins is fixed and guaranteed by the U.S. and Canadian governments, and they can be held in an IRA (Krugerrands and gold collectible coins cannot).[106] You will want to keep your gold holdings in an IRA if at all possible, because returns on gold are taxed at the collectibles rate of 28 percent. Your gold dealer should be able to help you through the process of establishing an IRA account for your gold. You should of course be sure to select a reputable gold dealer and one that will not charge you an arm and leg when you make trades.

Finding a good dealer, setting up an IRA, and physically securing your gold either at a bank or in your home all takes quite a bit of work. Fortunately, there is an alternative that makes buying, selling, and holding gold as easy as trading stock and bond funds. This alternative is the gold ETF. Two of the most popular and liquid of these are streetTRACKS Gold Shares (GLD) and iShares COMEX Gold Trust (IAU).

These ETFs work the same way as other ETFs, except that they invest in gold rather than stocks or bonds. Instead of taking physical possession of your gold, these ETFs give you ownership shares of gold held in the ETFs' vaults.

If you do decide to buy a gold ETF, you will have to pay the usual ETF costs, including broker commissions, bid/ask spreads, and the expense ratio. Of course, physical ownership of gold coins and bars also entails costs, including gold dealer commissions, rental costs on safe deposit boxes, or insurance costs if you are storing your gold at home. Whether you choose to buy gold coins, bars, or an ETF ultimately depends on your own personal preferences. Some may not be comfortable with only a paper claim to their gold, especially in the event of a crisis, while others may prefer the ease offered by ETFs.

Where to Hold?

Having considered the question of *what* funds to buy, we can now move on to the second question raised at the beginning of this chapter: *where* should we hold the mutual funds and ETFs we buy?

When you come home from the grocery store, you have to put each of the items you bought in its proper place. Some things belong in the refrigerator, some in the freezer, and some in the kitchen cabinets. If you make a mistake and put the ice cream in the cabinet, you will soon have a mess to clean up—and no ice cream to enjoy.

It's the same with mutual funds and ETFs. You probably have more than one place to store or hold these investments. The possible places might include, for example, a 401(k), a taxable brokerage account, a traditional IRA, or a Roth IRA. If you put the wrong funds in the wrong accounts, you will eventually be left with a mess to clean up. In this case, the mess will arrive by April 15, and you may have to clean it up by writing a big, fat check made payable to the IRS.

Different asset classes and funds have different tax consequences. Some get taxed at higher rates than others and need to be shielded in tax-deferred or tax-free accounts. Some generate tax credits and must be placed in taxable accounts to enable you to claim these credits. In short, where (in which accounts) you buy and hold different funds will have a significant impact on your tax bill. The question of where to hold must be given careful consideration. The answer to this question will depend in large part on what specific types of accounts you own: tax-free accounts (Roth IRAs and Roth 401(k)s), tax-deferred accounts (traditional IRAs and 401(k)s), and/or taxable accounts.

Basically, you should use your tax-deferred and tax-free accounts to hold those investments that are subject to high tax rates. These investments include bonds and gold. Bond dividends are taxed at your marginal income tax rate rather than the lower "qualified dividend" rate applied to most stocks, whereas gold is taxed at the collectibles rate of 28 percent.

Unfortunately, finding a place for your bond and gold investments is rarely as simple as the preceding guidance suggests. Suppose, for example, that you are using a 60/40 portfolio and that you have saved a total of $100,000 toward retirement, including $20,000 in tax-sheltered accounts and $80,000 in a taxable brokerage account. According to your 60/40 asset allocation plan, you should buy $40,000 worth of bonds. But you have only $20,000 available in your IRA(s) and 401(k)s. In this case, you will be able to shelter no more than half of your bond portfolio from taxes before you run out of room in your tax-advantaged accounts. Furthermore, after allocating your tax-sheltered savings to bonds, you will not have any money left in these accounts with which to buy gold.

If the room available in your tax-free and tax-deferred accounts is insufficient to hold your full allocation to bonds and gold, then your income level should determine which of these two asset classes should be given priority placement in these accounts. If your income is high enough to land you in a tax bracket greater than 28 percent, then allocate bonds to your tax-sheltered accounts before you make room for gold. If your tax bracket is less than 28 percent, start with gold, and if you have room left over, proceed to add bonds. Give TIPS the priority over other types of bonds when allocating space in your tax-sheltered accounts. As we discussed in Chapter 12, TIPS have some nasty features when it comes to taxation.

If you still have room in your tax-deferred and tax-free accounts after buying all of your bonds and gold, then you can proceed to add stock funds to these accounts. Give priority to U.S. small caps and U.S. value stock funds. Foreign stock funds should be last in line for placement in tax-sheltered accounts. You may be charged foreign taxes on these funds, but by placing them in your taxable account, you will be able to take a credit for these taxes on your 1040 form.

If you have a choice between a traditional (tax-deferred) account or a Roth (tax-free) IRA, put your stock funds in the Roth account. Unlike traditional IRAs, Roth IRAs do not force you to take required minimum distributions when you turn 70 ½. Your high-returning stock investments will be able to grow, undisturbed, beyond 70 ½ if you place them in a Roth IRA. (Unfortunately Roth 401(k)s do require you to take minimum distributions upon reaching the age of 70 ½.)

Meanwhile, Back in the Real World ...

The recommendations presented here represent *ideal* fund placements that do not take into account the real-world constraints you may face, such as limited investment options in your 401(k). While you can use these recommendations as a guide, understand that you may have to make compromises to fit all of your investments into the accounts you have available. In some cases, you may need to split your investment in a particular asset class across two different accounts, for example, by buying one U.S. small cap fund in your Roth IRA and another U.S. small cap fund in your traditional

401(k). In other cases, you may want to adjust your asset allocation so that it provides a better fit with your available accounts. Recall Patrick and Sandra from Chapter 11, who decided to place emerging-market bonds in their taxable account because this asset class was not available in Patrick's 401(k). They shifted their allocation away from emerging-market bonds and toward PME to reduce the impact of the former on their tax bill. Just as it is sometimes hard to fit all of the groceries into your refrigerator and kitchen cabinets, it can be a real challenge to fit all of your investments into your available accounts.

The key point here is that an ideal placement of all your funds will probably not be attainable. You should instead aim for the best placements possible given the real-world constraints you face. And do not despair if your initial fund placements fall far short of ideal, as you will have plenty of time and opportunity to make improvements over the course of your life. As just one example, the room inside your tax-sheltered accounts will grow as you make contributions to these accounts.

When to Buy?

We're almost there. We now know what to buy—low-cost index funds and ETFs—and where to put these investments. There's only one question left before you can take aim and click that "execute trade" button on your broker's website. *When* should you buy? Or more specifically, should you go ahead and buy *all* of the funds you need to implement your asset allocation plan now? Or should you wait to buy those asset classes that may be overpriced at present?

Let me rephrase these questions by putting them in context. Gold and PME enjoyed a huge price run-up during the Lost Decade. More recently, these assets have reversed course and suffered steep losses. Yet gold and PME prices still remain above their 2000 levels. They may still have much further to fall.

The case for gold and PME is uncertain, but there is less uncertainty with respect to bonds. Interest rates and bond yields are so low today, they can't go much lower. This means that they are either going to start rising—which will cause the prices of any bonds or bond funds you buy today to drop—or they are going to stay low, potentially for a long time. Either way, the bond investor can expect meager returns for the foreseeable future.

Given the current situation, should you buy your bond, gold, and PME funds now? Or should you wait until their prices come down?

I have a great deal of sympathy for those who would answer "wait." But I do not agree with them, and here's why. This book is not about trying to make money on *individual* investments. The entire purpose of this book is to teach you how to create a *portfolio* of investments that minimizes volatility without requiring too much compromise on returns. The key to accomplishing this goal is combining investments that zig with those that zag. In a well-diversified portfolio, you will often hold investments that are underperforming while your other investments are outperforming. It is precisely this combination of zigging and zagging investments that will enable your portfolio to dodge the worst of bear markets. If you do not implement your asset allocation in full and buy all your investments now, you will not get the full benefits of diversification. More specifically, if you wait to buy bonds, gold, and PME funds until their prices drop, your portfolio will completely lack the protection provided by both low-volatility and high-volatility hedges. Taking this route is very risky. You might get lucky—perhaps bond, gold, and gold mining stock prices will all drop to bargain-basement levels before the next bear market. But understand that the bear is very unpredictable. We do not know when she will arrive. All we know is that she *will* arrive. She always does. And it could take a long time—a very long time—for bond and gold prices to drop. It is best to be prepared at all times for the worst by buying all the investments you need now and holding them for the long run.

Again, I sympathize with those who are reluctant to buy asset classes that appear to be overpriced. After all, the way to make money in the markets is by buying low and selling high. But you will have many opportunities to do this *after* you buy your portfolio. The next two chapters explain two techniques—dollar cost averaging and rebalancing—that will give you simple, disciplined ways to buy low and sell high for the rest of your life.

But *now*, you need to take that first big step and implement your asset allocation plan. So place your cursor on the "buy" button. Take a deep breath. Ready, aim … CLICK.

CHAPTER 14

TECHNIQUES TO INCREASE RETURNS AND REDUCE COSTS

In this chapter, we learn how to do just a few important things to enhance your portfolio's performance. These techniques, including dollar cost averaging and tax loss harvesting, come with a lot of benefits and entail few, if any, costs. So read on.

Portfolio Optimization

The first technique we'll cover isn't really a technique. It's just a reminder that your real-world portfolio will probably fall short of the ideal but that opportunities will arise to improve and update it. We have already seen many of the types of compromises investors have to make owing to constraints such as limited 401(k) investment choices and lack of room in tax-deferred accounts. Recall Steve from Chapter 11, whose small nest egg could only accommodate four funds. Or Patrick and Sandra, who had to place investments taxed at a high rate—including gold and emerging-market bonds—in a taxable brokerage account.

Like them, you will probably not be able to fit your ideal portfolio into your real-world accounts. But you should always be aware of, and remember, the compromises you had to make—and be ready to fix those compromises when the opportunity arises. For example, for many years, I was unable to fit TIPS into my own portfolio. But when my 401(k) added a TIPS fund to our investment choices, I was finally able to make room for TIPS. Take advantage of these kinds of opportunities when they arise. If your 401(k) provider sends you a notice outlining new mutual fund choices, be sure to read the notice carefully and think about whether the new options might meet your needs better than your current 401(k) investments. If your broker advertises a new set of commission-free ETFs, compare them to your current investments and consider them as possible replacement options. As your savings grow, you may be able to improve your portfolio's asset class diversification or rearrange the investments in your various accounts to bring them more in line with the tax-based recommendations in the previous chapter. Always be on the lookout for these and other opportunities to improve your portfolio and grab them when they arise. (Your annual portfolio rebalancing exercise, discussed in the next chapter, is a good time to check whether these kinds of improvements can be made.)

In addition to improving your portfolio, you may need or want to update your asset allocation based on new information or changed life circumstances. In particular, remember to revisit your stock/bond split once you get within five years of your planned retirement. As we discussed in Chapter 11, the process used to decide on an appropriate stock/bond split is completely different for workers more than five years from retirement and workers within five years of retiring. The former should keep their percentage allocation to bonds as small as they can stomach. The latter should base their stock/bond mix on their expected withdrawal rate in retirement. Also, if you're a retiree, remember that you may be able to increase your allocation to bonds as you age. If you want to take advantage of this possibility, use Table 11.4 to guide any changes you make.

Finally, as you gain practical experience with your portfolio, you may want to adjust its volatility. It is difficult to know how you will react to bear markets until you experience them. If you learn, through hard experience, that your portfolio is too volatile, you may need to increase your allocation to bonds. Alternatively, you may find that you have no trouble at all handling your portfolio's volatility during bear markets. In this case, you should consider reducing your allocation to bonds.

In either of these situations, if at all possible, do *not* make your portfolio adjustments until the market has bottomed and the recovery rally is well advanced. Otherwise you could wind up either taking on more volatility than you can handle or selling low and locking in your losses forever. In fact, you should avoid making *any* improvements or other changes to your portfolio during a bear market or market correction. The mind is a funny thing—especially when it's operating under the stress that arises during a bear market. It can trick you into believing that you are adjusting your portfolio to take advantage of some new opportunity when you are really just responding to the fear caused by the market decline. Don't give your mind the chance to fool itself. The opportunities to improve your portfolio will still be available after the recovery rally has begun. Especially if you are considering adjustments to your stock/bond mix, you will be better able to judge the level of volatility you can handle in the calm following the storm. In the remainder of this chapter and in the next chapter, we discuss three techniques that you *should* continue to apply on a regular schedule regardless of what the market is doing. But limit your trades during a bear market or correction to those required by these three techniques: dollar cost averaging, tax loss harvesting, and rebalancing.

If during a market sell-off you or your significant other's stress level reaches a point where it is putting your health at risk, then by all means proceed immediately with the stock/bond adjustments needed to reduce your portfolio's volatility. But otherwise stand pat and make your adjustments later with the self-knowledge that should come with calm reflection and hindsight.

Dollar Cost Averaging and Tax Loss Harvesting

In the preceding section, we covered opportunities for improving and updating your portfolio. With just a few exceptions, these opportunities will not arrive on some set schedule. Instead, you will have to be on the lookout for them and, when opportunity knocks, be ready to open the door.

In this section, we cover two techniques that you *will* apply on a regular, set schedule (a third technique, rebalancing, is covered in the next chapter):

- Dollar cost averaging

- Tax loss harvesting

Dollar Cost Averaging

In the last chapter, I promised to give you two techniques you can use to buy low and sell high on a regular basis. Dollar cost averaging is one of these two techniques. Dollar cost averaging will enable you to buy low when you invest your savings. Anyone who is drawing a regular paycheck, and saving a portion of that paycheck, can use dollar cost averaging. Here's how it works. On a set schedule, you invest the same dollar amount in a fund (or funds). The share price of the fund(s) you've selected for investment will fluctuate, but by investing the same dollar amount every time, you will wind up buying more shares at lower than at higher prices.

For example, let's say that you are going to save $100 each month and invest it in fund X. In the first month, the share price for X is $10, so your $100 buys you ten shares of X. Let's say the share price increases to $20 when you invest your next $100, giving you an additional five shares. If the price of X subsequently goes to $15 per share, you might at first think that you have broken even on your two investments, because the price is now $5 higher than the price at which you invested your first $100 and $5 lower than the price at which you invested your second $100. But in fact, because you now own fifteen shares of X, the value of your investment at the current price of $15/share is (15 shares × $15/share) = $225. You have realized a net gain of $225 minus $200, or $25. You realize this gain because dollar cost averaging has lowered the weighted average purchase price of your investment in X. You bought most of your shares at the low price of $10 and fewer shares at the $20 high price. In other words, you bought low. Now all you need to do is hold on to your investment in X for the long haul, allowing it time to appreciate in value before, eventually, you sell high.

As this example illustrates, dollar cost averaging works particularly well for highly volatile investments. PME funds, emerging-market stock funds, and small cap funds are particularly good candidates for dollar cost averaging. ETFs, however, may not be good candidates, as the frequent buying required by dollar cost averaging may lead to excessive trading costs.

You should be able to completely automate the saving and dollar cost averaging process. Putting your saving and dollar cost averaging plan on autopilot will not only save you a lot of work, but by "fixing and forgetting" it, you will be less tempted to interfere with the plan.

Dollar cost averaging gives you a very simple, disciplined way to buy low. Be sure to take advantage of this neat technique.

Tax Loss Harvesting

If you hold investments in a taxable account, you can reduce your taxes using a technique called tax loss harvesting. Tax loss harvesting is easy. In late December of each year, simply sell those funds in your taxable account whose prices have fallen below their original purchase prices. This will enable you to realize a capital loss on these investments. After you sell them, wait thirty-one days and then repurchase the funds. You must wait the thirty-one days, as the IRS treats repurchases made *before* thirty-one days to be wash sales. You cannot claim the losses resulting from a wash sale.

The capital losses you realize can be used to offset capital gains on a dollar-for-dollar basis. In addition, if in any given tax year your capital losses exceed your capital gains, you may use the excess, up to $3,000, to reduce your taxable income. Losses in excess of this $3,000 can be transferred to the next tax year.

Suppose, for example, that in 2014 you realize $1,000 in capital gains and, through tax loss harvesting, $10,000 in capital losses. First, $1,000 of the losses would be applied to the $1,000 in gains, thereby eliminating your capital gains taxes. Next, your total income (including income from your job as well as interest and dividend income) would be reduced by $3,000 to compute your taxable income. Finally, the remaining $6,000 of capital losses will transfer to the 2015 tax year, where it can be used to reduce capital gains and income taxes in that year. If a portion of the $6,000 is left over after you use it in 2015, that portion will carry over to 2016. The capital losses never go away until you have used them all up.

Some people are reluctant to sell their losing investments and realize a loss because they view this as admitting that they made a mistake. *Don't be one of those people!* First of all, you didn't necessarily make a mistake. If you are a true black belt investor, it will often be the case that some of your investments will go down while others go up. That's the whole point of black belt investing using the principle of correlation. Second, *every* investor loses on some of his investments every now and then. Do you think Warren Buffet has never had a losing investment? Of course he has. It's not a sign of foolishness to realize a loss. But it is *very* foolish to pass up a guaranteed opportunity to save money on your tax bill. The smart investor recognizes that there are opportunities in every situation, good or bad. Stock prices drop through the floor in a major sell-off? That's a buying opportunity par excellence. You lost money in the sell-off? That's an opportunity to save on your taxes. Don't pass up the opportunities that come your way.

Tax loss harvesting works even better when you combine it with dollar cost averaging. Because the latter technique involves the purchase of investments at prices that fluctuate throughout the year, you may often find that you can realize a loss on the higher-priced shares you bought come December. To take advantage of this opportunity, you will need to use the specific share identification method to determine your tax cost basis. Speak to your broker or tax accountant about how to do this.

There is one disadvantage to tax loss harvesting—it requires you to be out of the market on some of your investments for a one-month period (to avoid a wash sale). As an alternative to holding the sale proceeds in a money market, you can instead purchase another fund that is not substantially identical to the fund you sold. What does the IRS mean by the term *substantially identical*? Unfortunately that's not entirely clear. Therefore I play it safe and just stay out of the market for the duration of the waiting period. For this reason, I don't use tax loss harvesting if the resulting tax savings will be small. But for larger amounts, the certainty of the tax savings are preferable to the *possibility* of an even larger gain by staying in the market.[107]

A Brief Word on Withdrawals

There is one other situation, besides portfolio optimization, dollar cost averaging, tax loss harvesting, and rebalancing (discussed in the next chapter), that will probably necessitate trading. Retirees making regular withdrawals from their nest egg to meet their living expenses will likely need to sell investments on a regular basis. In general, when it comes to making withdrawals, the advice offered by James Lange in his book *Retire Secure!* makes perfect sense. Lange's basic idea is that it is better to pay taxes later rather than now. To defer taxes as long as possible, Lange recommends that you first spend your income (including any dividend, interest, and capital gains distributions as well as income from Social Security and pensions) before either selling investments in your taxable account or making withdrawals from your 401(k) or IRA.[108] To implement this recommendation, you should set up your taxable account so that your fund distributions will *not* be automatically reinvested. (This is the opposite of what you should be doing when you are still working. Current workers who don't need to spend their distribution income should automatically reinvest this income back into the distributing funds.)

Many retirees will not be able to live on their income alone and will need to sell investments on a regular basis. The principle of "pay taxes later" suggests that asset sales should be made first in your taxable accounts, then in your tax-deferred (401(k) and IRA) accounts, and lastly in your tax-free (Roth) accounts. However, as Lange notes, the required minimum distributions (RMDs) that you must withdraw from 401(k)s and traditional IRAs starting at age 70 ½ is a complicating factor. RMDs may push you into a higher tax bracket, particularly if you have a lot of money stashed in your tax-deferred accounts. In this case, there *may* be advantages to withdrawing some of the money from your tax-deferred accounts in your sixties or, better, moving some of this money into a Roth IRA. However, this has to be done carefully or you will wind up in a higher tax bracket. In general, setting up and implementing a retirement withdrawal plan is one area where it may pay to seek the advice of a financial advisor or tax accountant. Taxes are a complicated subject, and one size does not fit all. The complications and potential pitfalls make a do-it-yourself approach risky.

Some retirees believe that the principal in their retirement accounts should *never* be touched. To avoid drawing down principal, these retirees may be forced to shift their portfolios toward investments that yield high dividends, such as junk bonds and high-dividend stocks. Chasing higher yields in this way has become a common practice in today's low interest rate environment. This is a major mistake. Your asset allocation should be based on the risk-reducing principles of correlation and compromise, not on an attempt to maximize dividend income. As we learned in Chapter 5, high-yield junk bonds are volatile and highly correlated with the stock market. And while high-dividend stocks can be good investments, some of these stocks have high yields because their share prices have been beaten down—for good reason. As long as you maintain a well-diversified portfolio and use a low withdrawal rate—preferably less than 4 percent—you can sell fund shares and even dip into principal on occasion without incurring undue risk.

CHAPTER 15

REBALANCING: THE SECRET SAUCE

In addition to tax loss harvesting and dollar cost averaging, there is a third technique that will help you to reduce volatility, buy low, and sell high: rebalancing. I'm giving rebalancing a separate chapter for two reasons. First, it is important that you rebalance your portfolio on a regular basis. And second, rebalancing will often be difficult to do (at times even more difficult than doing nothing). During bull markets, rebalancing will *feel* wrong to you. And during bear markets, it may feel downright terrifying. So I'm devoting an entire chapter to the task of convincing you that rebalancing is the right thing to do—regardless of what your feelings might tell you.

First, let's be sure we understand what exactly rebalancing is. Once you have bought your funds in accordance with your asset allocation plan, some of your investments will generate higher returns than others. As a result, your portfolio will drift away from your planned allocation. For example, if you originally planned on using a 60/40 allocation between stocks and bonds, but your stocks are outperforming your bonds, your portfolio may shift to 65/35 over time. In this situation, you will need to rebalance by moving some of your money out of stocks and into bonds to get back to 60/40. Similarly, you will need to rebalance *within* the stock and bonds portions of your portfolio to return your percentage allocations for each stock and bond investment back to your original plan.

Rebalancing is important for two reasons. First, the risk characteristics of your portfolio will change if you let it drift without rebalancing. Over the long run, stocks will likely yield higher returns than bonds, causing your portfolio to shift away from bonds and toward stocks. If you do not rebalance, your portfolio will suffer larger losses than you expected when a bear market hits. The result will be sleepless nights at best—and at worst too much negative volatility and a quick jog down John Stock-man's path to the poorhouse.

Rebalancing helps you maintain your portfolio's volatility level. But there is a second, excellent reason to rebalance. Rebalancing provides you with a safe, disci-plined way to buy low and sell high. Whenever you rebalance, you will be selling those investments that have outperformed (selling high) and buying investments that have underperformed (buying low). Buying low and selling high is, of course, the key to making money in the markets. Rebalancing is how buy-and-hold investors buy low and sell high.

In Part III, we studied the past performance of both basic and advanced portfo-lios that we built according to the principles of correlation and compromise. In all of the various tests we ran in Part III, we *rebalanced* our portfolios on an annual basis. Let's now consider what would have happened had we *not* rebalanced.

Volatility Reduction through Rebalancing

In Chapter 8 we met Anne, a twenty-five-year-old who inherited $100,000 in 1972. Anne put her inheritance in a retirement account and left it there until she retired at the end of 2013. Depending on which specific basic portfolio she used (conserva-tive, moderate, or aggressive), she would have wound up with somewhere between $2.44 million and $4.14 million by the time she retired (see Table 8.6).

But Anne rebalanced her portfolio every January. What would have happened had she never rebalanced?

First, her portfolio would have drifted far from its original allocation. For example, by the end of 2013, the 60/40 moderate portfolio would have wound up with an 81 percent allocation to stocks and only a 19 percent allocation to bonds. In other words, the moderate portfolio would have become an aggressive, 80/20 portfolio by the time she retired. Had Anne started with the conservative, 40/60 portfolio, her asset allocation would have shifted to 66 percent stocks and only 34 percent bonds by 2013—riskier even than the moderate 60/40 portfolio. And if Anne started with the aggressive 80/20 portfolio, she would have wound up with only 8 percent of her nest egg allocated to bonds by the time she retired.

These shifts away from bonds and toward stocks are not at all surprising. In the long run, stocks are expected to yield significantly higher returns than bonds. Stocks will likely come to dominate a portfolio that is never rebalanced. Such a portfolio will become increasingly volatile and subject to increasingly large losses with each new bear market. A person with a risk tolerance suitable to a 40/60 conservative portfolio is likely to experience increasingly intolerable losses as the portfolio drifts to 50/50, 60/40, and even higher stock allocations. Finding the right balance between stocks and bonds to fit *your* unique circumstances and risk tolerance is the most important step in asset allocation, and it takes a good deal of work (as we learned in

Chapter 11). Why in the world would you let your stock/bond split drift away from your chosen allocation after going through all that hard work?

The dangers resulting from a failure to rebalance do not begin and end with a drift away from bonds and toward stocks. Table 15.1 shows the drift that would have occurred within the stock portion of Anne's 60/40 moderate portfolio had she never rebalanced. While the allocations to U.S. large caps and small cap value stocks have held nearly constant, there has been a dramatic shift away from international stocks and toward precious metals equities (PME). In fact, the allocation to PME has nearly doubled by the end of 2011, to nearly 40 percent. This is much too large, and risky, an allocation to a highly volatile asset. PME are intended to hedge the stock portion of Anne's portfolio; by 2011, they have become Anne's core holding. Just how risky is this situation? Consider that from December 31, 2011, to December 31, 2013, the average PME fund suffered a 53.4 percent loss. This loss would have cost Anne $400,000. Annual rebalancing would have cut this loss in half. The one bit of good news in all this is that, owing to the massive losses suffered by the un-rebalanced portfolio, the allocation to PME would have dropped back to only 16 percent of Anne's stock portfolio by the end of 2013. The lesson here is simple—if *you* do not rebalance your portfolio, the *market* will rebalance it for you. But it will charge you a very hefty price for this service. Do it yourself, and save a boatload of money.

Table 15.1. Drift in the Stock Portion of the Moderate Portfolio Owing to Failure to Rebalance, 1972–2011

Asset Class	Original Intended Percentage Allocation (1972)	Final Percentage Allocation Owing to Drift (2011)
U.S. large cap blend	30%	29.4%
Foreign large cap blend	30%	9.7%
PME	20%	38.9%
Small cap value	20%	22.0%

Source: Developed by the author using data from www.morningstar.com.

The Rebalancing Bonus

It is no surprise that an un-rebalanced portfolio will tend to drift away from bonds and toward stocks, thereby becoming more volatile. What *is* surprising is that, in at least some circumstances, the un-rebalanced portfolio may generate *lower* returns than the same portfolio subject to annual rebalancing. Figure 15.1 compares the final values of Anne's basic portfolios in 2013 when annual rebalancing is used, against un-rebalanced versions of the same portfolios. For all three portfolios, conservative, moderate, and aggressive, annual rebalancing improves returns. This happens despite the fact that all three portfolios, if left untouched, shift significantly toward stocks over the course of the 42-year time frame. The differences in final portfolio values are significant, ranging from more than $250,000 for the conservative portfolio to more than $1 million for the aggressive portfolio.

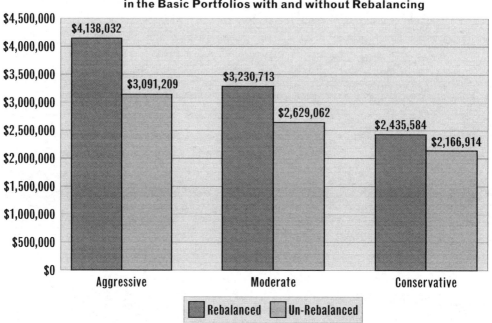

Figure 15.1. Final (2013) Value of a 1972 $100,000 Investment in the Basic Portfolios with and without Rebalancing

Source: Developed by the author using data from www.morningstar.com.

Figure 15.1 illustrates the second key advantage of rebalancing. Not only does this technique keep your portfolio from drifting away from your planned allocation, but it also provides you with periodic opportunities to buy low and sell high. Each year, you sell a portion of your higher-returning investments and use the proceeds to buy more of your lower-returning investments. This is the way you make money in the stock market. Sometimes it works so well that you can earn *higher returns with less volatility*.[109] While the un-rebalanced portfolios in Figure 15.1 gradually drifted toward higher stock allocations and increasing levels of volatility, the rebalanced portfolios remained closely fixed to their initial asset allocation levels but still managed to generate significantly better returns. Remember, you can't get high returns with low volatility from a single investment, but you can sometimes do this with a portfolio of investments—especially if you rebalance the portfolio.

Still, there might be something odd about the pattern of stock and bond returns for 1972 to 2013 that led to the surprising results in Figure 15.1. And in any event, forty-two years is a long time to wait for a strategy to pay off. Would rebalancing have produced higher returns with less volatility over shorter periods? Would it have

worked as well in both bull and bear markets? To answer these questions, I tested
the basic portfolios, with and without rebalancing, over rolling twenty-year periods.
The first test covered 1972 through 1991. The second test was for 1973 through 1992.
The third test covered 1974 through 1993. I continued to add one year to the test
period in this manner, until finishing with a test for 1994 through 2013. This approach
yielded a total of twenty-three tests of twenty-year time periods. For each test, I
determined which portfolio, the rebalanced or un-rebalanced one, yielded the most
money at the end of twenty years. Figure 15.2 shows the results. For the conservative
(40/60) portfolio, annual rebalancing yielded better returns than no rebalancing in
eighteen out of twenty-three tests. The rebalanced portfolio beat the untouched
portfolio in nineteen out of twenty-three tests for the moderate (60/40) allocation
and in twenty out of twenty-three tests for the aggressive (80/20) allocation.[110]

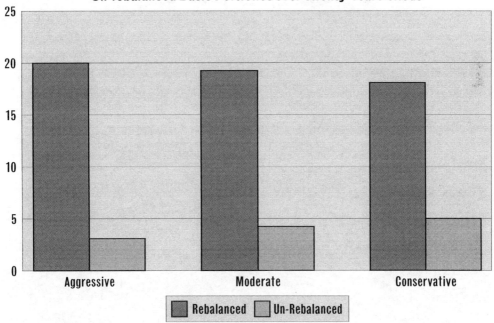

**Figure 15.2. Number of Wins for Rebalanced versus
Un-rebalanced Basic Portfolios over Twenty-Year Periods**

Source: Developed by the author using data from www.morningstar.com.

Figure 15.2 proves that the forty-two-year results in Figure 15.1 were *not* an
anomaly. In every single twenty-year period tested, the un-rebalanced portfolios
shifted away from bonds and toward stocks. For example, the moderate portfolio,
which began with a 40 percent allocation to bonds, wound up at the end of each
twenty-year period with a bond allocation ranging from 21 percent to at most 34
percent. Yet despite this shift away from bonds and toward higher-returning stocks,
the un-rebalanced portfolios usually produced lower returns than the rebalanced
portfolios.

Consider the implications of these results for an investor trying to minimize the retirement risk. As you now know by heart, there are two ways this risk manifests itself: too much (negative) market volatility and not enough returns to outpace inflation. During most of the twenty-year periods between 1972 and 2013, an investor could have reduced both components of the retirement risk, and put more money in her retirement accounts, simply by rebalancing on an annual basis.

Rebalancing the Advanced Portfolios

So far we have focused on the effects of rebalancing the simple, five-asset basic portfolios. But a rebalancing bonus is likewise earned by the advanced portfolios, at least over the shorter (1990–2013) time frame for which data are available for these portfolios. In fact, the rebalancing bonus appears to be much larger for the advanced than for the basic portfolios. This is shown in Figure 15.3. The rebalancing bonuses in this figure were calculated as the difference in the final (2013) values of a $100,000 investment made in 1990 in each portfolio, with and without annual rebalancing. For example, the advanced aggressive (80/20) portfolio wound up with $82,158 more by the end of 2013 with annual rebalancing than without, while rebalancing the basic aggressive portfolio yielded an additional $11,418.

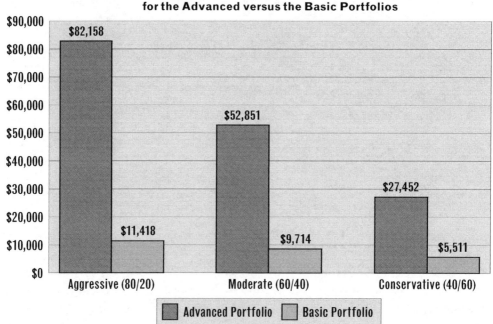

Figure 15.3. Rebalancing Bonuses, 1990–13, for the Advanced versus the Basic Portfolios

Source: Developed by the author using data from www.morningstar.com.
Gold returns based on London Gold Market Fixing prices.

Explaining the Rebalancing Bonus

Bigger returns with less volatility for both the basic and advanced portfolios—this is a neat trick, but we need to come to a better understanding of how, precisely, rebalancing manages to pull off this trick. William Bernstein did the original analyses that identified the existence of a rebalancing bonus. He listed the three key attributes that a portfolio should possess if it is to yield a rebalancing bonus:

- The correlations between the assets comprising the portfolio should be low

- The differences in returns among the assets comprising the portfolio should be small

- The volatility of the assets should be high[111]

Hmm, does this list remind you of anything? It should. Back in Chapter 2, we identified the three key attributes of a good hedge of large cap stocks, as follows:

- *Low correlation* with large caps

- *Expected returns* similar to those of large caps

- *High volatility*

The high-volatility hedges have the same three characteristics that help a portfolio to produce a rebalancing bonus. What a lucky coincidence!

It's almost too good to believe. Is it really true that adding high-volatility hedges to our portfolio will not only help to reduce our portfolio's volatility but also give us a rebalancing bonus to boot? Let's run another test and see.

The basic portfolios include a 20 percent allocation to one of the three high-volatility hedges: PME. And PME just happens to be the one asset class singled out by Bernstein as offering an unusually large potential rebalancing bonus.[112] What, then, would happen to our returns if we were to drop PME from the portfolio (and increase our allocation to U.S. large caps to make up the difference)? Table 15.2 answers this question for the moderate (60/40) portfolio over the forty-two-year period stretching from 1972 to 2013. The first column of this table shows that when we drop the PME fund from the portfolio, our annualized returns are 8.3 percent without rebalancing and 8.2 percent with rebalancing. This means that without the PME fund, we do not earn a rebalancing bonus, although the returns lost by rebalancing are a relatively small 0.1 percent per year (which works out to $126,000 less earned on a $100,000 initial investment by the end of 2013).

**Table 15.2. Annualized Returns of the 60/40 Basic Portfolio
with and without an Allocation to PME**

Rebalancing Procedure	Annualized Returns for Portfolio *Excluding* PME	Annualized Returns for Portfolio *Including* PME
Without rebalancing	8.3%	8.1%
With annual rebalancing	8.2%	8.6%

Source: Developed by the author using data from www.morningstar.com.

The second column of the table shows the returns for the original portfolio, with its 20 percent allocation to PME. Note, first, that simply adding the precious metals mining fund to the portfolio *without* rebalancing would have dragged returns down from 8.3 percent to 8.1 percent. But if we instead rebalance the portfolio with PME annually, returns increase from 8.1 percent to 8.6 percent. We earn a rebalancing bonus of 0.5 percent when we add our high-volatility hedge to the mix. For those who prefer dollars to percentages, this works out to an extra $602,000 by 2013—as compared with $126,000 *less* when we rebalance the portfolio that excludes the PME fund.

What you are seeing at work in Table 15.2 is nothing other than the long-promised secret sauce. We first mentioned this sauce back in Chapter 4. In that chapter, we found that adding a 50 percent PME allocation to a portfolio of large cap stocks would have *increased* the returns of the portfolio above the 8.8 percent annualized returns of the large caps—despite the PME fund earning only 6.5 percent. Similarly from Table 15.2, rebalancing the 60/40 basic portfolio *including* PME increases the portfolio's returns over what it would have earned *excluding* PME, even though PME's stand-alone returns would drag down the portfolio's returns without rebalancing.

Rebalancing is the secret sauce that makes these remarkable results possible. When you add this sauce to a portfolio that includes PME, it juices the returns above and beyond what you would expect from simply adding PME. How does rebalancing pull off this trick? The high volatility of PME funds creates many opportunities to sell the funds high (or buy low) when you rebalance, while the low correlation of these funds with the other investments in a well-diversified portfolio increases the chances that you will be using the sale proceeds to buy those other investments when they are low (or to sell them when they are high).

This is illustrated in Figure 15.4, which shows returns for the average large cap blend fund and PME fund for the first decade of the 1972–2011 time frame. (For illustrative purposes, we are leaving out of this figure the other three investments composing the basic portfolios.) As you can see, returns for the PME fund are much more volatile than those for the large cap blend fund.

The figure indicates with black dots the points on the PME fund's graph where the return trend reverses direction. Notice first that in 1974, the trend line tops out just as the large cap graph *bottoms* out. Up to this point, rebalancing would have involved selling the PME fund as it moved toward, and reached, its high (thereby selling high), and buying the large cap blend fund as it moved toward, and reached, its low (buying low). In 1976, the reverse situation occurs, as the PME fund bottoms out at the same time that the large cap blend fund reaches a top (it is difficult to see on the graph, but there is a slight drop in the large cap blend fund's trend between 1976 and 1977). Rebalancing between 1974 and 1976 would have resulted in the buying of shares of the PME fund as it moved toward and quickly reached a low (buying low) and the simultaneous selling of shares of the large cap blend fund as it moved toward and reached a high (selling high). In both 1974 and 1976, it is the low correlation between the two funds that sends them in opposite directions, thus enabling *both* buying low and selling high through rebalancing.

Figure 15.4. Growth of $1 Invested in the Average PME Fund and Large Cap Blend Fund, 1971–82

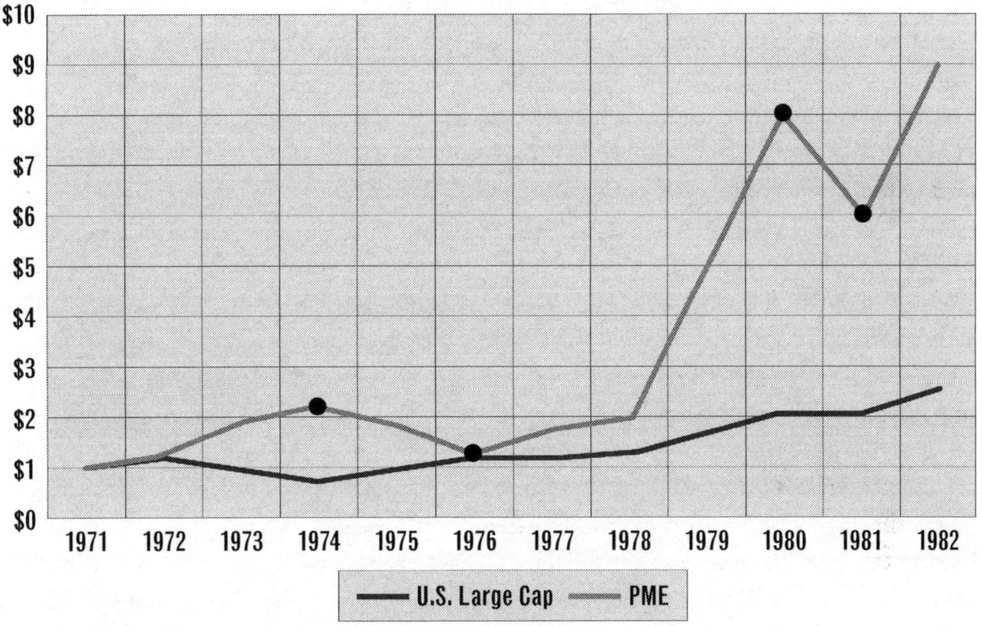

Source: Developed by the author using data from www.morningstar.com.

In 1980, after almost an eightfold increase in the PME fund, another reversal occurs. Although in this case the reversal does not correspond to an opposite reversal for the large cap blend fund, the selling of shares of the PME fund during the run-up would nonetheless have protected some profits from the steep downturn that occurred in 1981. And finally, the shifting of money out of the large cap blend fund and into the PME fund in 1981 would pay off when the PME fund once again took off like a rocket in 1982.

Of course, rebalancing will not always work out as well as it did in 1971–82. But rebalancing a portfolio that includes a PME fund will probably more often than not lead to buying low and selling high, given the high volatility and low correlation characterizing this asset class. With regard to volatility, it is the *frequency* as well as the magnitude of the reversals in PME's returns trend that helps produce large rebalancing bonuses. Between 1972 and 2013, the annual PME returns trend reversed itself a total of twenty-one times. That averages out to one reversal every two years. Had PME funds managed to generate more momentum, following up or down trends for longer time periods, annual rebalancing would have interrupted the momentum and might possibly have reduced returns. But with reversals occurring so frequently, there was no significant momentum to interrupt. Purchases of PME during a downtrend were soon rewarded with an uptrend, and sales of PME during an uptrend protected profits from the downtrend that usually quickly followed.

Other high-volatility hedges and the rebalancing bonus. You may at this point be wondering whether adding gold and emerging-market bonds to your portfolio might increase the size of the rebalancing bonus. At least over the last couple of decades, the answer appears to be no. Retesting the advanced portfolios over the 1990–2011 time frame with and without PME, gold, and emerging-market bonds, I found that only PME had a significant impact on the magnitude of the rebalancing bonus. Neither gold nor emerging-market bonds are as volatile as PME. The volatility of the latter asset class appears to result in a unique rebalancing bonus.

Bonds and the rebalancing bonus. As a portfolio's allocation to bonds increases, the chances of earning the rebalancing bonus will likely decline. For example, Figure 15.2 shows that rebalancing the aggressive (80/20) portfolio led to a rebalancing bonus in twenty of the twenty-three time periods tested. In contrast, the conservative (40/60) portfolio yielded a rebalancing bonus in only eighteen of the twenty-three tests. Furthermore, Figures 15.1 and 15.3 both indicate that as the allocation to bonds increases, the size of the rebalancing bonus declines. These results are to be expected given the three factors Bernstein identified as the source of the rebalancing bonus: low correlation between assets, similar returns across assets, and high volatility. Of these three factors, bonds share only one: low correlation. The *low* volatility and *low* returns of bonds mean that as you increase your allocation to bonds, you reduce both your chances of earning a rebalancing bonus and the size of the potential bonus.

Future Outlook for the Rebalancing Bonus

There is no *guarantee* you will earn a rebalancing bonus in the coming years. Whether you earn a bonus will depend on the extent to which the three factors Bernstein identified—low asset correlations, high volatility, and similar asset class returns—hold in the future. In fact, there is reason to think that that last factor—similar returns—may *not* hold up at least in the nearer term. Keep in mind that the historical analyses presented in this chapter cover a period of unusually high bond returns. During the three-decade bond bull market that began in 1982, intermediate-term bond funds averaged 8.1 percent annualized returns—not that much lower than the 11.0 percent returns generated by the S&P 500 over this same period. But with yields on bonds now at historic lows, the next few years may be characterized by a much wider gap between bond returns and stock returns. If bonds significantly lag stocks in the coming years, then the rebalancing bonus may disappear.

To get a sense of the potential impact a larger difference between stock and bond returns might have on the rebalancing bonus, we can look at a specific past period characterized by a large stock/bond return gap. During the latter half of the 1990s, the annualized returns of the bond portion of the advanced portfolios were a respectable 6.6 percent. But over this same 1995–99 period, the stock portion of the advanced portfolios generated 14.0 percent annualized returns—more than double the bond returns. And sure enough, over this limited five-year period, the rebalancing bonus failed to materialize. In fact, the advanced portfolios would have produced higher returns without rebalancing than they did with rebalancing. For example, the advanced moderate (60/40) portfolio would have drifted from 40 percent to 33.1 percent bonds from 1995 to 1999 if left un-rebalanced. The resulting shift to much higher returning stocks would have increased the portfolio's annualized returns by 0.4 percent over the returns produced by the annually rebalanced version of the same portfolio.

However, it is important to recognize that this increase in returns occurs only because the portfolio has been allowed to drift toward a more aggressive asset allocation. The 0.4 percent gain in returns would have been lost in the 2000–2002 bear market. The primary purpose of rebalancing is to keep the volatility of your portfolio under control. If you decide that your personal risk tolerance level calls for a 60/40 split between stocks and bonds, you must rebalance to retain that split. Otherwise, your portfolio will drift beyond your personal comfort zone. It stands to reason that constantly selling a portion of your stock portfolio to purchase bonds will result in a reduction in your returns. That is the price you pay to keep your portfolio from becoming too volatile. What is surprising is that under at least some conditions, you might not have to pay this price—and, indeed, you might even be rewarded with extra returns for taking steps to reduce your portfolio's volatility. By rebalancing, you might be able to reduce both aspects of the retirement risk.

Dr. Bernstein chose an apt term, bonus, to describe the extra returns that may come from rebalancing. In the business world, a bonus doesn't come with the same certainty as a regular paycheck. Your employer probably won't guarantee you that you'll get a bonus this year. Similarly, there's no guarantee that you'll receive the rebalancing bonus, especially in the next few years, when bond returns may lag far behind stock returns. But even the possibility that you might reap extra returns by limiting your portfolio's volatility should be welcome news. Investing does not offer many chances to increase returns without incurring greater volatility. Rebalancing is one such chance. And if and when bond yields return to more normal levels, the odds of cashing in on the rebalancing bonus will likely improve.

Keep in mind, also, that while low bond returns may possibly eliminate the rebalancing bonus in the coming years, PME and the secret sauce will still likely be working together, behind the scenes as it were, to increase the returns of the *stock* portion of your portfolio. As a result, any reductions in your portfolio's overall returns owing to rebalancing out of stocks and into bonds will be at least partially offset by the increased stock returns. In other words, the price you *may* have to pay to keep your portfolio's volatility under control will likely be a cut-rate bargain price.

So remember, you cannot win the bonus if you don't play the rebalancing game. And remember, too, that rebalancing is the secret sauce that brings out the best in PME. Be sure to combine this unique asset class with the secret rebalancing sauce in *your* gourmet portfolio.

When to Rebalance

There is one catch to the secret sauce. Its effects wear off, so you have to keep adding more of it to your portfolio. In other words, you must rebalance on a regular basis. The question therefore arises: *when* should you rebalance?

There are two basic approaches to rebalancing. The first approach is to rebalance on a regular schedule (such as annually). The second approach is to rebalance whenever your allocation drifts beyond established bounds. It is not possible to know, in advance, which approach will provide you with the best risk-adjusted returns. But the first approach has the advantage of being much simpler than the second. Keep things simple by using periodic rebalancing. Furthermore, I recommend that you rebalance annually. You do not want to rebalance too frequently or you will interrupt the momentum exhibited by the stock market in the short term. But by the same token, if you rebalance too infrequently, you will miss out on many of the opportunities to buy low and sell high. Annual rebalancing is a good compromise.

As far as when in the year to rebalance, I recommend January. This will allow you to combine rebalancing with the repurchasing of funds you sold for tax loss harvesting purposes in December. It's also easier to remember to rebalance if you get in the habit of doing it at the beginning of each year.

How to Rebalance

The four-step basic procedure for rebalancing is as follows:

1. Sum up the value of each of the investments in your portfolio.

2. Determine how the total amount calculated in step 1 should be allocated across stocks and bonds (based on your asset allocation plan).

3. Determine how the total stock and bond amounts calculated in step 2 should be allocated across each of your individual stock and bond fund investments (based on your asset allocation plan).

4. For each investment, compare the amount to be allocated (as calculated in step 3) to the actual current value of the investment. If the current value is larger than the step 3 amount, the difference is the amount that should be *sold*. If the amount allocated in step 3 is larger than the current amount, the difference is the amount that should be *bought*.

For example, suppose that the total current value of all of your investments is $100,000 (as calculated in step 1). Suppose, furthermore, that you are using a 60/40 portfolio and that your asset allocation plan calls for a 10 percent allocation of the stock portion of your portfolio to a small cap index fund. Finally, suppose that currently the total amount you have invested in the small cap index fund is $7,000. In this case, in step 2, you would calculate the total amount to be allocated to stocks as 60 percent of $100,000, or $60,000. In step 3, 10 percent of this total, or $6,000, would be calculated as the amount to be allocated to the small cap fund. Finally, in step 4, you would compare this $6,000 with the $7,000 currently invested in the small cap fund. A total of $1,000 worth of the small cap fund would need to be sold to bring this investment back in line with your asset allocation plan.

The preceding example is pretty straightforward, but rebalancing can get trickier when you have some or all of your investments in a taxable account. Selling taxable investments that have appreciated in value will trigger capital gains taxes. While such selling may sometimes be necessary to keep your portfolio from drifting too far from your asset allocation plan, allowing a *limited* amount of drift is warranted to avoid the tax implications. I allow investments in my own taxable account to drift up to 2 percentage points away from my planned allocation before rebalancing them. For example, I would allow a stock fund with a planned allocation of 10 percent to drift up to 12 percent if selling the fund would trigger capital gains taxes. Furthermore, if the fund drifted above a 12 percent allocation, I would only sell enough to get the fund back to 12 percent, not the planned 10 percent allocation. A certain amount of drift is acceptable and reasonable to avoid a taxable event. You can set your own limits on how much drift you will allow in your taxable account, depending on how much you love to rebalance — or hate to pay taxes. There is nothing special about the 2 percent rule; that is just a personal choice on my part.

Rebalancing gets tricky if you have investments in both taxable accounts and IRAs or 401(k)s. Appendix B provides a detailed example illustrating the process when multiple accounts are involved.

Rebalancing on the Go

If you are adding savings to your retirement portfolio on a regular basis, you can use your dollar cost averaging plan to help you rebalance as you save. Simply direct your regular savings to those investments that have fallen below your planned asset allocation. This will not only reduce the amount of rebalancing you will have to do in January, but because it involves directing savings to your lower-returning investments, it may also help you to buy low.

Similarly, if you are a retiree, you can limit your withdrawals to those investments that currently exceed your planned allocation, thereby helping you to sell high and rebalance as you go.

Summing Up

Rebalancing is important for two reasons. First, if you do not rebalance, your portfolio will drift away from your intended asset allocation. Over the long run, it will drift toward stocks and away from bonds, resulting in heightened volatility that will eventually surpass your risk tolerance. Second, you may in some situations earn excess returns—a bonus—simply by rebalancing. The chances of earning a rebalancing bonus, and the size of the bonus, increase if you include a PME fund in your portfolio. Rebalancing is the secret sauce that juices the returns of PME.

As we learned back in Chapter 2, you can take the great enemy of stock investors everywhere—volatility—and make it your friend. A black belt investor using the principle of correlation takes a highly volatile investment like PME and employs it to reduce his portfolio's volatility.

But this is not the only way volatility can be your friend. Volatility also offers excellent opportunities to buy low and sell high. Rebalancing provides a way to systematically exploit these opportunities. If you periodically rebalance a portfolio that includes relatively uncorrelated, highly volatile investments—especially a PME fund—you can further reduce portfolio volatility while possibly earning a rebalancing bonus.

You cannot change the fundamental, volatile nature of the stock market. But you can turn that volatility to your advantage. Make volatility your friend, or it will be your enemy.

★★★

In Parts I–III, we learned about the principles of correlation and compromise and why you should use them to protect your portfolio from the risk of outliving your money. In Part IV, we have turned from the question of why to the question of how, explaining the practical nuts and bolts of asset allocation, fund selection, saving for retirement, and portfolio maintenance techniques such as rebalancing. However, it is important to recognize that in the process of covering these practical issues, we have at the same time uncovered additional ways to mitigate the retirement risk. Let's now summarize these risk-reduction discoveries:

- Establishing a low initial withdrawal rate provides reliable protection from all components (investment and noninvestment related) of the retirement risk.

- Low-cost index investing and tax loss harvesting reliably reduce the risk of not earning enough returns to outpace inflation, without increasing volatility.

- The LMBP alternative virtually eliminates both investment-related components of the retirement risk, at least for a while and possibly for the length of your retirement.

- Dollar cost averaging reliably reduces the risk of not earning enough returns to outpace inflation, possibly without increasing volatility.

- Over the long term rebalancing reliably reduces the risk of volatility, while possibly also reducing the risk of not earning enough returns to outpace inflation (if a rebalancing bonus is earned).

Notice that in large part, these risk-reduction techniques share a key characteristic with the principle of correlation: they reduce one component of the retirement risk without increasing the other component. Some of them even reduce both risk components—a true win-win situation. Considered separately, each of them is more reliable than the correlation principle. But their real power as risk reducers lies not in their separate application but rather when they are all combined with an asset allocation plan built on the principles of correlation and compromise. Together, they complement and supplement each other, providing multiple lines of defense against the retirement risk.

In short, we have begun the process of building a very powerful "defense in depth" against the risk of outliving your money. But we have not yet completed this process. In Part V, we address the following key questions that all buy-and-hold investors should consider:

- Why should you hold your investments through thick and thin (addressed in Chapter 16)?

- How can you control your emotions and do nothing during market manias and crashes (Chapter 17)?

- When should you deviate from a do-nothing approach, and what specific actions should you take (Chapter 18)?

- If you sell your stock investments, for good reasons or bad, how and when should you reenter the market (Chapter 19)?

Like the questions we addressed in Part IV, the preceding questions are very practical ones. In the process of answering these questions (particularly the third question), we will discover yet a few more ways of mitigating the retirement risk. In the concluding section to Chapter 18, we combine these new discoveries with the ones made thus far, and finish building our defense in depth against the fates of John Stockman and Joe Bondsman.

PART V

HOW TO HOLD

CHAPTER 16

WHY HOLD?

Those who have knowledge, don't predict.
Those who predict, don't have knowledge.
—**Lao Tzu**

This book is all about designing and implementing a risk-reducing buy-and-hold investment strategy. So far, we have focused almost exclusively on the "buy" part of this strategy. But buying is only half of the buy-and-hold strategy. In the remainder of the book, we focus on holding. In Chapter 17, we discuss the two powerful emotions—desire and fear—that make holding so difficult and how to control them. In Chapter 18, we learn how to take the temperature of a portfolio to distinguish situations that pose a serious threat to your portfolio's survival from those that do not. We also consider a set of actions you can take in the former case, ranging from reducing your living expenses, up to and including selling your stock funds (or buying more stocks). And in Chapter 19, we learn about the market reentry plan you will need to follow if you *do* sell, to give your portfolio the best chance of recovering from its losses.

But before tackling the question of *how* to hold in the next chapter, a more basic question may have occurred to you—*why* should you hold? If the stock market is in freefall, why not sell and avoid further losses rather than trust to diversification, which will at best reduce, not eliminate, the losses? Or if some asset classes are clearly outperforming others, why not sell the underperformers and buy the outperformers?

These are reasonable questions. This chapter attempts to answer them. We begin by taking a close look at two of the most commonly used alternatives to buy and hold: performance chasing and market timing. Then we consider the key assumption that these two alternative strategies, and many others, have in common—and why that assumption is bound to prove false for the amateur investor. Finally, we turn to the buy-and-hold strategy and consider why it will almost certainly outperform any other strategy an amateur investor might employ.

Performance Chasing

When you see a stock rise high and fast in price, do you buy? When choosing a mutual fund in a particular asset class, do you pick the fund with the best returns over the past year? Do you dump market sectors when they underperform and put the money into high-flying sectors? Do you look to the financial media—TV pundits, magazines, newsletters, and such—to help you identify the latest hot stocks and fund managers?

If you answered yes to any of these questions, then you are chasing performance. Performance chasing is simply the strategy of buying into the latest hot stock, fund, or asset class.

Performance chasing often works—for a while. Certain stocks or sectors can gain real upward momentum, and you can enjoy nice returns as long as you don't wait too long to jump on, and off, the trend.

Why does performance chasing work, at least in the short run? Because a lot of traders, both professional and amateur, chase performance. It's a self-fulfilling prophecy. If enough people *believe* a stock or fund will continue to rise, then it *will* continue to rise.

To the investor (as opposed to the speculator), the value of owning a stock equals the stock's future earnings potential, that is, the sum of the stream of earnings the stock is expected to yield over the future.[113] At some point, a rising price trend, if it is to continue, *must* lead to a price that no longer reflects this underlying value. Yes, the fundamental value of a stock may be increasing along with its price, thereby justifying the price trend. The company may be increasing its market share, reducing its costs, bringing new products on line, making acquisitions, and otherwise growing its earnings per share. But there is *always* a limit to how far earnings can grow. Market share cannot exceed 100 percent; costs cannot be reduced to zero; the number of potentially profitable acquisitions is finite. And even if these and other barriers to perpetual growth did not exist, the business cycle of expansion and contraction would impose temporary interruptions to growth. If you can show me a stock with earnings that have never stopped growing and never will, I have some land I'd like to sell you just a few miles due west of Key West, Florida. At some point, a stock's underlying value will stop growing and hit a wall. At this point, either the stock's price must also hit the wall, or the price will diverge from the stock's value.

For those who believe that markets are always rational, and that a stock's price will always reflect its value, this is the end of the story—the price must stop rising when the stock's underlying value hits the wall. For those who believe that the market is at least partially swayed by human emotions and biases, it's possible that a stock's price could keep rising even after the stock's underlying value stalls. Let's suppose for the sake of argument that the latter folks, who belong to the behavioral finance camp, might have a point. We'll follow this line of reasoning through to its logical conclusion—at which point you can decide whether it makes sense to you.

A stock's price might keep rising regardless of its value, in part because there are many performance chasers focused solely on price. The performance chaser, swept up in the emotions surrounding a hot investment, simply assumes that the stock/fund/asset class will keep rising. She may not even be thinking of the possibility of a reversal when she makes her buys. Alternatively, she may expect a reversal to occur eventually but believe that she will be able to time the reversal and sell before she loses her profits. The true, pure performance chaser is not concerned with the underlying value of the stocks she buys or how a particular fund fits into her portfolio. What matters is a stock's recent price trend. A "media darling" stock with sharp upward momentum is a "buy," pure and simple.

But once a stock's price has diverged from its underlying value, the performance chaser is relying on *market psychology* to vindicate her buy. She is assuming, either explicitly or implicitly, that there are still plenty of other performance chasers who will follow her into her trade. She is following the "greater fool theory" of investing. According to this theory, she can always turn around and sell the stock to one of the greater fools willing to buy at an even higher price than the price she paid for it. Sure, some pessimists might start warning that the stock's price-to-earnings ratio is getting too high; that its price has therefore lost touch with its underlying value; that it is due for a reversal. But as long as the performance-chasing buyers outnumber the naysaying sellers, who cares? The price will keep rising.

The problem is that the supply of greater fools is finite—and there are plenty of other traders who *are* focused not just on price but on underlying value. As it becomes increasingly clear that the stock's price has risen beyond any possible justification based on its value, these traders will swing into action. Value investors who bought the stock before it became hot will now sell and take their profits. They will be joined by some of the performance chasers themselves, who either sense the beginnings of a reversal or simply start to get nervous. Eventually, as the supply of greater fools dries up, the sellers will outnumber the buyers and the price will start to decline. As the declining trend intensifies, a stampede to get out of the stock may ensue. Just as the stock's price overshot its value on the way up, it may *undershoot* its value on the way back down. Meanwhile, the herd of performance chasers will be off chasing some new hot stock.

The process by which stock prices rise through the roof only to fall has a name: *reversion to the mean*. Stated simply, reversion to the mean is the tendency of equity prices to revert back to norms over the long term. Stock prices can drift far above (or below) fundamental values in the short run. But in the longer run, prices will be pulled back toward underlying values.

Mean reversion is one of the most powerful forces at work in the stock market. Once mean reversion rears its head, the resulting shift in the direction of the price trend is often swift and dramatic. Consider the recovery rallies that follow bear markets. We have seen twelve stock market declines of 20 percent or more since 1926.[114] In the twelve months following these twelve bear markets, large cap stock returns have averaged 51.4 percent. Large cap total returns have exceeded 30 percent in the twelve months following nine of the twelve bear markets, and they have exceeded 40 percent for almost half (five of twelve) of the bear markets. In the twelve months following the 2007–9 financial crisis, the second worst bear market since 1926, large cap stocks returned 53.6 percent. And in the twelve months following the worst stock market decline of all, the 1929–32 Crash, large caps returned 162.8 percent.[115] It is as if the stock market sits atop a giant spring. The further down the market is pressed, the harder and faster it springs back.[116]

Mean reversion is the market's great self-correcting mechanism. It is the means by which the market pops bubbles and recovers swiftly from crashes. And it is the bane of performance chasers, especially those amateur investors who base their investment decisions on the advice of the financial media. These investors are usually the last to the party—and the ones left holding the bag when a stock's price mean reverts.

An old saw holds that if you can't tell who the sucker is at a poker game, *you're* the sucker. We might ask a performance chaser following the greater fool theory, how do you know *you're* not the greatest fool?

A Word on Momentum Investing

In Chapter 6, we learned about size and value premiums. Academic researchers have also identified a persistent, significant "momentum premium" across many different historical periods, asset classes, and countries. Specifically, researchers have found that investments tend to exhibit persistence in performance over limited time periods. In other words, stocks that have recently outperformed tend to continue this outperformance, whereas those that have a recent history of underperformance continue to underperform. Momentum investing involves buying stocks that have outperformed and selling short recent underperformers.

If this strategy sounds very similar to performance chasing, well, it is. Think of it as a more respectable, scientific version of performance chasing, because it is supported by many academic studies. The key difference between momentum investing and performance chasing is that the former uses clearly defined, empirically based rules to determine which hot stocks to buy, when to buy them, and when to sell them.

The existence of the momentum premium appears to directly contradict the efficient market hypothesis, according to which investors as a whole are rational and past price trends provide no information that could be used to predict future prices. Hence most of the various hypotheses proposed to explain the existence of the momentum premium are rooted in the behavioral finance view that markets are not entirely rational but rather exhibit behavioral biases. Of these various behavioral explanations, the most persuasive, to me at least, is that many traders and investors chase performance, thereby bidding up the prices of hot stocks. Momentum investors exploit this so-called bandwagon effect.

Although a great deal of research supports the existence of a momentum premium, I have to admit to nagging doubts about a strategy that essentially boils down to buying high and selling higher. Reversion to the mean makes it, to my mind, a risky approach that could just as easily lead to buying high and selling low. But my personal views aside, there are practical obstacles to implementing a momentum strategy. Very few funds are available that employ such a strategy, and of these, most charge high fees. I've felt compelled to discuss momentum investing here not because I recommend it (I do not) but rather because some might object that what I have been calling performance chasing could be viewed, in a more positive, scientific light, as momentum investing. However, if the majority of traders—professionals and amateurs alike—to whom I have been referring as performance chasers are actually momentum investors, then the evidence strongly suggests that the momentum premium is eluding most of them. In the case of professional fund managers, we have already seen the evidence indicating that very few can consistently beat an index fund. As for amateur momentum investors or performance chasers—whatever we choose to call them—the evidence follows.

The Evidence against Performance Chasing

What evidence do we have that amateur performance chasers (or momentum investors) do poorly? Morningstar has been gathering data on the actual returns mutual fund investors have captured, as distinct from the official returns the funds themselves have posted. The investors' returns are weighted to take into account the inflows and outflows a fund experiences. As a hypothetical example, suppose a fund achieved a return of −50 percent in the first half of 2009 and +100 percent in the second half of the year. In this case, the fund's *official* returns would be 0 percent in 2009, because the loss of half of the fund's value in the first part of the year was exactly offset by the doubling of its value in the second half.

But now, suppose that all the investors that owned the fund sold it after the first half of 2009, and no one else bought the fund until after the end of 2009. In this case, the *investors'* returns would be −50 percent, because no one was invested in the fund to enjoy the 100 percent returns achieved in the second half of the year. By comparing a fund's official returns with its investor returns, we can determine how well investors timed their investments.

In a recent article on the Morningstar website,[117] Russel Kinnel performed this comparison. The results were not pretty. Over the ten-year period ending in 2012, the official returns across all mutual funds averaged 7.05 percent, but the investor returns averaged only 6.1 percent.

In addition to measuring average returns across all fund categories, the article presents official and investor returns for six different fund categories, including U.S. stocks, sector stocks, international stocks, balanced (stock and bond) funds, taxable bond funds, and municipal bond funds. In every category, average investor returns lagged official fund returns over the ten years ending December 31, 2012. More telling, the biggest gap occurred for international stock funds, for which official returns averaged 10.0 percent, versus only 6.8 percent for investor returns. The Morningstar article notes that emerging markets are highly volatile, suggesting that a part of the explanation for the gap may lie in the large losses that performance chasers late to an emerging-market rally, and quick to sell in a downturn, might experience. On the flip side, balanced funds exhibited the smallest gap between official and investor returns (9.4 percent vs. 9.1 percent). These funds, which include bonds as well as stocks in their holdings, tend to be low in volatility. They are therefore the least likely to get hot and to attract performance chasers.

Kinnel concludes that "even funds with great returns get used poorly because people don't get in until after they've put up huge returns and then the funds fall flat, as often happens with any asset that has spiked in value."[118]

★★★

What's the moral of this story? If you are reading or hearing about a stock or fund that has been generating great returns, *you are probably already too late.* If you buy in now, you will be buying high—the exact opposite of what you should be doing. The only way you are going to make money is if you can sell even higher, before the stock mean reverts. If you have a doctorate in mass psychology, perhaps you will be able to figure out exactly when the market will decide to dump a high-flying stock. Otherwise, when you go up against mean reversion, you are playing with fire and likely to get burned. My advice to performance chasers: cancel your subscription to your "hot stock" tip sheet and buy and *hold* a well-diversified portfolio of low-cost index funds.

Market Timing

Market timing is the strategy of predicting which direction the market will move, and then taking action based on that prediction. Market timers sell their stocks when they believe the market will head down and buy when they expect it to rise.

Market timing is a fantastic strategy. I recommend it highly to everyone who knows the future. For you prophets, it is money in the bank. After all, how can you possibly *not* make a gazillion dollars if you can predict which way the market will move at any particular moment?

But you say you don't know the future? No worries—all you have to do is latch on to someone who does. There are apparently plenty of people who *do* know the future and who are willing to share their knowledge with the public. These extraordinarily generous souls have decided to give up the vast fortunes they could earn in the market so that they can devote their lives to selling their market timing predictions and techniques, at modest prices, to *you*. They advertise their newsletters, tip sheets, and websites by promising to make you rich quick, so you just *know* this has to be the real deal. It does make me wonder, though, why we have billionaires who made fortunes working sixteen hours a day, seven days a week starting and building their own businesses but no gazillionaires who simply sat at home reading the newsletters and timing the market?

OK, perhaps I'm going a bit overboard on the sarcasm. After all, we humans have become modestly adept at predicting some things, like the weather. Isn't it possible that at least some people have shown some limited ability to time the market? Let's consider this possibility before we dismiss market timing out of hand.

If we are going to look for moderately successful market timers, we should begin our search with the presumed experts—the people who invest for a living. And fortunately, we have some good evidence for one group of professionals: active mutual fund managers. In Chapter 13, we learned that active managers keep a portion of their assets in cash investments. By tracking their percentage allocation to cash, we can infer their skill at market timing. Specifically, we would expect them to hold high cash allocations at market tops, in anticipation of the stock market declines that immediately follow a peak. Similarly, we would expect them to hold low cash allocations at market bottoms, in expectation of the recovery rallies about to begin.

Well, guess what? The pattern of actual cash allocations is the opposite of what we would expect, assuming that fund managers are skilled at market timing. In *A Random Walk Down Wall Street*, Burton Malkiel presents the evidence:

> Mutual-fund managers have been incorrect in their allocation of assets into cash in essentially every recent market cycle. Caution on the part of mutual-fund managers (as represented by a very high cash allocation) coincides almost perfectly with troughs in the stock market. Peaks in mutual funds' cash positions have coincided with market troughs during 1970, 1974, 1982, and the end of 1987 after the great stock-market crash. Another peak in cash positions occurred in late 1990, just before the market rallied during 1991, and in 1994, just before the greatest six-year rise in stock prices in market history. Cash positions were also high in late 2002, at the trough of the market. Conversely, the allocation to cash of mutual-fund managers was almost invariably at a low during peak periods in the market. For example, the cash position of mutual funds was near an all-time low in March 2000, just before the market began its sharp decline.[119]

Malkiel concludes, "Clearly the ability of mutual-fund managers to time the market has been egregiously poor."[120]

It should not be surprising that fund managers as a group are terrible at timing changes in the market's direction. In fact, it *has* to be this way. As we've noted before, fund managers and other professional money managers *are* the market, in that they account for the vast majority of the market's trading volume. And the market cannot time itself. The market is a mechanism for pricing expectations about the future. Declining stock prices reflect pessimism about the future, while rising prices signal optimism. When the market bottoms, prices—and expectations about the future —reach their lowest point. Fund managers who raise their allocation to cash in market troughs are simply reflecting the market's consensus opinion about the future. As a group, they *must* reflect this market opinion, because they *are* the market. At the exact moment when the market is about to rally, the professionals who comprise the market peer into their crystal balls and conclude that the future looks even bleaker than it did a month ago, a week ago, and a day ago. They then bid down the prices of stocks to the lowest level they will reach. The money they raise selling their stocks goes to cash investments—hence the high allocations to cash Malkiel has observed at market bottoms. The same process happens in reverse, when the market reaches a top. The market cannot time itself; the pros that comprise the market are inevitably completely wrong in their future expectations at market tops and bottoms.

That said, the short-term returns earned by fund managers and other professional traders may benefit from their attempts to time the market. As stock positions are sold and cash allocations raised during a bear market, losses will be reduced. Similarly, additional gains will be realized by fund managers who lower their cash allocations during bull markets. Like performance chasing, market timing often works—as long as the market's trend continues uninterrupted. However, bear markets and bull markets share one characteristic in common—they always come to an end. Once the market changes direction, any market-beating short-term returns earned by market timers will usually lead to market-lagging long-term returns.

Why, then, would fund managers and other professional traders risk their long-term performance record trying to time the market? The pros may perhaps have a rational preference for short-term over long-term performance, because their incentives tend to be short-term in nature. For example, fund managers report their results on a quarterly, semi-annual, or annual basis, while investment bank traders receive much of their compensation in the form of year-end bonuses.

You and I, on the other hand, have no reason to prefer short-term over long-term results. And if fund managers and other professional traders can't time the market to their long-term benefit, what chance do we amateur investors have? The evidence indicates that our chances are poor. The Morningstar data on mutual fund investor returns likely reflect the impact of market timing predictions as well as performance chasing. As these data show, far from helping himself by moving in and out of the market, the typical amateur investor instead shoots himself in the foot and winds up with lower returns than he could earn simply by buying and holding his investments.

But granting that neither professional traders nor amateur investors, *as a group*, exhibit any market timing skills, isn't it possible that at least a few *individual* professionals possess such skills? Perhaps. But even if so, how could you identify which particular mutual fund managers might have this ability?

Or maybe, rather than searching for skilled market timers among fund managers, we should instead focus our search on newsletter writers and other market mavens who sell their prognostications to the public. Is it not possible that at least a few of these prognosticators have real ability? Or is it more logical to assume that if these prophets for hire could actually time the market, the *last* thing they would do is publicize their predictions?

Market timing, at least as practiced by amateur investors, is often less about a reasoned attempt to predict the market's future direction and more simply a way to stop the immediate pain of losses. During major sell-offs, amateurs (and, for that matter, many pros) join the exodus out of stocks in the same unthinking way that lemmings follow other lemmings over the cliff. I have a technical term for this kind of market timing: "panicking." We will have much more to say about panicking in the next chapter.

The Unknowable Future

Market timing and performance chasing share a number of key features. Above all, both are short-term, high-frequency trading strategies that seek to project the future based on the recent past. The performance chaser may recognize that eventually a stock or fund's price will mean revert, but in the short term, she expects upward price trends to continue. Although in theory, market timing does not necessarily involve an assumption that past trends will continue, in practice, the vast majority of market timers look backward and, seeing that the market has been rising (or falling), assume the trend will continue in the short run.

Although market timing and performance chasing are two of the most popular short-term strategies, there are many others. *All* short-term strategies share one characteristic in common: they all assume it is possible to make accurate predictions about the future. In some cases, including all performance chasing and most market timing, the predictions simply assume that the most recent trends will continue. In other cases, the predictions may be more sophisticated. But whether simple or complex, short-term strategies rely on some sort of prediction of the future.

However, the evidence indicates that amateur investors have no predictive ability. Put simply, *we don't know the future*. Therefore, we will not succeed using short-term strategies.

One more time, repeat after me: *I don't know the future*. Could anything be simpler or more obvious?

Buy and Hold: Investing for the Marathon

Fortunately, you don't need a crystal ball to be a successful investor. All you need is a *long-term* perspective. And a long-term perspective is precisely what almost everyone investing for or in retirement *should* have. If you are in your twenties, thirties, or forties, you have *decades* to go before you even reach retirement. If you are in your fifties, sixties, or seventies, chances are you have many years still ahead of you. Yes, the stock market will no doubt take a few nasty plunges along the way, but why should that matter to you? As long as the long-term trend is up, as it has *always* been going back to the early years of the Industrial Revolution, you should do OK. If, conversely, you choose to adopt the same short-term, high-turnover trading strategies that many of the pros employ, you can expect your long-term returns to suffer—and the risk you run of outliving your money to rise.

Short-Term versus Long-Term Volatility

But better returns aren't the only reason to cultivate a long-term perspective. Equally important, the volatility of annualized stock returns declines markedly as your perspective lengthens. This decline is illustrated in Table 16.1, which shows the best and worst annualized returns of the S&P 500 over one-year, five-year, ten-year, and twenty-year periods since 1972. Returns over a single year proved highly volatile, ranging from a low of −37.0 percent (for 2008) to a high of +37.4 percent (for 1995). But notice how quickly this volatility moderates as the time period lengthens. The worst average annual returns for a five-year period were only −2.3 percent (for 2000–2004), and none of the twenty-year periods between 1972 and 2013 yielded negative returns. In fact, over twenty years, returns fell within a narrow range of 7.8 percent (for 1992–2011) to 17.9 percent (for 1980–99).

Table 16.1. Best and Worst Returns for the S&P 500, 1972–2013

Return Category	1-Year Total Returns	5-Year Total Annualized Returns	10-Year Total Anualized Returns	20-Year Total Annualized Returns
Best returns	37.4%	28.6%	19.2%	17.9%
Worst returns	−37.0%	−2.3%	−1.4%	7.8%

Source: Developed by the author using data from www.morningstar.com.

Table 16.1 covers a relatively short historical period. But in his book *Stocks for the Long Run*,[121] Wharton professor Jeremy Siegel presents stock market return data going all the way back to 1802, showing the same pattern of declining volatility with increasing holding periods. Amazingly, over the last two hundred plus years, the *worst* annualized returns were never negative for a broadly diversified portfolio of U.S. stocks held for at least twenty years. What's more, the worst annualized return for a twenty-year period was still 1 percentage point higher than the rate of inflation. For a thirty-year period, the worst return beat inflation by 2.6 percent. In the long run, a well-diversified, buy-and-hold investor would *never* have lost money, *or* purchasing power, in the U.S. stock market over the past two centuries. In contrast, U.S. Treasury bonds and bills *have* fallen below the inflation rate over twenty- and thirty-year periods.[122] Stock prices are very volatile in the short term, but reversion to the mean, the stock market's great self-correcting mechanism, works to reduce long-term volatility. When stock prices get too high, investors bid them back down, and when they become too low, they are bid back up. Professor Siegel concludes that a diversified stock portfolio is the safest investment for preserving purchasing power over the long run.[123]

But you can protect your portfolio against the risk of inflation—one of the two key components of the retirement risk—only if you buy *and hold* a well-diversified stock portfolio. Investors with short-term perspectives, who chase performance or try to time the market, will almost certainly do worse than buy-and-hold investors and may well wind up losing out to inflation, even in the long term.

Nothing's Perfect: The Problems with Buy and Hold

To sum up, if you simply stick with a buy-and-hold strategy, you will almost certainly reap higher returns than is possible chasing performance, timing the market, or following any other strategy that requires you to trade on a frequent basis. And remember, one of the two components of the retirement risk is not enough returns to outpace inflation. When you hold your investments through thick and thin, you give yourself the best possible chance of earning the kinds of returns needed to beat inflation—the dreaded night thief.

But buy and hold is not perfect. In fact, it has a significant flaw, as John Stockman could attest. He held on to his stock investments through the worst financial storm in U.S. history, and it cost him everything he had. For that matter, Joe Bondsman held tight to his 100 percent bond portfolio, and he, too, was left bankrupt. True, they both made the major mistake of holding undiversified portfolios. Diversification would have saved their nest eggs, even in the face of the most extreme market decline and inflationary episode of the past century.

But what if the future brings even worse market crashes, and higher inflation, than the past? Isn't it possible that we could experience economic events so extreme they would destroy even a well-diversified portfolio? The answer is yes. Anything is possible including an event that, like a Category 5 hurricane, destroys everything in its path.

Doing nothing is the smartest thing an investor can do. But there is a point at which a portfolio's losses can become so severe that the portfolio will not recover.

If that point of no return is ever reached, doing nothing becomes the *dumbest* thing you can do.

Unfortunately, the buy-and-hold investor doesn't know where the danger point lies. This uncertainty leads to two problems. First, it makes buy and hold a very difficult strategy, emotionally, to implement. Many would-be buy-and-hold investors, fearing the worst, abandon the strategy when they are nowhere near the danger point. They wind up *increasing* their risk of not earning enough returns to outpace inflation.

Second, the uncertain location of the danger point exposes those investors who *do* manage to stick with buy and hold to the remote but potentially catastrophic risk posed by extreme events.

Taken together, these two problems have greatly reduced the potential application of the buy-and-hold strategy among amateur investors and the usefulness of the strategy to those who do try to follow it. The problems with buy and hold must therefore be addressed. The remainder of this book addresses them head-on. Chapter 17 focuses on the first problem: the emotional challenges posed by sticking with buy and hold through thick and thin. You will learn practical techniques to control the strong emotions of desire and fear evoked by bull and bear markets. These techniques should help you stay the buy-and-hold course.

In Chapters 18 and 19, we address the second problem: the remote risk of an event so extreme that it will bankrupt a buy-and-hold, well-diversified portfolio. Chapter 18 presents a series of tables providing survival rates for various portfolios emerging from past market declines. Using these tables, you will learn how to distinguish downturns that may truly threaten your portfolio's survival from downturns that will probably just scare the bejeebers out of you, without putting your portfolio at significant risk. You will also be given a hierarchy of actions you can take, up to and including selling your stocks, if and when you encounter the former situation.

In addition, Chapter 18 explains how to determine if the threat posed to your portfolio's survival comes, not from too much negative market volatility, but rather from not enough returns to outpace inflation. And again, a hierarchy of possible actions are provided for if and when the night thief of inflation threatens to bankrupt you.

Chapter 19 provides a market reentry plan you can use if you ever do decide to sell your stock holdings. You can use this plan whether you sell for the right reason (your portfolio was headed toward the danger zone) or the wrong reason (you panic). It will give you a decent chance—though by no means a guarantee—of finding a market reentry point that will reduce rather than increase the retirement risk.

It is possible that the future could bring situations so dire that a do-nothing investment strategy will fail. With the sole exception of such situations—worst cases that you may never encounter in your lifetime—the best way to minimize the retirement risk is to *maximize* your long-term returns by remaining fully invested at all times, in a well-diversified portfolio.

CHAPTER 17

HOW TO DO NOTHING

꤮

*Approximately 99% of the time, the single most important thing
investors should do is absolutely nothing.*
—**Jason Zweig, the** *Wall Street Journal's* **Moneybeat blog**[124]

The advantages of buying and then simply *holding* your investments should by now be clear. You will earn better long-run returns than those who try to time the market, chase performance, or otherwise trade frequently. And the longer you remain fully invested in a well-diversified portfolio, the less likely it is that you will suffer a long-term loss of your principal or purchasing power.

There is one additional, very important advantage to the buy-and-hold approach. It is a strategy that requires no particular skill or knowledge and very little work on your part. It is tailor-made for amateur investors who have neither the time nor the inclination to devote significant effort to studying the markets. There is no need to try to guess which way stocks are headed or to figure out which particular investments you should buy or sell on any given day. You just decide on an asset allocation, buy a set of index funds or exchange-traded funds (ETFs) to implement that allocation, and then ... do nothing. It is the perfect investment strategy for busy people, and for lazy people (like me).

You Will Be Tested

Well, at least it's perfect *most* of the time. But there will come a day when doing nothing will not be as easy as it sounds. In fact, when it comes to investing, doing nothing can be one of the most difficult things you will ever have to do.

Consider, for example, how difficult doing nothing would have been in 1999. In the preceding four years, the S&P 500's *worst* annual returns were 23.1 percent. And in 1999, the index was on track to beat 20 percent for the fifth year in a row. Yet the *best* returns for the advanced moderate (60/40) portfolio over those same four years were 15.3 percent. In 1998, this portfolio yielded a pathetic 1.1 percent—27.5 percentage points less than the S&P 500 in that same year. Imagine being at a New Year's Eve party on December 31, 1999, listening to all your friends and neighbors talking about the killings they made on this or that dot-com stock. And imagine if this was the *fifth* New Year's Eve party in a row where you had to listen to pretty much this same conversation. Wouldn't you have been tempted to ditch your boring, under-performing diversified portfolio and go for the gold?

Or even worse, imagine it is October 2008. The market has been gyrating wildly, up and down (mostly down), 5 percent or more per *day*. The S&P 500 has already dropped 40 percent from its 2007 high, and there is no end in sight. Normally calm government officials are waving their arms in the air, warning of a financial calamity, and the media is full of predictions of a new Great Depression. There is fear in the air; it is palpable. Would you be able to hold your allocation to stocks in the face of this fear?

Desire and fear are the most powerful of emotions. We all have a bit of John Stockman and Joe Bondsman in us. When times are good and the market is posting new record highs every other day, your inner John Stockman will come to you. He will show up dressed to the nines, with a blonde flapper on his arm, and whisper in your ear, "Come with us to the big party over at the stock market. We're all going to get rich!" When times are bad and stocks are plummeting toward oblivion, your inner Joe Bondsman may come to the fore. Dressed in a gray business suit and looking grim, he yells, "Sell, sell! Quick, before we lose everything!"

You can be sure of two things. First, sooner or later in your investing career, you will face a test similar to 1999 or 2008. And second, when that test comes, if you let your emotions get the better of you, they will betray you. There may perhaps be certain situations in life where it is wiser to follow your heart than your head. But investing is absolutely not one of those situations. Imagine if you had decided to dump your bonds, gold, and PME funds and put all your money in tech stocks in 1999. Your nest egg would have been crushed when the tech bubble burst in 2000. Imagine if you had sold your stock funds in October 2008 after they had lost 40 percent of their value. You would likely have missed out on the 2009 rally, thereby turning a temporary loss into a permanent one.

Of course, it is much easier for me to tell you that you should ignore your emotions than for you to actually do it. When a new test like 1999 or 2008 comes, ignoring the temptations posed by your inner John Stockman or Joe Bondsman will be one of the hardest things you will ever have to do. You must prepare yourself in advance for this test. You must *learn* how to do nothing, and you must have a plan in place that will prevent you from doing *something*. In this chapter we tackle the task of developing, and then sticking to, a do-nothing plan. Because behavioral finance researchers have shown that the fear of financial loss (loss aversion) is a more powerful psychological motivator than the desire for financial gain, we are going to focus mainly on the challenge posed by bear markets. However, the do-nothing plan we develop should also help you to control your emotions during bull markets and bubbles. Where necessary, we will tweak the plan a bit to deal more directly with the desire for gains that arise during the good times.

This chapter is the most important chapter in the entire book. Buying a well-diversified portfolio of index mutual funds and ETFs is easy. *Holding* that portfolio through good times and bad is the hard part. Many investors have started out fully intending to follow a buy-and-hold strategy, only to abandon the strategy after a few years or even months. Diversifying your portfolio using high-volatility and low-volatility hedges will smooth out some of the market volatility you experience, but it will not eliminate it. It will be up to *you* to ride out the volatility that cannot be diversified away. You may want to bookmark this chapter and reread it when your inner John Stockman or Joe Bondsman comes calling. Sooner or later, they *will* call. You *will* be tested.

Tigers, Bears, and Loose Rocks

But before we worry too much about the tests the stock market may have in store for us, let's count our blessings and keep things in perspective. The kinds of tests we modern folks face are *nothing* like those faced by our ancestors. Losing part of your savings in a bear market? Sorry, that doesn't begin to compare with losing your *life* to a real bear. Or a saber-toothed tiger. Like the one Bil the Caveman ran into one day, long, long ago.

It happened in the evening when Bil was commuting back to his cave after a long, hard day of hunting mastodons. He had with him his spear, his shield, and his trusty hunting dog, Dog. His commute took him up a mountain along a narrow ledge. As he rounded a bend, he noticed a spot where the ledge was starting to crumble. He carefully stepped over the spot and then made a mental note. This took him about five minutes of exhausting effort, but finally he had committed to memory an important warning to himself: "Me no fal down."

Bil turned to continue on his way, but after a couple more steps, suddenly something jumped onto the path ahead. It was a saber-toothed tiger! Bil froze in place. His pulse quickened; his muscles tightened; his pupils dilated to help him see the tiger in the fading light. His mind was filled with a single thought: "Me no cat fud." Unfortunately, this one thought crowded out all the other thoughts—including his recently completed mental note. He turned, took two steps, hit the loose rocks, and fell to his death. Life really was nasty, brutish, and short in those days.

As strange and tragic as Bil's death seems to us today, safe as we are from wild animals, there are some important parallels between Bil's experience and our own experiences with bear markets. First, bear markets are aptly named. Like real bears and saber-toothed tigers, you don't want to run into a bear market. They are scary.

Second, like Bil, when you do encounter a bear market, you basically have two choices. In Bil's case, the choices were to fight or run. In our case, the choices are "hold" (fight) or "sell" (run).[125]

Third, that second option—sell in our case, run in Bil's—*seems* the safer choice. But in fact, it comes with its own dangers—loose rocks in Bil's case, the difficulties of finding a market reentry point in ours. These dangers are nowhere near as scary as a saber-toothed tiger, or a growling bear market, but they can be just as great a threat to your portfolio.

And finally, like Bil, when confronted with a bear market, many of us are more likely to panic and flee the market rather than *think* before we act. Had Bil *thought* about his predicament before acting, he might have reached a different decision. First, instead of forgetting everything, except the tiger in front of him, he might have remembered his mental note and realized that escape back down the ledge was a treacherous option. And second, he would have realized that standing his ground wouldn't necessarily have led to his becoming cat food. He had his spear, his shield, and Dog (who was actually closer to a wolf than a modern dog and a pretty good match for saber-toothed tigers). Staying and fighting couldn't have turned out any *worse* than his decision to flee.

Panicking is a natural reaction to saber-toothed tigers—and to bear markets. The scientific term for the panic Bil felt is the fight-or-flight response. When it is triggered, the stress hormones adrenaline and noradrenaline are released, the heart beats faster, muscles tense in preparation for either fighting or fleeing, and, most importantly, the brain shifts its focus from all other tasks to the perceived source of danger. Back in Bil's time, when humans regularly faced the prospect of winding up as cat food, the fight-or-flight response usually worked to keep our ancestors alive. But Bil faced *two* dangers: a saber-toothed tiger in front and loose rocks behind. Only one of these dangers was scary enough to trigger the fight-or-flight response, and once it was triggered in Bil's rather small brain, his total focus on the tiger caused him to forget all about the danger behind. In the *complex* situation Bil encountered, the fight-or-flight response betrayed him.

Today, when the danger posed by wild animals has been replaced by the danger of tight deadlines, rush-hour traffic, and market crashes, the fight-or-flight response often does us more harm than good. It raises our stress level, clouds our thinking, and causes us to make snap decisions we later regret. Our modern environment is often too *complex* for our ancient instinctual responses. What we need to make the right choices in the face of this complexity is cool, calm, rational analysis, not panicky split-second decisions.

This is especially true in the complex environment of the securities markets. Like Bil, investors often face dangers both in front and in back. And like the saber-toothed tiger, the danger in front is often scarier, but the danger behind is usually worse. During a bear market, a decision to hold will likely result in a major, but *temporary*, loss. A decision to sell may reduce the size of the loss, but it will also likely make the loss *permanent*. This is especially true if the sell decision arises out of fear or the outright panic felt during the fight-or-flight response. To understand why, we need to review some of what we learned about market timing in the last chapter.

"Rational" Market Timing versus Panicking

We have already seen that market timing doesn't work. As practiced by active mutual fund managers, it might improve short-run returns, but it results in lower returns over the long run. Still, for fund managers and other professional traders, market timing may be a perfectly *rational* strategy. The pros are often judged primarily by their short-term results. Hence they may be more than willing to sacrifice long-term profits for short-term gains. Furthermore, fund managers and other pros have less reason to panic during a bear market than you or I, for one simple reason: it's not *their* money that's at risk. It is therefore reasonable to assume that the market timing decisions made by at least some professional traders are based on reason, not emotion. Let's refer to these decisions as *rational market timing*—not because they produce superior long-run returns (they don't) but because they are based on reason.

In contrast to the rational market timing practiced by at least some professionals, many amateurs sell during market downturns out of fear. In some cases, the sell decision may be an immediate outcome of the fight-or-flight response. In other cases, the investor may be able to suppress his fears for a period of time and continue to hold, until finally succumbing to his emotions. But in either case, fear rather than reason is driving the investor's decision to sell. To contrast this kind of market timing from the kind practiced by the professionals, we will refer to it simply as *panicking*.

When applied during a bear market, both rational market timing and panicking have one key feature in common: both result in a decision to *sell low*. There are only two ways this can work to the benefit of a long-term investor. First, if it takes *decades* for the stock market to return to the point at which the investor sold, then he will have avoided a loss from which he may never live to recover. But as we learned back in Chapter 8, in all of the major bear markets of the past 84 years, the U.S. stock market has recovered in a matter of years, not decades. In fact, across the globe, there are very few examples of developed-market countries that have experienced down markets lasting longer than a decade. It *is* true that the Japanese stock market has as yet failed to recover from a downturn that began in 1990, but the Japanese experience is the exception, not the rule. And as long as an investor holds a globally diversified portfolio of U.S., developed-market, and emerging-market stocks, it would take simultaneous, decades-long downturns in multiple countries to keep the investor's portfolio from recovering in fewer than ten years. This is not likely, and if it *does* happen, it may be the result of some catastrophe far worse than an economic downturn, such as a global military conflict or environmental disaster. In the event of such a catastrophe, the money saved by timing the market may prove worthless, and we will have much bigger things to worry about than retirement.

Assuming a normal recovery time, the only way a market timer who sells low during a bear market has a chance of benefitting from this move is by subsequently buying even lower. This is illustrated in Figure 17.1, which is a graph of the S&P 500's total returns from July 2007 to January 2011 (with the numbers removed for simplicity). Let's imagine an investor with an S&P 500 index fund who sticks with a buy-and-hold strategy through the early months of the 2007–9 bear market, only to panic and sell her fund at the beginning of October 2008 (point A in the figure). If she then waits to buy back her fund until the market has risen above point A—say, to point D—then she will have *permanently* lost the returns yielded by the market as it moved first down but then up from point A to point D. True, by selling, she would have avoided the additional losses incurred by the market between points A and B. But these losses were temporary. By selling at point A and buying at point D, she has permanently locked in a large portion of her losses.

Figure 17.1. Market Timing during the 2007–9 Bear Market

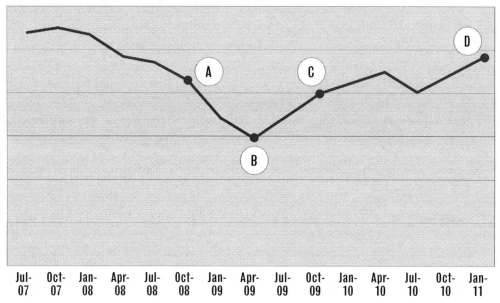

| Jul-07 | Oct-07 | Jan-08 | Apr-08 | Jul-08 | Oct-08 | Jan-09 | Apr-09 | Jul-09 | Oct-09 | Jan-10 | Apr-10 | Jul-10 | Oct-10 | Jan-11 |

Of course, if instead of buying back her index fund at point D, our hypothetical investor instead bought it back at point C, then she will have sold low but bought even lower. In this case, not only would she have avoided the temporary losses the market experienced as it moved from point A to point B but she would actually have *gained* the returns the market yielded as it climbed from point C back to the same price level as point A.

There's only one problem. Any investor who would have panicked and sold her stocks at point A is highly unlikely to have bought back at point C, or at any other point below point A. Rather, she would have waited until the market climbed back to point D or to some other point above point A—and by waiting, she would have permanently locked in her losses. How can I be so sure of this? The stock market is a mechanism for pricing expectations about the future. At points B, C, and all other points below point A, the market has priced the S&P 500 below its point A price. A lower price means that the millions of investors comprising the market have looked into the future and found it to be *bleaker* than it appeared at point A. If the market was worried about the future at point A, then it was even more concerned at point B. The market's increasing worries as we moved from point A to point B were reflected in a slew of bleak predictions of recession and even depression, published not only by the financial media but also the mainstream media between autumn 2008 and spring 2009. Even after the price rise between point B and point C, the market still had not reached the point A price level. And in fact, as we moved up from point B to point C, the media was filled with predictions of a double-dip recession. Many media reports predicted that the second leg down would be worse than the first.

If an investor, at point A, found the future to be so scary and bleak she abandoned buy and hold and sold her stocks, how likely is it that she would have bought them back at point B, C, or some other point below point A, when the future appeared even worse? Investors who succumb to the fight-or-flight response and sell in a panic are faced with an agonizing decision: *when* is it safe to buy stocks again? Such investors usually wait until the future looks much brighter and the market has risen well above the point at which they sold. This is certainly what we saw in the wake of the 2007–9 financial crisis. Far from repurchasing their stock funds while prices remained low, investors were *still* fleeing from equities in 2012—three years into the subsequent bull market. Between 2008 and 2012, investors in the world's ten largest economies sold $1.1 trillion worth of stock mutual funds, while adding $1.3 trillion to bond mutual funds.[126] Investors who sold their stocks in 2008 and waited until 2013 or later to repurchase them missed out on the 129 percent returns produced by the S&P 500 between the market bottom on March 9, 2009, and December 31, 2012. The retirees among these latecomers wound up increasing, rather than reducing, their risk of bankruptcy.

And just in case you don't quite believe that panicking and selling in a bear market is the financial equivalent of Bil's short trip over the cliff, consider this question. If fund managers and other professional traders lose money in the long run by practicing *rational* market timing, how in the world could you possibly avoid losing money with an *irrational, fear-driven* approach to market timing? When it comes to investing, decisions based on fear, or greed, are deadly. You must learn to suppress your emotions, your primitive fight-or-flight response, and act (or, more correctly, *not* act) based on reason and *the courage of your convictions*.

The Pledge

I hope at this point you have no doubt that market timing, whether based on fear or greed, is a losing proposition. If you are not *convinced* of this point, you should not even attempt to implement a buy-and-hold strategy. Make no mistake, buy and hold will test your nerves during bear markets and your patience during bull markets. You must be absolutely convinced that holding rather than selling is the *logical* thing to do or you *will* abandon buy and hold at the worst possible time.

But even if you are completely convinced of the logic behind buy and hold, unless you have ice water running through your veins, that won't be enough to protect you from yourself when the market goes into a tailspin. Our instinct is to protect our savings as we would our lives. In fact, for a few, money is more precious than life itself—as evidenced by those who committed suicide when they lost their life savings in the 1929 Crash. According to AARP, most people fear running out of money in retirement more than they fear death.[127] Reason is no match for the dread of losing everything. Like Bil the Caveman up on the cliff, we forget all about the danger behind us when the stock market bear rears up in front of us.

But let's consider a modification to Bil's story. Let's suppose that instead of being alone, Bil's wife and children were in front of him on the ledge, and the tiger was about to pounce. Would Bil still have turned and run, or would he have decided to fight to save his family? And let's also suppose Bil's entire tribe stood behind him, encouraging and pressuring him to fight. Would that have made a difference in his decision?

Your chances of facing down a bear market alone are poor. Conviction that holding is the rational, logical thing to do isn't enough. To face your fears, you need the *courage* of your conviction. And one way to bolster courage is to seek the support of your family and your peers. Let's now consider how this can be accomplished.

Seeking the Support of Your Family

Chances are you aren't the only one who has a lot riding on your investment decisions. If you are married, both you and your spouse face the retirement risk together. If you have children, it is they who may need to step in and provide for you if you outlive your money. This may in turn compromise their ability to provide for their own children or to save for their own retirements. I don't think many people retire with the goal of becoming a financial burden on their families. On the contrary, you would probably like to remain financially independent for the rest of your days, and maybe even leave a legacy to your heirs.

Given that your family members have a significant stake in the success of your retirement, you have a *responsibility* to them to try to hold true to your investment convictions. Making a promise to them, in writing, may help you to meet this responsibility. What I am suggesting is that you prepare and sign a written statement, pledging to your family to do your best to avoid making investment decisions based on emotion. If you are married, both you and your spouse could sign the pledge. The pledge might also be witnessed and signed by those of your family members old enough to understand the promise you are making.

Such a written pledge may give you the strength you will need to stand up to your fears during raging bear markets and to prevent greed from clouding your judgment during bull markets. Exhibit 17.1 provides an example of a "Rational Decision-Making Pledge" for a retired married couple. Let's go over some of the features of this pledge.

The first two sentences set forth the couple's reasons for making the pledge. Like this example, your pledge should also include an explicit statement of the risks of failing to adhere to a buy-and-hold strategy, not only to yourself but to the rest of your family. You will need to reread your pledge when you're tempted to break it, so having a reminder of why, and for whom, the pledge was made is very important.

**Exhibit 17.1. Example of a Rational Decision-Making Pledge
for a Retired Married Couple**

RATIONAL DECISION-MAKING PLEDGE

We understand that when it comes to investing, decisions based on emotion may cause us to abandon buy and hold in favor of market timing or performance chasing. Market timing and performance chasing reduce returns in the long run, increase the chances of bankruptcy, and put not only our own retirements but the financial well-being of our children and grandchildren at risk. We, (your name here) and (your spouse's name here), hereby pledge to each other, to our children (child's name here) and (child's name here), and to our grandchildren (grandchild's name here), (grandchild's name here) and (grandchild's name here), that we will strive, to the best of our ability, to avoid emotionally-based decisions and instead follow a rational investment decision process at all times. To help us in this endeavor, we also promise that, whenever we are tempted by fear or greed to abandon our buy and hold approach to investing, we will follow the 6-Step Process described in Chapter 17 of *The Death of Buy and Hold*. To confirm that we have completed the 6-Step Process we will fill out and sign the checklist presented in Exhibit 17.2 of that same book. We will complete the 6-Step Process and checklist however often may be necessary to avoid the temptation of emotional decision making.

Signed:

_____   _____
(Signature)   (Date)

_____   _____
(Signature)   (Date)

And witnessed by our adult children:

_____   _____
(Signature)   (Date)

_____   _____
(Signature)   (Date)

Notice that the pledge does *not* actually commit the couple to following the buy-and-hold approach. Rather, it commits them to trying to avoid the kind of emotional decision making that often results in the abandonment of buy and hold. This is an important distinction. There are certain situations where you may in fact have to deviate from buy and hold, temporarily, to protect either the health of your portfolio or you or your spouse's physical and mental health. But these situations can and should be identified and acted upon based on reason, not emotion. The Rational Decision-Making Pledge commits you not to buy and hold per se, but to a rational decision process to determine if and when you should deviate from buy and hold.

Finally, the pledge commits the couple to following a "Six-Step Process" and to filling out a checklist confirming completion of this process. We will learn all about the Six-Step Process and accompanying checklist later in this chapter. For now, all you need know is that the Six-Step Process is intended to help you make rational investment decisions and to calm yourself so that you can more easily maintain your commitment to buy and hold if you decide against selling.

You can use Exhibit 17.1 as a starting point for writing your own pledge. Note that even if you are single and childless, you can still make a written promise to yourself like that shown in the exhibit. However, if you do not have a family to fall back on for support—and even if you *do* have a family—you may want to seek the support of your peers. Bil the Caveman would have felt braver facing off against the tiger if his tribe had had his back. You might similarly feel more courageous facing down bear markets with your "tribe" behind you.

Seeking Peer Support

The example pledge shown in Exhibit 17.1 can be easily modified to accommodate a group of friends or like-minded investors. You might, for example, form a buy-and-hold investment club for the express purpose of providing peer support and encouragement to club members during trying times. Each member of the club could sign a club pledge to strive to avoid emotionally based investment decisions. Regular club meetings would provide the group with an opportunity to help and encourage each member to stay true to the pledge. Members could share their own techniques for reducing stress during market routs, tuning out the financial media, avoiding the temptations of performance chasing and market timing, and staying the course.

The Six-Step Process

Making a written pledge to yourself, your significant other, your children, your friends, or your fellow investment club members is a positive step you can and should take when the market is calm and you are thinking clearly and rationally. But making a pledge to follow a rational investment decision process isn't enough. You also need some way to help you *uphold* your pledge when a raging bull market or terrifying bear market comes along and you *can't* think straight for greed or fear. In this section, we will learn the Six-Step Process that you should promise to try to follow as a part of your pledge. The purpose of this process is to give you the inner calm and strength you will need to (1) avoid emotional decision making and (2) continue to follow the buy-and-hold approach whenever a rational analysis of the risks to your portfolio and your health warrant that approach. The six steps are simple to remember and can be summarized in just a few words, as follows:

1. **Stop!** (and calm yourself)

2. **Check Your Portfolio's Health** (Decision Point 1)

3. **Motivate Yourself**

4. **Seek (and Give) Useful Support**

5. **Tune Out Harmful Noise**

6. **Check Your Health** (Decision Point 2)

Let's now go over each of these steps.

Step 1: Stop!

You should *never, ever* buy or sell investments on an emotional whim. As soon as you feel yourself panicking during a market sell-off, or getting excited when the market's being irrationally exuberant, *do not act on your feelings*! Instead stop, take a deep breath, and calm yourself down. Meditate, take a long walk, go fishing, hit a bucket of golf balls—do whatever helps you to calm down.

Step 2: Check Your Portfolio's Health (Decision Point 1)

Once you've calmed down, the next step is to think through, rationally, what you should do. If you are in the midst of a bull market and are sorely tempted to dump your underperforming investments so you can chase performance, remind yourself of the dangers inherent in the greater fool theory of investing. (If you don't remember, go back and reread Chapter 16.) Consider what will happen if you sell your bonds and high-volatility hedges and the market suddenly turns and takes a dive. Consider what *did* happen to the many investors who got caught up in the irrational exuberance of the tech bubble, only to see their savings vanish when the market crashed in 2000. Remember that mean reversion is one of the most powerful forces at work in the market, and whatever high-flying stock, fund, or sector you jump on *will* reverse and fall back to earth. Finally, understand that what matters to your financial safety is *not* what the market's doing but how *your portfolio* is holding up. As long as you are not losing massive amounts of money (a highly unlikely situation in a bull market), you must come to the only rational conclusion you can and stick with buy and hold.

If instead of a bull you are face-to-face with a raging bear, step 2 is a little more complicated. There *are* situations in which it may possibly be better to act rather than to do nothing, to avoid a potential catastrophic loss. To determine whether you face such a dangerous situation, you will need to take the temperature of your portfolio. We will learn how to do this in Chapter 18. But briefly, you take your portfolio's temperature by calculating your current withdrawal rate and comparing it with a low-risk withdrawal rate you will select from the tables in Chapter 18. If your current withdrawal rate falls below the selected maximum actionable withdrawal rate (MAWR), then you should do nothing.

Note a key implication of this approach. If you are not yet retired or fewer than five years from retirement, your withdrawal rate should be zero. A zero withdrawal rate will always fall below your MAWR. Hence your portfolio should be able to recover from its losses *and you should do nothing.* Only those investors who are already retired or near retirement *may* encounter a situation in which it might possibly be better to take action than hold. (Investors within five years of retirement should calculate their current withdrawal rate using an estimate of their expected living expenses in the first year of retirement.)

If you are retired or nearing retirement and your current withdrawal rate rises to your MAWR, then there is a hierarchy of actions you should follow to protect your nest egg. Before abandoning buy and hold, you would first take steps to reduce your withdrawal rate. Such steps might, for example, include reducing your expenses or taking a part-time job until the bear market ends and the danger subsides.

If, after taking all possible steps to reduce your withdrawal rate, the market decline continues and your withdrawal rate once again rises to your MAWR, you will need to sell your stock investments. However, in this situation, you will be making the sell decision based on a rational analysis of the dangers facing your portfolio rather than an irrational response to fear. Furthermore, using the approach outlined in Chapter 19, you will have a decent chance (though not a guarantee) of timing your reentry into the market in such a way as to improve your portfolio's odds of survival.

If, after taking your portfolio's temperature, you find that your current withdrawal rate is less than your MAWR, then the rational decision is to hold. Understand, though, that this decision is by no means irrevocable. You can and should retake your portfolio's temperature frequently during a bear market. Each time you make a decision to hold rather than sell, that decision applies only until the next time you test your portfolio's temperature. You are committing yourself on a contingent basis to holding. If the temperature of your portfolio continues to rise, you will have many opportunities to reconsider your decision.

It is hoped that each time you calculate your portfolio's current withdrawal rate and find that it remains outside the danger zone, this knowledge will have a calming effect on you. And when you decide, based on this knowledge, to continue holding, then the understanding that you may revisit this decision as often as you like should help you to live with the decision. A revocable decision should be much easier and less stressful to make than an irrevocable one.

Step 3: Motivate Yourself

Assuming that you have completed Step 2, and that your current withdrawal rate remains below your MAWR, you now know that you are not inside the danger zone. This knowledge, however, is unlikely to completely quiet your fears. Therefore you must take action to screw up your courage—to motivate yourself to stick with the buy-and-hold approach. The place to begin this motivational effort is with your written pledge. Take your pledge out and carefully reread it. Think about each of the people—your significant other, each of your kids, each of your grandchildren—to whom you made the pledge. Realize that each of them is depending on you to do the right thing, the rational thing, the responsible thing—which in step 2 you have determined to be hold, not sell. Think about what might be the impact on each of them if you *fail* to hold. You may permanently lock in your losses, thereby increasing your risk of becoming a financial burden to them. This may in turn affect your children's ability to provide for their own families, to fund their kids' education, and to save for their own retirements. If it helps to motivate you, think of the bear market as a saber-toothed tiger, and imagine that you are up on Bil's ledge with your family in front of you. Then ask yourself, should you flee and leave your family to the tiger, or should you stand your ground and protect your loved ones?

Do not be afraid to get emotional in step 3. Step 3 is all about calling on the *right* emotions to overpower the *wrong* emotions. If reason alone were enough to counteract the strong emotions elicited by market crashes and market bubbles, there'd be no need for any steps beyond step 2. But for many people, reason is *not* enough. You must counteract the greed or fear triggered by the market with the similarly strong emotions you feel toward your loved ones. Remember, it is your responsibility to *protect* them as well as yourself from the financial mistakes you will be sorely tempted to make.

Step 4: Seek (and Give) Useful Support

Military commanders have known from time immemorial that a soldier's courage will be enhanced if he is part of a tight unit and can count on the morale-building support, and peer pressure, of his comrades in arms. Similarly, you can bolster your courage by seeking the support of family, friends, and peers. If you are married, you can look first to your spouse, who (should have) signed the same Rational Decision-Making Pledge you signed. Confide in and support each other.

If you are a member of an investment club committed to the buy-and-hold approach, seek out the support of your fellow club members whenever you feel yourself wavering in your own commitment. Providing support during both bull and bear markets should be the number one purpose of such clubs.

If forming or joining such a club is not an option for you in your area, there is good news. A group of like-minded investors already exists on the Internet. You will find them at the Bogleheads investment forum. The Bogleheads are so named in honor of John Bogle, the founder of the Vanguard Group and longtime champion of index investing. Bogle launched the Vanguard 500 fund (VFINX), the first successful index fund, back in the 1970s and has written extensively on the advantages of buying and holding a simple portfolio of low-cost index funds.[128] The Bogleheads take their inspiration from Bogle's teachings and provide investing and other financial advice for all those who post questions on their website.[129] They boast among their members a number of finance professionals, and their investment advice consistently exhibits to a high degree the same deep financial knowledge, savvy, and common sense that characterizes Bogle's own advice.

Most importantly, the Bogleheads as a group are committed to the buy-and-hold approach and to encouraging each other to "stay the course" during tough times. Indeed, the Bogleheads' existence is proof that buy-and-hold is *not* dead. You must be a member of the website to post questions and replies, but membership is free and it's easy to sign up. Once a member, you will have an online support group that will address your every fear and concern about the market with insight and wisdom, while challenging, encouraging, persuading, and admonishing you to stick with buy and hold through thick and thin. I encourage you to check out their website and sign up.

While seeking support from your spouse, your friends, fellow club members, or others, don't neglect to give support as well. Not only will you be helping others to stay the buy-and-hold course but *you too* can gain courage and inner calm from your own words of strength and wisdom.

Step 5: Tune Out Harmful Noise

"STOCK SHOCK FELT ROUND THE WORLD.
Gets 'nasty' as Lehman tanks, Merrill vanishes, AIG wobbles" [130]

**"Depression Coming? Boil Some Beans;
Ladies Who Quilt Give Tips on Surviving Tough Times"** [131]

"'Great Depression' closer than U.S. admits, report finds" [132]

"Will Bush become the new Hoover?" [133]

"Depression seen possible" [134]

"Behind Closed Doors, Warnings of Calamity" [135]

These are just a few of the dire headlines that greeted us from newsstands and websites during the dark days of September 2008. What better way to grab your attention, and sell you a newspaper, than with dire warnings of impending doom printed in big, bold letters? But while newspapers and magazines with these kinds of headlines may make you *want* to buy them, do you really *need* to buy them? Most of these headlines don't even convey actual facts. Rather, they are merely speculating on *possible* futures. Instead of useful news, what the media is often selling is at best useless noise. Of course, we now know that a depression was *not* in the offing, Bush did *not* become a new Hoover, and the quilting ladies were probably not reduced to a diet of beans. Given that none of these terrible things actually came to pass, would reading about them back in 2008 have made you any wiser? Or would it just have scared you into overreacting and doing something dumb?

If you are a buy-and-hold investor, *none* of the economic news, forecasts, and tips you read about in magazines, or hear on CNBC, will help you decide what you should or should not do during a market crash. The *only* factors that should matter in your decision process are how *your portfolio* and *your health* are holding up. If in step 2 you determine that your current withdrawal rate is still inside your safe zone, then the rational decision is to continue to hold—no matter how many stock market gurus on CNBC are predicting the end of civilization as we know it. If in step 4 your investment club, or the Bogleheads, have responded to all your concerns and calmed your nerves to the point where you can continue to hold, what will be gained by reading an article in your local paper that reawakens all the anxieties you worked so hard to quell?

We are all tempted to slow down and look when we pass a highway accident, but if you do, you'll at best just make the traffic jam worse, and you probably won't be able to see anything anyway. In the worst case, you *will* see something—and be sorry you did. The smarter move is to keep your eyes on the road ahead and speed away. So it is when it comes to the financial, and even mainstream, media during market crashes. Instead of tuning in to the latest dire predictions or advice about how to boil beans, the wiser move is to *tune out* all so-called news that is likely to cause anxiety and make it harder for you to stay the buy-and-hold course. When the market goes into a nosedive, or turns into a bubbly froth, cancel your subscription to *Forbes,* turn off CNBC, and walk rapidly past the corner newsstand with its headlines warning of Armageddon or promising Utopia. Instead of the newspaper, read a good book —it's more enjoyable, and you'll probably learn a lot more, too. Don't worry about being out of "the know" for a little while. You can catch up on the latest economic and financial news after the danger has passed and calm is restored to the markets.

Step 6: Check Your Health (Decision Point 2)

The Six-Step Process has two goals: (1) to give you a way to make a *rational* decision about whether to continue holding and, (2) *if* your decision is to hold in step 2, to reduce your stress level to the point where you will be able to safely follow through with this decision. In steps 2–5, the knowledge you gain that your withdrawal rate remains in the safe zone; the support of your family, friends, and fellow investors; and the avoidance of anxiety-inducing noise from the media should all combine to help ensure that the stress-reducing goal of the 6-Step Process is met.

However, it is possible that you will reach a decision to hold in step 2 but will *not*, despite your best stress-reducing efforts, be able to live with this decision without putting your health at risk. If you find yourself (or your significant other) in this situation, you *must* sell your stocks. Your health always comes before your money. You will not be doing yourself, or your family, any favors by giving yourself a heart attack. For that matter, you will not be doing your nest egg any good if you wind up with a big bill for an extended hospital stay. Allowing your anxiety to skyrocket to dangerous levels in an attempt to protect your savings is self-defeating behavior. It is for this reason that the Rational Decision-Making Pledge commits you only to completing the 6-Step Process, *not* to sticking with buy and hold if it endangers your health. If you complete the process in good faith and to the best of your ability, you have kept your promise to yourself and your family. If at the end of step 5 your stress level remains too elevated to allow you to safely continue holding, this is not a failure on your part but rather an indication that your portfolio's asset allocation is too aggressive for your personality. As is made clear back in Chapter 11, finding the right stock/bond mix to fit your risk tolerance level may take more than one try. It's OK if you find out, during a market crash, that you allocated too much of your nest egg to stocks, as long as you learn from this mistake and reduce your stock allocation going forward.

The last step of the 6-Step Process commits you to checking your stress level and making a *rational* decision as to whether you must abandon buy and hold, temporarily, for the sake of your (or your significant other's) health. It might seem that in step 6 you are making a decision based on emotion rather than reason, but this is not the case. Rather your goal is to make a decision based on a *rational* analysis of your *emotional* state and the implications for your health. Of course, there will be a good deal of judgment involved in evaluating your anxiety level and your ability to handle that anxiety. If you are unsure about what to do, a visit to your family doctor may help you decide. If you are still in doubt even after consulting with your physician, you should err on the side of caution and choose to sell rather than continue holding.

The Checklist

In addition to following the Six-Step Process, your Rational Decision-Making Pledge should commit you to *documenting* the specific actions you've taken, and the decisions you've made, at each step along the way. Exhibit 17.2 is an example of a checklist you (and your significant other) can use to document your actions and decisions. To check off a particular step, you must be able to document at least one concrete action you've taken to meet that step's goals. The checklist is intended to keep you honest and eliminate any wiggle room you might otherwise have to avoid the work required by the Six-Step Process. With the checklist as part of your pledge, you can't simply tell yourself that you've finished one of the steps if you cannot describe, in writing, what you've actually done.

Use the Six-Step Process (and Accompanying Checklist) as Often as Necessary

When you encounter a major bull or bear market, you may want to make *multiple* copies of the checklist in Exhibit 17.2. During a long bull market, you will likely face the temptation to deviate from your buy-and-hold strategy more than once. During a lengthy bear market, fear may often tempt you to sell. Your pledge should commit you to completing the Six-Step Process *each time* you are tempted to deviate from your buy-and-hold strategy; you should complete the accompanying checklist every time you complete the Six-Step Process. The Six-Step Process and accompanying checklist should help you control and reduce your anxiety each time you use them.

The Play Account

The Rational Decision-Making Pledge, 6-Step Process, and accompanying checklist should help you navigate the temptations posed by rising as well as declining markets. That said, our discussion has focused more on controlling the fear that arises during bear markets. This focus reflects the findings of behavioral finance, which indicate that loss aversion is a more powerful motivator than the desire for gain. But that is not to say that greed is not a powerful, difficult-to-control emotion in its own right. When the stock market is going gangbusters, fear wanes, our inner John Stockman comes to the fore, and we are tempted by visions of striking it rich. So before we leave the subject of how to do nothing, let's touch on one last technique that is geared more toward staving off our inner John Stockman than our Joe Bondsman.

Exhibit 17.2. Example Checklist for the Six-Step Process

6-STEP PROCESS CHECKLIST

Instructions: Place a check next to each step as you complete it. For Steps 1, 3, 4, and 5, document the specific actions you have taken to complete each step. For Steps 2 and 6, document the decisions that you made.

☐ **Step 1: Stop! (and calm yourself)**

Describe the specific actions you took to calm yourself that helped you to continue holding: _____

☐ **Step 2: Check Your Portfolio's Health**

Check the Step 2 decision you reached on the list below, and the reason(s) for that decision:

  ☐ Continue to hold, since my (our) portfolio did not experience any investment losses (bull market)
  ☐ Continue to hold, since I am (we are) not yet retired or near retirement (hence my/our withdrawal rate is zero and safe)
  ☐ Continue to hold, since my (our) current withdrawal rate of ___% is less than my (our) Maximum Actionable Withdrawal Rate (MAWR) of ___% specified in my (our) Investment Plan
  ☐ Continue to hold, because although my (our) current withdrawal rate of ___% has risen to the MAWR of ___%, I (we) have taken steps to reduce my (our) withdrawal rate by reducing expenses or increasing non-investment income
  ☐ Sell my (our) stock mutual funds and ETFs because my (our) current withdrawal rate of ___% has risen to the MAWR of ___%
  ☐ Other (explain): _____

☐ **Step 3: Motivate Yourself**

Describe the actions you've taken to complete Step 3:

  ☐ Re-read my (our) Rational Decision-Making Pledge
  ☐ Thought through potential impacts to family members of failing to hold
  ☐ Other (describe): _____

Exhibit 17.2. Example Checklist for the Six-Step Process *(continued)*

☐ **Step 4: Seek (and Give) Useful Support**

List those fellow buy-and-hold investors to whom you turned to for support, or gave support to:

☐ Spouse
☐ Other family members (Provide names): _____
☐ Friends/Peers (Provide names): _____
☐ Investment club members
☐ Bogleheads online forum
☐ Others (Provide Names): _____

☐ **Step 5: Tune Out Harmful Noise**

Describe the specific actions you took to tune out noise:

☐ Stopped watching (or continued to stop watching) the financial news networks
☐ Stopped reading (or continued to stop reading) news about the stock market
☐ Other (describe): _____

☐ **Step 6: Check Your Health**

Check the decision you reached on the list below:

☐ Continue to hold, because I (we) judge that my (and my spouse's) current stress level does not put my (and/or my spouse's) health at risk
☐ Sell all stock mutual funds and ETFs, because I (we) judge that my (and my spouse's) current stress level puts my (and/or my spouse's) health at risk
☐ Other (explain): _____

If you find yourself frequently tempted to roll the dice by chasing performance, timing the market, or trying to discover the next Microsoft or Apple, then allow yourself to indulge these desires—within strict limits. Set up a brokerage account separate from your other accounts and funded with a *small* percentage of your nest egg. This will be your play account, which you can use to pursue any short-term trading strategy, hot stock tip, or get-rich-quick scheme that grabs your fancy. Use your play account to let off steam, have fun, and play the stock market, while you follow a strict buy-and-hold approach in your main retirement accounts. If your play account makes you rich, fantastic! If not, it will at least give you the chance to get your wilder ideas and strategies out of your system.

There are a few rules you need to follow if you do decide to set up a play account. First, you must limit the funds you deposit in the account to an amount you can afford to lose. One to 2 percent of your retirement nest egg is a reasonable amount, and certainly no more than 5 percent. Second, you must limit all experimentation, short-term trading, and stock picking to your play account, while following a strict well-diversified, buy-and-hold strategy in your main accounts. Third, you cannot count money in your play account as part of your retirement nest egg, because you are essentially gambling with this money, and it may not be there when you need it. Should you eventually decide to close your play account, you can then add any money remaining in the account to your retirement nest egg. Fourth and finally, you must not add any additional money to the play account after you open it with your initial funds. *This last rule is very important.* If you start adding funds to your play account, you run the risk of slowly (or quickly) draining your retirement savings on a series of long-shot gambles. If you happen to lose all the money in your play account, you must close the account—once your play money is gone, it's gone for good.

While a play account should prove particularly effective in helping you to deal with the desires that arise during bull markets and bubbles, it may also help you control your fears. Remember, you can do anything you want with the money in your play account, and that includes using trading strategies and derivatives to hedge your main accounts. If, for example, you are worried that the stock market will crash, you can sell the stocks in your play account and use the proceeds to short the market or buy put options.[136] If your hedging trades pay off, you can then transfer the profits from these trades to your main retirement accounts to offset your losses. (Although you should not add more money to your play account once it has been funded, you can always *withdraw* money from this account.) In this way, your play account gives you an opportunity to time the market, without doing damage to your main retirement accounts.

A Brief Word on Rebalancing

Doing nothing in the midst of a market crash or raging bull market is one of the hardest things you will ever have to do. But there is one thing that is even harder: rebalancing. Yes, rebalancing gives you an opportunity to buy low and sell high. But this is precisely why it is so hard to do. During a bull market, it just *feels wrong* to pull money out of high-flying investments, only to put the money back into laggards. And it can be scary, in the extreme, to sell your safe bonds and rebalance into stocks during a bear market.

What, then, should you do if it is time to rebalance but you are already having a lot of emotional difficulty just holding? In this situation, concentrate on holding, and postpone rebalancing until the markets—and you—calm down. Chasing performance during a bull market or panicking and selling your stock funds during a bear market are big mistakes. But failing to rebalance on time is more a missed opportunity than a major mistake. If your emotions are under control and you are able to hold with little difficulty, then by all means try to rebalance your portfolio. If need be, use the 6-Step Process to help calm your nerves as you take on the rebalancing effort. But if you are already struggling with the stress of holding, do not add to that stress by attempting to rebalance. Instead, give yourself a break.

However, if you are a retiree and the stock market is crashing, you *should* rebalance on the go by taking your withdrawals from your bond portfolio rather than your stock portfolio. When the market has weakened your stock portfolio, it is very important to avoid selling shares of your stock funds. This will only further weaken your financial situation and make recovery that much longer and more difficult.

CHAPTER 18

MAINTAINING YOUR PORTFOLIO'S HEALTH IN RETIREMENT

⤴

Examine the record of history, recollect what has happened within the circle
of your own experience, consider with attention what has been the conduct
of almost all the great unfortunate, either in private or public life, whom you may
have either read of, or heard of, or remember; and you will find that the misfortunes
of by far the greater part of them have arisen from their not knowing
when they were well, when it was proper for them to sit still and be contented.
—**Adam Smith,** ***The Theory of Moral Sentiments***

U ntil now, I have strongly advocated a buy-and-*hold* investment strategy, with annual rebalancing. Over the long run, such a strategy is almost certain to produce better returns than any strategy that requires frequent buying and selling. We learned this lesson in Chapter 16.

We also learned that as long as what you buy and hold is a well-diversified portfolio of large cap stocks, high-volatility hedges, low-volatility hedges, and return boosters, your risk of going broke in retirement will be minimized. Such a portfolio, purchased and then held for the long run, will reduce the risk of too much (negative) volatility, without unduly increasing the risk of not realizing enough returns to outpace inflation.

But buying and holding a well-diversified portfolio will not eliminate the retirement risk. Once you've saved any money—be it millions of dollars or a single penny —you risk losing it. Nothing can ever eliminate this risk. And although buy and hold will prove the wisest strategy the vast majority of the time, extreme circumstances might make it better to take action than to do nothing. John Stockman (and many real-life investors) should have sold, not held, his stocks during the catastrophic market crash that brought the Roaring Twenties to an end. Joe Bondsman should have sold some of his bonds and used the proceeds to buy stocks during the Great Inflation of the 1970s. Doing nothing is the right move for investors almost all of the time—*almost*.

But how can you know the difference between situations that require action and those that do not? Knowing when it is probably safe to hold your investments is critically important. This knowledge should help you to overcome your fears, to "sit still and be contented," in Adam Smith's words, when it is "proper" to do so. Knowing when it is probably not safe to do nothing is even more important. This knowledge can help you to avoid a catastrophic, unrecoverable loss.

By "knowing," I do not mean having *all* of the relevant information to choose action, or inaction, with absolute certainty. In investing, you will never have all of the information you need to act with certainty. In this chapter, though, you will gain the kind of partial, fuzzy knowledge that will help you tell the difference between situations that may pose a real danger to your portfolio and situations that may be scary but are likely not dangerous. You will also learn what specific actions you should take to save your portfolio in the former cases.

Before delving into this helpful knowledge, it will be instructive to consider systems that cannot provide you with the kind of knowledge you need. By learning what doesn't work, you will come to a better understanding of what does work, and why.

Sell Signal Systems That Miss the Mark

Countless systems claim to identify market *sell signals*. The books written on this subject could fill entire libraries. We cannot possibly discuss all of these systems, nor is it necessary to do so. Instead, a subset can serve as an illustrative example. We focus on systems that can best be termed *moving average systems*. Such systems involve selling equities when an index such as the S&P 500 crosses below its moving average[137] (e.g., the two-hundred-day moving average) and repurchasing them when the index crosses above the same moving average. These systems are designed to avoid the worst of bear market losses. They require you to sell low as the selected index declines. They may enable you to buy lower, but if the buy signal comes too late, you might wind up buying high—and permanently locking in your losses. It all depends on where the index crosses its moving average as it declines relative to where it crosses the average again on the way back up.

Moving average systems are examples of market timing, pure and simple. We already considered the evidence against market timing in Chapter 16. Like all market timing strategies, moving average systems will likely harm your long-term returns. After all, if you are looking for high returns, selling low whenever the market crosses below its moving average is not a good way to start. Furthermore, if the chosen index keeps crossing back and forth over its moving average, the frequent buy and sell signals will result in heavy trading costs.

Nonetheless, moving average systems have shown some ability to reduce bear market losses. And while these short-term loss reductions may well come at the expense of long-run returns, such a trade-off might be worth making if the losses thus avoided are of the truly dangerous, as opposed to the merely scary, kind. However, even assuming that moving average systems have some ability to reduce bear market losses, there is no reason to believe that these systems can distinguish temporary losses from catastrophic, unrecoverable losses. In fact, by focusing exclusively on the market, moving average systems, like all market timing strategies, completely miss the only factor that should matter to you: the health of your portfolio.

A couple of examples will help to illustrate this point. Ted retired five years ago at the age of seventy, using an initial withdrawal rate of 2.5 percent. Since his retirement, a combination of high returns and low inflation has worked to reduce his withdrawal rate to 1.5 percent. Let us now suppose that the market enters a nosedive that rivals the 1929 Crash. Let's further suppose that a particular moving average system Ted has investigated would generate a sell signal once the market has declined 15 percent. But Ted has remained a strict buy-and-hold investor and does nothing. The market continues its downward spiral, until the S&P 500 has lost 90 percent of its value.

Has Ted made a huge mistake? Not at all, because he has been monitoring the health of his portfolio, and it has remained in good shape throughout the crash. The 90 percent loss applies to the S&P 500, but Ted has a well-diversified portfolio of large caps, high-volatility hedges, low-volatility hedges, and return boosters. As a result, his personal losses are limited to 50 percent. Furthermore, because he entered the crash with a withdrawal rate of only 1.5 percent, his withdrawal rate when the market hits bottom still stands at a low 3 percent. As we will soon see, a portfolio with a 3 percent withdrawal rate at a market bottom has a 100 percent probability of surviving at least thirty more years. As the recovery rally picks up steam, Ted's withdrawal rate quickly drops back to its 2.5 percent starting point. The market crash never posed a true danger to Ted's portfolio, so there was no reason for him to sell.

Might he have done better had he been using the moving average system? Possibly, if the signal to repurchase equities occurred in time for Ted to "sell low" and "buy lower." If the buy signal came late, though, Ted would have permanently locked in a portion of his losses. He would have also incurred heavy trading costs had the system generated frequent buy and sell signals. There was no reason for Ted to risk the potential permanent losses and trading costs, given that his portfolio was never in any danger.

Let's consider a second example. Lisa retired at age sixty-five with an intention to follow the same moving average system Ted investigated but rejected. Unfortunately, the first ten years of her retirement were marred by stagflation—low economic growth and high inflation reminiscent of the 1970s. As a result, her withdrawal rate has steadily risen and now stands at 8 percent. At this point, the market enters into a correction. After a 10 percent decline, the S&P 500 begins a slow rally. The index does not cross below its moving average, a sell signal is never generated, and hence Lisa continues to hold.

However, despite Lisa having a well-diversified portfolio, she has incurred a 20 percent loss by the time the market bottoms (it could happen). Making matters worse, the high inflation of the preceding ten years continues, and Lisa's withdrawal rate reaches 12 percent. This rate is unsustainable and puts Lisa in grave danger of bankruptcy. Had she been monitoring the health of her portfolio rather than relying on the moving average system, she would have received a signal to take action and avoided what was for her a catastrophic loss.

In both these examples, the moving average system worked, in the sense that it correctly distinguished a major market crash from a minor downturn. It generated a sell signal in the former, but not the latter, case. Yet this same system would have put Ted at risk of a permanent, avoidable loss. And much worse, it would have failed to prevent Lisa from suffering a catastrophic loss.

The fundamental flaw in moving average systems should now be clear. Such systems focus entirely on predicting the future direction of the market while completely ignoring what really matters: the current health of your portfolio. Even if they manage to get their market predictions correct, those predictions may be irrelevant to you for three reasons. First, moving average systems track an index like the S&P 500, but the performance of a well-diversified portfolio can differ dramatically from that of a market index. As an extreme example, during the 2000–2002 bear market, some of the portfolios we tested in Part III actually had positive returns. Using a moving average system during 2000–2002 probably would have meant missing out on these gains.

Second, moving average systems fail to account for the strength or weakness of your position. If, like Ted, you enter a major market decline in a strong financial position, a moving average system may put you at risk of suffering a permanent loss and high trading costs when holding would keep your losses temporary. If, like Lisa, you encounter a minor bump when your portfolio has been significantly weakened, you may be better off selling than holding, but a moving average system might not generate a sell signal. When it comes to avoiding the retirement risk, what should matter to you is the health of your portfolio, not the health of the market.

Third and finally, moving average systems are designed to protect you from only one of the two components of the retirement risk: negative market volatility. But as Joe Bondsman could tell you, the second component—not enough returns to outpace inflation—is just as important.

We have used moving average systems as an example, but our conclusions apply equally to all market timing systems. All such systems generate sell signals based on some prediction of the market's direction. Even assuming they have predictive ability—a big *if*—none of them take into account the health of your portfolio. Hence none of them can help you to distinguish dangerous situations that require action from merely scary situations that are best met by doing nothing.

★★★

As the preceding examples demonstrate, an effective approach must focus on how your portfolio, not the market, is performing. But these examples also offer a more specific hint as to *how* to construct a better alternative. It was the withdrawal rate that provided real insight into the health of Ted's and Lisa's portfolios. In Chapter 10, we learned that *lowering* your initial withdrawal rate is the best way to minimize all aspects of the retirement risk. We also learned that an *elevated* withdrawal rate increases your risk of going broke in retirement. Thus you can use your current withdrawal rate to assess the overall health of your portfolio.

An approach based on withdrawal rates has two major advantages over moving average and other market timing systems. First, such an approach focuses not on the market but on what really matters: your portfolio and how it is holding up. And second, unlike the market's future direction, you can measure your withdrawal rate with a high degree of certainty and precision. Over time, your withdrawal rate will change. If your savings grow faster than your inflation-adjusted expenses, your withdrawal rate and your risk of bankruptcy will decrease. If your savings grow more slowly than your inflation-adjusted expenses, or if you suffer losses, your withdrawal rate will increase, along with your risk of going broke. At any point in time, you can calculate your withdrawal rate simply by dividing your annual budget by the amount of money in your retirement portfolio. You can think of this current withdrawal rate as the temperature of your portfolio. A high withdrawal rate indicates illness, just as an elevated body temperature indicates illness in a person. As we shall see, an elevated withdrawal rate may indicate either that a portfolio is overheating because of too much negative volatility or that it is becoming too cold as a result of insufficient returns. We will refer to the former illness as portfolio fever and to the latter as portfolio hypothermia. Portfolio fever arises only during market downturns, whereas portfolio hypothermia occurs when the market is flat or rising. In the next section, we learn how portfolio fever can be diagnosed and treated. After considering portfolio fever, we turn to the diagnosis and treatment of portfolio hypothermia.

Portfolio Fever

Diagnosis

Suppose you are experiencing a bear market and your portfolio's temperature is rapidly rising as your losses mount. How do you know when the rising temperature, or withdrawal rate, indicates portfolio fever? As long as the portfolio will probably survive, then portfolio fever is not indicated. If there is a significant risk that the portfolio will be bankrupted, then the temperature has reached a danger zone. If you can determine in advance the withdrawal rates that lie within the danger zone, then you can take action to save your portfolio *before* it reaches this zone. Thus the key to developing a strategy that will help distinguish safe from threatening conditions is to determine, in advance, the withdrawal rate that marks the boundary of the danger zone.

In Chapter 11, we developed guidelines for determining appropriate stock/bond mixes for retiree portfolios using the initial withdrawal rate. These guidelines were based on the Trinity Study. In this study, three professors at Trinity University tested the survival rates of various portfolios of stocks and bonds. Using data on stock and bond returns from 1926 through 2009, the Trinity Study authors subjected their portfolios to backtests posed by some of the most difficult conditions of the past eighty-four years, including the 1929 Crash and the stagflation of the late 1970s and early 1980s. The Trinity Study provides portfolio survival rates for various retirement lengths, stock/bond mixes, and initial withdrawal rates. Its results confirmed the well-known rule of thumb that an initial withdrawal rate of 4 percent or less is probably safe from bankruptcy.[138]

Similar to the Trinity Study, we can use historical backtests to determine the withdrawal rates that will result in portfolio survival — or end in bankruptcy — for each of the recoveries from the bear markets and market corrections we have experienced since 1926. On the basis of these results, we can determine historical portfolio survival rates for different withdrawal rates.

Consider, for example, the October 1929 Crash, which lasted nearly three years. The market finally bottomed in July 1932. Suppose that a retiree with a 60/40 portfolio saw his withdrawal rate rise to 6 percent by July 1932. Would the portfolio have then been able to survive an additional thirty years, until July 1962? Or would the damage done to it during the Crash cause it to go broke sometime between 1932 and 1962? We can answer these questions by setting a 60/40 portfolio's withdrawal rate to 6 percent as of July 1932, adjusting the withdrawals for subsequent inflation, and backtesting the portfolio over the July 1932 through July 1962 time frame. We can repeat this same test for other withdrawal rates (e.g., 6.2 percent, 6.4 percent) and other stock/bond mixes. Then, the same set of tests can be repeated starting in March 1938 (the bottom of the 1937–38 bear market), April 1947 (the 1946–47 bear market bottom), and all of the other bear market and market correction bottoms we experienced between 1926 and 1982.[139] Finally, we can combine the backtest results to show the percentage of times that a particular portfolio, with a particular withdrawal rate, managed to recover from its losses and survive at least thirty more years.

Table 18.1 shows the results of this analysis. The nineteen bear markets and market corrections used as the starting points for measuring the portfolio survival rates in this table include all market declines of at least 10 percent, based on the total returns (capital losses plus dividends) of U.S. large cap stocks. The table was developed using the same data source used by the Trinity Study authors: the *Ibbotson®* *Stocks, Bonds, Bills, and Inflation®* (*SBBI®*) *Classic Yearbook*, published on an annual basis by Morningstar.[140] This source was used rather than the mutual fund return data provided on Morningstar's website because the *Yearbook* covers a much longer time period. Most important, the monthly return data in the *Yearbook* begins in 1926, allowing the analysis to extend all the way back to the historic 1929 Crash, thereby capturing the impact of the most extreme financial storm of the past nine decades on portfolio survival rates. The available bond mutual fund return data on the Morningstar website do not extend back to the 1930s.

Table 18.1. Portfolio Survival Rates for Thirty-Year Retirements
Following Historic Market Bottoms (1926–2012)

Withdrawal Rate (%)	Stock/Bond Mix				
	100% Stock	80/20	60/40	40/60	20/80
Less than 3.0	100%	100%	100%	100%	100%
3.0	100%	100%	100%	100%	100%
3.2	100%	100%	100%	100%	100%
3.4	100%	100%	100%	100%	100%
3.6	100%	100%	100%	100%	95%
3.8	100%	100%	100%	100%	95%
4.0	100%	100%	100%	100%	89%
4.2	100%	100%	100%	100%	63%
4.4	100%	100%	100%	95%	47%
4.6	95%	95%	95%	84%	42%
4.8	95%	95%	95%	84%	32%
5.0	95%	95%	95%	79%	26%
5.2	95%	95%	89%	63%	26%
5.4	95%	95%	79%	53%	26%
5.6	95%	89%	79%	53%	26%
5.8	95%	84%	74%	47%	11%
6.0	84%	79%	68%	42%	5%
6.2	84%	79%	63%	32%	5%
6.4	84%	79%	63%	32%	5%
6.6	79%	68%	58%	21%	5%
6.8	79%	68%	47%	11%	5%
7.0	79%	68%	47%	11%	5%
7.2	79%	58%	42%	11%	5%
7.4	68%	58%	37%	11%	5%
7.6	68%	53%	32%	11%	5%
7.8	63%	53%	26%	11%	5%
8.0	55%	53%	26%	5%	5%
8.2	55%	37%	21%	5%	5%
8.4	55%	30%	16%	5%	5%
8.6	50%	30%	15%	5%	5%
8.8	45%	30%	14%	5%	0%

**Table 18.1. Portfolio Survival Rates for Thirty-Year Retirements
Following Historic Market Bottoms (1926–2012)** *(continued)*

Withdrawal Rate (%)	Stock/Bond Mix				
	100% Stock	80/20	60/40	40/60	20/80
9.0	40%	30%	10%	5%	0%
9.2	35%	30%	10%	5%	0%
9.4	30%	30%	10%	5%	0%
9.6	30%	24%	9%	5%	0%
9.8	30%	24%	9%	5%	0%
10.0	30%	24%	9%	0%	0%
10.2	30%	19%	9%	0%	0%
10.4	29%	14%	9%	0%	0%
10.6	29%	14%	5%	0%	0%
10.8	29%	14%	5%	0%	0%
11.0	27%	14%	5%	0%	0%
11.2	27%	14%	0%	0%	0%
11.4	23%	9%	0%	0%	0%
11.6	18%	9%	0%	0%	0%
11.8	18%	9%	0%	0%	0%
12.0	18%	9%	0%	0%	0%
12.2	18%	9%	0%	0%	0%
12.4	17%	4%	0%	0%	0%
12.6	17%	4%	0%	0%	0%
12.8	13%	4%	0%	0%	0%
13.0	13%	0%	0%	0%	0%
13.2	13%	0%	0%	0%	0%
13.4	9%	0%	0%	0%	0%
13.6	9%	0%	0%	0%	0%
13.8	4%	0%	0%	0%	0%
14.0 to 15.0	4%	0%	0%	0%	0%
Greater than 15.0	0%	0%	0%	0%	0%

Source: Developed by the author using historical stock and bond total returns data from *2013 Ibbotson® Stocks, Bonds, Bills, and Inflation® (SBBI®) Classic Yearbook*, Morningstar, Inc., 2013, pages 220–21 and 232–33, and historical CPI-U (inflation) data published by the Bureau of Labor Statistics, U.S. Department of Labor, www.bls.gov/cpi/#tables.

Although Table 18.1 is based on the same data source as the Trinity Study, it reflects an adjustment to one of the asset classes used by the Trinity Study authors. Whereas they used corporate bonds, Table 18.1 uses intermediate-term government bond return data to represent the bond portion of the various portfolios. Large cap stock returns represent the stock portfolios, in the table as in the Trinity Study. Because the data source is limited to only a few asset classes, we cannot capture the impact that other assets, including high-volatility hedges, might have on portfolio survival rates. However, to the extent that survival rates are reduced by this limitation, the table can be considered to provide conservative guidance. Such conservativeness adds an additional layer of protection against the possibility of catastrophic losses.

In addition to the thirty-year survival rates shown in Table 18.1, the same procedure was used to develop twenty-five-, twenty-, fifteen-, and ten-year survival rates. These shorter-term rates are provided in Tables 18.2–18.5. Note that as the recovery period shortens, it is possible to add more recent market bottoms to the nineteen covered in Table 18.1. For example, given that the return data extend through 2012, all twenty-three market bottoms that occurred between 1926 and 2002 (ten years prior to 2012) are included in the analysis of the ten-year survival rates shown in Table 18.5.

A more detailed description of the methodology used to develop Tables 18.1–18.5, as well as the rationale behind this methodology, can be found in Appendix C.

Table 18.2. Portfolio Survival Rates for Twenty-Five-Year Retirements Following Historic Market Bottoms (1926–2012)

Withdrawal Rate (%)	Stock/Bond Mix				
	100% Stock	80/20	60/40	40/60	20/80
Less than 4.0	100%	100%	100%	100%	100%
4.0	100%	100%	100%	100%	95%
4.2	100%	100%	100%	100%	95%
4.4	100%	100%	100%	100%	95%
4.6	100%	100%	100%	100%	80%
4.8	100%	100%	100%	95%	65%
5.0	95%	95%	95%	95%	55%
5.2	95%	95%	95%	85%	45%
5.4	95%	95%	95%	85%	40%
5.6	95%	95%	90%	75%	35%
5.8	95%	95%	85%	65%	30%
6.0	95%	85%	80%	55%	30%
6.2	90%	85%	75%	55%	20%
6.4	85%	85%	75%	50%	20%

Table 18.2. Portfolio Survival Rates for Twenty-Five-Year Retirements Following Historic Market Bottoms (1926–2012) *(continued)*

Withdrawal Rate (%)	Stock/Bond Mix				
	100% Stock	80/20	60/40	40/60	20/80
6.6	85%	85%	75%	40%	10%
6.8	85%	80%	65%	40%	10%
7.0	85%	75%	60%	30%	10%
7.2	85%	75%	50%	25%	10%
7.4	80%	70%	50%	20%	5%
7.6	75%	60%	45%	20%	5%
7.8	75%	60%	40%	15%	5%
8.0	67%	55%	35%	15%	5%
8.2	62%	55%	35%	10%	5%
8.4	57%	48%	35%	10%	5%
8.6	57%	38%	29%	10%	5%
8.8	57%	33%	24%	9%	5%
9.0	52%	33%	14%	5%	5%
9.2	48%	33%	14%	5%	5%
9.4	43%	33%	14%	5%	5%
9.6	33%	33%	14%	5%	0%
9.8	33%	29%	14%	5%	0%
10.0	33%	29%	9%	5%	0%
10.2	33%	29%	9%	5%	0%
10.4	29%	23%	9%	5%	0%
10.6	29%	18%	9%	5%	0%
10.8	29%	18%	9%	0%	0%
11.0	27%	14%	9%	0%	0%
11.2	27%	14%	5%	0%	0%
11.4	27%	14%	4%	0%	0%
11.6	27%	14%	4%	0%	0%
11.8	27%	13%	4%	0%	0%
12.0	23%	13%	0%	0%	0%
12.2	18%	13%	0%	0%	0%
12.4	17%	13%	0%	0%	0%
12.6	17%	9%	0%	0%	0%
12.8	17%	9%	0%	0%	0%

Table 18.2. Portfolio Survival Rates for Twenty-Five-Year Retirements
Following Historic Market Bottoms (1926–2012) *(continued)*

Withdrawal Rate (%)	Stock/Bond Mix				
	100% Stock	80/20	60/40	40/60	20/80
13.0	17%	9%	0%	0%	0%
13.2	13%	4%	0%	0%	0%
13.4	13%	4%	0%	0%	0%
13.6 to 14.2	13%	0%	0%	0%	0%
14.4 to 15.0	9%	0%	0%	0%	0%
15.2 to 15.6	4%	0%	0%	0%	0%
Greater than 15.6	0%	0%	0%	0%	0%

Source: Developed by the author using historical stock and bond total returns data from *2013 Ibbotson® Stocks, Bonds, Bills, and Inflation® (SBBI®) Classic Yearbook*, Morningstar, Inc., 2013, pages 220–21 and 232–33, and historical CPI-U (inflation) data published by the Bureau of Labor Statistics, U.S. Department of Labor, www.bls.gov/cpi/#tables.

Table 18.3. Portfolio Survival Rates for Twenty-Year Retirements
Following Historic Market Bottoms (1926–2012)

Withdrawal Rate (%)	Stock/Bond Mix				
	100% Stock	80/20	60/40	40/60	20/80
Less than 4.8	100%	100%	100%	100%	100%
4.8	100%	100%	100%	100%	95%
5.0	100%	100%	100%	100%	95%
5.2	100%	100%	100%	100%	90%
5.4	95%	100%	95%	95%	86%
5.6	95%	95%	95%	95%	76%
5.8	95%	95%	95%	90%	67%
6.0	95%	95%	95%	90%	57%
6.2	95%	95%	95%	81%	52%
6.4	95%	95%	90%	81%	43%
6.6	95%	90%	81%	76%	43%
6.8	90%	90%	81%	67%	29%
7.0	90%	90%	81%	62%	24%
7.2	90%	86%	81%	57%	19%
7.4	90%	81%	81%	43%	19%
7.6	86%	81%	71%	38%	19%
7.8	86%	81%	57%	29%	19%

**Table 18.3. Portfolio Survival Rates for Twenty-Year Retirements
Following Historic Market Bottoms (1926–2012) (continued)**

Withdrawal Rate (%)	Stock/Bond Mix				
	100% Stock	80/20	60/40	40/60	20/80
8.0	77%	76%	57%	29%	14%
8.2	77%	71%	52%	29%	14%
8.4	73%	64%	43%	24%	10%
8.6	73%	59%	36%	24%	5%
8.8	68%	59%	36%	23%	5%
9.0	68%	55%	36%	18%	5%
9.2	64%	36%	36%	14%	5%
9.4	59%	36%	32%	9%	5%
9.6	55%	36%	27%	9%	5%
9.8	55%	36%	27%	9%	5%
10.0	45%	36%	27%	9%	5%
10.2	36%	36%	14%	9%	4%
10.4	36%	36%	14%	5%	4%
10.6	36%	36%	14%	5%	4%
10.8	36%	36%	14%	4%	0%
11.0	36%	27%	14%	4%	0%
11.2	36%	23%	9%	4%	0%
11.4	36%	23%	9%	4%	0%
11.6	36%	14%	9%	4%	0%
11.8	27%	13%	9%	4%	0%
12.0	27%	13%	9%	0%	0%
12.2	27%	13%	9%	0%	0%
12.4	26%	13%	9%	0%	0%
12.6	26%	13%	4%	0%	0%
12.8	17%	13%	4%	0%	0%
13.0	17%	13%	4%	0%	0%
13.2	17%	13%	0%	0%	0%
13.4	17%	13%	0%	0%	0%
13.6	17%	13%	0%	0%	0%
13.8	13%	9%	0%	0%	0%
14.0	13%	9%	0%	0%	0%
14.2	13%	9%	0%	0%	0%

Table 18.3. Portfolio Survival Rates for Twenty-Year Retirements Following Historic Market Bottoms (1926–2012) *(continued)*

Withdrawal Rate (%)	Stock/Bond Mix				
	100% Stock	80/20	60/40	40/60	20/80
14.4	13%	4%	0%	0%	0%
14.6	13%	4%	0%	0%	0%
14.8 to 15.2	13%	0%	0%	0%	0%
15.4 to 16.2	9%	0%	0%	0%	0%
16.4 to 16.6	4%	0%	0%	0%	0%
Greater than 16.6	0%	0%	0%	0%	0%

Source: Developed by the author using historical stock and bond total returns data from *2013 Ibbotson*® *Stocks, Bonds, Bills, and Inflation*® *(SBBI*®*) Classic Yearbook*, Morningstar, Inc., 2013, pages 220–21 and 232–33, and historical CPI-U (inflation) data published by the Bureau of Labor Statistics, U.S. Department of Labor, www.bls.gov/cpi/#tables.

Table 18.4. Portfolio Survival Rates for Fifteen-Year Retirements Following Historic Market Bottoms (1926–2012)

Withdrawal Rate (%)	Stock/Bond Mix				
	100% Stock	80/20	60/40	40/60	20/80
Less than 6.2	100%	100%	100%	100%	100%
6.2	100%	100%	100%	100%	95%
6.4	100%	100%	100%	100%	95%
6.6	100%	100%	100%	100%	95%
6.8	100%	100%	100%	100%	90%
7.0	95%	95%	95%	90%	76%
7.2	95%	95%	95%	86%	76%
7.4	95%	95%	90%	86%	76%
7.6	95%	90%	86%	86%	71%
7.8	90%	90%	86%	86%	52%
8.0	86%	90%	86%	86%	43%
8.2	86%	86%	86%	71%	33%
8.4	86%	82%	86%	71%	29%
8.6	86%	82%	82%	67%	24%
8.8	82%	82%	77%	50%	23%
9.0	82%	82%	73%	41%	23%
9.2	82%	77%	68%	36%	18%
9.4	82%	77%	59%	32%	18%
9.6	77%	73%	50%	27%	18%

Table 18.4. Portfolio Survival Rates for Fifteen-Year Retirements
Following Historic Market Bottoms (1926–2012) *(continued)*

Withdrawal Rate (%)	Stock/Bond Mix				
	100% Stock	80/20	60/40	40/60	20/80
9.8	77%	73%	45%	27%	18%
10.0	77%	68%	45%	27%	14%
10.2	73%	64%	41%	27%	13%
10.4	68%	50%	41%	27%	9%
10.6	68%	45%	36%	23%	9%
10.8	68%	45%	27%	22%	4%
11.0	64%	41%	27%	13%	4%
11.2	45%	41%	27%	13%	4%
11.4	41%	41%	26%	9%	4%
11.6	41%	41%	26%	9%	4%
11.8	41%	35%	22%	9%	4%
12.0	41%	35%	22%	9%	4%
12.2	41%	35%	22%	9%	4%
12.4	39%	30%	17%	9%	0%
12.6	39%	30%	13%	9%	0%
12.8	39%	22%	13%	9%	0%
13.0	35%	22%	9%	9%	0%
13.2	35%	17%	9%	9%	0%
13.4	35%	17%	9%	4%	0%
13.6	30%	17%	9%	0%	0%
13.8	30%	17%	9%	0%	0%
14.0	26%	13%	9%	0%	0%
14.2	22%	13%	9%	0%	0%
14.4	22%	13%	9%	0%	0%
14.6	22%	13%	4%	0%	0%
14.8	22%	13%	4%	0%	0%
15.0	17%	13%	4%	0%	0%
15.2	13%	13%	4%	0%	0%
15.4	13%	9%	4%	0%	0%
15.6	13%	4%	4%	0%	0%
15.8	13%	4%	0%	0%	0%
16.0	13%	4%	0%	0%	0%

**Table 18.4. Portfolio Survival Rates for Fifteen-Year Retirements
Following Historic Market Bottoms (1926–2012)** *(continued)*

Withdrawal Rate (%)	Stock/Bond Mix				
	100% Stock	80/20	60/40	40/60	20/80
16.2	13%	4%	0%	0%	0%
16.4	13%	4%	0%	0%	0%
16.6	9%	4%	0%	0%	0%
16.8	9%	4%	0%	0%	0%
17.0	9%	4%	0%	0%	0%
17.2	9%	4%	0%	0%	0%
17.4	9%	4%	0%	0%	0%
17.6	9%	4%	0%	0%	0%
17.8	9%	4%	0%	0%	0%
18.0 to 19.8	4%	0%	0%	0%	0%
Greater than 19.8	0%	0%	0%	0%	0%

Source: Developed by the author using historical stock and bond total returns data from *2013 Ibbotson*® *Stocks, Bonds, Bills, and Inflation*® *(SBBI*®*) Classic Yearbook*, Morningstar, Inc., 2013, pages 220–21 and 232–33, and historical CPI-U (inflation) data published by the Bureau of Labor Statistics, U.S. Department of Labor, www.bls.gov/cpi/#tables.

**Table 18.5. Portfolio Survival Rates for Ten-Year Retirements
Following Historic Market Bottoms (1926–2012)**

Withdrawal Rate (%)	Stock/Bond Mix				
	100% Stock	80/20	60/40	40/60	20/80
Less than 9.4	100%	100%	100%	100%	100%
9.4	100%	100%	100%	100%	96%
9.6	100%	100%	100%	100%	96%
9.8	100%	100%	100%	100%	96%
10.0	100%	100%	100%	96%	91%
10.2	100%	100%	100%	96%	83%
10.4	100%	100%	96%	91%	78%
10.6	96%	96%	91%	87%	65%
10.8	96%	96%	91%	83%	61%
11.0	96%	91%	83%	83%	61%
11.2	91%	87%	83%	74%	52%
11.4	83%	83%	83%	74%	52%
11.6	83%	83%	83%	74%	43%

Table 18.5. Portfolio Survival Rates for Ten-Year Retirements Following Historic Market Bottoms (1926–2012) *(continued)*

Withdrawal Rate (%)	Stock/Bond Mix				
	100% Stock	80/20	60/40	40/60	20/80
11.8	78%	78%	78%	61%	39%
12.0	78%	78%	74%	52%	26%
12.2	78%	78%	65%	48%	22%
12.4	78%	78%	65%	48%	22%
12.6	78%	78%	65%	39%	22%
12.8	78%	70%	61%	35%	22%
13.0	78%	65%	61%	35%	17%
13.2	74%	65%	52%	30%	17%
13.4	74%	65%	43%	26%	13%
13.6	74%	65%	39%	26%	13%
13.8	65%	57%	39%	17%	9%
14.0	65%	57%	35%	17%	9%
14.2	61%	48%	35%	17%	9%
14.4	61%	43%	26%	17%	9%
14.6	57%	43%	22%	17%	9%
14.8	52%	35%	22%	13%	9%
15.0	39%	35%	22%	13%	9%
15.2	39%	30%	22%	13%	9%
15.4	39%	30%	22%	13%	9%
15.6	39%	30%	22%	9%	4%
15.8	39%	26%	17%	9%	4%
16.0	35%	22%	17%	9%	0%
16.2	30%	22%	13%	9%	0%
16.4	30%	22%	13%	9%	0%
16.6	30%	22%	13%	9%	0%
16.8	30%	17%	13%	9%	0%
17.0	30%	17%	13%	9%	0%
17.2	26%	17%	13%	4%	0%
17.4	26%	17%	9%	4%	0%
17.6	26%	17%	9%	4%	0%
17.8	17%	17%	9%	4%	0%
18.0	17%	17%	9%	4%	0%

Table 18.5. Portfolio Survival Rates for Ten-Year Retirements
Following Historic Market Bottoms (1926–2012) *(continued)*

Withdrawal Rate (%)	Stock/Bond Mix				
	100% Stock	80/20	60/40	40/60	20/80
18.2	17%	17%	4%	4%	0%
18.4	17%	17%	4%	4%	0%
18.6	17%	13%	4%	4%	0%
18.8	17%	9%	4%	0%	0%
19.0	17%	9%	4%	0%	0%
19.2	17%	9%	4%	0%	0%
19.4	17%	4%	4%	0%	0%
19.6	17%	4%	4%	0%	0%
19.8	17%	4%	4%	0%	0%
20.0	13%	4%	4%	0%	0%
20.2	13%	4%	4%	0%	0%
20.4	9%	4%	4%	0%	0%
20.6	9%	4%	4%	0%	0%
20.8	9%	4%	4%	0%	0%
21.0	4%	4%	4%	0%	0%
21.2	4%	4%	4%	0%	0%
21.4	4%	4%	4%	0%	0%
21.6	4%	4%	0%	0%	0%
21.8	4%	4%	0%	0%	0%
22.0	4%	4%	0%	0%	0%
22.2	4%	4%	0%	0%	0%
22.4	4%	4%	0%	0%	0%
22.6	4%	4%	0%	0%	0%
22.8	4%	4%	0%	0%	0%
23.0	4%	4%	0%	0%	0%
23.2	4%	4%	0%	0%	0%
23.4	4%	4%	0%	0%	0%
23.6	4%	4%	0%	0%	0%
23.8	4%	4%	0%	0%	0%
24.0	4%	0%	0%	0%	0%

Source: Developed by the author using historical stock and bond total returns data from *2013 Ibbotson® Stocks, Bonds, Bills, and Inflation® (SBBI®) Classic Yearbook*, Morningstar, Inc., 2013, pages 220–21 and 232–33, and historical CPI-U (inflation) data published by the Bureau of Labor Statistics, U.S. Department of Labor, www.bls.gov/cpi/#tables.

Interpreting the tables. Tables 18.1–18.5 provide historical guidance on the odds that any particular portfolio will be able to survive following a market decline. For example, Table 18.1 indicates that a 60/40 portfolio experiencing a market decline that raises its withdrawal rate to 4.4 percent has a 100 percent chance of surviving for at least thirty more years, based on historical data. In other words, the portfolio would be able to recover from its losses and survive an additional thirty years, even if the subsequent recovery proves to be as weak as the most anemic recovery we have experienced over the last eighty-seven years.

In contrast, the same 60/40 portfolio has a 0 percent chance of recovery, based on history, if its withdrawal rate rises to 12 percent during a market decline. At such an elevated temperature, the portfolio is almost certain to be bankrupted within thirty years, unless the subsequent recovery exceeds the strength of all past recoveries.

You may have noticed that as the proportion of bonds in the tested portfolios increases, the portfolio survival rate tends to decline. This phenomenon is most noticeable at elevated withdrawal rates. For example, Table 18.1 shows that at a 6 percent withdrawal rate, the odds of portfolio survival steadily decline as the bond allocation increases, from 84 percent for a 100 percent stock portfolio to a mere 5 percent for a 20/80 stock/bond portfolio. This result shouldn't be surprising, as it reflects the double-edged nature of bonds that we discussed previously. Tables 18.1–18.5 show the survival rates of portfolios during the *recoveries* that follow market declines. During recovery rallies, bonds act as a drag on portfolio returns. Keep in mind, however, that although adding bonds to a portfolio will slow down its recovery, the low volatility of bonds will also reduce the losses experienced during crashes. Although a 20/80 portfolio is much less likely than a 100 percent stock portfolio to recover from a crash that raises the portfolio's withdrawal rate to 6 percent, the former bond-heavy portfolio is also much less likely to experience a crash that raises its withdrawal rate to such a high level. Notice, too, that at lower withdrawal rates —especially those at or below 4 percent—the odds that a portfolio will survive are high, regardless of the portfolio's percentage allocation to bonds.

Shortly we consider how retirees can use the tables to determine whether to hold or sell stocks when the market goes into a decline. But first, we need to address a very important implication of the tables. As Table 18.1 shows, all portfolios have a 100 percent survival rate for withdrawal rates of 3.4 percent or less. Of course, the lower the withdrawal rate below 3.4 percent, the safer the portfolio from the retirement risk. And the lowest possible withdrawal rate is zero. Logically, if you are not withdrawing any money from your retirement portfolio, then for all practical purposes, you are completely safe from contracting portfolio fever. You will experience temporary losses on occasion, but you can expect a full and complete recovery from these losses. The available historical data confirm that the U.S. stock market has fully recovered from every past decline and gone on to new highs. In fact, the recoveries tend to be rapid, as we learned in Chapter 8.

Therefore, if you are not retired or within five years of retiring, and your withdrawal rate is zero, *there are no circumstances in which you should consider selling your stocks*. Tables 18.1–18.5 are for retirees and near-retirees only. Those who are still far from retirement should hold their stock investments at all times.

Tables 18.1–18.5 provide portfolio survival rates *measured from market bottoms forward*. They capture the impact of damage sustained by a portfolio during a market decline on that portfolio's chances of survival *after* the decline has ended and the recovery rally has begun. The survival rates in the tables do not consider the possibility that a portfolio could fail *before* the market bottoms out. However, this is a remote possibility for anyone using the tables to guide the decision process. On the basis of Table 18.5, a 100 percent stock portfolio with a 24 percent withdrawal rate has only a 4 percent chance of surviving ten years; for the other stock/bond mixes, this survival rate drops to 0 percent. Given these extremely poor odds, it is highly unlikely that anyone using the tables will *not* sell long before reaching a 24 percent withdrawal rate. However, let's suppose that despite these impossible odds, someone decides to wait until he hits a 24 percent withdrawal rate before selling. Assuming that the returns this person earns on his cash and bonds after he sells at least match the inflation rate, his portfolio should still last four more years (because he will be withdrawing slightly less than one-fourth of the portfolio's value each year). The longest cyclical bear market the U.S. has experienced since 1926 was the 1929 Crash, which lasted fewer than three years. A bear market exceeding four years in length is unprecedented. Hence even a person selling at a 24 percent withdrawal rate is unlikely to be bankrupted *before* the market bottoms out. And based on Table 18.5, it would be foolish indeed to allow your withdrawal rate to rise that much before taking action. As long as you are using Tables 18.1–18.5 to guide your decision process, there is virtually no chance that you will be bankrupted before the market reaches a bottom. In this way, the tables will serve to protect you from bankruptcy during, as well as following, market crashes.

For retirees and people nearing retirement, the survival rates in Tables 18.1–18.5 should be used as guidelines, not guarantees, of future performance. They are based on past history and provide reliable guidance to the future only to the extent that future market recoveries will prove similar to past recoveries. Of course, we can never know how well the future will mirror the past. But though imperfect, history is still the best guide to what may come. As in so many of life's decisions where certainty is absent, in investing we must be content to rely on probabilities.

How to use the tables. Tables 18.1–18.5 provide you with a means of (1) identifying the danger zone for your own portfolio and (2) avoiding that danger zone. Before we delve into the details of how to define and avoid the danger zone, let's consider an example illustrating the general process. Diane is a seventy-year-old retiree with a 60/40 portfolio. Her first step is to choose the table she will use to define her danger zone. Because she wants to avoid bankruptcy even if she lives to age one hundred, Diane selects Table 18.1 for a thirty-year retirement. Next, Diane decides that she is comfortable with a portfolio survival rate of 75 percent but no less. From Table 18.1, 5.8 percent is the lowest withdrawal rate corresponding to a portfolio survival rate less than 75 percent. Therefore, Diane's danger zone begins at a withdrawal rate of 5.8 percent. During market declines, Diane will monitor her withdrawal rate and take action before it rises to 5.8 percent. To ensure that she will act before it is too late, she defines the maximum temperature (withdrawal rate) she will allow her portfolio to reach before she takes action to cool it down. Diane picks 5.4 percent as her maximum actionable withdrawal rate (MAWR), leaving a safety cushion between the rate at which she will act and the 5.8 percent rate marking the boundary of her danger zone. (The size of the safety cushion used is a matter of personal preference; a reasonable cushion might range anywhere from 0.4 to 0.8 percent.)

As Diane grows older, she updates her danger zone and her MAWR. For example, at age seventy-five, she will be able to update using Table 18.2, the twenty-five-year table. This table shows that Diane's danger zone—a portfolio survival rate less than 75 percent—begins at a 6.8 percent withdrawal rate for a 60/40 portfolio. Leaving a 0.4 percent safety cushion, Diane updates her MAWR to 6.4 percent.

Like Diane, you will first need to select a specific table to use. Your selection should be made primarily on the basis of your age, but you may want to consider other factors, including your health and risk tolerance. For example, a healthy eighty-year-old retiree who wants to be sure not to run out of money even if he lives to one hundred would want to use the twenty-year retirement table (Table 18.3).

Once you've picked a table, define your danger zone and your MAWR. To do this, you must consider not only the risk of holding but also the risk of acting. As we will soon see, there is a hierarchy of actions you can take to avoid the danger zone. Some of these actions, such as reducing your expenses, entail no risk (though they do require sacrifice). However, the final action in the hierarchy—the option of last resort—is to sell your stock investments. This is the action you must consider when defining the zone you will seek to avoid at all costs. And selling comes with its own risks. For one, if you reenter the market too late, you may wind up permanently locking in losses that you would have recovered had you held. Additionally, you may incur substantial trading costs. As we discuss in the next chapter, there are ways to reduce the trading costs and the possibility of reentering the market too late. However, neither trading costs nor the potential for a late reentry can be eliminated. Together, these two risks may outweigh the risk of continuing to hold.

Tables 18.1–18.5 show portfolio survival rates assuming that you will hold. Ideally, there would be another set of tables that show portfolio survival rates assuming that you sell your stocks. If this second set of tables existed, you could compare, for any given withdrawal rate, the survival rate for holding and the survival rate for selling and simply choose the option that gives the best survival rate. For example, from Table 18.1, the survival rate for a 60/40 portfolio with a 7 percent withdrawal rate is 47 percent. This represents the probability that the portfolio will survive assuming you do *not* sell. If a similar table existed that gave a survival rate of, say, 55 percent for *selling* a 60/40 portfolio at a 7 percent withdrawal rate, then your decision would be a no-brainer. A 55 percent survival rate is better than a 47 percent rate, so you should sell.

But unfortunately, it is not possible to meaningfully quantify portfolio survival rates when you choose to sell. Hence portfolio survival rate tables for selling cannot be developed. This means that when deciding where to place your danger zone, you must compare the known risks of holding (from Tables 18.1–18.5) to the unknown risks of selling. As former defense secretary and amateur philosopher Donald Rumsfeld might put it, you must compare a risk you know you know with a risk you know you do not know. This is necessarily a subjective process, based on your personal attitudes toward risk and uncertainty. However, a couple of guidelines may help you zero in on your personal danger zone. First, remind yourself that you cannot improve on a survival rate of 100 percent. At best, selling when your estimated survival rate for holding is 100 percent will not improve your odds of beating the retirement risk. At worst, selling may reduce your odds of survival to less than 100 percent. Therefore you should always choose to hold at withdrawal rates showing 100 percent portfolio survival in the tables. Second, you have nothing to lose by selling, and at least a *chance* of improving your odds, when the survival rate for holding is 0 percent. You should therefore choose to sell at withdrawal rates corresponding to 0 percent portfolio survival rates.

Survival rates between these two extremes fall into a large gray area. But you can follow a logical process to help find your danger zone within this gray area. Begin the process by asking yourself the following question: does it make sense to take a chance with an option (selling) carrying unknown risk when there is a 95 percent probability that my portfolio will survive if I simply hold? Presumably, most people will choose to accept the known, small 5 percent risk of bankruptcy over the unknown risk that comes with selling. If you answer no to the question, then repeat the question, but this time with a 90 percent survival probability instead of 95 percent. Continue to ask yourself the question, reducing the survival probability in 5 percent increments, until you answer yes.

If you reach a 50 percent probability and are still answering no, keep in mind that at probabilities less than 50 percent, the odds that your portfolio will survive if you do not sell are less than even. I suspect many, if not most, people will prefer to take their chances selling when the alternative is a less-than-50/50 chance of outliving their money.

Whether it comes above or below the 50 percent probability level, at some point you will reach a survival probability for holding that is so low that you will prefer the unknown risks of selling. This point will mark the beginning of your danger zone.

Before choosing your danger zone, read the next chapter. Although it is impossible to quantify the risks of selling, Chapter 19 will give you some qualitative insight into these risks. Also, take this issue into account when defining your danger zone: portfolios irreparably damaged by fever during a market decline rarely, if ever, fail suddenly. On the contrary, bankruptcy is a gradual process that plays out over years, even decades. Table 18.5, which shows portfolio survival rates over the ten years following a market decline, proves this point. As the table indicates, even when withdrawal rates have risen as high as 9 percent, all tested portfolios, from 100 percent stock to 20/80, have a 100 percent ten-year survival rate. From a practical standpoint, this means that even if a market decline sets your portfolio on a path toward bankruptcy, you will more than likely have plenty of time to take the steps needed to get off this path before you reach this unwanted destination.

In fact, you can get a rough estimate of the amount of time you will have by looking up your withdrawal rate on each of the tables. Suppose, for example, that you are using a 60/40 portfolio and your current withdrawal rate has risen to 6 percent during a market decline. Table 18.1 shows a 68 percent chance that this portfolio will survive for at least thirty more years. Although your current risk of bankruptcy is therefore slightly less than one in three, you can estimate the amount of time you still have in the event that you are among the unlucky one-third by looking up the 6 percent withdrawal rate in the other tables. From Table 18.2, a 60/40 portfolio with a 6 percent withdrawal rate has an 80 percent survival rate over twenty-five years. Table 18.3 shows that the survival rate rises to 95 percent over twenty years, and Table 18.4 gives a 100 percent survival rate over fifteen years. Again, chances are the portfolio will survive for at least thirty years, but if the portfolio in this example does fail, the failure is not likely to occur until at least fifteen years have elapsed.

Returning to our earlier example, let's suppose that Diane encounters a bear market after updating her MAWR to 6.4 percent. When the market bottoms out, Diane's withdrawal rate stands at 5.2 percent. Because her withdrawal rate never reaches her MAWR, Diane continues to hold her stocks throughout the bear market. From Table 18.2, we can see that when a 60/40 portfolio reached a withdrawal rate of 5.2 percent during past market bottoms, it went on to survive for at least another twenty-five years 95 percent of the time. This is a high survival rate. But let's suppose that Diane gets unlucky and experiences a very weak market recovery. Unknown to her, her portfolio is now on a path to bankruptcy before she reaches the age of one hundred. She will, however, continue to monitor her portfolio's temperature, to diagnose both portfolio fever during future market declines and portfolio hypothermia (discussed later in this chapter) during bull markets. Because her portfolio's temperature will reach her MAWR or signal hypothermia before it is bankrupted, Diane will have another chance to make the corrections needed to avoid the retirement risk. In fact, she will most likely have plenty of time to make the needed changes. From Table 18.3, for a twenty-year retirement, we can see that a 60/40 portfolio that reaches a 5.2 percent withdrawal rate, like Diane's, has a 100 percent survival rate over twenty-year periods. Therefore, based on history, Diane's portfolio is most likely to be bankrupted between twenty and twenty-five years following the bear market bottom. This will take her into her late nineties, giving her plenty of time to make the needed corrections.

Because Diane recognizes that she will have more than one opportunity to fix her portfolio, if necessary, she is willing to define her danger zone as less than a 75 percent survival rate rather than a higher rate such as 90 percent. For this same reason, I have not included tables for retirement lengths exceeding thirty years. If you are a relatively young retiree in your sixties or fifties, as long as you choose a MAWR that gives you reasonable confidence that your portfolio will survive at least thirty years using Table 18.1, you will have plenty of time to make any needed corrections should you live longer.

Conversely, an older retiree using the ten- or fifteen-year table (Table 18.4 or 18.5) will have less time to fix a portfolio heading toward bankruptcy. This being the case, you may want to tighten your definition of the danger zone as you grow older. For example, a sixty-year-old retiree who has defined his danger zone as a portfolio survival rate of less than 75 percent may want to change his definition to, say, less than 90 percent upon reaching age eighty-five.

Do not wait to define your danger zone and MAWR until the market is in the grips of a bear. You should establish your MAWR when the market is calm and you are thinking clearly and rationally. If you are using a stock/bond mix not shown in the tables, you should use the portfolio closest to yours to find your danger zone and MAWR. For example, if you are using a 55/45 portfolio, refer to the 60/40 columns of the tables to establish your MAWR. (Or, if you are a math wizard, you can interpolate to estimate the portfolio survival rates that apply to your stock/bond mix.) Be sure to write down your MAWR in your Investment Plan (see Exhibit 11.1).

Once you've defined your danger zone and MAWR, you are ready for whatever the market throws at you. Sooner or later, that will no doubt include a market correction or bear market. Don't panic. Simply follow the Six-Step Process outlined in Chapter 17. In step 2 of the process, you will compare your current withdrawal rate to your MAWR. Calculate your current withdrawal rate using your current annual withdrawal amount and the total current value of your retirement portfolio (excluding your emergency fund). If you are planning to retire in the next five years, use an estimate of the amount you expect to withdraw in your first year of retirement to calculate your withdrawal rate.

If during step 2 you find that your current withdrawal rate is less than your MAWR, you should continue to do nothing. You can take comfort from the insight that your portfolio is not in the danger zone. Yes, the market may continue its decline, but your decision to hold is by no means irrevocable. If the market continues on a downward path, you will continue to take your portfolio's temperature by periodically calculating your current withdrawal rate and comparing it to your MAWR. Eventually the market will bottom out and begin its recovery. If your current withdrawal rate is still less than your MAWR at the bottom, your nest egg has a good chance of surviving going forward. If at any point before the market hits bottom your withdrawal rate reaches your MAWR, you will be able to take action to save yourself from the retirement risk.

Remember, you can and should repeat the 6-Step Process as often as necessary to remain calm. In general, you should repeat the process and check your portfolio's temperature more frequently as your withdrawal rate approaches your MAWR. You will also need to check for portfolio fever more frequently when the market's volatility rises. If the market is heading downward in a calm and orderly fashion, and your withdrawal rate is nowhere near your MAWR, it may be sufficient to check your portfolio's temperature once a month. But if the market is fluctuating wildly and you are closing in fast on your MAWR, you may need to check the temperature weekly or, preferably, even daily. Remember, you want to avoid entering the danger zone. The closer you get to that zone, the more closely you will need to monitor your portfolio's health.

Treatment of Portfolio Fever

I hope your portfolio will always remain outside your danger zone. But what should you do if your withdrawal rate *does* reach your MAWR? Selling your stock funds should always be your last resort. Selling will at best stabilize, not reduce, your portfolio's fever. And, as we will see more clearly in the next chapter, reentering the market after you sell is a process fraught with uncertainty. If you are unlucky, selling may increase rather than reduce your chances of bankruptcy.

Rather than unloading your stocks, the best, safest course of action is to directly reduce your portfolio's temperature. In other words, take steps to reduce your withdrawal rate before you consider selling your stocks.

You can do this in two ways: reduce your expenses and/or increase your income. If you have built some luxury items into your budget, say, an annual trip, you should be able to cut back on expenses without too much pain and sacrifice. Alternatively, you may be able to take a part-time or seasonal job to boost your income. Neither option need be permanent. You need only reduce your withdrawal rate just long enough for the market to bottom and the recovery rally to pick up steam. Once the recovery is well under way, your stock returns will rebuild your nest egg. Then you can quit your job or take that trip you put off during the crash.

If you are a near-retiree rather than already retired, you have options for reducing your *future* withdrawal rate. First, you can make cuts to your planned retirement budget. If you choose this option, be realistic: you will need to adopt the reduced budget upon reaching your retirement date if your nest egg has not yet recovered its losses. Second, you can delay retirement until your nest egg has recovered. Finally, to speed up the recovery process, you can increase your savings.

Whether you are a retiree or a near-retiree, you need not wait until your withdrawal rate reaches your MAWR before taking the steps necessary to reduce expenses and/or increase income. As an alternative, you can define *two* MAWRs: a lower MAWR, which you will use to decide when to reduce your withdrawal rate, and an upper MAWR, which, if reached, will trigger a stock sell-off. Setting your lower MAWR will require balancing the risk of doing nothing (which can be estimated from Tables 18.1–18.5) against the sacrifices involved in reducing your expenses or increasing your income. This balancing act is necessarily personal and subjective in nature.

Suppose you have already reduced your expenses and increased your income to the maximum extent possible. If the market decline continues and your withdrawal rate once again rises to your MAWR (or upper MAWR), you will need to sell your stock funds as your last resort. I recommend selling the entire stock portion of your portfolio (including your investments in gold and emerging-market bonds). Leave your bond portfolio intact. Keep the cash you raise from the sell-off in a money market fund or other highly liquid investment. You will need to access this money immediately once you reach your market reentry point. We cover the market reentry process in depth in the next chapter.

Portfolio Hypothermia

If you follow the preceding process of defining a danger zone, choosing a MAWR, and checking your portfolio's temperature during market crashes, you should be able to diagnose and effectively treat the disease we're referring to as portfolio fever. Portfolio fever is caused by too much negative market volatility. It is the same portfolio illness that brought ruin to John Stockman.

But what about the sickness that broke Joe Bondsman? Too much negative market volatility is only one side of the coin that is the retirement risk. The second component of the retirement risk—not enough returns to outpace inflation—is just as dangerous. If too much negative market volatility can cause a portfolio to overheat and suffer a deadly fever, then insufficient returns can result in an equally deadly condition: portfolio hypothermia. We need a procedure to diagnose and treat this dangerous condition if we don't want to wind up like Joe Bondsman.

Diagnosis

Portfolio hypothermia can be identified using the same measure we use to diagnose portfolio fever: the current withdrawal rate. An elevated withdrawal rate can signal a portfolio that is too cold as well as one that is overheating. Consider, for example, that Joe Bondsman's withdrawal rate steadily rose from 4 percent in 1962 (the year he retired) to 10.3 percent in 1977 and a whopping 51.5 percent in 1983.

But if portfolio hypothermia exhibits the same symptom—a rising withdrawal rate—as portfolio fever, how do we distinguish these two diseases? The answer lies in the context within which the withdrawal rate is rising. Portfolio fever occurs only when the stock market exhibits a declining trend, such as a correction or a bear market. Portfolio hypothermia, conversely, *cannot* occur during a market decline. Hence, if a retiree experiences an elevated withdrawal rate when the market is crashing, her portfolio is suffering from fever. If the same retiree experiences an elevated withdrawal rate when the market is *not* declining, her portfolio may be suffering from hypothermia.

I use the word "may" in the previous sentence because diagnosing portfolio hypothermia is a bit tricky. Portfolios can exhibit heightened withdrawal rates during bull markets without necessarily being in danger of bankruptcy. For example, a portfolio that has recently experienced a bear market may continue to exhibit an elevated withdrawal rate for months, or even years, after the market has bottomed and begun its recovery. Such a portfolio is not necessarily in danger; rather, it may be slowly recovering.

Diagnosing portfolio hypothermia is therefore not as straightforward as identifying portfolio fever. That said, we can turn to the Trinity Study for guidance once again. In Chapter 11, we used the Trinity Study results to identify those stock/bond allocations that offered the highest degree of safety from the retirement risk. The safest stock/bond mixes thus identified varied depending on the retiree's age and the withdrawal rate. Table 18.6 is a slightly modified version of Table 11.4, showing the Chapter 11 guidelines.

Table 18.6. Guidance on Lower-Risk Stock Allocations for Retirees

Current Withdrawal Rate	Lower-Risk Stock Allocation Ranges for Retirees in Their		
	Sixties and Younger	Seventies	Eighties and Beyond
3.5% and less	20% to 100%	20% to 100%	20% to 100%
3.51% to 4%	50% to 100%	25% to 100%	20% to 100%
4.01% to 5.5%	75% to 100%	50% to 100%	20% to 100%
5.51% to 6.5%	75% to 100%	75% to 100%	25% to 100%
6.51% to 7.5%	100%	75% to 100%	50% to 100%
7.51% to 8.5%	100%	100%	50% to 100%
8.51% to 9.5%	100%	100%	75% to 100%
Greater than 9.5%	100%	100%	100%

The gray-shaded cells in Table 18.6 identify withdrawal rates that come with a heightened risk of bankruptcy regardless of the stock allocation chosen. For example, if you are in your seventies, you should avoid withdrawal rates greater than 4 percent.

However, if circumstances force you to adopt a 5 percent withdrawal rate, the table indicates that a stock allocation in the 50 to 100 percent range offers the best chance of avoiding bankruptcy. In short, the best way to mitigate the retirement risk is to stay inside the white zone, but if this is not possible you can still reduce (though not minimize) your risk by selecting a stock allocation that falls within the range given in the gray-shaded cell that applies to your age and withdrawal rate.

By the same token, if you are in the white zone but using a stock allocation that falls outside the ranges shown in the table, you face a heightened risk of bankruptcy. For example, if you are in your sixties with a 4 percent withdrawal rate, you are not safe from the retirement risk unless you are using a stock allocation of 50 percent or higher.

Notice that Table 18.6 is for retirees and people within five years of retiring. If you are neither retired nor near retirement and your withdrawal rate is zero, you are not in any significant danger of either portfolio hypothermia or portfolio fever.

If you are retired or soon will be, you can use Table 18.6 to check your portfolio for signs of hypothermia whenever the stock market is not experiencing a significant decline. (You should *always* use Tables 18.1–18.5, not Table 18.6, when the market is in decline.) When the market is stable or rising, I recommend checking your portfolio's temperature once a year, right before you complete your annual rebalancing. To conduct this annual checkup, calculate your current withdrawal rate and use it to determine the low-risk stock allocation range for someone your age from Table 18.6. As long as you are (1) not inside the gray zone and (2) your planned stock allocation falls within the lower-risk range shown in the table, your portfolio is not hypothermic. Suppose, for example, that a sixty-five-year-old retiree using a 60/40 portfolio has a current withdrawal rate of 3.75 percent. From Table 18.6, retirees in their sixties with a withdrawal rate between 3.51 percent and 4 percent should be at a relatively low risk of bankruptcy as long as their stock allocation falls somewhere between 50 percent and 100 percent. Because our sixty-five-year-old has a planned stock allocation of 60 percent, his portfolio is safe from hypothermia.

If, in this example, the retiree were instead using a 30/70 stock/bond mix, his portfolio might be showing signs of hypothermia. But there are other possible explanations. Rather than jumping to conclusions, if you find that your stock allocation falls outside the range of lower-risk allocations shown in Table 18.6, wait at least one year (and maybe two) before taking any action. Portfolio hypothermia does not require the same urgency and close monitoring as portfolio fever. When the market is in decline and volatility is on the rise, your withdrawal rate may move rapidly toward the danger zone. In this situation, you must be vigilant and check your portfolio's temperature often. In contrast, your withdrawal rate will decline slowly (if at all) when the market is rising. In this situation, it is best to allow a significant period of time to pass before rechecking your portfolio's temperature so as to better capture the long-term trend in your withdrawal rate.

Hypothermia is no longer indicated if your withdrawal rate puts you back within the lower-risk ranges shown in Table 18.6 after a year passes. (You may need to wait a few years if the market enters a long-running decline. In this case, you must suspend checking for hypothermia and instead focus on fever until the market begins its recovery.) Even if you find that your stock allocation remains outside the lower-risk range, as long as your withdrawal rate has declined or held steady, there is no need for concern or action. Simply continue to monitor your withdrawal rate annually to ensure that it keeps moving in the right (downward) direction.

Treatment of Hypothermia

If, however, your withdrawal rate continues to rise, hypothermia is a possibility. There are three possible courses of action you can take. The first course is *inaction*.

Inaction. Physicians sometimes let certain illnesses run their course when they expect a full recovery and recognize that the treatment may be worse than the disease. Some forms of portfolio hypothermia can likewise safely run their course and are best left untreated. A couple of examples will illustrate why, and when, inaction is sometimes the best course of action.

Ralph is a seventy-seven-year-old retiree with a 60/40 portfolio. His annual portfolio checkup reveals that, because of a recent market crash, his withdrawal rate has risen from its original value of 3.8 percent to 5.7 percent. On the basis of Table 18.6, a retiree in his seventies with a 5.7 percent withdrawal rate falls in the gray zone indicating a heightened danger of bankruptcy regardless of his portfolio's stock allocation. Furthermore, the table indicates that, given his elevated withdrawal rate, Ralph would be *safer* (though still not necessarily *safe*) with a 75 percent than a 60 percent stock allocation. However, Ralph follows the hypothermia-diagnosis guidelines given earlier and waits one year before rechecking his withdrawal rate. Unfortunately, he finds that it has risen to 5.8 percent, suggesting that his portfolio may indeed be hypothermic. However, Ralph will turn eighty in just two years. From Table 18.6, retirees in their eighties with a withdrawal rate between 5.5 percent and 6.5 percent are not in the gray danger zone. Furthermore, these retirees can use a stock allocation as low as 25 percent and still have a low risk of bankruptcy. If Ralph simply waits and his withdrawal rate stabilizes, his portfolio may be back in the lower-risk white zone in just a couple years. Therefore, rather than taking immediate action, Ralph waits another year, and upon rechecking his portfolio, he finds that his withdrawal rate has dropped back down to 5.7 percent. By the time he reaches age eighty, his withdrawal rate has remained at 5.7 percent, and any danger posed by portfolio hypothermia has dissipated.

Laura is a sixty-three-year-old early retiree with a conservative 40/60 portfolio. Her annual portfolio checkup reveals a current withdrawal rate of 3.55 percent.

After waiting one year and rechecking, her withdrawal rate has risen to 3.6 percent. Although she is not in the high-risk gray zone, this is the second year in a row her withdrawal rate has put her outside the lower-risk range of stock allocations (50 to 100 percent) for someone her age. Although by age seventy, her 40/60 portfolio would once again become safe if her withdrawal rate were to remain below 4 percent, unlike Ralph, she still has a long way to go (six years) before reaching her seventies. However, her withdrawal rate increased only slightly over the course of the year (0.05 percentage points), and it is only 0.1 percentage points above the <3.5 percent range that would put her portfolio back in the safe zone. For these reasons, she decides to wait before taking action. Her withdrawal rate subsequently drops below 3.5 percent and remains at this level until she reaches her seventies.

If your current withdrawal rate puts your portfolio outside the lower-risk zone, but you (like Ralph) will soon reach an age that will put it back inside that zone, it may be better to wait and continue annual monitoring for hypothermia than to take action. Similarly, if your withdrawal rate puts you only slightly outside a low-risk zone (like Laura), or if your withdrawal rate is rising slowly (again, like Laura), waiting (with continued annual monitoring) may be your best option. Bankruptcy due to portfolio hypothermia is a slow process, and you will generally have plenty of time to take corrective action if further monitoring shows that such action is warranted.

Withdrawal rate reduction. But beyond these situations, you should take action if, after waiting one year, your withdrawal rate is elevated and rising. Most especially, if your withdrawal rate reaches the high single digits (greater than 7 percent) and your stock allocation falls outside the lower-risk allocations in Table 18.6, you should act rather than wait. As withdrawal rates approach and then exceed 10 percent, even a 100 percent stock portfolio may not be able to generate long-run returns sufficient to fund your expenses. Unless you take corrective action, such circumstances will necessitate a continual drawdown of principal—an unsustainable situation.

As with portfolio fever, the most effective way to actively address hypothermia is to reduce your withdrawal rate, by cutting expenses and/or increasing income. However, whereas the elevated withdrawal rates caused by portfolio fever typically return to normal quickly during the rallies that follow bear markets, hypothermic withdrawal rates can remain stubbornly high over much longer periods. Understand, therefore, that any sacrifices you make to "warm up" your portfolio may need to be maintained over the long haul—or at least until you reach an age that allows for a higher withdrawal rate.

Stock/bond allocation adjustment. If you are unwilling or unable to make the potentially long-term sacrifices needed to reduce your withdrawal rate—or if you make these sacrifices but your withdrawal rate once again rises to hypothermic levels—your final option is to increase your allocation to stocks, if possible to a level that puts you within the lower-risk ranges shown in Table 18.6.

Suppose, for example, that Valerie, a seventy-year-old retiree with a 40/60 portfolio, has an elevated withdrawal rate hovering around 6 percent. She takes steps to reduce expenses and increase income, but her withdrawal rate once again rises to 6 percent. Assuming Valerie has exhausted all options to lower her withdrawal rate, she should consider moving to a 75 percent stock allocation. Although this higher stock allocation will still leave her in the gray zone, indicating a heightened risk of bankruptcy, it will at least reduce this risk as far as possible given her elevated withdrawal rate. If she is too loss averse to be able to handle a 75/25 portfolio comfortably, she should move to the highest stock allocation that would still allow her to sleep at night.

In the case of portfolio fever, whether the treatment you choose is to reduce the withdrawal rate or sell stocks, this treatment is typically short term in nature. However, the treatment options for portfolio hypothermia typically require a longer-term commitment. This is true of adjustments to your stock/bond mix as well as reductions to your withdrawal rate. In some cases, once you have increased your stock allocation, you may need to maintain the new allocation permanently. In other cases, you may be able to return to your former allocation as you age. Returning to our previous example, Table 18.6 shows that after ten years, when Valerie reaches her eighties, she will be out of the gray danger zone and be able to return to a 40 percent stock allocation (or even lower), assuming her withdrawal rate declines or at least stabilizes at 6 percent.

Defense in Depth: Bringing It All Together

Tables 18.1–18.6 will help you solve a key problem that has always plagued the buy-and-hold strategy. Although it is true that holding your investments is *almost* always the best way to protect yourself from the retirement risk, exceptions to this rule are possible. Given a big enough drop in the stock market, you may suffer losses so large that recovery becomes impossible. Or if the night thief—inflation—goes on a rampage, you may not be able to earn returns sufficient to cover your expenses, forcing you to draw down on your principal until it is entirely gone.

The problem is, how do you *know* when you may need to take action and when doing nothing entails less risk? Moving average systems and other market timing strategies attempt to answer this question by predicting the direction of the market. But can a market prediction ever amount to knowledge? And even if it somehow were possible to predict the market's direction with a reasonable degree of confidence, would knowledge of what the market will do necessarily help you to understand the risks to your portfolio?

Tables 18.1–18.6 make no attempt to predict the market's future movements. Instead, they focus on your portfolio and help you understand whether it is probably safe at the present time. This understanding confers two major benefits. First, if you know that your portfolio has a good chance of surviving, this knowledge should help you to stay the buy-and-hold course. Uncertainty is a major enemy of the buy-and-hold investor, sowing doubt in his do-nothing strategy. Although uncertainty can never be eliminated, it can be reduced significantly. Tables 18.1–18.6 replace uncertainty with probabilities.

Second, if you know that your portfolio is skirting a danger zone, you can take corrective action before it is too late. This ability to identify situations in which a passive do-nothing strategy may be dangerous adds a whole new dimension to your defenses against the retirement risk. We have identified many such defenses in the preceding chapters of this book, but these defenses are all passive. Even rebalancing, dollar cost averaging, and tax loss harvesting, although requiring a limited amount of work on your part, are essentially passive in nature because they are undertaken on a set schedule, not in response to heightened dangers to your portfolio's health. In contrast, the treatments of portfolio fever and portfolio hypothermia covered in this chapter provide you with additional active lines of defense should your passive lines of defense fail. Separately, each line of defense, whether passive or active, will provide your portfolio some protection against one or more components of the retirement risk. But when combined, they will complete a powerful "defense in depth," including multiple fail-safe mechanisms should your first lines of defense fail. We began building this defense in depth in Chapter 15. It is time now to complete the construction by adding the active to the passive lines of defense, to see how the resulting edifice will protect your portfolio from each of the two components of the retirement risk —too much (negative) market volatility, and not enough returns to outpace inflation.

Defense against Market Volatility

Consider first the risk of portfolio fever posed by too much negative market volatility. Table 18.7 summarizes all of the various defenses we've now considered to protect your portfolio against volatility. This table also indicates how reliable each defense is as a volatility reducer, and it shows the impact each defense has on the other component of the retirement risk—not enough returns to outpace inflation.

The first five lines of defense listed in the table are passive in nature; they are implemented within the framework of a buy-and-hold, do nothing strategy. The high-volatility hedges form your first line of defense against volatility. If your high-volatility hedges fail to reduce your losses, your low-volatility hedges—bonds—provide the second line of defense. Bonds provide more reliable protection from losses than PME, gold, and emerging-market bonds, although they do come with a higher cost in terms of lower returns. Your third, and best, line of defense against portfolio fever is to establish a low initial withdrawal rate for the beginning of your retirement —no more than 4 percent and preferably 3 percent to 3.5 percent. Unlike the other passive defenses listed in Table 18.7, a low initial withdrawal rate will not directly reduce the volatility of returns earned by your portfolio, but it will reduce the odds that this volatility might lead to bankruptcy. If you are willing to take on the extra work involved, your fourth line of defense is a liability-matching bond portfolio (LMBP). Finally, annual rebalancing forms your fifth and last passive line of defense against portfolio fever.

Table 18.7. Lines of Defense against Market Volatility (Portfolio Fever)

Line of Defense	Impact on Inflation Risk	Reliability
Passive Defenses:		
High-volatility hedges	Limited, if any	Low
Low-volatility hedges	Increases risk	High
Low initial withdrawal rate	Reduces risk	High
LMBP	Eliminates risk as long as bond ladder lasts	High
Rebalancing	May reduce or increase risk (depending on rebalancing bonus)	High in the long term, although may increase volatility in the short term (if undertaken during stock market declines)
Active Defenses:		
Reduce withdrawal rate	Reduces risk	High
Sell stock portfolio	May reduce or increase risk (depending on success of market reentry)	High

If you are retired or nearing retirement and your passive lines of defense fail to keep your withdrawal rate from rising to your MAWR, you can switch to an active defense. Reducing your expenses and/or increasing your income is your sixth line of defense. And finally, if you reduce your withdrawal rate but it once again rises to your MAWR, you can activate your seventh, final line of defense and sell your stocks.

Notice that with one exception (the high-volatility hedges), all of the defense mechanisms listed in Table 18.7 are highly reliable at reducing the risk posed by portfolio volatility. Furthermore, all but one of them (the low-volatility hedges) offer volatility risk reduction with at least the possibility of simultaneously reducing (or at least not increasing) the risk posed by inflation. Together, these multiple lines of passive and active defense mechanisms offer formidable protection against the risk of portfolio fever posed by negative market volatility.

Defense against Inflation

But your defense in depth does not end there. You also have both passive and active defense mechanisms to guard against the second component of the retirement risk

—not enough returns to outpace inflation. In fact, as Table 18.8 shows, you have even more lines of defense against inflation—ten in total—than volatility. Some of these defenses work by increasing your returns (for example, the return boosters), while others (such as tax loss harvesting) work by lowering your investment expenses. The key to defeating inflation risk, what we have referred to in this chapter as portfolio hypothermia, is to ensure that your portfolio includes a good helping of stocks. Equity is the only asset class that has consistently outpaced inflation over the long term. Therefore your first line of defense consists of large cap stocks, whereas your second line is built out of return boosters. You can generally count on the latter to produce higher inflation-beating returns over the long haul, but this greater reliability may come at a higher cost in terms of increased volatility.

Table 18.8. Lines of Defense against Inflation (Portfolio Hypothermia)

Line of Defense	Impact on Volatility Risk	Reliability
Passive Defenses:		
Large cap stocks	Increases risk	High
Return boosters	Increases risk	High
Low initial withdrawal rate	Reduces risk	High
LMBP	Eliminates risk as long as bond ladder lasts	High
Index investing	No impact	High
Tax loss harvesting	No impact	High
Dollar cost averaging	May reduce or increase risk	High
Rebalancing	Reduces risk over long run	Low
Active Defenses:		
Reduce withdrawal rate	Reduces risk	High
Sell bonds and buy stocks	Increases risk	High

Your third line of defense, once again, is to establish a low withdrawal rate at the start of your retirement. A low initial withdrawal rate is the best protection against all aspects of the retirement risk, including the risk of portfolio hypothermia posed by inflation. If you so choose, you can use an LMBP as your fourth line of defense. By reducing your investment costs and increasing the portion of returns you get to keep yourself, index investing and tax loss harvesting provide fifth and sixth lines of defense against the risk posed by inflation. Dollar cost averaging provides a seventh line of defense, and rebalancing forms the last passive line of defense. Because the effectiveness of rebalancing depends on whether you earn a rebalancing bonus, it is the one and only defensive line listed in Table 18.8 that cannot be considered highly reliable as a reducer of inflation risk.

If you are retired or near retirement and your withdrawal rate indicates portfolio hypothermia, you can switch from a passive to an active defense. In this case, reducing expenses and/or increasing income is your ninth line of defense. And if that fails, you can activate your tenth and last line of defense by shifting your portfolio allocation from bonds to stocks, using Table 18.6 as your guide.

As Table 18.8 shows, only three of the ten lines of defense against the risk of inflation will unambiguously increase the risk you face from market volatility (large caps, return boosters, and shifting your allocation toward stocks). The remaining seven inflation defense mechanisms offer at least the possibility of either a reduction or no change in volatility.

In addition to the defense mechanisms shown in Tables 18.7 and 18.8, don't forget to make sure that you have adequate insurance coverage and a separate cash fund for emergencies. Insurance and an emergency fund will help to protect you against a non-investment-related aspect of the retirement risk: large unexpected expenses. (The risk posed by large unexpected expenses will also be reduced by those defenses that reduce the inflation risk without increasing volatility—including index investing, tax loss harvesting, and possibly rebalancing and dollar cost averaging. Furthermore, while these defenses won't directly reduce the risk that you will live a long life, they will increase the chances that you will earn the returns necessary to sustain a long life.)

You can never completely eliminate the risk of outliving your money. But with multiple lines of defense, both passive and active, you will have built a mighty castle to protect yourself and your loved ones from all aspects of the retirement risk. Within this castle, you may reasonably look forward to a comfortable retirement free from money worries, for as long as you live.

CHAPTER 19

MARKET REENTRY PLAN

ᴥ

I have a strange wish to relate: I sincerely hope the plan outlined in this chapter proves completely useless to you. You see, this is the "break glass in case of fire" chapter. You will need to use the plan herein detailed *only* if an emergency, real or imagined, causes you to sell your stock funds. My hope is that you never find yourself in a situation that necessitates selling—and that your emotions never betray you into selling when you shouldn't.

But stuff happens. If you ever *do* sell your stocks, either because you failed to hold when you should have or because your current withdrawal rate reached your maximum actionable withdrawal rate (MAWR), the material in this chapter will immediately go from useless to absolutely crucial. It will be crucial because you will have only begun the process of saving your portfolio from the retirement risk.

Let's suppose for a moment that the market is crashing and you just sold your stock funds. Having sold, you may *think* the danger to your nest egg has passed and you can now rest easy. But even if you sold for the right reason (a withdrawal rate that has reached your MAWR or a threat to your health), be assured the risk to your portfolio has *not* passed—at least not yet. You have completed only one-half of the action needed to save your nest egg. (On a more positive note, if you panicked and sold for the *wrong* reason, all is not yet lost. You have completed only one-half of the action needed to shoot yourself in the foot.)

Do you remember Bil the Caveman? When last we saw him, he was tumbling down the side of a mountain. Bil chose to flee rather than fight the saber-toothed tiger. Selling during a bear market is the modern equivalent of Bil's choice. And attempting to reenter the market after you've sold is like trying to grab on to something while crashing down the side of a mountain. You might get a hold of a rock or a tree trunk only to feel your grip loosen once again. It may take a number of tries before you finally break your fall. The longer it takes you to find a firm market re-entry point, the more bruised and battered you will be. If it takes too long, you may never recover from the wounds.

Most of the time, buy-and-hold investing is about as hard and stressful as a day at the beach. But once you've abandoned buy and hold and sold your stocks, everything changes. Selling is the easy part. It's the buying back into the market that's treacherous. To have any chance of successfully pulling it off, you must roll up your sleeves and go to work. The market reentry plan described in this chapter will show you what you need to do.

Tumbling Down the Mountain with Bil the Caveman

To illustrate just how difficult reentering the market is, let's consider an example. Figure 19.1 shows a hypothetical price chart for a stock mutual fund. The figure captures the fund's price trajectory over the course of a major market decline and the beginnings of a recovery rally. A seventy-year-old retiree, Wayne, owns 1,200 shares of the fund. At point A, before the market crash, Wayne's investment is worth $50 per share, or $60,000 total. Wayne also owns a bond fund worth $40,000, giving him total savings of $100,000. His annual withdrawal amount is $4,000 (or $333 per month). His withdrawal rate is therefore ($4,000/$100,000) 4 percent.

After one month (point B on the graph), the stock fund's price has dropped to $25 per share, and Wayne has lost half of his $60,000. He decides to sell the fund at this point. He takes the $30,000 proceeds from the sale and puts it in a money market fund, while continuing to hold the bond fund. We'll assume that Wayne withdrew his $333 in monthly expenses from the bond fund, which had zero percent returns over the course of the month. Hence, at point B, Wayne has $30,000 in the money market fund and ($40,000 − $333) $39,667 in the bond fund, for a total of $69,667. Wayne's withdrawal rate has now increased to ($4,000/$69,667) 5.7 percent.

After selling the fund, Wayne must continue to withdraw money from his nest egg to pay his living expenses, at the rate of $333 per month. After four more months have elapsed (point E in the figure), his withdrawals total (4 × $333) $1,333. Wayne withdraws the entire $1,333 from the bond fund. This is a smart move on Wayne's part, as it enables him to leave the $30,000 in the money market fund untouched and ready whenever he decides to repurchase his stock fund.

Let's suppose that four months after selling (point E in the figure), Wayne repurchases the stock fund at his $25 per share selling price. He thus is able to get back all 1,200 shares he sold. He now has $30,000 in the stock fund—the same amount he had when he sold the fund. For simplicity, we'll assume the bond fund produced zero total returns in the four months Wayne spent out of the stock market, thus leaving him with a total bond investment of $38,334 (the $39,667 he had at point B minus the $1,333 in expenses). The total value of his portfolio is $68,334, and his withdrawal rate is ($4,000/$68,334) 5.9 percent.

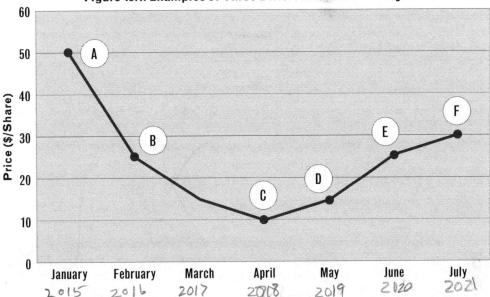

Figure 19.1. Examples of Three Different Market Reentry Points

Eventually the stock fund will return to its former high of $50 per share. Assuming he isn't bankrupted in the interim, Wayne's 1,200 shares will then be worth $60,000—the same amount they were worth at point A, before the market crashed. By repurchasing the stock fund at the same price at which he sold it, Wayne will have thus recovered all of his losses. But—and here is the real kicker—Wayne's risk of bankruptcy is now exactly the same as it would have been had he never sold the fund!

To see that this is true, let's suppose that instead of selling, Wayne held the fund throughout the bear market. At the bottom (point C), the fund's price has dropped to $10 per share, leaving Wayne with (1,200 × $10) only $12,000 left in the fund. He will also have incurred three months' worth of expenses, or $1,000. Assuming Wayne draws all of the expenses from the bond fund (as he should to avoid further weakening his stock portfolio), he will have $39,000 in bonds, and $51,000 total, at the market bottom. His withdrawal rate at the bottom will be ($4,000/$51,000) 7.8 percent. From Table 18.1, a 7.8 percent withdrawal rate for a planned 60/40 stock portfolio has only a 26 percent chance of surviving thirty more years. Clearly, had Wayne held, he would have probably put himself on a path to bankruptcy. Wayne's financial ruin would not have come quickly—from Table 18.5, a portfolio with a 7.8 percent withdrawal rate has a 100 percent chance of surviving ten more years. But at some point between ten and thirty years, Wayne is likely to go broke.

However, the fund now begins to recover, and by the time it reaches point E, it has more than doubled in price, from $10 to $25. Wayne's 1,200 shares are now worth $30,000, and, having withdrawn another two months' worth of expenses from the bond fund, that fund is valued at $38,334. The total value of his portfolio is $68,334, and his withdrawal rate is ($4,000/$68,334) 5.9 percent. This is exactly the same amount he would have had after selling and repurchasing the fund at point E! And likewise at point F, when the fund's price has risen to $30 per share, Wayne will have the same amount of money ($74,000[141]) and the same withdrawal rate (5.4 percent[142]) regardless of whether he sold or held. Either way, his portfolio is on the exact same path. And because we know that if he had *held*, the path he was on had only a 26 percent chance of leading to his portfolio's survival, it follows that by *selling* at point B and repurchasing at point E, his odds of survival are likewise 26 percent. While repurchasing his portfolio at the same price he sold it enabled Wayne to avoid locking in his losses, it did nothing to reduce his risk of bankruptcy.

But it gets worse. For simplicity, we have ignored trading costs, but these costs would have eroded his financial position still further had he sold rather than held the stock fund. And as we shall see, it may well take multiple attempts to reenter the market, driving trading costs ever higher. Also, we have ignored the stock fund dividends Wayne missed out on for the four months he was out of the market. At least currently, these dividends would have almost certainly been larger than the interest Wayne would have earned on the money market fund. Wayne's portfolio would have had a 26 percent chance of surviving had he held. But, taking trading costs and lost dividends into account, his chances would have been less than 26 percent had he sold at $25 per share and then reentered the market at the same price.

As you can probably guess, if Wayne had waited to get back into the market until the price of the fund rose above the $25 sale price his risk of bankruptcy would have been even greater. At point F, Wayne would have had (1,200 × $30) $36,000 invested in the stock fund had he held on to his 1,200 shares throughout the market crash. But had he sold at $25 and repurchased at $30 (point F), the $30,000 in his money market fund would have bought only 1,000 shares, worth $30,000. Only if Wayne buys back into the market at a lower price than his selling price will he have a *chance* to improve his portfolio's odds of surviving beyond 26 percent. For example, at a $15 per share repurchase price—point D in the figure—Wayne could have purchased 2,000 shares of the fund, putting him in a better position than if he had held his 1,200 shares. But even in this case, his portfolio's odds of surviving will be improved *only* if his gains outweigh his losses in trading costs and dividends.

If the dangers of selling during a market crash haven't been apparent before, they should now be crystal clear. Like Bil eying the tiger, it may *seem* that the real danger lies in standing your ground and facing down a bear market. But those loose rocks behind you are every bit as treacherous as the bear in front. Even if you manage to repurchase your stocks at the same price you sold, and thus avoid permanently locking in your losses, you haven't improved your portfolio's chances of survival going forward. Yes, you have avoided the risk of going bankrupt *before* the market bottoms. But you've likely *increased* the risk that you will be bankrupted at some point *after* the market bottoms out, as a result of the damage done to your portfolio during the bear market. Assuming the goal of selling is to reduce the retirement risk both *before* and *after* the market hits bottom, you must act quickly and repurchase your stock funds as close to the bottom as possible.

Unfortunately, many, if not most, investors who panic and sell become paralyzed with uncertainty. As the recovery rally begins, they wonder, "Is it safe to reenter the market?" As the rally proceeds and picks up more steam, many continue to sit on the sidelines, still agonizing over this same question. Like deer in the headlights, they freeze in place, until finally the question becomes, "Is it too late to reenter the market?" For these people, it was too late long before they even began to ask themselves this latter question.

How do you avoid the "deer in the headlights" syndrome? By having a clear market reentry plan long before you are ever faced with the task of reentering the market, and by faithfully executing that plan, if and when the time comes. Whether you sold for the right reason (your withdrawal rate reached your MAWR or you judged your health to be at risk) or the wrong reason (you panicked), the following market reentry plan is designed to give you a decent chance of emerging from your decision at a lower, not higher, risk of bankruptcy. But it must be stressed that there are no guarantees when it comes to reentering the market, and luck will play a major part in the outcome.

The Plan

We will assume, for now, that upon selling, the market continues its decline (later we'll consider the possibility that the market instead rises). As the price of each fund you sold declines, establish a "trigger price" midway between your sale price and the lowest price reached by the fund. For example, if you sell a fund at $22 per share and the price drops to $20, your trigger price will be $21. If the price continues down, say, to $16, the trigger price will move to $19. If the fund price then increases, say, to $18, the trigger price will not move. In effect, the trigger price will trail the fund's price as the latter moves down toward the bottom.

If the fund's price increases more than 1 percent above the trigger price, then repurchase the fund. For example, if the trigger price is $19 per share, then repurchase the fund if its price rises above $19.19.

If you originally sold the fund for the wrong reason (you panicked), once you've repurchased it, you should attempt to hold it without making any further sales. However, if you originally sold the fund because your withdrawal rate reached your MAWR, or because you judged that your health was in jeopardy, then you may need to sell it again and must continue to monitor its price. If, after repurchasing the fund, the price drops more than 1 percent below the trigger price ($18.81 if the trigger price is $19), sell the fund again. If the price then continues to decline to a new low (say, $10), move the trigger price down so that it always remains halfway between the original selling price and the low.

The more closely you monitor the market, the better the plan will work. If you are using mutual funds, you should check closing prices, reestablish your trigger price, and execute any required purchases or sales daily when the market closes. If you are using exchange-traded funds (ETFs) and have the time during the day, you may want to follow prices and make your trades even more frequently (especially when the market is volatile).

Reentry Plan Example

Table 19.1 provides an example of how the plan would work for a hypothetical mutual fund using daily closing prices. In this table, each time a new trigger price is set, that price is shown in bold text. Buy and sell decisions (in the last two columns) are also shown in bold text.

On day 1, the fund is sold at a price of $100 per share. This original sale price is recorded and will be used to calculate the trigger price on all subsequent days.

On day 2, the fund's price drops to $99, and the first trigger price is established halfway between $99 and the $100 original sale price. On days 3 and 4, the fund price drops to new lows. Whenever a new low is set, the trigger price is moved so that it remains halfway between the original sale price and the new low price. On day 5, the fund's price rises, but not high enough to cross the trigger price. The trigger price remains at $95 and will not move again until a new low is set on day 7.

On day 9, the fund's price rises to $96, which is higher than the $94.94 "trigger price plus 1 percent." Therefore the fund is repurchased. If the fund was originally sold for the wrong reason (the investor panicked), the reentry would now be complete and the investor would (it is hoped) return to a buy-and-hold strategy.

But let's assume that the investor originally sold the fund for good reason (either the current withdrawal rate reached the investor's MAWR or continuing to hold would have put his health at risk). In this case, the repurchase may not be the last one needed and the investor must continue to monitor the fund's price. Upon repurchasing the fund, its price drops below the trigger price minus 1 percent (on day 12). At this point, the fund must be once again sold. On day 14, the fund's closing price reaches a new low, and so the trigger price is once again moved to halfway between the new $86 low and the original $100 sale price. The plan will continue to be executed in this same manner until finally the fund's price crosses above the trigger price plus 1 percent and remains above this point.

To help guide you through the reentry process, you may want to use tables similar to Table 19.1 to track each of your fund's current prices, lows, trigger prices, and "buy" and "sell" decisions.

**Table 19.1. Example of Market Reentry Plan in Action
for a Hypothetical Stock Mutual Fund**

Day	Daily Closing Price	Trigger Price	Trigger Price Plus 1%	Trigger Price Minus 1%	Buy?	Sell?
1	$100.00	—	—	—	—	Yes, Original Sale
2	$99.00	$99.50	$100.49	$98.51	No	—
3	$98.00	$99	$99.99	$98.01	No	—
4	$90.00	$95	$95.95	$94.05	No	—
5	$93.00	$95	$95.95	$94.05	No	—
6	$92.00	$95	$95.95	$94.05	No	—
7	$88.00	$94	$94.94	$93.06	No	—
8	$93.00	$94	$94.94	$93.06	No	—
9	$96.00	$94	$94.94	$93.06	Yes	—
10	$97.00	$94	$94.94	$93.06	—	No
11	$95.00	$94	$94.94	$93.06	—	No
12	$92.00	$94	$94.94	$93.06	—	Yes
13	$91.00	$94	$94.94	$93.06	No	—
14	$86.00	$93	$93.93	$92.07	No	—

Supposing the Price Goes Up

What should you do if, instead of going down, the price of a fund you have sold goes up immediately after you sell it? You should wait, at least a while, for the price to go back down. Selling constitutes a bet that the market has not yet reached bottom (after all, if you think the market has bottomed out, there's no point in selling). This is actually a good bet. Since 1945, the average bear market has lasted 393 days.[143] Even the shortest market correction in recent times—the 1998 correction—lasted forty-five days. The chances that, out of at least forty-five days, you will happen to sell on the *one* day the market hits bottom are low.[144]

The reentry plan therefore assumes that the market has not yet reached its low point when you sell. If this assumption proves wrong, then, unfortunately, you are out of luck. But the odds are strongly in your favor. If the market rises immediately after you sell, wait for a reversal. Once the market has reversed and the price drops below the original price at which you sold, you will establish a trigger price and follow the reentry procedure described previously.

However, there is a limit to how long you can wait for the market to reverse direction and head back down. If the price of a fund you sold fails to decline but instead rises more than 10 percent (plus 1 percent) above the original sale price, then repurchase the fund. While market increases of 10 percent or more do happen within bear markets, they are relatively rare.[145] It is likely that once the price rises by 10 percent, it is not going to drop back down. In effect, you are setting your trigger price at 10 percent above the sale price.

If you originally sold the fund because you panicked, your reentry into the market is now complete and you should continue to hold. However, if you had a rational reason for selling the fund in the first place (i.e., your withdrawal rate rose to your MAWR or you judged your health to be at risk), then you must continue to monitor the fund's price. If the fund's price continues to rise and remains above the trigger price (which is now 10 percent above the original sale price), then your reentry will be complete. However, if the fund's price drops below the trigger price minus 1 percent, then you should resell the fund and move the trigger price to the midpoint between your original repurchase price and the recent low the fund has set. From this point on, simply follow the same procedure illustrated in Table 19.1.

Table 19.2 provides an example of the procedure to be used in the event of a sale followed immediately by a price rise. On day 1, a hypothetical fund is sold at a price of $100. On day 2, the fund's price increases rather than declines. The trigger price is therefore set at 10 percent above the sale price ($110). The investor will now wait for the price of the fund to reverse and head back down. As soon as the price acts as expected and drops below the original sale price, the trigger price will be reestablished halfway between the sale price and the new low.

However, in this example, the fund price does the unexpected and continues to rise. On day 4, it rises above the trigger price plus 1 percent. At this point, the fund must be repurchased. If the original sale was based on emotion rather than reason, the market reentry has now been completed, and the investor should return to the buy-and-hold strategy.

However, we will assume that the investor originally sold the fund for a good, rational reason (either the withdrawal rate reached the investor's MAWR or his health was at risk). In this case, the reentry may not yet be finalized, and monitoring of the fund's price must continue. On day 5, the price goes up once again. On day 6, the price heads down to $111. On day 7, the price crosses below the $108.90 level, representing the trigger price minus 1 percent, and therefore the fund is resold. On this same day, a new trigger price is established midway between the $110 original repurchase price and the new low of $106 just established. From this point on, the investor will follow the same procedure illustrated in Table 19.1, keeping the trigger price midway between the $110 original repurchase price and the low price.

Table 19.2. Example of Market Reentry Plan for a Hypothetical Stock Mutual Fund, in the Event that the Fund's Price Rises After It Is Sold

Day	Daily Closing Price	Trigger Price	Trigger Price Plus 1%	Trigger Price Minus 1%	Buy?	Sell?
1	$100.00	—	—	—	—	Yes, Original Sale
2	$101.00	$110	$111.10	$108.90	No	—
3	$104.00	$110	$111.10	$108.90	No	—
4	$112.00	$110	$111.10	$108.90	Yes	—
5	$113.00	$110	$111.10	$108.90	—	No
6	$111.00	$110	$111.10	$108.90	—	No
7	$106.00	$108.00	$109.08	$106.92	—	Yes
8	$102.00	$106.00	$107.06	$104.94	No	—

Possible Options to Reduce Trading Costs

Unless you're unlucky and sell at the market bottom, the preceding plan, followed diligently on a daily basis, ensures that your final repurchase will be made at a price below your original sale price. However, this does not guarantee that you will avoid increasing your risk of bankruptcy over what it would have been had you not sold. Nor does it guarantee that you will avoid incurring permanent losses.

The wild card in the plan is trading costs. These costs may more than offset the gains you realize by repurchasing at a price lower than your sale price. As the example in Table 19.1 shows, you may have to purchase and then resell each of your funds multiple times before you find your final market reentry point. There is no way to know, in advance, how many trades you will need to execute and how much each trade will cost. (This is one of the reasons why, as explained in the last chapter, it is impossible to estimate the risks of selling during market declines.)

In addition to ETF commissions and bid/ask spreads, the reentry plan's trading costs will include "slippage." Table 19.1 provides an example of slippage. Notice that on day 9, the fund is repurchased at a price of $96, only to be sold again, on day 12, at $92. The $4 loss represents slippage.[146]

At a minimum, given the 1 percent band above and below the trigger price, slippage will cost you 2 percent every time you buy and then resell a fund. The loss to slippage *per trade* can be reduced by minimizing, or even eliminating, the band around the trigger price—but this will more than likely cause an increase in the number of trades you must execute.

However, by consolidating your portfolio you may be able to reduce both slippage and other trading costs. Attempting to reenter the market may be the one and only situation where less diversification is better than more diversification. If you are using a well-diversified stock portfolio with large caps, high-volatility hedges, and return boosters, you will incur trading costs on *each* of these investments as you attempt to repurchase them. By consolidating your stock portfolio into a single investment, just for the duration of the emergency that caused you to sell, you may be able to dramatically reduce your market reentry costs. You will also greatly simplify the reentry process by eliminating the need to establish multiple price triggers for each of your investments.

One approach to consolidation is as follows. First, as you prepare to sell your stock funds, identify a single large cap index fund that you will repurchase in place of your stock portfolio. Record the price of this fund at the time you make your original sales. Then, use the selected fund's price to determine a single trigger price for your entire stock repurchase. When the fund's price crosses above the trigger price (plus 1 percent), you will use the proceeds from all of your funds' sales to buy the selected large cap fund. Once your market reentry has been finalized and the bear market is clearly visible in the rearview mirror, you can then sell the selected fund and repurchase your diversified set of investments.

Besides significantly reducing the number of trades you need to complete, consolidating your purchases into one fund may also enable you to significantly reduce your costs *per trade*. For one, if you use ETFs to implement your stock portfolio, you may be able to identify a single replacement ETF that can be purchased without a commission. A number of brokers offer zero-commission trades for a select set of ETFs. Furthermore, by choosing a heavily traded large cap ETF, you should be able to minimize the bid/ask spread on your trades.

Or alternatively, you could switch from an ETF portfolio to a single, large cap mutual fund and potentially eliminate trading costs other than slippage. However, many mutual funds charge a penalty for frequent trading, and some even prevent you from repurchasing them within a specified time after they've been sold. You would need to make sure the mutual fund you select allows penalty-free frequent trading.

Rather than using a mutual fund, you may be better off sticking with an ETF, or even switching to an ETF if you normally use mutual funds to implement your portfolio. An ETF *may* enable you to reduce trading costs below what is possible using a no-penalty mutual fund, *if* you are able and willing to track the ETF's price throughout the day. In fact, if you can access a zero-commission ETF with a minimal bid/ask spread, it may make sense to eliminate the 1 percent band around the trigger price. This will in turn significantly reduce, if not eliminate, slippage costs. Yes, it may also significantly increase the number of trades you will have to make. But as long as you can keep the trading costs to a small fraction of 1 percent on each trade, the reduction in slippage losses will likely be worth the additional trading. You can, of course, eliminate the 1 percent band if you are using a no-penalty mutual fund rather than an ETF, but it is your ability to trade an ETF throughout the day that would allow you to reduce slippage to a bare minimum. Keep in mind, though, that to make the most of this advantage, you will need to follow the ETF's price closely—at least on those days when the price is hovering near your trigger price.

Finally, if you can reduce your trading costs to a bare minimum using either an ETF or a mutual fund, one other very important option should be considered. Rather than placing the trigger price midway between the original sales price and the low price, you can keep it closer—much closer—to the low price. You might, for example, move the trigger price to a point 90 percent of the way from the sales price to the low price. (For example, if the original sale price is, say, $100 per share, and the price has since reached a low of $90 per share, then the trigger price would be set to $91 rather than $95.) Moving the trigger price closer to the low price will likely result in more frequent trading, but it will also enable you to obtain a much lower price for your final purchase. The closer you can get to the market bottom on your final reentry, the lower your risk of bankruptcy going forward. If your costs per trade are minimal, it may make sense to accept the likelihood of more frequent trading in exchange for a lower final purchase price.

★★★

By following the market reentry plan in this chapter, and taking as many of the preceding steps as possible to minimize your trading costs, you will give yourself a decent chance of reentering the market having reduced rather than increased your exposure to the retirement risk. Once you have repurchased your stock portfolio, and can clearly see the big, bad bear market in the rearview mirror, you should return to the best strategy ever devised for amateur investors: the buy-and-hold strategy. Despite rumors to the contrary, it is still very much alive.

AFTERWORD

✑

We are still masters of our fate.
—**Winston Churchill**

We began with a short story, and we will end with another. This one is true. On October 24, 1929, as the crowds gathered in lower Manhattan and the fictional John Stockman jostled for a spot near the ticker tape at his broker's office, a few blocks away, a future British prime minister held a front-row seat to the unfolding catastrophe. Winston Churchill had an uncanny knack for appearing wherever history was being made, and Black Thursday found him in the visitors' gallery at the New York Stock Exchange. He was nearing the end of a three-month cross-continent tour of the United States and Canada that had included sightseeing at California's redwood forest and the Grand Canyon, memorial dedications, speechmaking, and visits with William Randolph Hearst, Charlie Chaplin, and President Hoover, among others. He was now spending one last week in New York before his October 30 departure date.[147]

Exchange officials closed the visitors' gallery at 12:30, causing Churchill to miss the day's turning point by one hour. At 1:30, the acting president of the Exchange, Richard Whitney, appeared on the floor among the shaken traders, confidently strode to the post where U.S. Steel was traded, and bid for ten thousand shares at $205. He then proceeded to buy large blocks of other stocks. Word had already gone out over the wire that the city's major bankers, led by Thomas Lamont of J. P. Morgan and Company, were meeting, and the floor traders quickly and correctly surmised that Whitney was acting on their behalf. His actions electrified the market. As word spread that organized support had finally arrived, the panic gave way to a big rally. By the end of the day, the market stood just slightly down from its opening.[148]

Although he got to witness the morning panic, if not the afternoon recovery, Churchill was rarely content observing events from the sidelines. He preferred action.

During his stay in New York, he visited the office of his friend, the financier Bernard Baruch, and let it be known that he wanted to play the market. Baruch sensed trouble but nonetheless acquiesced.

As Churchill placed his trades, the situation quickly went from bad to worse. He tried to make up for his initial losses by plunging in deeper, but prices kept dropping relentlessly. This was, after all, October 1929, and despite the brief respite purchased by Whitney and the bankers, the market's main trend was now unstoppable. Churchill's usually impeccable timing had failed him; his ship literally sailed too late.

> At the end of the day he confronted Baruch in tears. He was, he said, a ruined man. Chartwell [his home] and everything else he possessed must be sold; he would have to leave the House of Commons and enter business.[149]

Not so, replied Baruch. For he had given his staff secret instructions to take the opposite side of every trade Churchill placed. He took the gains he realized betting against Churchill and gave them all to his friend.[150] Churchill was made whole again.

Thus, to the many remarkable events that made up Churchill's life, we must add one more. He was quite probably the only person ever to have speculated in stocks without any risk of loss. That he did so in the midst of the worst market crash in history makes it all the more remarkable. [151]

***

We should all be so fortunate. But assuming you lack a rich friend as generous—and shrewd—as Bernard Baruch, risk will be an inescapable, omnipresent fact of your investing career. And as Churchill's story demonstrates, the really big risk—the possibility of financial ruin—*ought to be* the dominant fact guiding your every move as an investor. This possibility brought to tears the man who faced down Adolf Hitler. And it's brought lesser men to far worse, such as Richard Whitney, who, deep in debt following a long string of bad investments, turned to embezzlement. By 1938, he had embarked on an all-expenses-paid retirement—at Sing Sing Prison.[152]

Investing is not about getting rich. It's about not getting poor. Should you outlive your money, the resulting misery may well spill over from your life into the lives of your loved ones. Your first, last, and most important job as an investor is to guard against this possibility—what we have termed the retirement risk.

To protect yourself and your loved ones, you must begin by coming to a full and complete understanding of the retirement risk. As Einstein taught us, you cannot solve a problem until you truly understand it. But the retirement risk plays tricks on our minds. One aspect of it—the risk of too much (negative) market volatility—grabs all our attention. Our fear of possible future Black Thursdays blinds us to the more mundane, but equally dangerous, risk of not earning enough returns to outpace inflation. As a result, we wind up fleeing the one asset that has never failed to beat inflation over the long run. That asset is stocks.

But once you fully understand and internalize the fact that the retirement risk comes in two varieties, the best solutions to this risk become clear. These solutions will reduce the risk of stock market volatility while simultaneously reducing (or at least not increasing) the risk posed by inflation. One such solution is to make a friend of your enemy. Like a black belt in judo who turns his opponent's superior size and strength against him, you can take the one characteristic of the stock market that makes it so frightening to so many—volatility—and turn it to your advantage. Stocks are inherently volatile; there is no way you can change this fundamental fact. But by applying the principle of correlation, and adding high-volatility hedges to your portfolio, you can actually reduce your portfolio's volatility while still capturing the kind of returns you need to beat inflation.

The principle of correlation works some of the time, but you cannot count on it to work all the time. Therefore you must back it up with the more reliable principle of compromise. When you include low-volatility hedges in your portfolio, you give up some returns in exchange for less volatility. But once you accept this compromise, you can then afford to add some additional volatility to your portfolio in the form of small cap and value stocks. These stocks will boost your returns and reduce the inflation risk.

Buying and holding a well-diversified portfolio of large caps, high-volatility hedges, low-volatility hedges, and return boosters will go far toward protecting you against both investment-related components of the retirement risk: too much (negative) market volatility and not enough returns to outpace inflation. But there are many other ways to reduce the risk you face of outliving your money. If you are still working, you can gain further protection by diligently saving for retirement using dollar cost averaging. This in turn will help you to establish a low initial withdrawal rate when you retire. Like the high-volatility hedges, a low initial withdrawal rate will reduce the risk posed by too much volatility without increasing the risk of earning returns insufficient to outpace inflation. In fact, by keeping your initial withdrawal rate below 4 percent (and preferably to 3.5 percent or less), you will reduce both the investment-related components of the retirement risk and the other noninvestment components (longevity risk and the risk of large unexpected expenses). A low initial withdrawal rate is the most reliable and effective solution to all aspects of the retirement risk—better even than the principle of correlation.

If you use a liability-matching bond portfolio (LMBP) you can virtually eliminate the investment-related components of the retirement risk—at least for a while, and perhaps for the remainder of your life. Purchasing a portfolio of low-cost index funds is similar to black-belt investing using the principle of correlation, in that it enables you to reduce one of the investment-related components of the retirement risk (not enough returns to outpace inflation) without simultaneously increasing the other component (too much negative volatility). Tax loss harvesting will likewise help you to outpace inflation without increasing your portfolio's volatility.

Rebalancing your portfolio on a regular basis is yet another solution that will reduce the risk of volatility while *possibly* also reducing the risk of not earning enough returns to outpace inflation. And the beauty of this solution is that it works best in tandem with one of the high-volatility hedges: precious metals equities (PME). You are not guaranteed extra returns when you rebalance. But by combining rebalancing with PME, you give yourself the best possible chance of earning such a bonus. Why *wouldn't* you grab this chance?

The above solutions are best implemented within the framework of a buy-and-hold, passive strategy. However, on rare occasions action may be better than inaction. Once you have retired, you can use your current withdrawal rate to monitor your portfolio's health and to determine if and when action may be necessary. By lowering your withdrawal rate when either portfolio fever or portfolio hypothermia is indicated, you will reduce all components of the retirement risk, both investment and noninvestment related. And finally, in extreme circumstances, you can sell your stocks if you are threatened by too much volatility (portfolio fever), or you can sell bonds and buy stocks if the problem you face is insufficient returns (hypothermia).

These many solutions to the retirement risk—the principles of correlation and compromise, a low initial withdrawal rate, an LMBP, index investing, dollar cost averaging, tax loss harvesting, rebalancing with PME, and monitoring your portfolio's health and taking action when needed—work well separately. But when they are all combined within a buy-and-hold investment strategy, they form a very powerful "defense in depth" protecting your nest egg from most, if not all, possible eventualities.

Finally, to benefit from the power of this holistic defense-in-depth approach, you must add your own personal strength and conviction to the mix. You can bolster the courage of your investing convictions by committing to a Rational Decision-Making Pledge and the 6-Step Process.

Risk is a part of life, and a big part of investing. You can never eliminate the risk of outliving your money. But you can manage it, and minimize it. Here's wishing you a secure, comfortable, and fulfilling retirement.

THE MORNINGSTAR HISTORICAL MUTUAL FUND RETURN DATA

For readers interested in checking the data used in this book, or conducting their own backtests, this appendix presents a guide to finding and using the Morningstar historical mutual fund return data.

Locating the Data on the Morningstar Website

Morningstar's website can be found at www.morningstar.com. To access the historical data, begin by entering the ticker symbol of a mutual fund with a lengthy history in the "Quote" box at the top center of the website's home page. If I want to access data going back to the mid-1970s, I use VFINX (the ticker symbol for Vanguard's 500 Index mutual fund); if I want to go further back in time, I use VWELX (for Vanguard's Wellington fund).

Once you have the initial quote page for VFINX or VWELX on your screen, scroll down to the chart showing the growth of a $10,000 investment in the selected fund. At the top right of this chart, click on "More." You should now see a full-screen version of the chart. At the top right of this full-screen chart, you will see options for how far back in time you can extend the chart, ranging from one month ("1M" on the screen) to "Maximum." You should click the option that best suits your purpose. If you click on "Maximum" for VFINX, the chart will extend itself from August 31, 1976, to yesterday's date. For VWELX, the chart will extend all the way back to July 1, 1929.

Once you have chosen "Maximum" or another time option, you can customize the specific time period. At the top left-hand corner of the chart, you will see two boxes showing the beginning and end dates for the customized chart. By clicking inside these boxes, you can revise the dates. First click on the beginning date box, make your revisions (you must enter a date after, not before, the default date shown on the screen), and then use the tab key to go to the end date box. After making your revisions to the end date, hit Enter, and the chart will then show the growth of $10,000 for the time period you have specified.

Once you've customized the chart to cover your specified beginning and end dates, you can obtain data for the specific asset class of interest to you. To do so, put your cursor on top of the word "Benchmark" toward the top left of the chart. A drop-down box will appear giving you six options from which to choose. If you choose the first option, "Morningstar Category," a second drop-down box will appear giving you a new set of categories. Most of the asset classes covered in this book are included in the first four of these categories: "Stock Style Box," "Other U.S. Stock," "International Stock," and "Taxable Bond." Placing your cursor on any one of these four options will give you a third drop-down box that will list the specific asset classes you can select. For example, under the "Stock Style Box" option, you will find the data for U.S. large cap blend funds, U.S. large cap value funds, U.S. small cap blend funds, and U.S. small cap value funds. Click on the asset class of interest, and a new trend line will appear on the chart. This new trend line will show the total growth of $10,000 invested in the selected asset class over the specified time period. The growth data are calculated using the average total returns (including reinvested dividends) of all mutual funds included in the particular asset class you selected. The end-date value of the $10,000 investment is given for the asset class you selected in the color-coded legend along the top of the chart. You can also obtain values for dates prior to the end date by moving your cursor along the trend line of the chart. When you do this, the date corresponding to the location of your cursor will appear in the top left corner of the chart, and the total value of the $10,000 investment as of that date will appear next to the selected asset class in the color-coded legend at the top of the chart.

The specific asset class you select may not have data extending all the way back to the beginning date you specified, in which case, you will need to determine how far back the data extend and redraw the chart accordingly. To determine whether the data for your asset class extend all the way back to the beginning date, place your cursor at the very beginning (extreme left-hand end) of the trend line, and slowly move it to the right. As you move the cursor, watch the dollar amount shown next to your asset class in the color-coded legend. If the amount shown remains 10,000 even after you have moved the cursor, then the available data do not extend all the way back to the beginning date you specified. In this case, continue to move your cursor along the trend line until you find the first date that yields an amount other than 10,000. This date will represent the first date for which data are available for the asset class you've chosen. You should then redraw the chart using this date as your beginning date, as you will not be able to obtain data for your asset class prior to this date.

Using the Growth Data to Calculate Returns

To calculate cumulative total returns over the entire period considered, use the following formula:

$$CR = 100\% \times (EV - \$10{,}000)/\$10{,}000 \tag{A.1}$$

where

> CR = Cumulative average returns of all mutual funds in the selected asset class (%)
>
> EV = Value of $10,000 original investment in the asset class as of the specified end date ($)

To calculate average annualized returns, use the following formula:

$$EV = \$10{,}000 \times (1 + ACR)^n \tag{A.2}$$

where

> EV = Value of $10,000 original investment in the asset class as of the specified end date ($)
>
> ACR = Average annualized returns of all mutual funds in the selected asset class (fraction)
>
> n = Length of time period from beginning date to end date (years)

Equation A.2 can be solved for ACR, average annualized returns, using either an iterative approach or a financial calculator.

Example

The following is an example applying Equations A.1 and A.2 to actual data obtained from Morningstar.

> Asset Class: Small cap value
> Beginning date = June 30, 2010
> End date = December 31, 2013
> Total length (n) of time period considered = 3.5 years

Ending value (EV) of $10,000 investment, from the historical return data on Morningstar = $18,995.18

Using the preceding equations,

CR = 100% × ($18,995.18 − $10,000)/$10,000 = 89.95%

$18,995.18 = $10,000 × (1 + ACR)$^{3.5}$

Solving the preceding equation iteratively for ACR, we obtain 0.2012, which, when multiplied by 100%, yields an annualized return of 20.12 percent.

DETAILED REBALANCING EXAMPLE

This appendix provides a detailed example of the rebalancing process when multiple accounts are involved.

We will assume an investor, Jane, is using the basic moderate (60/40) portfolio with one modification—she has added an intermediate-term bond fund to the portfolio's short-term bond holding. The first column of Table B.1 shows the planned asset allocation for this modified version of the portfolio. Jane has two accounts: a 401(k) and a taxable brokerage account. As Table B.1 indicates, all of Jane's stock funds are located in the taxable account, whereas the two bond funds are in Jane's 401(k).

Following a recent market downturn, Jane has lost money in all of her stock funds except her precious metals equities (PME) fund. She has had modest gains in her two bond funds. It is January and time for Jane to rebalance her portfolio. The second column of Table B.1 shows the current amounts in each of her investments. Notice that Jane has no money in her small cap value fund. This is because she sold the fund in December to harvest tax losses. The $6,000 she raised from this sale is now in the money market fund (see first row of the table) and ready for reallocation.

Applying step 1 of the four-step rebalancing procedure (from Chapter 15), Jane first calculates the total current value of her portfolio. The result is $90,000 (see last row, second column of table). Column 3 of the table shows how this amount should be reallocated to stocks and bonds (step 2) and to individual investments within the stock and bond portions of her portfolio (step 3). For example, of the $90,000 total, 60 percent, or $54,000, should be allocated to stocks. Of this $54,000, 30 percent, or $16,200, should be allocated to the U.S. large cap fund, and another 30 percent ($16,200) should go to the foreign large cap fund. The PME and small cap value funds should each be allocated 20 percent, or $10,800.

Table B.1. Basic Rebalancing Example

Account	Asset	COLUMN 1 Planned Allocation	COLUMN 2 Current Value	COLUMN 3 Rebalanced Value	COLUMN 4 Amount to Be Sold	COLUMN 5 Amount to Be Bought
	Stocks	60%	$47,000	$54,000	$8,200	$15,200
Taxable	Money market	0%	$6,000	$0	$6,000	$0
Taxable	U.S. large cap	30%	$13,000	$16,200	$0	$3,200
Taxable	PME	20%	$13,000	$10,800	$2,200	$0
Taxable	U.S. small cap value	20%	$0	$10,800	$0	$10,800
Taxable	Foreign large cap	30%	$15,000	$16,200	$0	$1,200
Total taxable	–	–	$47,000	–	$8,200	$15,200
	Bonds	40%	$43,000	$36,000	$7,000	$0
401(k)	Short-term	50%	$21,000	$18,000	$3,000	$0
401(k)	Intermediate	50%	$22,000	$18,000	$4,000	$0
Total 401(k)	–	–	$43,000	–	$7,000	$0
Grand total	–	100%	$90,000	$90,000	$15,200	$15,200

Next, Jane completes step 4 by calculating the amount of each fund that should be sold or bought. The results are shown in columns 4 (for sales) and 5 (for purchases). For example, the current amount allocated to the short-term bond fund ($21,000, see column 2) exceeds the amount that should be allocated to this fund ($18,000, see column 3). Therefore, $3,000 worth of this fund should be sold, as shown in column 4. In contrast, the current amount allocated to the U.S. large cap fund ($13,000) is less than the amount that should be allocated to this fund ($16,200). The difference ($3,200) is the amount that should be bought.

Columns 1–5 of Table B.1 simply apply the basic four-step rebalancing procedure described in Chapter 15. Notice that the total amount to be sold (last row, column 4) equals the total amount to be bought (last row, column 5). If this example involved a single account with no potential taxable issues, Jane would now be finished with her rebalancing calculations and could proceed with making the trades shown in columns 4 and 5.

However, two issues complicate the rebalancing process, and will necessitate some adjustments to the results shown in Table B.1. First, as the table shows, Jane should sell $2,200 of the PME fund (the difference between the fund's current value of $13,000 and reallocated value of $10,800). This fund is located in the taxable account, and therefore selling it could possibly trigger a taxable event. Jane checks her trade confirmation records and finds that she originally purchased the fund for only $7,000. Because this is less than the fund's current value ($13,000), the sale would trigger capital gains taxes. Jane has adopted the rule that she will sell a taxable investment to rebalance *only* if the current allocation to the investment exceeds 2 percentage points more than the planned allocation. In this case, the $13,000 currently allocated to the PME fund represents 24.1 percent of the $54,000 to be allocated to stocks. This amount does exceed, by more than 2 percentage points, the 20 percent to be allocated to the PME fund according to Jane's asset allocation plan. Therefore she should proceed with the sale. However, to limit her tax liability, Jane will sell only enough of the fund to get her to a 22 percent allocation—within 2 percentage points of her 20 percent planned allocation. This, for Jane, is a reasonable compromise between paying taxes versus allowing her allocation to drift too far from plan. Table B.2 is a copy of Table B.1, but with the needed correction (shown in bold) to the sale amount for the PME fund.

Table B.2. Rebalancing Example Revised to Limit Capital Gains Tax

Account	Asset	COLUMN 1 Planned Allocation	COLUMN 2 Current Value	COLUMN 3 Rebalanced Value	COLUMN 4 Amount to Be Sold	COLUMN 5 Amount to Be Bought
	Stocks	60%	$47,000	$54,000	~~$8,200~~ **$7,120**	$15,200
Taxable	Money market	0%	$6,000	$0	$6,000	$0
Taxable	U.S. large cap	30%	$13,000	$16,200	$0	$3,200
Taxable	PME	20%	$13,000	~~$10,800~~ **$11,880**	~~$2,200~~ **$1,120**	$0
Taxable	U.S. small cap value	20%	$0	$10,800	$0	$10,800
Taxable	Foreign large cap	30%	$15,000	$16,200	$0	$1,200
Total taxable	–	–	$47,000	–	~~$8,200~~ **$7,120**	$15,200

Table B.2. Rebalancing Example Revised to Limit Capital Gains Tax *(continued)*

Account	Asset	COLUMN 1 Planned Allocation	COLUMN 2 Current Value	COLUMN 3 Rebalanced Value	COLUMN 4 Amount to Be Sold	COLUMN 5 Amount to Be Bought
	Bonds	40%	$43,000	$36,000	$7,000	$0
401(k)	Short-term	50%	$21,000	$18,000	$3,000	$0
401(k)	Intermediate	50%	$22,000	$18,000	$4,000	$0
Total 401(k)	–	–	$43,000	–	$7,000	$0
Grand total	–	100%	$90,000	$90,000	~~$15,200~~ **$14,120**	$15,200

Notice, however, that because Jane is reducing the amount to be sold for the PME fund, the grand total amount to be sold ($14,120, from the last row of Table B.2, column 4) no longer matches the grand total to be bought ($15,200, last row, column 5). These two numbers must match or Jane will not have enough money from the sales to make all the required purchases. Therefore, she will need to pare down her purchases to get the grand total in column 5 down to $14,120—the total amount she will have available after making her sales. In Table B.3, Jane has reduced her purchases of the other three stock funds by a total of $1,080 to achieve the required balance between total sales and purchases. Although it is possible to calculate precisely how the reduction in purchases should be distributed across the three funds, this level of precision is not required—Jane has simply reduced the purchases for each of the three stock funds by an equal amount ($360). These new revisions are shown in bold in Table B.3. Notice that no changes have been made to the planned allocations in column 1 to reflect the revisions shown in columns 3, 4, and 5. These minor revisions are strictly temporary; Jane's planned asset allocation remains unaffected by them, and she will continue to use the planned allocation as the basis for rebalancing her portfolio in future years.

Table B.3 completes the revisions to the rebalancing calculations to reduce Jane's capital gains taxes. But as previously noted, a second issue requires further revisions. Focusing specifically on Jane's 401(k) account, notice that the rebalancing calculations require selling $7,000 worth of the two bond funds. But *within* the 401(k), there are no purchases shown in column 5. At the same time, the purchases that need to be made in the taxable account ($14,120, see column 5) exceed the sales ($7,120, see column 4) by $7,000. To complete the transactions shown in the table, Jane would need to transfer the $7,000 raised from the bond fund sales in the 401(k) to the taxable account. But clearly this would be a mistake, as Jane would need to pay taxes on the amount withdrawn from the 401(k) and possibly an early withdrawal penalty as well (depending on Jane's age).

Table B.3. Rebalancing Example:
Further Revisions Required to Limit Capital Gains Tax

Account	Asset	COLUMN 1 Planned Allocation	COLUMN 2 Current Value	COLUMN 3 Rebalanced Value	COLUMN 4 Amount to Be Sold	COLUMN 5 Amount to Be Bought
	Stocks	60%	$47,000	$54,000	$7,120	~~$15,200~~ $14,120
Taxable	Money market	0%	$6,000	$0	$6,000	$0
Taxable	U.S. large cap	30%	$13,000	~~$16,200~~ $15,840	$0	~~$3,200~~ $2,840
Taxable	PME	20%	$13,000	$11,880	$1,120	$0
Taxable	U.S. small cap value	20%	$0	~~$10,800~~ $10,440	$0	~~$10,800~~ $10,440
Taxable	Foreign large cap	30%	$15,000	~~$16,200~~ $15,840	$0	~~$1,200~~ $840
Total taxable	–	–	$47,000	–	$7,120	~~$15,200~~ $14,120
	Bonds	40%	$43,000	$36,000	$7,000	$0
401(k)	Short-term	50%	$21,000	$18,000	$3,000	$0
401(k)	Intermediate	50%	$22,000	$18,000	$4,000	$0
Total 401(k)	–	–	$43,000	–	$7,000	$0
Grand total	–	100%	$90,000	$90,000	$14,120	~~$15,200~~ $14,120

To get around this problem, Jane can purchase a *new* stock fund in her 401(k) with the money raised from the bond fund sales. Let's suppose that her 401(k) does not offer a PME fund but that it does offer a U.S. large cap blend, a U.S. small cap value, and a foreign large cap blend fund. The small cap value fund is actively managed and has a high expense ratio, making it an unappealing option. However, we'll suppose that both the U.S. and the foreign large cap funds are low-cost index funds. In this situation, Jane's best option would be to use the $7,000 from the sale of the bond funds to buy the U.S. large cap fund in her 401(k). She can then *reduce* her allocation to the U.S. large cap fund in her *taxable* account by $7,000. This will free up an additional $7,000 in the taxable account to complete the required purchases in that account. In effect, Jane is shifting part of her allocation to the U.S. large cap asset class from her taxable account to her 401(k). At the same time, she is keeping her entire allocation to the foreign large cap asset class in her taxable account, which will allow her to claim a credit for any foreign taxes she incurs on her 1040 form.

Table B.4 shows these latest revisions to the rebalancing calculations in bold. A new row has been added to the 401(k) account for the new U.S. large cap fund Jane will buy in that account. Furthermore, Jane has reduced her allocation to the U.S. large cap fund in her taxable account to ensure that the purchases and sales in this account will balance out. With this changed taxable fund allocation, instead of *buying* $2,840 worth of the large cap fund (column 5), she will now *sell* $4,160 of the fund (see column 4).

With these changes, the purchases and sales balance not only across both accounts but *within* each account as well. Note, also, that despite all of the various revisions, Jane's rebalanced allocation will meet her overall 60 percent stocks/40 percent bonds target allocation. By limiting her temporary deviations from her allocation plan to the *stock* portion of her portfolio, she has successfully kept her stock/bond mix from deviating from her 60/40 target. When it is necessary to deviate from your planned asset allocation to avoid triggering capital gains taxes, you should try to keep the deviations limited to *within* the stock and/or bond portions of your portfolio, while holding your overall stock/bond mix to plan. The overall stock/bond mix is a more important determinant of a portfolio's volatility level than the allocations to individual investments *within* the stock or bond portions of the portfolio.

Table B.4 completes all of the revisions needed to accommodate Jane's tax situation and multiple accounts. She need only make the purchases and sales indicated in columns 4 and 5 of this final revised table to complete her rebalancing effort for the year.

Table B.4. Rebalancing Example:
Final Revisions Required to Enable Rebalancing Across Accounts

Account	Asset	COLUMN 1 Planned Allocation	COLUMN 2 Current Value	COLUMN 3 Rebalanced Value	COLUMN 4 Amount to Be Sold	COLUMN 5 Amount to Be Bought
	Stocks	60%	$47,000	$54,000	~~$7,120~~ **$11,280**	~~$14,120~~ **$11,280**
Taxable	Money market	0%	$6,000	$0	$6,000	$0
Taxable	U.S. large cap	**30% (to be split between this fund and 401(k) fund)**	$13,000	~~$15,840~~ **$8,840**	~~$0~~ **$4,160**	~~$2,840~~ **$0**
Taxable	PME	20%	$13,000	$11,880	$1,120	$0
Taxable	U.S. small cap value	20%	$0	$10,440	$0	$10,440
Taxable	Foreign large cap	30%	$15,000	$15,840	$0	$840
Total taxable	–	–	$47,000	–	~~$7,120~~ **$11,280**	~~$14,120~~ **$11,280**
401(k)	U.S. large cap	**30% (to be split between this fund and taxable fund)**	–	**$7,000**	**$0**	**$7,000**
	Bonds	40%	$43,000	$36,000	$7,000	$0
401(k)	Short-term	50%	$21,000	$18,000	$3,000	$0
401(k)	Intermediate	50%	$22,000	$18,000	$4,000	$0
Total 401(k)	–	–	$43,000	–	$7,000	~~$0~~ **$7,000**
Grand total	–	100%	$90,000	$90,000	~~$14,120~~ **$18,280**	~~$14,120~~ **$18,280**

DETAILED METHODOLOGY USED TO DEVELOP TABLES 18.1–18.5

This appendix documents the methodology used to develop Tables 18.1–18.5, and it provides the underlying rationale for this methodology.

Methodology

Tables 18.1–18.5 show portfolio survival rates for various time periods, ranging from 10 to 30 years, following stock market bottoms that occurred between January 1926 and December 2002. Stock market bottoms were defined using the monthly total return index for U.S. large cap stocks presented in the *2013 Ibbotson® Classic Yearbook* by Morningstar.[153] A market bottom was defined as the month in which the index, following a decline of 10 percent or more, reached a low from which it subsequently fully recovered its losses before declining lower. This definition eliminated "false bottoms," which occur when a market decline is interrupted by a period of rising stock prices before returning to the declining trend and establishing a new low. Consider, for example, the period stretching from August 1932 to April 1933. The value of the large cap index for each month in this period is given in Table C.1. Notice that after declining 20 percent, from 0.933 to 0.746, the market reaches a false bottom in November 1932. This is a false bottom, according to the definition used to construct Tables 18.1–18.5, because although the index rises after November to 0.795 in January 1933, it does not fully recover to the value of 0.933 established in August 1932 at the beginning of the decline. The market bottom for the 1932–33 bear market is not reached until February 1933, when the index hits its low of 0.654 (29.9 percent below the market top reached in August 1932). February is the bottom for the 1932–33 bear market, because the index fully recovers from this decline (by April 1933, in this example) without first reaching a value below its February value of 0.654.

Table C.1. Example of a Bear Market with a False Bottom

Month and Year	Large Cap Index	Comments
August 1932	0.933	Market reaches a top; decline exceeding 10% begins
September 1932	0.900	
October 1932	0.779	
November 1932	0.746	False bottom
December 1932	0.789	
January 1933	0.795	Market fails to fully recover
February 1933	0.654	Bear market bottom
March 1933	0.678	Full recovery begins
April 1933	0.966	Full recovery achieved

Source: *2013 Ibbotson® Stocks, Bonds, Bills, and Inflation® (SBBI®)*
Classic Yearbook, Morningstar, Inc., 2013, Table B-1, p. 220.

Table C.2 shows all of the market declines and market bottoms between January 1926 and December 2002 meeting the described definition. Note that although the adopted definition of a market bottom prevents declines from overlapping, it allows new bottoms to be established within the full recovery period following a prior bottom. For example, the large cap index does not fully recover from the 1929–32 bear market until January 1945; during the long June 1932 to January 1945 recovery, seven new declines occur with market bottoms meeting the definition described earlier.[154] The result is a series of overlapping or rolling-period backtests similar to the backtests used in the Trinity Study.[155] However, unlike the Trinity Study backtests, the rolling periods used to develop Tables 18.1–18.5 are not evenly spaced; instead, the spacing is determined by the definition used to identify market bottoms.

It should be noted that the dates defining bear markets and market corrections in Table C.2 may differ in some cases from the dates used in the main text, as may the size of the market losses. This reflects the fact that Table C.2 is based on monthly large cap index data, whereas the dates/losses in the main text are based on daily S&P 500 data. For example, the 1973–74 bear market to which the main text refers began on January 11, 1973, and lasted until October 3, 1974. However, the less precise monthly index data used to develop Table C.2 show this same bear market as lasting from December 1972 to September 1974. The loss of precision resulting from the use of monthly data is more than counterbalanced by the fact that these less precise data allow an extension of the analysis much further back in time (to 1926) than would be possible using the available daily index data.

Table C.2. The Twenty-Three Market Declines and Market Bottoms Used to Develop Tables 18.1–18.5

Bear Market or Market Correction	Market Top	Market Bottom	Total Large Cap Index Loss from Top to Bottom
1929–32	Aug 1929	Jun 1932	−83.4%
1932–33	Aug 1932	Feb 1933	−29.9%
1933	Aug 1933	Oct 1933	−18.8%
1934	Jan 1934	Jul 1934	−20.7%
1934–35	Nov 1934	Mar 1935	−10.1%
1937–38	Feb 1937	Mar 1938	−50.0%
1938–39	Dec 1938	Apr 1939	−16.3%
1939–42	Sep 1939	Apr 1942	−30.3%
1946–47	May 1946	Apr 1947	−21.0%
1948–49	Oct 1948	May 1949	−10.0%
1956–57	Jul 1956	Feb 1957	−10.2%
1957	Jul 1957	Dec 1957	−15.0%
1961–62	Dec 1961	Jun 1962	−22.3%
1966	Jan 1966	Sep 1966	−15.6%
1968–70	Nov 1968	Jun 1970	−29.3%
1972–74	Dec 1972	Sep 1974	−42.6%
1975	Jun 1975	Sep 1975	−11.0%
1976–78	Dec 1976	Feb 1978	−14.3%
1980–82	Nov 1980	Jul 1982	−16.5%
1987	Aug 1987	Nov 1987	−29.6%
1990	May 1990	Oct 1990	−14.7%
1998	Jun 1998	Aug 1998	−15.4%
2000–2002	Aug 2000	Sep 2002	−44.7%

Source: Developed by the author using data from *2013 Ibbotson® Stocks, Bonds, Bills, and Inflation® (SBBI®) Classic Yearbook*, Morningstar, Inc., 2013, Table B-1, pages 220-21.

Total returns for large cap stocks and intermediate-term U.S. government bonds were used to develop Tables 18.1–18.5. Total returns were calculated for each twelve-month period following a market bottom, based on the monthly indices in the *2013 Ibbotson Classic Yearbook*.[156] For example, annual returns for the recovery following the June 1932 market bottom were calculated from June of each year to June of the following year. Each portfolio was assumed to be rebalanced at the market bottom, and it was rebalanced at the end of each twelve-month period following the market bottom. Again, for the June 1932 bottom, rebalancing was done in June. Annual withdrawals were taken from each portfolio at the beginning of each twelve-month period. Withdrawals were increased by the arithmetic average of the rate of inflation over the coming twelve months and the prior twelve months. This average rate of inflation was calculated based on the monthly Consumer Price Index (CPI-U) data published by the U.S. Bureau of Labor Statistics.[157] Hence portfolio values at the end of each twelve-month period were calculated as follows:

$$V_{taw} = V_{t-1} - (W_{t-1})\{1 + [(IR_{t-1} + IR_t)/2]\} \tag{C.1}$$

$$V_t = (V_{taw})(1 + R_t) \tag{C.2}$$

where

V_{taw} = Value of portfolio at the beginning of twelve-month period t, after removing withdrawal for period t (dollars)

V_t = Value of portfolio at the end of twelve-month period t (dollars)

V_{t-1} = Value of portfolio at the end of twelve-month period $t - 1$ (dollars)

W_{t-1} = Withdrawal for period $t - 1$ (dollars)

IR_{t-1} = Rate of inflation over period $t - 1$ (fraction)

IR_t = Rate of inflation over period t (fraction)

R_t = Rate of return for the portfolio over period t (fraction)

Portfolio values were calculated for ten-, fifteen-, twenty-, twenty-five-, and thirty-year periods following each of the market bottoms listed in Table C.2; if at the end of each of these five recovery lengths the value of the portfolio was greater than zero, then the portfolio was deemed to have survived. All twenty-three market bottoms were included in the ten-year calculations (Table 18.5). For longer recovery lengths, the maximum possible number of market bottoms was included for each withdrawal rate. For example, the thirty-year recovery period included at a minimum all market bottoms through December 1982. In addition, market bottoms ending in portfolio failure prior to December 2012 were also included. Suppose that for a particular withdrawal rate and stock/bond mix the November 1987 market bottom ended in failure prior to December 2012. In this case, the November 1987 bottom was included in the portfolio survival rate calculation for this particular withdrawal rate and portfolio, because it could be determined with certainty that this portfolio would not have survived for thirty years. However, suppose that for a different withdrawal rate and/or stock/bond mix, the portfolio value for the November 1987 market bottom was still positive as of December 2012. In this case, the November 1987 bottom was not included in the portfolio survival rate calculation, because although the portfolio survived twenty-five years, it could not be determined whether it would survive an additional five years (to November 2017). In this manner, all available information that could be determined with certainty was included in the calculation of the survival rates.

For each withdrawal rate, stock/bond mix, and recovery period length covered in Tables 18.1–18.5, the number of market bottom recoveries ending in portfolio survival was calculated as a percentage of the total number of market bottoms considered. The results are provided in Tables 18.1–18.5.

Rationale

The preceding methodology implicitly assumes that portfolio survival rates during the recoveries following market bottoms differ significantly from the survival rates published in the Trinity Study. If this assumption were not true, then there would be no reason to develop a new set of survival rates, separate from the Trinity Study results, for use during market declines.

The Trinity Study calculated survival rates for retirements beginning in January of each of the years stretching from 1926 through 1980 (for thirty-year retirements). Hence, whereas the selection of the twenty-three periods used to construct Tables 18.1–18.5 was constrained to periods beginning with a market bottom, no such market-based constraint applied to the Trinity Study results. The recovery rallies that form the beginning of each of the periods considered in Tables 18.1–18.5 will therefore differ, by definition, in important ways from the early stages of the periods used in the Trinity Study. For one, by definition, large cap returns in the first month of each period used in the construction of Tables 18.1–18.5 must be positive; no such limitation applied to the Trinity Study. Furthermore, the time periods used for Tables 18.1–18.5 must, by definition, begin with a full recovery from the market decline that preceded each market bottom. During this recovery, the value of the large cap index cannot have dropped below its value at the beginning of the period (i.e., at the market bottom). Again, no such constraints apply to the Trinity Study, and in fact, many of the periods considered in that study began with large cap losses.

Beyond these key definitional differences, there appear to be important differences that distinguish returns during recovery rallies from typical or average returns. Specifically, at least in the first month of recovery rallies, returns appear to be significantly larger than average returns across all months. Table C.3 presents the one-month and one-year returns following each of the twenty-three market bottoms represented in Tables 18.1–18.5. The one-month returns averaged 8.4 percent. By definition, this one-month rally average excludes months with negative returns, and so to obtain a comparative value, it is first necessary to exclude all months with negative large cap returns between January 1926 and December 2002. A total of 644 months had positive returns over this seventy-seven-year time frame. The average of these 644 positive returns was 3.9 percent.

Hence the twenty-three months immediately following market bottoms yielded average large cap returns more than double the average returns of all (positive-return) months. On the basis of this result, it appears that recovery rallies are characterized by unusually high returns, at least in their early stages. However, it is possible that the observed difference between the two averages arose as a result of random variation in the population of positive-return months. If so, it should be possible to replicate the unusually high returns produced during the first month of recovery rallies simply through random sampling. To test this possibility, a total of one thousand samples, of 23 months each, were randomly drawn from the 644 positive-return months. The average return across the twenty-three months was then calculated for each of these samples. None of the one thousand samples yielded an average return equal to or greater than the 8.4 percent average return produced during the first month of the recovery rallies. The largest average return for the one thousand samples was 7.4 percent — 1 full percentage point less than the average for the twenty-three one-month rallies. It is concluded that the unusually large returns observed during the first month of recovery rallies is highly unlikely to be the result of random variation.[158] These large first-month returns no doubt contributed to the abnormally high returns (averaging 41.8 percent, see Table C.3) observed for the first twelve months following a bottom.

In short, there are both definitional and empirical reasons to expect that the returns earned by large caps during recovery rallies will significantly outpace returns earned during periods selected without market-based constraints. It is true that once full recovery has been achieved, the market-based constraints on returns imposed by the preceding definition of a market bottom will no longer apply; hence there is no reason to expect that the larger-than-normal returns earned during the first months and years following a market bottom will continue beyond the point of full recovery. However, for portfolios subject to withdrawals, the sequence of returns has a significant impact on the risk of portfolio failure. The higher-than-normal returns earned during the months and years immediately following market bottoms will, all else being equal, reduce the chances of portfolio failure during periods beginning with a bottom relative to periods selected without market-based constraints.

Therefore, we would expect the portfolio survival rates in Tables 18.1–18.5 to be consistently higher than the results found in the Trinity Study, given the same withdrawal rates and stock/bond mixes. This is in fact the case. As just one example, at a 5 percent withdrawal rate, thirty-year portfolio survival rates from the Trinity Study range from 80 percent for a 100 percent stock portfolio to 67 percent for a

50/50 portfolio.[159] In contrast, thirty-year portfolio survival rates from Table 18.1 for a 5 percent withdrawal rate equal 95 percent for all stock/bond mixes ranging from 100/0 to 60/40; for a 40/60 portfolio, the survival rate is 79 percent.

**Table C.3. First Month and First Twelve-Month Returns
Following Market Bottoms, 1926–2002**

Bear Market or Market Correction	Market Bottom	Large Cap Returns in First Month Following Market Bottom (%)	Large Cap Returns in First 12 Months Following Market Bottom
1929–32	Jun 1932	38.0	162.8
1932–33	Feb 1933	3.7	98.9
1933	Oct 1933	11.3	2.9
1934	Jul 1934	6.1	34.0
1934–35	Mar 1935	9.7	83.8
1937–38	Mar 1938	14.5	35.1
1938–39	Apr 1939	7.3	17.6
1939–42	Apr 1942	8.0	61.3
1946–47	Apr 1947	0.1	12.4
1948–49	May 1949	0.2	42.4
1956–57	Feb 1957	2.1	-1.7
1957	Dec 1957	4.4	43.4
1961–62	Jun 1962	6.5	31.2
1966	Sep 1966	4.9	30.6
1968–70	Jun 1970	7.7	41.8
1972–74	Sep 1974	16.8	38.1
1975	Sep 1975	6.5	30.4
1976–78	Feb 1978	2.9	16.6
1980–82	Jul 1982	12.1	59.3
1987	Nov 1987	7.6	23.3
1990	Oct 1990	6.5	33.5
1998	Aug 1998	6.4	39.8
2000–2002	Sep 2002	8.8	24.4
Average		**8.4**	**41.8**

Source: Developed by the author using data from *2013 Ibbotson® Stocks, Bonds, Bills, and Inflation® (SBBI®) Classic Yearbook,* Morningstar, Inc., 2013, Table B-1, pages 220–21.

In conclusion, although the Trinity Study provides the most appropriate results for assessing portfolio survival probabilities over any period selected without constraints based on market events, the Trinity Study will tend to underestimate portfolio survival rates for periods that begin in months marking market bottoms. For this reason, Tables 18.1–18.5, which have the specific purpose of providing estimated probabilities of portfolio survival in the years following a market decline of 10 percent or more, were developed based on a methodology similar in general approach to that of the Trinity Study but focused on the recovery periods that begin at market bottoms.

RECOMMENDED READING

Investing Classics

The Four Pillars of Investing: Lessons for Building a Winning Portfolio, by William Bernstein.

The Intelligent Asset Allocator: How to Build Your Portfolio to Maximize Returns and Minimize Risk, by William Bernstein

A Random Walk Down Wall Street: The Time-Tested Strategy for Successful Investing, by Burton G. Malkiel.

Other Books on Investing

Common Sense on Mutual Funds: New Imperatives for the Intelligent Investor, by John C. Bogle.

Stocks for the Long Run: The Definitive Guide to Financial Market Returns and Long-Term Investment Strategies, by Jeremy J. Siegel.

The Bogleheads Guide to Investing, by Taylor Larimore, Mel Lindauer, and Michael LeBoeuf.

Bond Investing for Dummies, by Russell Wild.

Exchange-Traded Funds for Dummies, by Russell Wild.

All About Asset Allocation: The Easy Way to Get Started, by Richard A. Ferri

Morningstar Complete Investor, by Christine Benz and Pat Dorsey.

Books on Retirement Planning

The Bogleheads Guide to Retirement Planning, by Taylor Larimore, Mel Lindauer, Richard A. Ferri, Laura F. Dogu, and others.

Work Less, Live More: The New Way to Retire Early, by Bob Clyatt.

Books on Financial and Market History

Devil Take the Hindmost: A History of Financial Speculation, by Edward Chancellor

The Panic of 1907: Lessons Learned from the Market's Perfect Storm, by Robert F. Bruner and Sean D. Carr.

When Money Dies: The Nightmare of Deficit Spending, Devaluation, and Hyperinflation in Weimar Germany, by Adam Fergusson.

Lords of Finance: The Bankers Who Broke the World, by Liaquat Ahamed.

The Great Crash 1929, by John Kenneth Galbraith.

Rainbow's End: The Crash of 1929, by Maury Klein.

Once in Golconda: A True Drama of Wall Street 1920-1938, by John Brooks.

A Colossal Failure of Common Sense: The Inside Story of the Collapse of Lehman Brothers, by Lawrence G. McDonald with Patrick Robinson.

Too Big to Fail: The Inside Story of How Wall Street and Washington Fought to Save the Financial System—and Themselves, by Andrew Ross Sorkin.

The Big Short: Inside the Doomsday Machine, by Michael Lewis.

Misunderstanding Financial Crises: Why We Don't See Them Coming, by Gary B. Gorton.

Crisis Economics: A Crash Course in the Future of Finance, by Nouriel Roubini and Stephen Mihm.

This Time Is Different: Eight Centuries of Financial Folly, by Carmen M. Reinhart and Kenneth S. Rogoff.

Book on the Psychology of Investing

Your Money & Your Brain: How the New Science of Neuroeconomics Can Help Make You Rich, by Jason Zweig.

ACKNOWLEDGEMENTS

First-time authors are in need of much help navigating the many steps that separate a blank Word document from a finished book. This new author was fortunate to receive sound advice and guidance at each step along the way. My brother Jay Minnucci, my friend and former colleague Michael Mondshine, and senior freelance editor Paul Dinas all took time out of busy schedules to review drafts of the manuscript. They provided just the right mix of encouragement, ideas for improvement, and constructive criticism. The book has been greatly enriched by their insights, although any errors, omissions and shortcomings that remain are solely my responsibility.

While I had at least some inkling of what I was doing when I set out on this writing journey, the processes of publishing and promoting a book were unknown territory to me. Luckily Susan McCullough, a published author who knows this terrain well, was willing to act as my guide. Her explanations of the requirements and pitfalls of traditional publishing were instrumental in my decision to go the self-publishing route. She pointed out a number of excellent resources on self-publishing, and got me moving in the right direction toward promoting the book. I owe her a great debt for her advice and guidance.

A team of top-notch professionals turned the draft manuscript into a published book. My editor, Holly Monteith, quickly grasped my informal writing style, and approached the editing process accordingly, while still saving the book from my many egregious grammatical and punctuation errors. She also provided numerous suggestions that enhanced both the substance and clarity of my writing. David Moratto, book designer, is a consummate professional who took a complicated manuscript of text, tables, figures, and exhibits and turned it into beautiful final product, with an unusual and very cool cover. Pierre L'Abbé adapted David's design to an eBook format, and Wendy Catalano created the thorough-going index, proofread the entire book, and crafted a much more market-savvy synopsis than I ever could have written on my own. I am also indebted to Andrew Garman at Pipedream Marketing & Design for giving my new website a very classy design, and to Alex Nye and Brittney Karpovich at Smith Publicity for teaching an old dog a few new tricks.

Finally, this book would not have been possible without the treasure trove of mutual fund data available on Morningstar's website. I am very grateful to Morningstar for permission to use these data in my analyses and calculations, and to Kyle Oesterle and Dexter McAuley at Morningstar for their help in obtaining this permission.

NOTES

∾

Introduction

1   Annualized returns are defined as the rate of return earned per year, averaged over a period longer or shorter than a year. Annualized returns take into account compound growth, and in this book, unless stated otherwise, all annualized return figures represent total returns, including re-investment of dividends.

2   According to investment growth data on Morningstar's website.

3   Bernard Condon, "Families Hoard Cash 5 Years after Crisis," October 7, 2013, http://money.msn.com/business-news/article.aspx?feed=AP&date=20131007&id=16970156.

4   Karen Aho, "Why Older People Work: For Money," April 2, 2013, http://money.msn.com/retirement/why-older-people-work-for-money.

5   A. Barry Rand, "Retirement at Risk," *AARP Bulletin* 54, no. 2 (March 2013): 30.

6   Blake Ellis, "More Americans Delaying Retirement until Their 80s," *CNN Money*, October 23, 2012, http://money.cnn.com/2012/10/23/retirement/delaying-retirement/index.html/.

7   Mebane T. Faber and Eric W. Richardson, *The Ivy League Portfolio* (Hoboken, NJ: John Wiley & Sons, Inc. 2009), 3.

8   Over the last five years, the returns earned by the Yale and Harvard endowments have trailed the S&P 500 by a significant margin. The endowments rely heavily on alternative investments such as hedge funds and private equity to implement MPT, and it appears that these alternatives have dragged down the endowments' overall returns. It is possible that the recent poor performance of hedge funds and other alternatives is a temporary phenomenon, but some have argued

that the rising popularity of hedge funds in particular has put a squeeze on the opportunities for outperformance available to hedge fund managers. In any event, in this book, we will be avoiding alternative investments (many of which can be accessed only by the wealthy) and will instead rely on standard investments (accessible to all investors) to implement the principle of correlation.

9   At www.morningstar.com. For those readers who may be interested, Appendix A explains how the Morningstar historical mutual fund returns data can be accessed.

Chapter 1

10   Noelle E. Fox, "Comparing a Bucket Strategy and a Systematic Withdrawal Strategy," *The American Association of Individual Investors Journal*, April 2012.

11   Maury Klein, *Rainbow's End: The Crash of 1929* (New York: Oxford University Press, 2001), 28.

12   John Kenneth Galbraith, *The Great Crash 1929* (New York: Mariner Books/ Houghton Mifflin Harcourt, 1954), 52.

13   Ibid., 99.

14   Ibid., 99–100.

15   Calculated by the author from the Social Security Administration's 2009 Actuarial Life Table, www.ssa.gov/oact/STATS/table4c6.html.

16   For the mathematically inclined, the chances that at least one spouse will make it to age eighty-seven is equal to 100 percent minus the chance that *both* spouses will die before age eighty-seven, or $[1 - (1 - 0.33) \times (1 - 0.46)] \times 100\% = 64\%$.

Chapter 2

17   According to historical return data from Morningstar's website.

18   Please don't get me wrong and conclude that ETFs are to be avoided. As we shall see in Part IV, ETFs are a great investment product. I use them extensively in my own portfolio. They just happen to have an unfortunate side effect.

19   Unless otherwise noted, all mutual fund and S&P 500 index return data presented in this book represent total returns, including reinvested dividends as well as capital gains.

Chapter 3

20   According to investment growth data on Morningstar's website.

21   The 2000–2002 downturn actually consisted of two bear markets separated by a short-lived (three-and-a-half-month) bull market rally, but for simplicity, we will treat it as a single bear market in this book.

22   As calculated by the author using data from Morningstar's website.

23   Joseph H. Davies, Roger Aliaga-Diaz, C. William Cole, and Julieann Shanahan, *Investing in Emerging Markets: Evaluating the Allure of Rapid Economic Growth*, (Valley Forge, PA, The Vanguard Group Inc., 2010).

24 Wade D. Pfau, "An International Perspective on Safe Withdrawal Rates from Retirement Savings: The Demise of the 4% Rule?," Discussion Paper 10-12, GRIPS Research Center, 3.

25 Just as a U.S. investor's returns on Japanese stocks are adjusted downward when the yen declines relative to the dollar, a foreign investor's returns on U.S. bonds are adjusted downward when the dollar declines.

26 As calculated by the author using data from Morningstar's website.

Chapter 4

27 Quoted in William L. Silber, *Volcker* (New York: Bloomsbury Press, 2012), 42.

28 Timothy Knight, "Peculiar Facts from 500 Years of Finance," *American Association of Individual Investors (AAII) Journal* 36, no. 5 (2014): 28.

29 World Gold Council, "Gold Demand Trends, First Quarter 2009," May 2009, www.gold.org/investment/research/regular_reports/gold_demand_trends/.

30 These funds may include investments in other precious metals mining companies, such as silver mining companies; however, gold companies comprise the vast majority of the investments in most precious metals funds.

31 During this forty-year period, six stock market downturns have officially qualified as S&P 500 bear markets—defined as a price loss of at least 20 percent. However, because two of these downturns (in 2000–2001 and 2002) were separated by a mere three-and-a-half months, for simplicity, we have grouped them together as a single bear market (running from March 24, 2000, to October 9, 2002). Also, we treat the 1980–82 bear market as a market correction. As the table shows, the S&P 500's total returns (dividends plus capital gains) were negative 19.7 percent during the 1980–82 downturn. These losses are much closer to the losses for the three worst market corrections post-1970 than to the losses incurred during the four bear markets (a market correction is defined as a loss of 10 to 20 percent). Therefore we refer to the 1980–82 downturn as a market correction throughout this book.

32 American investors would not have been able to benefit directly from gold's rise in 1973–74, as it was illegal for U.S. citizens to own gold prior to 1975. However, they could have benefited indirectly by investing in the stocks of gold mining companies.

33 It is possible that we have not yet emerged from this secular bear market (only time will tell), but for our purposes, we will treat it as the nine years stretching from the market top reached on March 24, 2000, to the most recent bottom of March 9, 2009.

34 It took the dividend-adjusted version of the Wilshire 5000 Index (the index that best represents the entire U.S. stock market) only four-and-a-half years to fully recover from the 2007–9 bear market. And while the Dow Jones Industrial Average didn't fully recover from the 1929 Crash until 1954, the Dow provides a very

distorted image of the real recovery time, given that it includes a mere thirty stocks, does not include dividends, and is not adjusted for the deflation that occurred during the Great Depression. According to Ibbotson Associates, the deflation-adjusted total return U.S. stock market index took only a little more than seven years to return to its pre-Crash 1929 high. Mark Hulbert, "Bear Market Losses Have Been Erased," April 5, 2012, http://money.msn.com/investment-advice/bear-market-losses-have-been-erased-marketwach.

35 That gold outperformed inflation over the last five decades may in large part be due to a one-time, unrepeatable event that occurred in the early 1970s. Prior to 1971, the price of gold had been kept artificially low under the Bretton Woods agreement that governed international monetary relations. When this agreement was scrapped in 1971, the resulting release of years of pent-up price pressure led to rapid run-up in the price of gold. Between 1971 and 1975, the metal's price more than tripled. The end of Bretton Woods was a one-time event, and the resulting jump in the price of gold is not likely to be repeated.

36 That PME funds yielded significantly lower long-term returns than the S&P 500 is surprising, given that precious metals equities are *much* more volatile than the broader market. The capital asset pricing model (CAPM) may provide an explanation for this result. According to CAPM, investors are not compensated for the entire risk (i.e., volatility) of an investment, but only for that portion of the risk (volatility) that cannot be diversified away. Because PME are not closely correlated with the stock market, much of the risk associated with this asset class can be diversified away when PME are held in a well-diversified portfolio of large caps and other stocks. CAPM holds that the investor in PME will be rewarded only for the nondiversifiable portion of the risk.

37 Carmen M. Reinhart and Kenneth S. Rogoff, *This Time Is Different: Eight Centuries of Financial Folly* (Princeton, NJ: Princeton University Press, 2009), 93.

38 "The King of Con-Men," *The Economist*, December 22, 2012, www.economist.com/node/21568583/print.

39 A default occurs when a bond issuer fails to pay all or a portion of the principal and/or interest it owes on its bond.

40 Reinhart and Rogoff, *This Time Is Different*, 93–94.

41 In a debt rescheduling, one or more payments owed by a bond issuer are made later than originally scheduled.

42 Reinhart and Rogoff, *This Time Is Different*, 96–97, 99–100.

43 "King of Con-Men."

44 Reinhart and Rogoff, *This Time Is Different*, 95–96, 271.

45 "Power Shift," *The Economist Online*, August 4, 2011, www.economist.com/blogs/dailychart/2011/08/emerging-vs-developed-economies/print.

46 Reinhart and Rogoff, *This Time Is Different*, 278.

47 Ibid., 98, emphasis added.

48 Ibid., 80.

49   Ibid., 72.

Chapter 5

50   Roger C. Gibson and Christopher J. Sidoni, *Asset Allocation: Balancing Financial Risk* (New York: McGraw-Hill Education, 2013), 37.
51   Inflation-protected bond funds may include some corporate and international bonds; however, TIPS comprise the dominant holdings of these funds.
52   Via www.treasurydirect.gov.
53   To open a TreasuryDirect account, go to www.treasurydirect.gov/indiv/myaccount/myaccount_treasurydirect.htm.
54   Again, based on Morningstar data.

Chapter 6

55   Eugene F. Fama and Kenneth R. French, "The Cross-Section of Expected Stock Returns," *The Journal of Finance* XLVII (1992): 427-465.
56   According to investment growth data on Morningstar's website.
57   According to investment growth data on Morningstar's website.
58   Richard A. Ferri, *All about Asset Allocation* (New York: McGraw-Hill, 2006), 89, 96–97.
59   According to investment growth data on Morningstar's website.
60   Larry Swedroe, "Risk-Based Explanations of the Size and Value Premiums," January 2, 2007, www.indexuniverse.com/sections/research/920.html?fullart=1&start=2.
61   Based on return data for value and growth stocks from Ken French's website, http://mba.tuck.dartmouth.edu/pages/faculty/ken.french/data_library.html.
62   Jeremy J. Siegel, *Stocks for the Long Run: The Definitive Guide to Financial Market Returns and Long-Term Investment Strategies*, 4th ed. (New York: McGraw-Hill, 2008), 157–58.
63   Ferri, *All about Asset Allocation*, 125–26.

Chapter 7

64   In 1979, there was a short delay in the repayment of Treasury bills owing to a technical glitch at the Treasury Department. The bill holders were repaid with interest for the delay. Yalman Onaran, "US Default Seen as Disaster Dwarfing Lehman's Fall," October 7, 2013, http://money.msn.com/top-stocks/post--us-default-seen-as-catastrophe-dwarfing-lehmans-fall.
65   William J. Bernstein, *Rational Expectations* (2014), Figure 1-7.

Chapter 8

66   For example, for the 1973–74 bear market, which began on January 11, 1973, and lasted until October 3, 1974, I've rebalanced each portfolio to return it to the percentage allocations shown in Tables 8.3–8.5 on January 1, 1974.

67   Assuming a fund with zero fees.

68   Mark Hulbert, "Bear Market Losses Have Been Erased," April 5, 2012, http://
      money.msn.com/investment-advice/bear-market-losses-have-been-erased-
      marketwach.

69   Charles D. Ellis, *Winning the Loser's Game: Timeless Strategies for Successful Investing*,
      6th ed. (New York: McGraw-Hill Education, 2013), 141.

70   In the case of the 1980–82 correction, full recovery came very quickly (less than
      three months) for the S&P 500. Our portfolios matched, but could not improve
      upon, this performance. But the S&P 500 recovered much faster than our
      portfolios from the other three market corrections. In the case of the 1990
      correction, the S&P 500 achieved full recovery in four months, versus six
      months for all three of our portfolios. The S&P 500 fully recovered from the
      1998 correction in less than three months, whereas our portfolios took from
      four and a half months (in the case of the conservative portfolio) to longer than
      eight months (the aggressive portfolio). And whereas the S&P 500 fully
      recovered from the 2011 correction in less than five months, our aggressive and
      moderate portfolios had not yet achieved full recovery as of December
      2012 — more than a year after the market bottomed in October 2011.

Chapter 9

71   U.S. large cap value counts as a large cap asset as well as a return booster.

72   Small companies tend to be less dependent on exports than larger companies,
      and hence they are tied more closely to the local than the global economy.

73   The Morningstar website does not provide separate return data for the interna-
      tional small cap asset class; instead, it provides two sets of data for (1) small *and*
      mid cap value funds and (2) small *and* mid cap growth funds. I have calculated
      the average returns of these two categories to obtain an approximation of
      returns for international small cap blend funds. However, because the two
      Morningstar categories combine mid cap with small cap funds, it is likely that
      the return estimates I have calculated slightly underestimate the returns for
      international small cap funds. For 1990 and 1991, data are not available for the
      international small and mid cap value category; for these two years, I have used
      return data for the international small and mid cap growth category to
      approximate returns for international small cap blend funds.

Chapter 10

74   One way you *can* reduce longevity risk is by delaying claiming your Social Secu-
      rity benefits. We will discuss this option in more detail later.

75   Ratings are provided by A. M. Best Company (www.ambest.com) as well as
      Moody's Investor Services (www.moodys.com), Standard & Poors (www.standar-
      dandpoors.com), and Fitch Ratings (www.fitchratings.com).

76   In addition to your emergency fund, CDs may have another place in your

investment strategy if you are saving money for a large *planned* expense, such as a college education for your children or a down payment on a house. If you are within just a few years of incurring such an expense, it makes sense to move the money you've saved for that purpose from stocks and bonds into FDIC-insured CDs. Because in this case the expenses are planned, you can match the CDs' maturity(ies) to the date(s) the bills will come due. For example, if your child is one year away from entering a four-year college, you can buy four CDs with maturities of one, two, three, and four years.

77 Assuming returns are a constant 3 percent per year over the length of the bear market.

78 Philip L. Cooley, Carl M. Hubbard, and Daniel T. Walz, "Portfolio Success Rates: Where to Draw the Line," *Journal of Financial Planning* 24, 4 (April 2011), www.fpanet.org/jounal/CurrentIssue/TableofContents/PortfolioSuccess-Rates/.

79 Those who are already retired and are using the formula to calculate their *current* withdrawal rate do not need to make any adjustments for inflation.

80 For the mathematically inclined, the multiplier to adjust for inflation = $(1 + i/100\%)^y$, where i is the annual percentage inflation rate and y is the number of years until retirement.

81 Alternatively, if you still remember your high school math, you can calculate a more accurate estimate of the inflation factor using interpolation, as follows: $1.81 + (21 - 20) \times (2.09 - 1.81)/(25 - 20) = 1.87$.

82 Because Social Security benefits are adjusted to account for inflation, you must adjust your expected Social Security income using Table 10.1. However, other types of retirement income, such as pension income, may not include an inflation adjustment. If you expect to receive a pension, you should adjust the amount for inflation *only* if your expected payout includes an inflation adjustment like Social Security.

83 If you are a wizard at math, you can use interpolation to calculate a more precise multiplier for a 75/25 portfolio and a retirement in twenty-two (as opposed to twenty) years.

84 See, for example, www.socialsecuritychoices.com/info/social_security_as_investment.php.

85 Discounted to the present.

86 John B. Shoven and Sita Nataraj Slavov, "The Decision to Delay Social Security Benefits: Theory and Evidence," Working Paper 17866, National Bureau of Economic Research, February 2012, www.nber.org/papers/w17866.

87 William Meyer and William Reichenstein, "How the Social Security Claiming Decision Affects Portfolio Longevity," *Journal of Financial Planning* 27 no. 4 (April 2012), www.fpanet.org/journal/HowtheSSClaimingDecisionAffectsPortfolio-Longevity/.

88 If you have not yet reached retirement age and are in the process of calculating

the amount of money you will need in retirement, you should assume that you will begin collecting Social Security as soon as you retire. You cannot be sure that your initial withdrawal rate will be low enough to allow you to retire but delay collecting Social Security. Therefore, the assumption that you will need Social Security immediately upon retirement is the better (more conservative) assumption to make.

89   See AARP's website at www.aarp.org.

Chapter 11
90   Cooley et al., "Portfolio Success Rates."
91   Ibid.
92   Ibid.
93   That is, withdrawal rates in the first year of retirement.

Chapter 12
94   Taylor Larimore, Mel Lindauer, Richard A. Ferri, and Laura F. Dogu, *The Bogle-heads Guide to Retirement Planning*, (Hoboken, NJ: John Wiley and Sons, 2009), 108.
95   In the event of an insurance company default, many states guarantee the pay-outs from annuities, but there are caps on the amount guaranteed. Furthermore, the annuity may be transferred to another company. The new insurer may reduce the payout. William J. Bernstein, *The Ages of the Investor*, 2012), 25.
96   The situation is slightly different for ETFs, which are priced by the market; however, ETF prices normally closely follow their net asset values (NAV). An ETF's NAV is calculated using the market prices of the bonds held by the ETF.
97   www.ssa.gov/oact/STATS/table4c6.html.
98   Health care cost increases have slowed markedly in the wake of the 2008 financial crisis, but these costs are still rising significantly faster than the inflation rate. It is unclear whether the slowing growth in health care costs represents a long-term structural change or a temporary phenomenon.

Chapter 13
99   Christopher B. Phillips, Francis M. Kinniry Jr., and Todd Schlanger, *The Case for Index-Fund Investing* (Valley Forge, PA: Vanguard Group, 2013).
100   The authors defined "low cost" as those index funds with expense ratios of 0.2 percent or less.
101   All ending on December 31, 2012.
102   Phillips et al., *Case for Index-Fund Investing*, 16. The sole exception was the fifteen-year returns for emerging markets; data for this asset class/time period were not available and hence a comparison was not made.
103   Phillips et al., *Case for Index-Fund Investing*, 14.
104   Ibid., 12.
105   Christopher B. Philips, Joanne Yoon, Michael A. DiJoseph, Ravi G. Tolani, Scott

J. Donaldson, and Todd Schlanger, "Emerging Market Bonds—Beyond the Headlines," Vanguard Research Paper, May 2013, 10.

106 Paul Mladjenovic, *Precious Metals Investing for Dummies* (Hoboken, NJ: John Wiley, 2008), 135, 142.

Chapter 14

107 Don't try to get tricky and, in anticipation of the sale, purchase the same fund days *before* you sell it. The same fund purchased thirty days or earlier *before* the sale will also count as a wash sale. Also, don't sell the fund in one account and repurchase it in another account (including an account owned by your spouse) before the thirty-one days are up. All of these are wash sales that will result in the disallowance of your capital losses.

108 James Lange, *Retire Secure! Pay Taxes Later* (Hoboken, NJ: John Wiley and Sons, 2006), 54–55.

Chapter 15

109 There is a second reason the rebalanced portfolios in Figure 15.1 generate higher returns than the un-rebalanced portfolios. Lowering the volatility of a portfolio increases the portfolio's *compound* returns, all else being equal. Volatility interferes with the mechanics of compounding, as a simple thought experiment will demonstrate. Consider two investments, one of which generates positive returns every year, while the other generates negative returns every other year. The returns from the first investment will compound every year, but there will be no compounding of returns for the second investment in those years when it yields losses instead of gains. The rebalanced portfolios in Figure 15.1 generated larger *simple average* returns than the un-rebalanced portfolios, as a result of buying low and selling high, but the *compound* returns of the rebalanced portfolios were larger still, owing to the reduction in volatility brought about by rebalancing.

110 The few tests in which the rebalanced portfolios lost out to the un-rebalanced ones all clustered around the periods running from 1978 to 2001. These periods included the dot-com bubble of the late 1990s, while excluding the worst year (2002) of the 2000–2002 bear market. As would be expected, the shift toward stocks due to portfolio drift helped to power the outperformance of the un-rebalanced portfolios during the bubble years.

111 William J. Bernstein, "Case Studies in Rebalancing," www.efficientfrontier.com/ef/100rebal100.htm.

112 William J. Bernstein, "The Longest Discipline," www.efficientfrontier.com/ef/adhoc/gold.htm.

Chapter 16

113 The stock's future stream of expected earnings must be discounted to the present before being summed to yield the stock's underlying value.

114   Based on U.S. large cap total return data in Morningstar, *2013 Ibbotson® Stocks, Bonds, Bills, and Inflation® (SBBI®) Classic Yearbook* (Chicago, IL: Morningstar Inc., 2013).

115   Based on U.S. large cap total return data in ibid.

116   Appendix C presents a more formal analysis of the returns experienced in the early stages of past recovery rallies. The analysis provides evidence indicating that the abnormally high returns observed in the first month of a rally are unlikely to be explained by random variations in monthly returns.

117   Russel Kinnel, "Mind the Gap: Why Investors Lag Funds," February 4, 2013, http://news.morningstar.com/articlenet/article.aspx?id=582626.

118   Ibid.

119   Burton Malkiel, *A Random Walk Down Wall Street: The Time-Tested Strategy for Successful Investing* (New York: W.W. Norton and Company, 2007), 171–72.

120   Ibid., 172.

121   Siegel, *Stocks for the Long Run*.

122   Ibid., 25.

123   Ibid.

Chapter 17

124   http://blogs.wsj.com/moneybeat/.

125   There is a third option, "buy," but only those with nerves of steel (and ready cash) will consider it.

126   Condon, "Families Hoard Cash."

127   Fox, "Comparing a Bucket Strategy and a Systematic Withdrawal Strategy."

128   If I haven't persuaded you of the advantages of sticking with index funds, I urge you to read Bogle's very persuasive book *Common Sense on Mutual Funds*. If Bogle can't convince you that index investing is the way to go, no one can.

129   The Bogleheads website can be found at www.bogleheads.org/forum/index.php.

130   *New York Daily News*, September 16, 2008.

131   *Albuquerque Journal*, September 21, 2008.

132   *Pittsburgh Tribune-Review*, September 27, 2008.

133   *Politico*, September 19, 2008.

134   *Florida News-Press*, September 27, 2008.

135   *The New York Times*, September 20, 2008.

136   A put option gives you the right to sell shares of a stock or ETF at a predetermined "strike price," even if the market price falls below the strike price.

Chapter 18

137   A moving average is an average that is recalculated on a daily basis to capture the most recent day's returns.

138   Cooley et al., "Portfolio Success Rates."

139   The analysis of thirty-year survival rates necessarily excludes bear markets and

market corrections that have occurred since 1982, because we do not yet have thirty years of data following these more recent market declines. However, I have added the more recent market declines, up to and including the 2000–2002 bear market, for the analyses of survival rates over shorter time periods (see Tables 18.2–18.5).

140 Tables 18.1–18.5 are based on the 2013 version of the *Ibbotson® SBBI® Classic Yearbook*, which provides return data from 1926 through 2012.

Chapter 19

141 At this point, he would have twelve hundred shares in the stock fund, worth $36,000 ($30 × 1,200), and $38,000 in the bond fund ($38,334 minus another $333 in expenses).

142 $4,000/$74,000 = 5.4%.

143 Bespoke Investment Group, "An Historic Look at Past Bull and Bear Markets," September 6, 2007, http://seekingalpha.com/article/46477-an-historic-look-at-past-bull-and-bear-markets.

144 You can improve your chances of avoiding a bottom sale by checking your current withdrawal rate on a frequent—preferably daily—basis as you approach your MAWR.

145 There have been only seven increases of more than 10 percent during past bear markets, based on the 1926 through 2012 monthly capital appreciation data for large cap stocks in Morningstar, *2013 Ibbotson® Stocks, Bonds, Bills, and Inflation® (SBBI®) Classic Yearbook*, 188–89.

146 If you are trading in a taxable account, you will be able to recover a portion of your slippage losses come tax time, because slippage represents a capital loss.

Afterword

147 William Manchester, *The Last Lion: Winston Spencer Churchill—Visions of Glory: 1874–1932* (New York: Dell Publishing, 1988), 824–28.

148 Galbraith, *The Great Crash 1929*, 100, 102.

149 Manchester, *Last Lion*, 14.

150 Ibid.

151 This incident raises a fascinating, if chilling, what-if question. What if Baruch had not come to Churchill's rescue and his losses forced him to quit politics in 1929? Would Britain still have stood alone against Nazi Germany in 1940? "No" is at least a plausible answer, given that Churchill's main rivals for the office of prime minister—most notably Lord Halifax—appeared amenable to the peace treaty Hitler wanted with Britain after the fall of France. (I suspect, though, that Churchill would have found a way to continue his political career despite his financial losses.)

152 John Brooks, *Once in Golconda: A True Drama of Wall Street 1920–1938* (1969; repr., New York: John Wiley & Sons, 1999), 277.

Appendix C

153 Morningstar, *2013 Ibbotson® Stocks, Bonds, Bills, and Inflation® (SBBI®) Classic Yearbook*, Table B-1, 220–21.

154 The value of the large cap index at these new bottoms in all cases exceeds the value of the index in June 1932; hence June 1932 is not a false bottom.

155 Cooley et al., "Portfolio Success Rates," Table 2.

156 Morningstar, *2013 Ibbotson® Stocks, Bonds, Bills, and Inflation® (SBBI®) Classic Yearbook*, Tables B-1 and B-7, 220–21, 232–33.

157 Bureau of Labor Statistics, www.bls.gov/cpi/#tables.

158 To test whether this conclusion might be limited to the 1926–2002 time period, a second test, using data for January 2003 through December 2012, was performed. A total of seventy-nine months were characterized by positive large cap returns during this ten-year period; these seventy-nine returns averaged 3.0 percent. Three months met the definition of a market bottom during this time period: February 2009, June 2010, and September 2011. Large cap returns averaged 8.9 percent during the first month following these three bottoms. None of one thousand three-month samples selected randomly from the seventy-nine positive-return months produced average returns equal to or greater than 8.9 percent. The largest average return for the one thousand samples was 8.4 percent—a half percentage point less than the average returns during the first month of recovery rallies. It appears, based on this second out-of-sample test, that the unusually high returns associated with the early stage of recovery rallies is not an artifact of history; rather, similarly high rally returns are observed for more recent times as well.

159 Cooley et al., "Portfolio Success Rates," Table 2.

INDEX

*Page numbers in bold indicate figures or tables

ABOUT THE AUTHOR

Chris Minnucci is an early retiree and self-taught investor, living in southeastern Pennsylvania. Chris was formerly a mining engineer at a large consulting company. In addition to *The Death of Buy and Hold*, he writes a blog to help early retirees maximize their healthcare benefits and minimize their costs under the Affordable Care Act (Obamacare). His website is at www.ChrisMinnucci.com.

Made in the USA
Middletown, DE
03 May 2015